Contingency Management

FOR SUBSTANCE ABUSE TREATMENT

Contingency Management

FOR SUBSTANCE ABUSE TREATMENT

A Guide to Implementing This Evidence-Based Practice

Nancy M. Petry

Routledge
Taylor & Francis Group
New York   London

Routledge
Taylor & Francis Group
711 Third Avenue
New York, NY 10017

Routledge
Taylor & Francis Group
27 Church Road
Hove, East Sussex BN3 2FA

© 2012 by Taylor & Francis Group, LLC
Routledge is an imprint of Taylor & Francis Group, an Informa business

Printed in the United States of America on acid-free paper
Version Date: 20110506

International Standard Book Number: 978-0-415-88289-7 (Paperback)

Library of Congress Cataloging-in-Publication Data

Petry, Nancy M.
    Contingency management for substance abuse treatment : a guide to implementing this evidence-based practice / Nancy M. Petry.
        p. ; cm.
    Includes bibliographical references and index.
    ISBN 978-0-415-88289-7 (pbk. : alk. paper)
    1. Substance abuse--Treatment. 2. Behavior therapy. 3. Evidence-based psychiatry. I. Title.
    [DNLM: 1. Substance-Related Disorders--therapy. 2. Behavior Therapy--methods. 3. Evidence-Based Practice. 4. Reinforcement (Psychology) WM 270]

RC564.P477 2011
616.86'06--dc22
                                                                                        2011001063

Visit the Taylor & Francis Web site at
http://www.taylorandfrancis.com

and the Routledge Web site at
http://www.routledgementalhealth.com

For Billy, Hannah, and Noah

Contents

The Author

Nancy M. Petry earned a Ph.D. in psychology from Harvard University in 1994. In 1996, she joined the faculty of the University of Connecticut Health Center, where she is Professor of Medicine in the Calhoun Cardiology Center. Dr. Petry conducts research on the treatment of addictive disorders, ranging from substance use disorders to pathological gambling, and is expanding her research on contingency management to the prevention and treatment of behavioral cardiovascular health issues. She has published over 200 articles in peer-reviewed journals, and the National Institute on Drug Abuse, the National Institute on Alcohol Abuse and Alcoholism, and the National Institute of Mental Health fund her work. Dr. Petry serves as a consultant and advisor for the National Institutes of Health, is a member of the Substance Use Disorders Workgroup for *The Diagnostic and Statistical Manual of Mental Disorders-Revision V,* and is an editorial board member for six academic journals. Her first book, *Pathological Gambling: Etiology, Comorbidity, and Treatment,* received the Choice Magazine Award for Top Academic Titles in 2005. Dr. Petry received the American Psychological Association Distinguished Scientific Award for Early Career Contributions to Psychology in 2003 and the Joseph Cochin Award from the College of Drug Dependence in 2007.

Author's Note and Preface

Contingency management (CM), the application of tangible positive reinforcers to change behavior, and specifically substance-using behavior, is both an old and a new intervention. In some senses, it has been around since the beginning of time, as reinforcement is a central process related to learning and shaping behavior in many populations and contexts. It has also been researched, in one form or another, for treating substance abuse for over 35 years.

CM is an intervention that has only recently gained attention in community-based substance abuse treatment settings. With the conduct and publication of the National Institute on Drug Abuse Clinical Trials Network studies of CM, clinicians across the United States have been exposed to CM and seen firsthand its benefits. With the dissemination of these research findings, more and more program administrators and clinicians in the United States, as well as internationally, are gaining interest in adapting and applying CM to the patients they treat.

Unfortunately, there has been a dearth of informational sessions and training materials related to CM. Although many clinicians have heard of CM at conferences or via word of mouth, no empirically based training programs have been available on a large-scale basis, and very few clinicians have been trained in the background and administration of CM. Much of the information provided about CM is secondhand, or based upon informal applications using well intentioned, but not necessarily well informed, non-empirically validated applications. For example, many proponents of CM have claimed they are using CM when they provide encouraging verbal feedback or when they give an occasional tangible incentive (e.g., a gift card or candy bar) to patients.

Although these applications of incentives may have some modest positive effects on patient or clinician morale, incentives when provided in these manners are unlikely to have substantive benefits on patients or their drug abuse treatment outcomes. A vast empirical literature on CM demonstrates that basic behavioral principles need to be followed for CM to have significant beneficial effects. One relates to awarding appropriate magnitudes of tangible reinforcement. Thus, positive verbal statements, while necessary for the appropriate administration of CM, are not going to substantially improve outcomes on their own; similarly, candy bars and very low magnitude reinforcers are unlikely to impact outcomes. Another basic principle of CM is to provide tangible positive reinforcers each time the behavior targeted for change is objectively observed. Many current applications of incentive-type procedures do not select a priori specific behaviors to reinforce, and many only intermittently—and often with long delays—provide the reinforcers. For example, good attitudes or contributions to group may be rewarded in some contexts, but these are not objectively defined behaviors. Awarding a certificate of completion or even a $20 gift card for finishing a phase of treatment poses a lengthy delay (e.g., 4, 8, or 12 weeks or even longer) between the behaviors necessary to receive the reinforcement (regular attendance at treatment) and its receipt. The behavioral literature has well established that learning is maximized when time between the behavior and the reinforcer is minimized. Thus, much of what is considered CM in community practice is incongruent with behavioral principles and is unlikely to substantially alter patients' behaviors.

This book is designed to dispel myths related to what CM is and what it is not. It is written as a practical guide to provide clinicians, administrators, and researchers with background in applied behavioral research so that they can design, administer, and achieve the best possible outcomes with CM. Although research studies provide the basis of the work presented in this book, this book and its exercises are designed to assist professionals in applying CM to address issues of clinical significance within their own unique settings. Thus, it is expected that research protocols will not be blindly adapted for use in treatment settings. Rather, this book was written to teach administrators, clinicians, and researchers how best to adapt or integrate CM protocols to improve outcomes of their own patients.

The exercises and training materials outlined in this book have been utilized in over 50 training sessions that I've conducted with thousands of community-based providers over the past 10 years. I have learned to adapt and shape these trainings toward the most common clinical needs expressed by the therapists. My hope is that by providing these materials in the format of a book, more therapists and ultimately patients can benefit from well-designed and well-administered CM approaches.

Chapters 1 through 4 focus on introducing the concept and basic principles of CM. They also describe some of the seminal research studies that demonstrate the efficacy of the intervention, and they highlight different populations and settings in which CM has proven successful. Chapters 5 through 9 outline specific steps for designing a CM protocol; they teach you how to narrow down a behavior to reinforce, choose a patient population with whom to apply CM, design a monitoring and reinforcement schedule, and select reinforcers. Worksheets and exercises are included with these chapters to guide the processes. Chapters 10 and 11 relate to estimating costs of CM protocols and raising funds to support them. Chapter 12 gives detailed advice on what is needed to start a CM program. For readers who want to implement pre-existing and "standard" CM protocols that reinforce either drug abstinence or attendance at groups (the two most popular CM approaches), specific implementation guidelines are provided in Chapters 13 and 14. If few or no modifications from these procedures are needed, the reader can move directly to Chapters 12 and then Chapters 13 or 14, with earlier chapters serving as rationale for why these interventions are designed in the manner they are. Finally, Chapter 15 provides guidance on supervising CM administration, including information related to keeping track of reinforcers and reinforcement delivery. Together, these chapters comprise a comprehensive source for understanding, designing, and implementing CM.

I am thankful to the National Institute of Drug Abuse (P30-DA023918, R01-DA13444, R01-DA016855, R01-DA14618, R29-DA12056, R01-DA027615, R01-DA022739, R01-DA024667, R01-DA018883, R01-DA021567, U10-DA13034, and P50-DA09241) and the National Institute on Alcohol Abuse and Alcoholism (P60-AA03510) for funding the projects that are described in this book. Colleagues and research staff have been instrumental in conducting these and related studies, including but not limited to Dr. Sheila Alessi, Dr. Danielle Barry, William Blakey, Matt Brennan, Ellen Ciesielski, Marcia DeSousa, Anne Doersch, Trish Feery, Karen Gilliam, Damaris Hernandez, Dr. Elise Kabela-Cormier, Dr. Ron Kadden, Lindsey Kelley, Dr. David Ledgerwood, Dr. Mark Litt, Steve MacKinnon, Amy Novotny, Betsy Parker, Dr. Carla Rash, Sean Seirra, and Julie Urso. In addition to my colleagues at University of Connecticut Health Center, I acknowledge friends and colleagues who have helped to shape my interests in CM: Drs. Warren Bickel, Kathleen Carroll, Steve Higgins, John Roll, Bruce Rounsaville, and Maxine Stitzer. I am also thankful for the many clinicians and administrators at clinical treatment sites who supported CM projects throughout the years, including Alcohol and Drug Recovery Centers, Inc., Baystate Medical Center Carlson Recovery/Behavioral Health Network, Inc., Community Substance Abuse Centers, Inc., Connecticut Renaissance, Inc., Connections, The Dispensary, Hospital of Central Connecticut, Hospital of Saint Rapheal Substance Abuse Services, Liberation Programs, Inc., Morris Foundation, New York State Office of Alcohol and Substance Abuse Services and affiliated centers, St. Mary's Hospital Behavioral Healthcare Services, Regional Network of Programs, and the National Institute of Drug Abuse Clinical Trials Network treatment sites: Arapaho-Douglas, Charleston, Circle Park, Crossroads, Harbel, Jefferson, Guenster LMG, Matrix, Act II, Aegis, Glenwood, Greenwich, LESC, and Oasis.

Perhaps most of all, I am indebted to my husband, a physician who was initially one of the greatest skeptics of CM but who now sees its application to a variety of health behaviors, and our 1-year-old daughter and new baby on the way. Children are constant reminders of the robustness of behavioral principles. They also provide invaluable lessons about how even the youngest infants can modify their own behaviors—and those of their parents—depending on appropriate (and also the inevitable inappropriate) use of behavioral principles.

Foundations for Understanding

I

Chapter 1

Introduction

We have all encountered patients who do not succeed in treatment. Often, we can spot them right away. They come to their initial evaluation with limited motivation to change. External circumstances, such as a family member threatening to leave them or a recent arrest with a court case pending, may prompt their coming into treatment. Some minimize their drug use, and others proclaim they will overcome their problems. But, we know for many, this will not be the case. We know many will not even show up for treatment tomorrow.

Others present to treatment, and we really have hope that they will make it. They have lost a lot—friends, family, jobs, health, material goods, and perhaps even their freedom—because of their drinking and drug use. They attribute their losses directly and conclusively to their substance use. They know they are better off without it. They have already made it through the withdrawal stages, and they have even been sober for a few days or weeks before beginning treatment. They have started attending Alcoholics Anonymous meetings and report that it seems to be working for them. They indicate that they have thrown out all their old alcohol bottles and their drug-using paraphernalia. They want to know your success rates, and they ask you what more they can do to stay sober.

Although some patients who begin substance abuse treatment do succeed and stop using substances in both the short and the long term, many others do not. We have no way of knowing conclusively who will succeed and who will not. Unfortunately, we encounter many patients for whom we have high hopes, but who, despite all their efforts and ours, still relapse.

What if there were something that helped? What if there were an intervention that improved retention and more patients got better? Wouldn't it be worth investing the effort to try it?

There is such an intervention. It is met with a great deal of controversy, and it is not a magic bullet. However, this intervention does improve outcomes of substance-abusing patients. In fact, in a large independent analysis, this intervention was found to be the *most* effective psychosocial treatment for substance use disorders (Dutra, Stathopoulou, Basden, Leyro, Powers, & Otto, 2008).

On some levels, the intervention is very straightforward and simplistic. Basically, it involves rewarding desired or therapeutically appropriate behaviors. This intervention has been tested repeatedly

3

in controlled clinical research trials with virtually every substance-abusing patient population and in every type of clinical setting. The research evidence for this intervention is outstanding, yet the technique has rarely been integrated into clinical settings. This gap between research and practice has resulted from a host of factors, ranging from costs of the procedure, to lack of experience and knowledge, to ideological concerns.

You may have heard of this intervention, and you may even have strong feelings about it. It is called contingency management (CM), and more recently it has also been termed "motivational incentives." Simply stated, it involves providing tangible and concrete reinforcers or incentives to patients for evidence of objective behavior change. The reinforcers most often consist of vouchers, exchangeable for retail goods and services, or the chance to win a variety of prizes, such as bus tokens, candy bars, toiletry items, radios, and televisions.

Some have criticized the procedure as using bribery to reward drug abusers for what they should be doing anyway. Others contend that patients will simply sell their goods and buy more drugs. Still others acknowledge the efficacy of the procedure but state it is impractical or too expensive to use in real world clinical settings.

These concerns are all valid issues, especially among those with limited familiarity with the technique. The purposes of this book are to help dispel some of the myths about CM and to assist clinicians in developing CM programs that will be useful in their own settings and with their own patients. The book will detail the background and history of CM treatments, along with their similarity to procedures used in everyday settings ranging from childrearing to employment. Solutions to potential problems, such as selling incentive items for drug money, have long been overcome in the research about CM. This book will assist clinicians in designing CM programs that do not backfire in such manners.

Effective examples of CM, when designed and implemented by clinicians in practice, are becoming abundant. The National Institute on Drug Abuse's Clinical Trials Network (CTN) studies (Peirce et al., 2006; Petry, Peirce, et al., 2005) have spurred interest nationwide in adapting CM in practice settings. These studies are described in detail in Chapter 3. Following the conclusion of the CTN trials, the Health and Hospital Corporation in New York City integrated CM in five large substance abuse treatment programs (Kellogg, Burns, Coleman, Stitzer, Wale, & Kreek, 2005). Each clinic designed its own CM system, selecting different behaviors to reinforce and reinforcement systems, similarly to what you will do in the context of this book. Most clinics developed a reinforcement system that provided reinforcers contingent upon attendance at particular groups alone or in combination with abstinence. Patients could earn tangible reinforcers, such as gift cards and subway tokens. As outlined below, both patients and staff became very enthusiastic about the CM program.

Initially, some patients were in disbelief that they would receive something for attending groups, and they had to actually see the reinforcer before they believed it was real. One patient quoted in Kellogg et al. (2005) stated, "In Russia, we were forced into treatment—Now (crying), my God, I'm getting treatment and $25.00!" Another man with chronic alcohol dependence cried when he received his first McDonald's coupon. He said that no one had ever given him anything for working on his recovery, and he achieved sobriety for the first time in eight years. In a number of poignant stories, patients gave their earned reinforcers to other patients or used their gift certificates to buy presents or needed items for their children or other family members. Patients who earned gift cards for movies would go together in groups, connecting with one another in a manner therapists had never seen previously.

Once the staff overcame their initial resistance toward CM, many clinicians became strong supporters of it. An important part of this transformation was a changing perspective on the use of reinforcers. As clinicians began to see the benefits of tangible reinforcers, many who were initially skeptical became vocal proponents of CM. Instead of seeing CM as bribery, a clinician interviewed by Kellogg et al. (2005) stated, "We came to see that we need to reward people where rewards in their lives were few and far between. We use the rewards as a clinical tool—not as bribery—but for recognition."

An unexpected benefit of CM, staff and administrators reported that their morale increased as they began to see greater group attendance. Clinicians found larger groups were easier to conduct and more satisfying to run. When patients publicly, and sometimes tearfully, thanked a therapist for his or her help, the staff felt a sense of personal fulfillment.

Clinicians further note (Kellogg et al., 2005) that patients who are positively reinforced show increases in self-esteem and become more empowered. They report that patients began to speak about pursuing goals, including vocational and educational aspirations, with CM treatments. These sorts of "turnarounds" are clearly gratifying to the clinicians.

Patients with long histories of treatment resistance who responded well to CM are particularly inspiring to clinicians. In my initial CM project (Petry, Martin, Cooney, & Kranzler, 2000), the very first patient assigned to CM treatment was a chronic recidivist alcohol-dependent man, who was well known to staff but had never before remained in outpatient treatment longer than a week. With CM, he continued in treatment—and sustained abstinence—for the entire duration of the program. Staff were amazed at his engagement. Years after the CM program had ended, a staff member ran into him at a community event, to which he had taken his grandson. The patient reported no lapses to alcohol use for years, and attributed his abstinence to a tradition he began during his CM program—spending every Saturday with his grandson.

A large treatment provider in Wisconsin provides another example of successful integration of CM in an adolescent program (Petry & Bohn, 2003). Michael Bohn, director of this program, noted,

> The parents had often reported having great difficulty setting limits with their substance-abusing children, and they had become frustrated by battles that often deteriorated into power struggles over the adolescent's behavior…. We began … to persuade individual parents that it would be helpful to try to reward their child for doing well. We helped them begin to use objective measures of specific behaviors, such as attendance at school and treatment sessions, to reward their kids.
>
> We have also begun to use coupons for things that kids like— such as free pizzas, passes to water parks and laser tag arcades, fast food restaurants…. Using these coupons…, we saw more of the adolescents staying in treatment. And it wasn't costing us anything. The parents were giving the same rewards they would otherwise have given outright, such as permission to the use the car, money for dates, and the like—but using them now as contingencies. So it really was a revenue-neutral proposition… the reward system has significantly reduced our dropout rate among adolescents and has substantially increased parental involvement and satisfaction. (pp. 56–57)

Such personalized stories are convincing on many levels. However, others want to know about the financial implications of implementing CM when parents or others are not funding the reinforcers. The director (M. Boyle, personal communication, February 11, 2004) of a clinic in Illinois began implementing CM in a residential detoxification program. He set aside funds for the CM program in hopes that it would enhance retention and improve reimbursement rates. Before CM, over 30% of patients left treatment against medical advice. This rate decreased to 12% with the introduction of CM. Importantly, this reduction in premature discharges resulted in a substantial increase of $166,000 in revenue to the clinic over a six-month period.

The Office of Alcohol and Substance Abuse Services in the State of New York received a grant to implement CM in a variety of clinical settings. After a one-day training, similar to that outlined in this book, four large outpatient providers participated in a CM implementation phase in which they provided reinforcers, using the Name-in-the-hat CM procedure detailed in Chapter 14, for attendance at group sessions. All four programs were able to readily implement CM. With this initial success, all chose to integrate additional rounds in new or continuing group sessions. The clinics documented increases in group attendance ranging from 13% to 42%, which translated directly into increased provider revenue (McCorry, Brandau, & Morone, 2009). At the time of this writing, three of four programs made programmatic decisions to continue to sustain and spread CM throughout their organizations.

Lott and Jenicus (2009) implemented CM in an outpatient adolescent treatment program in Illinois. The CM reinforced abstinence and attendance at treatment. They compared attendance rates, drug-free urine samples, and billings in the three months before CM to the 12 months during which CM was operative. On average, adolescents attended 13 days of treatment before CM, and attendance increased significantly to 15 days during CM; proportions of negative urine samples increased significantly as well, from 66.7% to 76.6% between the pre-CM and CM phases. Further and important from a cost perspective, the amounts billed for clinical services increased significantly from $3,671 per patient before CM to $4,395 per patient during CM. Thus, CM was not only effective in improving outcomes, but also cost-effective to the program.

These case studies reveal what research has long shown. CM is effective in changing patients' behaviors. It can have profoundly positive effects for both patients and the clinicians who institute it. However, CM is an intervention in the crossroads; it is an empirically validated treatment, yet one that has only recently infiltrated into practice settings. As CM moves more and more into the hands of clinicians, it is imperative that its users understand circumstances under which it will work well and conditions under which it will not. This is a practical book that will help you design CM interventions to best serve the needs and improve the outcomes of the patients you treat. In doing so, you will be empowered to positively impact your patients.

Chapter 2

Background of Behavioral Therapies and the Evolution of Contingency Management

Behavioral principles serve as the foundation for CM interventions. This chapter reviews some basic behavioral principles and how they relate to impacting behavior change. The chapter initially describes how behavioral principles are operative in everyday life. In the context of CM treatments, these principles are also applied to substance abusers, and I describe the relevance of these behavioral procedures to drug abuse treatment. The chapter ends with a detailed description of how CM interventions have been adapted on a wide-scale approach in methadone maintenance settings.

2.1 BASIC BEHAVIORAL PRINCIPLES

2.1.1 Positive Reinforcement

One of the basic principles of behavioral therapy relates to positive reinforcement. Simply put, providing reinforcers, or rewards, will increase the frequency of a behavior. For example, if a parent provides a tangible reinforcer, such as a candy bar, a small toy, or a dollar bill, each time his eight-year-old child makes her bed, the child will increase the frequency with which she makes the bed. If a child receives a sticker each time he brushes his teeth, and seven stickers can be exchanged for a toy, a child will learn to brush his teeth. All parents use some forms of CM to shape or alter their children's behavior.

Similarly, a variety of settings, including classrooms as well as work and employment situations, use CM techniques. Teachers provide smiley faces and stars on homework or tests on which a child has performed well. Passing grades and special privileges in the classroom (extra recess time, special helper status, etc.) are common examples of reinforcers that encourage studying and cooperative classroom behaviors. In some professions, such as sales, those who achieve high performance receive extra income in the form of bonuses or commissions. These are all examples of positive reinforcers used to increase the frequency of specific behaviors.

2.1.2 Negative Reinforcement

In contrast to positive reinforcers that increase the frequency of a behavior, negative reinforcers reduce the frequency of behaviors. In school settings, small children receive time-outs when they are exhibiting aggressive or inappropriate behaviors. As children get older, teachers withhold recess privileges or send children to detention or the principal's office if problem behaviors arise. In employment settings, employees who arrive late for work may lose their hourly pay, forgo promotions, or be subjected to demotions and reductions in salaries or even the loss of a job for continued poor performance.

Both positive and negative reinforcers can effectively alter behaviors. However, everyone prefers to receive something positive rather than have it taken away. In the context of clinical settings and CM treatments, the emphasis is on positively reinforcing appropriate patient behaviors.

2.2 APPLICATION OF BEHAVIORAL TREATMENTS TO CLINICAL SETTINGS

2.2.1 Non-Substance-Abusing Populations

Many examples exist of the use of behavioral therapies to modify behaviors in clinical settings. For example, autistic children receive social or tangible reinforcers for vocalizations (Wolf, Risley, & Mees, 1964), and mentally retarded patients earn concrete, specific, and immediate reinforcers, such as food or access to entertainment, for completing learning tasks (Bijou & Orlando, 1961; Glover, Roane, Kadey, & Grow, 2008). The therapeutic culture of Boys Town for conduct disordered adolescents is another example of behavioral principles applied clinically (Resetar-Volz & Cook, 2009). It awards points or tokens for positive and pro-social behaviors and removes these points or tokens when negative or undesired behaviors occur.

2.2.2 Residential Substance Abuse Treatment

"Contingency management" is a term that describes adaptation of the token economy for substance-using populations. Most token economies are relevant only in "closed" settings. Staff can monitor and closely regulate token economies within restrictive settings, and such procedures work well when all residents have equal opportunities to earn privileges.

Residential substance abuse treatment settings make use of similar procedures. Points or privilege systems are nearly ubiquitous in Therapeutic Communities and residential substance abuse treatment programs. Patients can earn privileges such as visitor passes, phone calls, and more appealing chores, depending on progress and behavior in the residential setting.

2.2.3 Outpatient Substance Abuse Treatment

In outpatient settings, however, such extreme control over many facets of life is not possible. Patients come and go into the clinic, and their financial and social situations vary outside of the therapeutic setting. Earning a star or a token exchangeable for something one can readily gain access to outside of the clinic may not be particularly appealing or effective for altering behavior among outpatients. Further, the nature of the desired items and privileges that serve as reinforcers is vastly different in outpatient settings compared with inpatient or residential ones. Outpatients have less desire for clinic privileges, as phone calls and status in the clinic may not be particularly meaningful beyond the few hours a day or week spent there.

In outpatient settings and 12-step meetings like Alcoholics Anonymous (AA), the use of positive reinforcers is commonplace, although the reinforcers differ. Coffee and food may reinforce attending meetings, and the structure of AA calls for verbally reinforcing each day of abstinence. Statements related to days of non-drinking achieved (e.g., "My name is Michael and I've been sober for 42 days") result in clapping and congratulations. Specific anniversaries of abstinence lead to special celebrations, and sponsor status is granted to those with long-term regular attendance at meetings and abstinence. Thus, reinforcement is used in the context of 12-step meetings, the most popular intervention for substance abuse in the United States.

2.3 BASIC PRINCIPLES OF CM

Contingency management treatments refer to utilizing the principles and processes of reinforcement that are routinely applied in everyday settings, including 12-step interventions, and adapting them so that they more clearly align to behavioral principles. In this manner, the reinforcers have a greater likelihood of encouraging the desired behaviors. There are three basic premises of a CM intervention. The three key principles of CM are the following:

1. Frequently monitor the behavior that you are trying to change.
2. Provide tangible, immediate positive reinforcers each time that the behavior occurs.
3. When the behavior does not occur, withhold the positive reinforcers.

Each of these principles is more thoroughly described below. The remainder of this book refers back to these three principles, which will become critical to the design of your own CM program.

2.3.1 Frequently Monitor the Behavior That You Are Trying to Change

In the case of substance abuse treatment, the behavior most often targeted for change is drug use. Objective and easy-to-use methods exist for assessing use of most substances, and clinicians are familiar with these procedures. They typically involve urine drug screening. Most urine drug tests can detect abstinence (or use) over a two- to three-day period. Hence, if a patient used cocaine on a Monday, his urine samples would test positive that day and until Wednesday or Thursday. Because of this window over which abstinence can be detected, most CM systems rely upon thrice-weekly urinalysis testing: Mondays, Wednesdays, and Fridays. If samples are collected and tested according to this schedule, each instance of cocaine use, and each two- or three-day period of cocaine abstinence, can be detected. Abstinence is positively reinforced, which in turn results in the behaviors leading to abstinence increasing in frequency.

2.3.2 Provide Tangible, Immediate Positive Reinforcers Each Time That Behavior Occurs

In terms of the second principle of CM, positive reinforcers need to be provided each time the targeted behavior occurs. The key is to make use of widely applicable and universally appealing reinforcers. In closed systems such as residential treatment programs, privileges can be appealing and highly desired, but in outpatient settings, different forms of reinforcers are needed to have a substantial impact on behavior. Thus, reinforcers could be money, vouchers exchangeable for retail goods and services, or chances to win prizes of monetary value.

Each time the patient tests negative for the targeted substance, she earns a reinforcer. As noted earlier, I caution against the exclusive use of privileges as reinforcers in outpatient settings, as not all patients desire clinic privileges, and many types of privileges are things upon which patients will satiate or tire over time. For example, some (but certainly not all) patients will enjoy being a group leader or being allowed to use the clinic's phone for a call occasionally. However, if these are the only possible reinforcers, patients will grow less enthused with them over time. Chapter 8 describes the types of reinforcers that are possible to include in CM interventions, and the advantages and disadvantages of each. The key to a successful CM intervention is to select reinforcers that *all* patients will desire and work to achieve.

2.3.3 When the Behavior Does Not Occur, Withhold the Positive Reinforcers

In terms of the third key strategy of CM interventions, patients who do not exhibit the desired behavior (i.e., fail to submit a negative urine sample) do not receive the reinforcer. There is no direct punishment involved, as patients who are punished for using (or exhibiting other negative behaviors) are unlikely to remain engaged in treatment in voluntary settings. Hence, punishment will serve to disengage patients from the treatment process, rather than encourage the behavior that one is attempting to increase. A good analogy relates to AA. When an AA member relapses, they are not punished for the relapse, but rather congratulated for re-engaging in the meetings, even if the current duration of abstinence is short (e.g., hours or days). A similar approach is necessary in CM treatments. When relapses occur, the patient forgoes the tangible reinforcers but is strongly encouraged to regain abstinence and again achieve the reinforcer.

On the surface, CM is as simple as the three steps outlined above. Nevertheless, decades of research and clinical experience have gone into designing and evaluating the efficacy of CM for reducing substance use. Protocols for the most effective CM interventions involve nuances that integrate some additional, and sometimes rather subtle, behavioral principles. The remaining chapters outline these issues to encourage development of the most effective CM approach for your clinical setting.

2.4 ADOPTING CM FOR CLINIC PRACTICE: A CAUTIONARY TALE

2.4.1 Early CM Studies in Methadone Clinics

As noted above, researchers and clinicians have adapted and implemented CM for substance-abusing populations, and Chapter 3 reviews results from these studies and experiences. With the ever-growing demand for implementation of evidence-based treatment in clinical practice, more and more clinicians desire to learn about and implement CM procedures in practice. Although CM can be very effective in altering drug use behaviors, one must adhere to the three principles outlined earlier, or the desired benefits may not be achieved. A historical tale described below illustrates a less-than-ideal dissemination of CM into practice.

Contingency management interventions began during the late 1960s and early 1970s. They were not explicitly referred to by this terminology, but they shared the three central features of CM outlined above. Researchers conducted the initial CM studies in methadone maintenance clinics that were just beginning to emerge as an effective treatment for heroin dependence at that time. Although methadone substantially reduces heroin use when administered at the appropriate dosage (Ball & Ross, 1991), not all patients who receive methadone cease using heroin. In fact, continued heroin use among methadone patients is a common clinical concern.

In this context, CM treatments developed and grew. Initial studies of CM for methadone-maintained heroin-dependent patients used properties of the methadone-dosing regimen itself to reinforce heroin abstinence. Whenever patients tested negative for heroin, they received a reinforcer, and one of the possible reinforcers was a take-home dose of methadone. Because methadone clinics require daily attendance, take-home doses allow patients a day off from the clinic, while still receiving benefits of methadone. All methadone patients desire take-home doses, and importantly, the value of take-home doses does not diminish over time. The initial studies using contingencies in methadone patients found benefits of take-home doses as reinforcers.

As an example of an early CM study, Maxine Stitzer and colleagues (Stitzer, Bigelow, & Liebson, 1980) applied CM to seven methadone maintenance patients, who chronically used heroin while maintained on methadone. In a five-week pre-treatment phase in which urine samples were collected and tested for heroin use twice weekly, the patients tested positive for heroin at least 30% of the time (range 30% to 85% positive). During the CM intervention phase, urine samples continued to be collected twice weekly, and patients could earn a reinforcer (e.g., a take-home dose of methadone or $15 cash) immediately after they tested negative for heroin. The proportion of urine samples positive during the contingent phase was lower than during the pre-treatment phases in all seven of the patients, with five of the seven patients showing dramatic reductions in heroin use in the contingent relative to pre-treatment phase; three patients submitted fewer than 10% heroin-positive samples during the contingent phase, and two others submitted only about 20% positive samples. Thus, a strong positive effect of CM was noted in about two-thirds of the patients.

Note that this CM study closely adhered to the three basic principles of CM outlined earlier. The behavior targeted for change (heroin abstinence) was monitored often (two times per week). Each time abstinence was detected, clinicians reinforced abstinence with a highly desired reinforcer (e.g., a take-home dose of methadone). Every time the desired behavior did not occur (i.e., the patient tested positive), the reinforcer was withheld.

2.4.2 Moving Research Into Practice: What Went Wrong

Early studies of CM in methadone patients paved the way for future legislation and today's clinical practice guidelines for methadone treatment. A common practice in methadone clinics today is to allow for take-home doses when patients have achieved abstinence, and it is easy to see how this practice evolved from the initial research with CM.

Although well intended, the adoption of this CM technique into practice occurred with some changes relative to its use in the original research studies. Typically, in methadone clinics in the United States today, patients must not miss any clinic visits and they must submit negative urine samples for a three-month or longer period in order to receive take-home privileges.

Some patients benefit from these procedures, and some achieve abstinence and earn take-home privileges. However, the vast majority of patients maintained on methadone do not receive take-home doses. Rates of illicit drug use in methadone treatment can be as high as 60% to 80% or greater (Ball & Ross, 1991). About half of all patients who begin methadone treatment drop out, with most dropouts continuing to abuse heroin. The relatively poor success rates of the reinforcement-based procedures used today in practice are in stark contrast to the benefits of CM noted in the early trials, which used take-home doses as reinforcers.

2.4.3 Failure to Apply the Three Basic Principles of CM in Methadone Clinics

There are a number of reasons the take-home dosing guidelines used today do not perform as well in practice as CM procedures did when they were implemented in early research studies. Many of the reasons relate directly to the three basic principles of CM outlined earlier. The first is simple. The behavior targeted for change (heroin abstinence) is generally not monitored frequently in practice settings. On average, patients in methadone clinics leave only one urine sample per month, not two or three per week as was the standard in the research trials. Hence, heroin abstinence goes undetected and is not reinforced. Conversely, much use of heroin occurs throughout the month, but the "random" monthly urine tests infrequently detect it.

The second premise of CM is to frequently reinforce—with tangible reinforcers—each instance of the targeted behavior. As noted above, issues with the monitoring schedule prevent appropriate reinforcement and reduce the likelihood that the desired behavior will increase in frequency. In addition, the reinforcer (a take-home dose) is not provided immediately after the target behavior (heroin abstinence). Patients need to maintain abstinence for three months to earn even one take-home dose in methadone clinics, while each instance of abstinence resulted in a take-home dose in the CM studies. Hence, far more take-home doses were available to patients in the studies, and they received reinforcement in greater temporal proximity to the behavior.

The third principle of CM is that whenever the behavior does not occur, the reinforcer is immediately removed. In initial research studies, any missed or positive sample resulted in a forfeiting of take-home privileges. Because patients provided samples multiple times each week, detection of use occurred fairly rapidly. In the system practiced in many methadone clinics today, patients can go weeks, and sometimes even months, using heroin before they test positive on the "random" monthly urine screens and lose their take-home privileges.

A parallel example would be in using reinforcement to encourage your child to make her bed. If you checked her bed every day right before she came down to breakfast and, if it was made, immediately gave her some amount of money, it is likely she would begin making her bed every day. In contrast, if you checked her bed only once per month, and she had to have the bed made on random monthly checks three months in a row prior to receiving any reinforcement, it is highly unlikely that she would ever make her bed regularly.

The above example is just one of many demonstrating that appropriate behavioral procedures are needed in order for a CM protocol to exert its desired effects. It highlights the lessons that can be learned when attempting to adapt empirically validated treatments into clinical settings without a full understanding of the basis of the intervention. Had methadone clinics applied CM procedures as described in the research studies, they would have been more successful in decreasing drug use. This is a naturally occurring example of a less-than-ideal attempt of translating an evidence-based treatment into practice.

2.5 PREPARING FOR THE FUTURE: A NEW GENERATION OF CM ADOPTION

Clinicians should learn from this historical example as newer versions of CM are adopted into practice. The remainder of this book provides concrete examples of good and less-than-ideal CM protocols. It critiques their strengths and weaknesses. Clearly, some issues are unique to patients and settings and require modifications of strictly research-based interventions. Highly controlled research methodology is difficult to implement within the challenges of modern-day substance abuse and mental health treatment. However, one can make some modifications without comprising effectiveness, so long as basic principles and procedures remain intact.

Much can be gained by implementing CM, especially when it is done correctly. Patients can and do get better, and clinicians feel successful and more fulfilled. Reimbursement rates to clinics can also increase as patients attend more sessions and premature discharges decrease. In sum, designing and implementing CM in practice can have substantial benefits, but the key is to develop strategies in an informed manner to maximize the potential for success.

Chapter 3

Empirical Evidence of the Efficacy of Contingency Management

Contingency management interventions for treating substance abusers began in the context of methadone maintenance clinics, as noted in Chapter 2. The reinforcer was typically take-home doses of methadone, and providing this reinforcer contingent upon drug abstinence was very effective in decreasing heroin use. Since these initial studies were conducted, CM approaches have been adapted to reduce drug use in other substance-abusing populations as well. This chapter details some studies that utilized CM to reduce drug use in a variety of patient populations to provide you with the scientific basis of evidence of CM. By the end of the chapter, you should have a good understanding of the benefits of CM.

3.1 VOUCHER CM FOR COCAINE ABUSE

3.1.1 Background

In the mid to late 1980s, the United States was struck by the cocaine and HIV epidemics. Cocaine use was growing markedly throughout the United States during this period. The National Institute on Drug Abuse (NIDA, 1989) estimated that the number of persons using cocaine once a week or more increased 33% between 1985 and 1988. Further, one to two million persons in the United States were dependent on cocaine (Committee on the Judiciary, 1990; NIDA, 1990).

HIV was also becoming increasingly recognized during that time. As HIV infection rates rose, epidemiologists quickly discovered that intravenous drug use was responsible for large proportions of cases of HIV transmission. Nearly all methadone-maintained heroin users were intravenous drug users, with many injecting not only heroin but also cocaine. Hence, this patient population was substantially impacted by the HIV epidemic. Methods for reducing intravenous use of drugs became a public health priority.

Further, cocaine-dependent patients were initiating outpatient drug abuse treatment in record numbers. By the early 1990s, the Drug

Abuse Treatment Outcome Study found that cocaine was the most commonly used illegal drug among individuals entering treatment programs (Simpson, Joe, Fletcher, Hubbard, & Anglin, 1999). Most substance abuse treatment clinics at that time were accustomed to treating alcohol-dependent patients, not illicit drug users. Dropout and relapse rates among cocaine abusers were extraordinarily high, and clinicians were unfamiliar with working with this generally younger population. The treatments traditionally used with alcohol-dependent patients did not appear very successful with the cocaine-abusing patients (Gawin & Kleber, 1987). No pharmacotherapy to this day has demonstrated consistently positive results in treating cocaine dependence, further necessitating effective psychotherapies or behavioral therapies.

By the early 1990s, not a single clinical trial applying traditional substance abuse strategies evidenced successful outcomes with cocaine-abusing outpatients (Budney, Higgins, Hughes, & Bickel, 1992). Studies evaluated supportive therapies, 12-step interventions, cognitive-behavioral therapy or other skills-based trainings, but none demonstrated consistently beneficial effects. Given the increasing concerns surrounding the HIV epidemic, there was a pressing need to find an efficacious intervention for cocaine-abusing outpatients.

3.1.2 Introduction of Voucher-Based CM

In this context, Dr. Stephen Higgins developed a CM intervention for cocaine abusers. Dr. Higgins studied at Johns Hopkins University and participated in the early CM studies with methadone-maintained patients. When Dr. Higgins moved to the University of Vermont, he was no longer working with methadone-maintained patients, making take-home doses of methadone inappropriate as reinforcers. He developed a voucher-based procedure, integrating the token economy approach and applying it to outpatient substance abuse treatment populations.

Voucher-based CM provides points worth a specific amount of money whenever a patient submits a urine sample negative for cocaine. Points are recorded on vouchers so that patients do not receive money directly. Vouchers are analogous to having a bank account within the clinic. Patients "deposit" their earned vouchers into their account, in which they have a running tally of amounts earned and spent. Patients can save vouchers for a large value item (e.g., an iPod or stereo), or they can spend them as quickly as they earn them. They simply ask clinic staff to purchase any item or service that they want, once they have accumulated a sufficient amount in vouchers to cover its costs. Items appropriate for voucher spending were required to be of therapeutic value, such that a patient could request new clothes for a job interview or tuition for a continuing education class. Vouchers are also commonly spent on social and recreational activities such as cameras, tickets to the movie theater, or gift cards to stores. Clinicians can deny voucher requests. Examples of inappropriate voucher spending include weapons, alcohol or tobacco products, or tickets to a rock concert in which substance use would be likely.

An important component of a voucher program is that the value of vouchers earned increases with each consecutive instance of the desired behavior. The first cocaine-negative urine sample submitted earns 10 points, and each point is worth 25 cents, for a total of $2.25. The second negative sample in a row earns 15 points or $3.75, the third negative sample in a row results in 20 points or $4.50, and so on. Whenever the target behavior does not occur (e.g., a negative sample is not submitted), voucher values are reset to the initially low level of $2.25 for the next negative sample, thus providing a powerful incentive to sustain abstinence over time.

To allow for the greatest probability of this intervention being successful in decreasing cocaine use, Dr. Higgins arranged for large magnitudes of vouchers. In the initial studies of this approach, patients could earn up to a total of about $1,000 in vouchers if they maintained abstinence throughout a 12-week treatment episode.

3.1.3 Comparing Voucher CM to 12-Step Therapy

The first study evaluated voucher CM when combined with another effective therapy: the community reinforcement approach (CRA). CRA involves changing environmental contingencies in the patient's life (Hunt & Azrin, 1973). Employment, recreation, and family systems are addressed to promote a lifestyle that is more reinforcing than substance use. Rather than being entirely office-based, CRA (as its name implies) occurs, at least in part, in the community. If patients do not attend treatment or fail to follow through with an employment or recreational goal, the therapist may go to their homes, accompany them to interviews, or help them try a new activity.

In the initial study of voucher CM (Higgins et al., 1991), the first 13 cocaine-abusing outpatients received voucher CM plus CRA therapy, and the next 15 patients received a 12-step intervention. Significantly more patients who received CM plus CRA remained in treatment for 12 weeks. Eighty-five percent of patients who receive CM plus CRA, versus only 33% in the 12-step group, remained involved in treatment for 12 weeks. Patients receiving CM plus CRA also achieved significantly longer periods of continuous cocaine abstinence; 75% of those receiving CM plus CRA achieved four or more weeks of cocaine abstinence compared to 0% of the patients receiving 12-step therapy. This initial study suggested benefits of voucher CM, but because the study was not randomized, one could not conclusively attribute the improvements to CM plus CRA treatment.

Higgins, Budney, Bickel, Hughes, Foerg, and Badger (1993) next conducted a randomized study comparing these two treatments in a sample of 38 cocaine-dependent patients. Half of the patients were assigned to CM plus CRA and half to 12-step counseling. This trial lasted for 24 weeks. The CM plus CRA treatment provided escalating vouchers for submission of cocaine-negative urine samples for the first 12 weeks, and $1 lottery tickets were reinforcers for cocaine abstinence in the last 12 weeks. Fifty-eight percent of patients randomly assigned to CM plus CRA completed 24 weeks of treatment, compared to 11% of patients assigned to 12-step counseling. Groups also differed significantly with respect to rates of continuous abstinence; 68% of patients receiving CM plus CRA achieved eight weeks or more of continuous cocaine abstinence versus 11% of those assigned to 12-step counseling.

As is common in clinical trials, researchers invited, and paid, patients to come back to the clinic for follow-up evaluations, at which time drug use was assessed by both self-report and objective indices (urine toxicology). The goal is to get as many patients as possible to complete follow-up assessments so that long-term effects of the interventions can be evaluated in a non-biased fashion. If patients miss the follow-up evaluations, one is unsure whether they relapsed or remained abstinent. In this study, Higgins, Budney, Bickel, Badger, Foerg, and Ogden (1995) were able to contact and interview 79% of patients one year following study participation. Group differences in substance use outcomes favored the CM plus CRA treatment at each assessment throughout the follow-up period. Patients who received CM plus CRA were more likely to report abstinence in the 30 days prior to each interview and to submit cocaine-negative urine samples compared to patients who received 12-step counseling. For example, 96% of patients who had earlier received CM plus CRA and who completed the one-year follow-up were abstinent from cocaine at the time of the evaluation compared with 69% of those who received 12-step counseling. Fifty-eight percent of patients who received CM plus CRA maintained cocaine abstinence throughout the one-year follow-up period versus 26% of patients who received 12-step counseling.

Thus, this first randomized study of the efficacy of voucher-based CM demonstrated strong and long-lasting benefits of CM plus CRA treatment. However, patients who received the CM differed from the comparison condition not only with respect to the availability of vouchers but also in terms of the psychotherapy (CRA or 12-step). CRA therapy itself is an evidence-based treatment, with controlled trials showing its benefits to other psychotherapies (Azrin, 1976; Roozen, Boulogne, van Tulder, van den Brink, De Jong, & Kerkhof, 2004). Thus, the next step in this series of investigations was to examine the effects of CM in conjunction with CRA versus CRA alone, without vouchers for abstinence.

3.1.4 Isolating the Effects of CM versus CRA

To dismantle the effects of contingent vouchers versus those of CRA, Higgins, Budney, Bickel, Foerg, Donham, and Badger (1994) randomized 40 cocaine-dependent outpatients to CRA alone or CRA plus voucher CM. In both conditions, the CRA was delivered in twice-weekly individual counseling sessions in weeks one through 12 and in once-weekly individual sessions in weeks 13 through 24. Patients assigned to CM plus CRA received vouchers when they submitted cocaine-negative urine samples during weeks one through 12. During the final 12 weeks, both groups earned $1 lottery tickets for provision of cocaine-negative urine samples. Again, there was a significant difference between patients assigned to the two treatments with respect to the proportion who remained in treatment for 24 weeks. Three-quarters of those receiving CM plus CRA completed treatment compared with 40% of those receiving CRA alone. Longest duration of continuous cocaine abstinence differed significantly between the groups as well. Patients in the CM plus CRA group achieved an average of 11.7 weeks of continuous abstinence from cocaine, whereas patients in the CRA alone group achieved an average of 6.0 weeks. About 72% of CM patients achieved at least a month of continuous cocaine abstinence and 55% two or more months. In contrast, only about 55% and 25% of those in the CRA alone group attained at least one or two months of abstinence, respectively. Further, the average duration of continuous abstinence was longer during the first 12 weeks of treatment when they received vouchers, and during the second 12 weeks of treatment when patients in both groups received lottery tickets, but those in the CM plus CRA group were no longer receiving vouchers. This result suggested that the early abstinence achieved with voucher-based reinforcement contributed to sustained abstinence when the high magnitude voucher reinforcers were no longer available.

3.1.5 Contingent versus Non-Contingent Vouchers

A number of studies have demonstrated that *contingent* delivery of the reinforcer, rather than just access to vouchers or greater retention in treatment, engenders reductions in drug use. Silverman, Higgins, et al. (1996) randomly assigned 39 cocaine-abusing methadone patients to one of two treatments: vouchers contingent upon submission of cocaine-negative urine specimens, or vouchers regardless of urine toxicology results. Patients in the non-contingent group received the same overall amount of vouchers, and at the same frequency, as those in the contingent group, and retention rates were similar. Of patients in the contingent group, however, 42% achieved at least eight weeks of continuous cocaine abstinence compared with 0% in the non-contingent group.

Higgins, Wong, Badger, Ogden, and Dantona (2000) reported similar results in cocaine-dependent patients who were not opioid dependent (and not maintained on methadone). Seventy patients were randomized to contingent vouchers or to vouchers regardless of results of toxicology screens. Retention was similar between the groups, because even those in the non-contingent condition were required to come to treatment to obtain vouchers; 56% of those in the contingent condition and 53% of those in the non-contingent condition remained in treatment for 24 weeks. Of those randomized to the contingent condition, 37% achieved 12 or more weeks of continuous cocaine abstinence, compared with only about 10% of patients receiving non-contingent vouchers. Beneficial effects of contingent vouchers were noted a year after treatment ended. At each time point of assessment after treatment ended, numerically higher proportions of patients who had earlier received vouchers tested cocaine negative and self-reported no cocaine use for the prior 30 days.

Thus, this series of elegantly designed studies demonstrates that voucher-based CM increases durations of abstinence. These studies also show that effects of CM can persist beyond the period in which patients receive the reinforcers. In fact, one of the best predictors of long-term abstinence is the duration of abstinence one is able to achieve during treatment (Higgins, Badger, & Budney, 2000). Most studies of voucher-based CM led to statistically significant increases in durations of abstinence (Lussier, Heil, Mongeon, Badger, & Higgins, 2006; Prendergast, Podus, Finney, Greenwell, & Roll, 2006).

3.2 GROWTH OF RESEARCH ON VOUCHER-BASED CM

3.2.1 Substance-Abusing Populations

With the exciting findings of voucher-based CM approaches, this technique spread to other research-based settings and populations. A number of independent investigators have replicated the efficacy of voucher CM for decreasing stimulant use in non-opioid, as well as opioid-maintained, stimulant abusers (Epstein, Hawkins, Covi, Umbricht, & Preston, 2003; Kirby, Marlowe, Festinger, Lamb, & Platt, 1998; Rawson et al., 2002, 2006; Silverman, Chutuape, Bigelow, & Stitzer, 1999; Silverman, Higgins, et al., 1996; Silverman, Wong, Umbricht-Schneiter, Montoya, Schuster, & Preston, 1998). Further, large meta-analyses of CM studies confirm the efficacy of CM in 47 independent trials (Lussier et al., 2006; Prendergast et al., 2006).

Not only is CM efficacious in decreasing cocaine use, but provision of contingent vouchers decreases use of many other substances as well. Voucher-based CM is efficacious in decreasing opioid use in opioid-dependent patients, whether they are maintained on methadone (Iguchi, Belding, Morral, & Lamb, 1997; Piotrowski et al., 1999; Preston, Umbricht, & Epstein, 2000; Silverman, Wong, et al., 1996) or LAAM or buprenorphine (Kosten et al., 2003; Oliveto et al., 2005). Voucher-based CM also reduces opioid use in patients undergoing outpatient medication-assisted opioid detoxifications (Bickel, Amass, Higgins, Badger, & Esch, 1997; Katz, Chutuape, Jones, Jasinski, Fingerhood, & Stitzer, 2004), as well as among patients in treatment programs following detoxifications (Chutuape, Silverman, & Stitzer, 1999; Katz, Gruber, Chutuape, & Stitzer, 2001).

Likewise, beneficial effects of contingent vouchers appear in studies of treatment for marijuana (Budney, Higgins, Radonovich, & Novy, 2000; Budney, Moore, Rocha, & Higgins, 2006; Kadden, Litt, Kabela-Cormier, & Petry, 2007) and benzodiazepine abuse (Stitzer, Iguchi, & Felch, 1992). Polydrug use can also be reduced when vouchers are provided contingent upon abstinence (Dallery, Silverman, Chutuape, Bigelow, & Stitzer, 2001; Iguchi et al., 1997; Kosten et al., 2003; Stitzer et al., 1992).

Finally, even in the treatment of cigarette smokers who do not wish to stop smoking, large proportions of smokers significantly reduce or stop smoking when voucher or cash reinforcers are provided for negative carbon monoxide samples (e.g., Alessi, Badger, & Higgins, 2004; Corby, Roll, Ledgerwood, & Schuster, 2000; Gilbert, Crauthers, Mooney, McClernon, & Jensen, 1999; Heil, Tidey, Holmes, Badger, & Higgins, 2003; Robles et al., 2005; Roll & Higgins, 2000; Roll, Higgins, & Badger, 1996; Roll, Higgins, Steingard, & McGinley, 1998; Schmitz, Rhoades, & Grabowski, 1995). These CM-induced decreases in smoking are noted even without concurrent pharmacotherapy and even among difficult-to-treat populations such as patients with schizophrenia (Roll et al., 1998; Tidey, O'Neill, & Higgins, 2002). Thus, voucher-based CM is a widely applicable and powerful method for decreasing drug use.

3.2.2 If Voucher-Based Reinforcement Is So Effective, Why Is It Not Used in Clinical Settings?

Despite its efficacy in clinical research trials, voucher CM has rarely been implemented in clinical practice settings. A number of reasons exist for this disconnect between research and practice. One issue relates to the fact that vouchers have most often been applied in tightly controlled research studies conducted within research-based treatment facilities. For example, Higgins and colleagues' trials (1991, 1993, 1994, 2003; Higgins, Wong, et al., 2000) are conducted in a NIDA-funded research clinic. The ratio of staff to patients is about 1 to 7. Staff are hired based upon their prior experience with behavioral interventions and willingness to utilize these reinforcement procedures. Substantial training is provided, and adherence to study procedures is closely monitored. In real world practice settings, the staff-to-patient ratio is substantially lower (e.g., 1:40 or even more), and the staff has a wide range of education and experience, often with little or no training in behavioral therapy. Detailed and personalized feedback to staff regarding implementation of therapeutic procedures is rarely provided.

In addition to the need for training and experience, voucher CM programs are expensive to employ and manage. In many voucher studies (Bickel et al., 1997; Higgins et al., 1994; Higgins, Wong, et al., 2000; Rawson et al., 2002; Silverman, Higgins, et al., 1996), each patient can earn about $1,000 in goods during treatment, and earnings average about $600 (e.g., Higgins et al., 1994, 2003; Higgins, Wong, et al. 2000; Silverman, Higgins, et al., 1996). These costs may preclude the use of this procedure in many community settings. If the amounts of vouchers available are reduced, the effects are not nearly as strong. Studies have examined if magnitude affects outcomes, and simply reducing magnitude of available vouchers reduces efficacy (Dallery et al. 2001; Higgins, Heil, Dantona, Donham, Matthews, & Badger, 2007; Silverman et al., 1999; Stitzer & Bigelow, 1983, 1984). For example, Silverman et al. (1999) found that although 45% of cocaine-abusing methadone patients achieved four or more weeks of abstinence when exposed to a CM condition that provided up to $3,480 in vouchers, only 3% maintained this duration of abstinence when exposed to a CM condition that provided only $382 in vouchers. Thus, reinforcer magnitude is positively associated with outcomes, but higher magnitude reinforcers are even more expensive to integrate into clinical settings.

Several strategies have been utilized to apply less costly contingencies rather than vouchers. Changes in methadone dose (Calsyn & Saxon, 1987; Stitzer, Bickel, Bigelow, & Liebson, 1986), take-home privileges (Stitzer et al., 1992), and continued treatment as opposed to administrative discharge (Dolan, Black, Penk, Robinowitz, & DeFord, 1985; McCarthy & Borders, 1985) have been used as reinforcers in methadone programs. Although these reinforcers are not costly, they are only applicable in settings that apply agonist pharmacotherapies such as methadone or buprenorphine.

A benefit of vouchers is that, except for the issue of cost, they can complement any existing treatment structure. They are applicable in outpatient, inpatient, and residential treatment settings. As noted earlier, vouchers are efficacious in every patient population in which they have been evaluated, so long as adequate magnitudes of vouchers are provided and behavioral principles are taken into account. The struggle between cost and efficacy is long-standing. Reducing amounts of vouchers available reduces the effectiveness of CM (Lussier et al., 2006). Methods for reducing costs, without diminishing efficacy, are needed.

3.3 EVOLUTION OF PRIZE-BASED CM

In 1997, I developed an adaptation to the voucher-based CM reinforcement approach (Petry, 2000; Petry et al., 2000). Rather than earning vouchers, patients earn the chance to draw from a "fishbowl" or prize bowl and win prizes. Prizes range from small $1 items (choice of bus tokens, fast food coupons, toiletries) to large $20 prizes (choice of watches, Walkmans, gift certificates, and phone cards), and jumbo $100 prizes (choice of TVs and stereos). Not every draw results in a prize, and some slips state "good job." This system is less expensive than the voucher system as only a proportion of behaviors is reinforced with a tangible reinforcer (a prize), and average earnings are about $100 to $200 per patient. Thus, prize CM may be a relatively inexpensive variant of the voucher system, and one that may be well suited to community settings.

I have thus far conducted and published numerous studies on the efficacy of prize-based CM in a variety of clinical populations and settings. Specifically, I and others (e.g., Ghitza, Epstein, Schmittner, Vahabzadeh, Lin, & Preston, 2007; Helmus, Saules, Schoener, & Roll, 2003; Lott & Jencius, 2009; Preston, Ghitza, Schmittner, Schroeder, & Epstein, 2008; Squires, Gumbley, & Storti, 2008) have demonstrated that the technique is effective in a variety of substance-dependent populations. In the next section, I highlight some of the prize-based CM studies and describe how they are integrated with standard care procedures in practice settings.

3.3.1 Populations in Which Prize CM Has Been Evaluated

3.3.1.1 Alcohol-Dependent Patients

In my first prize CM study (Petry et al., 2000), 42 alcohol-dependent patients initiating treatment at a Veterans Administration outpatient substance treatment clinic were randomly assigned to one of two eight-week conditions: standard care or standard care plus prize CM. Standard care was group-based treatment, consisting of 12-step sessions, daily planning activities, life skills training, health education, and cognitive-behavioral and skills training treatment.

In addition to standard care, all patients in the study also met regularly with a research assistant, usually a bachelor's-level staff member with some clinical experience. The meetings occurred daily (five days a week) for the first four weeks, and then at least weekly for the next four weeks. Each time patients met with the research assistant, they provided a breath sample that was screened for recent alcohol use. Further, at weeks four and eight, they received a small payment for completing structured interviews and providing objective indicators (breath and urine toxicology screens) of substance use. Over 93% of patients enrolled in the study completed these evaluations.

Patients assigned to the standard care condition received the treatment and substance use monitoring detailed above. In addition, a research assistant provided about 15 minutes of psychoeducation about drug use once a week. These meetings involved the use of brochures and ensured that patients in both conditions received similar amounts of individual attention.

Patients assigned to CM received the same standard care and substance abuse monitoring described above. CM patients were intermixed with and participated in the same group sessions as patients assigned to standard care. Non-study patients (those who were ineligible for the study because they were not alcohol dependent) also participated in these same groups.

There were only a couple of differences in the treatments provided to study patients assigned to CM and those not assigned to CM. Each time CM patients provided a breath sample that tested negative for alcohol, they earned a chance to draw from a bowl and win prizes. Patients in the CM condition did not receive the psychoeducation, but instead they contracted with the research assistant each week to complete three sobriety-related activities. They also received chances to win prizes ranging in value from $1 to $100 for completing these activities, a procedure described in greater detail in Chapter 5.

On average, patients assigned to the prize CM condition could expect to win $240 worth of prizes, if they submitted all negative breath samples and completed all 24 activities throughout the eight-week treatment period. On average, patients earned $200 in prizes. This prize CM system was efficacious in enhancing retention in treatment. Eighty-four percent of the CM patients were retained in treatment for the entire eight-week period compared with only 22% of the standard treatment patients. The prize CM system also increased time to first drink and lengthened time to first heavy drinking episode, defined as self-reports of consuming five or more drinks on a single occasion or submission of a positive breath alcohol sample. By the end of the treatment period, 69% of those receiving CM maintained continuous abstinence from alcohol versus only 39% of those receiving standard treatment. Further, only 26% of those assigned to CM had relapsed to heavy alcohol use compared with 61% of the patients assigned to standard care. In addition, the prize CM approach was beneficial in suppressing other drug use, even though alcohol abstinence was the only substance upon which reinforcement was based in this study. Only 10% of patients assigned to the CM group submitted a sample positive for an illicit drug, but 43% of patients assigned to the standard treatment group submitted one or more samples positive for illicit opioids, stimulants, marijuana, or benzodiazepines.

Thus, this prize-based CM approach had similar benefits for alcohol-dependent patients as did the voucher CM procedure for cocaine-dependent patients. Subsequent studies, as noted below, also found evidence of the efficacy of prize CM for stimulant abusers.

3.3.1.2 Stimulant Abusers

Treatment providers associated with NIDA's Clinical Trials Network (CTN) selected prize CM to be implemented and studied in the first wave of projects conducted in this national initiative. The CTN is a network of academic and community providers designed to test and improve treatment for substance abuse. Over 800 stimulant abusers from 14 clinics in the country participated in the CTN trial of CM.

The trial was conducted in two types of clinics—psychosocial clinics that do not provide medications (Petry, Peirce, et al., 2005) and methadone maintenance clinics (Peirce et al., 2006). Because of differences between these settings and patient populations, the trials differed slightly with respect to procedures, and the outcomes were presented separately. In both types of settings, stimulant-abusing or stimulant-dependent patients were randomly assigned to standard care or standard care plus prize CM. In the CM conditions, patients had to provide a breath sample that tested negative for alcohol and a urine sample that tested negative for cocaine and methamphetamine to receive any draws from the prize bowl. Number of draws earned began at one draw, and draws increased by one for each consecutive week in which negative samples were submitted. In total, up to 156 draws were possible if all samples tested negative for alcohol and stimulants. Samples were collected and tested twice per week for 12 weeks, and sample collection procedures did not differ by group.

In addition to earning draws for submitting alcohol and stimulant free samples, patients randomly assigned to the CM condition earned additional draws if they also tested negative for other, secondary drugs. In the psychosocial clinics (Petry, Peirce, et al., 2005), patients could earn two additional draws if they tested negative for both opioids and marijuana in addition to testing negative for cocaine and alcohol. In the methadone clinics (Peirce et al., 2006), opioid-negative samples resulted in additional draws. In both types of settings, patients could earn up to 204 draws in total: 156 for submitting alcohol and stimulant negative samples, plus 48 additional draws (two draws per sample × two samples per week × 12 weeks = 48 draws) if they also tested negative for the secondary drug(s).

Benefits of prize CM were noted among those recruited from psychosocial treatment settings (Petry, Peirce, et al., 2005), as well as those recruited from methadone clinics (Peirce et al., 2006). In the psychosocial clinics, prize CM significantly enhanced retention in treatment. By the end of 12 weeks, 49% of patients assigned to CM remained engaged in treatment versus only 35% of patients assigned to standard care. The mean number of weeks of consecutive abstinence from stimulants was 4.4 weeks for those assigned to CM and 2.6 weeks for those assigned to standard care. Further, the prize CM condition had approximately twice as many patients with at least four weeks of documented sustained abstinence from stimulants compared to the standard care condition (39.7% vs. 21.0%). Percentage of patients who sustained stimulant abstinence throughout the full 12-week treatment period was nearly four times greater for the prize CM condition (18.7% vs. 4.9%). Overall, patients earned an average of $203 in prizes.

3.3.1.3 Stimulant-Abusing Methadone-Maintained Patients

In the methadone arm of the CTN study (Peirce et al., 2006), durations of continuous cocaine abstinence achieved were also significantly enhanced in the prize CM condition relative to the standard care condition. On average, patients assigned to prize CM achieved 2.8 weeks of continuous stimulant abstinence versus a mean of 1.2 weeks among standard care patients. Patients in the CM condition were nearly three times more likely than those in the standard care condition to attain four or more weeks of continuous stimulant abstinence (23.7% vs. 9.0%) and 11 times more likely to maintain continuous abstinence throughout the 12-week study period (5.6% vs. 0.5%). The lower overall rates of stimulant abstinence in methadone-maintained patients relative to those in drug-free programs relate to the more chronic use of cocaine in this population. Rates of cocaine-positive samples in methadone-maintained patients assigned to standard care were 61% versus about 10% in patients recruited from drug-free programs. The average amount of prizes earned was $120, reflecting the lower overall stimulant abstinence achieved in this population. Nevertheless, prize CM had significant effects on reducing stimulant use in general, as well as use of a specific stimulant: methamphetamine.

3.3.1.4 Methamphetamine Abusers

Roll et al. (2006) analyzed data from the 113 patients in the CTN trials who were diagnosed with methamphetamine abuse or dependence. Patients randomly assigned to the prize CM condition achieved an average of 13.9 weeks of stimulant abstinence compared with 9.9 weeks for those in standard care. These statistically significant results show that prize CM is also efficacious in treating methamphetamine patients.

In sum, prize CM has been demonstrated efficacious in decreasing use of a variety of drugs in a number of different patient populations and settings. As outlined above, prize CM decreases alcohol, cocaine, and methamphetamine use, in both drug-free psychosocial settings and methadone clinics. Other studies have also noted benefits of this approach in reducing opioid use in methadone-maintained patients (Petry & Martin, 2002) and in abating smoking in cigarette smokers (Alessi, Petry, & Urso, 2008). Thus, prize CM, similar to voucher CM, has a great deal of efficacy and generalizes across populations.

3.3.2 Comparing Voucher and Prize CM

I have also conducted a series of studies that demonstrate prize CM is as efficacious as voucher CM (Petry, Alessi, Marx, Austin, & Tardif, 2005). In an initial study comparing the two CM approaches, I randomized 152 cocaine-abusing patients from three community clinics to standard care, standard care plus prize CM, or standard care plus voucher CM. Both prize and voucher CM retained patients in treatment longer than standard care alone, with trends toward improved retention with prize CM over voucher CM. On average, patients assigned to prize CM remained in treatment for 9.3 weeks versus 8.2 for those assigned to voucher CM and 5.5 for those assigned to standard care. Both CM conditions were equally efficacious in reducing drug use; patients in the prize CM condition attained an average of 7.8 weeks of continuous abstinence and those in the voucher CM condition achieved an average of 7.0 weeks of continuous abstinence, compared with an average of only 4.6 weeks for those in standard care. The proportions of patients who achieved at least four weeks of continuous abstinence were 64.7%, 62.3%, and 39.5% in the prize CM, voucher CM, and standard care conditions, respectively. The respective proportions who maintained abstinence throughout the 12-week study period were 45.1%, 26.4%, and 7.9%, and these rates also differed significantly across conditions. Further, patients who achieved greater durations of abstinence during treatment were significantly more likely to be abstinent at the long-term follow-up. Each week of consecutive abstinence achieved during treatment was associated with a 24% increase in the probability of abstinence at the most distal follow-up conducted nine months later.

Thus, these data demonstrate evidence of efficacy of prize and voucher CM. In this study, magnitude of expected maximal earnings was similar between the two CM conditions, about $800 over 12 weeks. On average, patients in the prize CM condition earned about $295 in prizes, and those in the voucher CM condition earned about $335 in vouchers.

In a follow-up study (Petry, Alessi, Hanson, & Sierra, 2007), I compared voucher and prize CM when the expected magnitude of reinforcement was substantially lower in the prize CM treatment compared to the voucher CM treatment. The maximal expected reinforcement was $240 in the prize condition versus $560 in the voucher condition. Seventy-four cocaine-dependent methadone patients were randomly assigned to standard care or one of the two CM conditions. As in the above study, prize CM worked at least as well as voucher CM. The mean duration of consecutive abstinence was 2.7 weeks in the standard care, compared with 5.8 weeks in prize CM and 5.7 weeks in voucher CM. Those assigned to prize CM achieved significantly greater durations of abstinence than those assigned to standard care, whereas the difference between the voucher and standard groups did not reach significance. This study shows that even when the overall magnitude of prizes available is lower, prize CM is as efficacious as voucher CM in reducing drug use.

Although prize CM improves outcomes relative to standard care even at a lower magnitude of overall arranged reinforcement than voucher CM, the magnitude of prize reinforcement affects outcomes in prize CM, similarly as it does in voucher CM. In another study, I (Petry, Tedford, Austin, Nich, Carroll, & Rounsaville, 2004) randomly assigned 120 cocaine-abusing patients to standard care, standard care with CM with an average maximum of $240 in prizes, or standard care with CM with an average maximum of $80 in prizes. In the two CM conditions, probabilities of winning were identical between groups, but the most frequently won prizes in the $80 condition were of a lower value ($0.33 and $5 prizes) than those in the $240 condition ($1 and $20 prizes). jumbo ($100) prizes were available in both conditions at equal probabilities.

The mean weeks of continuous abstinence were 2.5, 3.7, and 4.9 for patients in the standard care, $80 CM, and $240 CM conditions, respectively. Only the $240 CM condition differed significantly from standard care. Because the lower value condition did not improve outcomes relative to standard care, I recommend including $1, $20, and $100 prizes rather than lower valued items.

To summarize, tightly controlled research studies find that prize CM is efficacious in decreasing use of a variety of substances across a number of treatment settings. Prize CM, even at lower overall costs, is at least as efficacious as voucher CM. This treatment advance is important for moving CM into practice settings. One of the primary obstacles to adoption of CM has related to its costs. Direct costs of prize CM are about $200 per patient over a 12-week period, and this level of prize reinforcement can have pronounced effects on decreasing drug use.

3.3.3 Moving from Randomized Trials to Clinic-Wide Implementation

All the prize-based CM studies described above were conducted in community-based treatment programs. The CM was added to standard care, and there were no difficulties associated with providing the CM as an adjunct. Many clinics have participated in these studies (over 30 drug-free or psychosocial clinics and at least 15 methadone maintenance programs), so the efficacy of CM has been generalized to many types of populations and settings.

However, in the above studies, CM was applied individually with patients. Most often, a highly trained and closely supervised research assistant—as opposed to clinical staff at the programs—delivered CM. In contrast, most substance abuse treatment in community clinics is provided in a group format.

One of my early studies designed to address the issue of integrating CM in the context of groups and when delivered by community-based clinicians used a randomized design (Petry, Martin, & Simcic, 2005). Seventy-seven cocaine-dependent methadone patients were randomly assigned to 12 weeks of standard care, including attendance at a weekly group therapy session, or standard care with CM. Group therapy sessions in both conditions covered the same psychoeducational and skills training materials. The difference was that the CM groups provided draws from the prize bowl for each attendee, with increasing draws for consecutive weeks of group attendance. Those randomized to the non-CM condition did not earn draws for attendance. The CM resulted in about twice the rate of group therapy attendance. On average, patients attended the standard care groups only about 30% of the time compared with about 80% of the time in the CM condition. The average number of groups attended by patients assigned to the standard care condition was 3.0 sessions versus 6.6 sessions for those assigned to the prize CM condition.

Another study did not employ a randomized design (Petry, Martin, & Finocche, 2001), but compared attendance before, during, and after clinic-wide implementation of CM. Before CM, an average of less than one patient per session (range zero to four) attended drug abuse treatment groups at an HIV drop-in center. When CM was implemented with increasing draws for consecutive weeks of attendance, attendance increased to an average of seven patients (range two through 12) per session.

However, when more patients were attending groups and each patient was drawing between one and 20 times (based on weeks of consecutive attendance), the drawing time exceeded 30 minutes of the 1.5 hour session. Furthermore, patients argued over who got to choose first from the prize cabinet and who selected which prizes. Thus, in subsequent studies that reinforced attendance at groups, I institute a new CM procedure—the Name-in-the-hat prize CM approach for group attendance.

Briefly, in this procedure, everyone who attends group puts his or her name in a hat. The number of times one's name goes in the hat increases based on weeks of consecutive attendance. Patients who have attended for the first time or for just one week in a row put their name in the hat once. Those who have come two weeks in a row put their name in the hat twice, those who have come for three weeks in a row put their name in the hat three times, and those who have come four weeks in a row put their name in the hat four times, and so on. The group leader draws names from the hat at each session. Typically, half as many names are drawn as there are people in attendance at group. Those whose names are drawn get to win a prize by selecting slips from a prize bowl.

In this system, about half the people in attendance at group draw, and that many draws are awarded (rather than the hundreds of draws that occur if each person in attendance draws 10 times or more). In this format, the prize bowl is proportioned differently compared to when each person earns increasing numbers of draws. In the individualized prize CM system, half the slips state "good job!" but are not associated with a prize. In this Name-in-a-hat procedure, the prize bowl contains all winning slips, with greater probabilities of winning across all categories of prizes, especially the more desirable categories. Typically, 100 prize slips are in the bowl, and one is the jumbo (prizes worth up to $100 in value), 10 are larges (prizes worth up to $20 in value), 20 are mediums (prizes worth up to $5 in value), and the remaining 69 are smalls (prizes worth up to $1 in value). Overall costs are about $4 per draw. If five draws are awarded in a group session that 10 people attend, that number of draws (five) translates to about $20 in prizes per week.

This Name-in-the-hat procedure improves group attendance. Ledgerwood, Alessi, Hanson, Godley, and Petry (2008) evaluated the effectiveness of this procedure, with no involvement from research staff. Clinicians at four sites in

Maine, New Hampshire, and Illinois participated in a two- to three-hour training session about how to implement this CM approach. All sites then implemented CM and standard care, in a randomized order, for 16 weeks each. Patients who were in treatment at these clinics during the time when CM was in effect attended a significantly greater proportion of their sessions (80.4%) than patients who did not receive CM (68.9%). This study provides good evidence of the ability of clinicians to integrate CM into group sessions, and this approach is further detailed in Chapter 14.

In addition to this research study, the Name-in-the-hat prize CM procedure for group attendance has been implemented in over 20 separate clinics in the states of New York and Connecticut. Many of these clinics worked exclusively with dual diagnosis patients. Providers attended two one-day trainings in CM background and administration, and they then selected the groups in which they wanted to implement CM. Although there was no random assignment procedure in place, the vast majority of clinics reported the procedure to be effective in enhancing attendance at groups. Providers associated with the New York State sites compared pre-CM with during-CM attendance rates, and reported increased attendance ranging from 13% to 42% (McCorry et al., 2009). Even patients with chronic and persistent mental health problems were able to understand the contingencies and looked forward to attending groups. A total of $500 to $1,000 in start-up funds was sufficient to provide reinforcers for at least three or four separate 12-week groups.

SUMMARY

In conclusion, substantive data suggest that CM is effective in changing patient behavior. Research on CM that began in the context of tightly controlled studies has moved toward community-based clinical settings and has focused on issues that directly affect practice. CM procedures are now available that can positively affect patient behavior at relatively low cost and that can be administered in a group context. In the next chapter, I review special populations and settings in which CM has been integrated, and I also discuss behaviors beyond attendance and abstinence that can be impacted.

Chapter 4

Applications of Contingency Management in Novel Settings and With Special Populations

This chapter will describe evidence for, and applications of, CM beyond primary substance–using populations. CM can be effective with dual diagnosis patients, patients enrolled in vocational rehabilitation programs, criminal justice system patients, homeless adults, pregnant women, and adolescents.

Although CM programs usually reinforce abstinence, CM can be adapted to reinforce other behaviors as well. Such behaviors include attendance at treatment, medication adherence, and compliance with goal-related activities, such as activities related to obtaining employment, increasing exercise, and reducing weight. This chapter will provide an overview of studies that applied CM procedures to behaviors and patient populations beyond primary substance abusers as examples of the generalization of CM techniques. In situations in which CM approaches were not effective, I describe how the CM intervention failed to take into account the three central tenets of CM, as outlined in Chapter 2, Section 2.3, and important characteristics of the patient population.

4.1 SPECIAL SUBSTANCE-ABUSING POPULATIONS

4.1.1 Dual Diagnosis

Many published studies support the use of CM in a variety of special populations who abuse substances. Dual diagnosis patients are the subgroup with whom CM has been most widely implemented, and multiple studies of successful CM implementation exist in patients with severe mental illness. These studies are described below.

Bellack, Bennett, Gearon, Brown, and Yang (2006) randomized 110 outpatients with severe and persistent mental illness and cocaine, heroin, or marijuana dependence to a group-based behavioral intervention that included CM for submission of negative samples or to a supportive group therapy treatment without CM. Each group met twice weekly for six months, and all patients submitted urine samples twice weekly. Patients assigned to the CM condition increased total and continuous abstinence, and they submitted higher proportions of negative toxicology screens compared to patients assigned to the supportive therapy group. For example, 54.1% of CM patients compared with 16.3% of supportive therapy patients achieved at least a month of continuous abstinence, and CM patients submitted negative samples 58.9% of the time versus only 24.7% of the time for supportive therapy patients. The CM patients also showed improved quality of life, had more funds available for living expenses, and evidenced fewer hospitalizations.

Helmus et al. (2003) used a non-randomized reversal design to evaluate the effects of prize CM in dual diagnosis patients. In the baseline phase, attendance was measured and breath samples were monitored for four weeks; then a CM procedure was introduced that reinforced attendance and negative breathalyzer samples for 12 weeks. Following the CM phase, the reinforcers were removed, and attendance and breath samples were again monitored in a second baseline phase. In the initial baseline phase, attendance rates were 45%, and they increased to 65% during CM, and remained high—at 68%—during the second baseline phase. Although the CM had clear and persisting effects on attendance, no positive breath alcohol samples were collected in either of the baseline phases, or during CM, so no impact on substance use was noted. These results underscore the importance of targeting reinforcement to a behavior that is likely to show improvement with the introduction of CM (see Chapter 5).

Sigmon, Steingard, Badger, Anthony, and Higgins (2000) used a similar reversal design to evaluate the effects of CM on marijuana use in 18 patients with psychotic disorders. Patients submitted urine samples twice weekly during a baseline, a CM, and a second baseline phase. This population had high rates of substance use in the baseline period. The average proportion of negative samples submitted was 13% during the first baseline phase, and this rate increased to 45% during the CM phase. Proportion of negative samples reverted to 18% during the second baseline phase. The average number of consecutively negative samples was 0.9 during the first baseline phase, and this increased significantly to 3.9 during the contingent phase but reduced to 1.4 during the second baseline phase. Other drug use (opioids, cocaine, or benzodiazepines) did not change when patients were being reinforced for marijuana abstinence.

Another study found similar effects. Sigmon and Higgins (2006) used a baseline, CM, baseline design to evaluate the effects of CM on marijuana use in seven patients with serious mental illness, primarily schizophrenia (86%). In all phases, patients provided urine samples twice a week. During the 12-week CM phase, patients could earn up to $930 in vouchers for submitting marijuana-negative urine samples. The mean percentage of negative samples was 9% in the first baseline period, 46% during CM, and then it dropped to 0% in the second baseline phase.

Roll, Chermack, and Chudzynski (2004) examined CM for reducing cocaine use among three individuals with schizophrenia. Again, a baseline, CM, baseline design was employed, and urine samples were collected three times per week in each phase. Although only about 8% of samples were negative for cocaine during the baseline phases, the average proportion of negative samples during the CM phase was about 23%. Thus, these reversal design studies all found beneficial effects of CM during the period in which contingencies were in effect. Three studies failed to show persisting effects of CM on substance use after reinforcers were removed, but the Helmus et al. (2003) study demonstrated persistent effects of CM on attendance, even when the reinforcers were no longer provided.

Ries, Dyck, Short, Srebnik, Fisher, and Comtois (2004) randomized 41 patients to contingent or non-contingent benefit management for 27 weeks. Patients were severely mentally ill, had active substance use disorders (primarily alcohol), and were receiving mental disability payments. During the study, payees paid for their rent using their disability payments and dispersed the remaining funds between once a month and up to five times per week, with more frequent but smaller payments for patients with more significant substance use problems. The payment plan was consistent with each patient's usual recommendations for those in the non-CM condition. Those in the CM condition could receive their remaining payments in cash if the case manager noted no substance use and if they were adherent with therapy and other goals. For moderate adherence, CM patients received a mixture of cash and food gift cards, and in cases of poor adherence or substance abuse they received their remaining funds in the form of food gift cards only. Alcohol use decreased significantly in the CM group, along with combined alcohol and drug use. In addition, ratings of appropriate money management ratings improved among those receiving benefits contingently. This study is an interesting adoption of CM that requires no upfront funds for reinforcement, as the reinforcers were different forms of the patients' own disability funds.

Patients with schizophrenia suffer from extraordinarily high rates of nicotine dependence, and traditional psychotherapies and pharmacotherapies effective for smoking in most populations have much lower rates of (or no) efficacy in patients with schizophrenia. Roll et al. (1998) used a baseline, CM, baseline design to evaluate the effects of CM to promote nicotine abstinence in 11 patients with schizophrenia. Abstinence was significantly greater during the CM compared to the baseline phase, with mean carbon monoxide (CO)-negative readings of 0.7 in the baseline phase and 2.7 in the CM phase, and 0.6 during the second baseline condition. Tidey et al. (2002) examined the combined effects of transdermal nicotine and CM on smoking cessation in individuals with schizophrenia. Fourteen patients participated in each of three conditions in a randomized manner: CM combined with transdermal nicotine, CM combined with placebo patch, and non-contingent reinforcement combined with placebo patch. Each condition lasted five days, and CO levels were measured three times daily. CM reduced smoking, but the transdermal nicotine did not enhance the effect. These results offer evidence for CM for reducing smoking among people with schizophrenia, but longer term studies are needed, as well as development of methods to extend the benefits of CM.

In addition to these studies conducted explicitly in patients with severe mental illness who also have substance use disorders, two retrospective analyses of studies conducted in primary substance–abusing populations have examined the effects of severity of psychiatric symptoms on treatment outcomes during CM and non-CM treatments. Tidey, Mehl-Madrona, Higgins, and Badger (1998) divided 123 cocaine-dependent patients into groups of low, medium, and high psychiatric symptom severity based on Addiction Severity Index psychiatric composite scores. As expected, patients with high psychiatric symptom severity reported poorer functioning and more adverse consequences of cocaine use than the lower severity groups. Nevertheless, psychiatric symptom severity failed to influence treatment outcome within or across CM and non-CM treatment conditions. Thus, in this study, the authors found no evidence to indicate that high psychiatric severity is associated with poorer response to CM treatment.

Weinstock, Alessi, and Petry (2007) also examined the relationship between psychiatric symptom severity and treatment outcomes in 393 substance-abusing patients who were randomized to standard care or standard care plus CM conditions. Patients in the high psychiatric severity group again reported poorer baseline psychosocial functioning. However, in this study, a significant interaction between psychiatric severity and treatment modality was found with respect to treatment retention. Patients assigned to standard care were more likely to drop out of treatment sooner as psychiatric severity increased, but patients assigned to CM remained in treatment for similar durations, regardless of level of psychiatric severity. CM was equally effective across all psychiatric severity groups in terms of enhancing drug abstinence. These findings suggest CM is an efficacious and appropriate intervention for substance use disordered individuals across a range of psychiatric problems, and CM may be particularly useful for enhancing retention in treatment among those with more pronounced psychopathology.

Some individual reports also suggest that CM is especially effective in dual diagnosis populations. In a sample of cocaine-abusing buprenorphine-maintained patients, Gonzalez, Feingold, Oliveto, Gonsai, and Kosten (2003) found that CM increased drug-negative urine submission rates more among patients with a history of major depressive disorder than among those with no history of major depression. Lester, Milby, Schumacher, Vuchinich, Person, and Clay (2007) reported that, among 118 homeless cocaine-dependent adults, those with trauma exposure and posttraumatic stress disorder

(PTSD) symptoms had significantly greater reductions in trauma-related symptoms when assigned to CM than when assigned to non-CM treatments. Ford, Hawke, Alessi, Ledgerwood, and Petry (2007) examined outcomes of 142 substance abusers randomized to standard care or standard care plus CM. They found that patients with high levels of PTSD symptoms were more likely to be abstinent at a nine-month follow-up assessment than those with less severe PTSD symptoms in the CM condition only. Thus, patients with trauma-induced symptomology may be particularly responsive to CM interventions with respect to long-term drug abstinence outcomes.

In sum, a number of demonstration projects and some larger randomized studies have all found benefits of CM in patients with severe and persistent mental illness. In addition, retrospective analyses find that CM is effective, and perhaps particularly effective, in patients with more significant psychopathology. Contingencies are, therefore, not too difficult for patients to comprehend. To the contrary, patients with substantial mental illness and even psychotic disorders respond well to positive contingencies. Some reviews point toward the promise of CM for these difficult-to-treat populations. For example, Drake, O'Neal, and Wallach (2008) reviewed the literature of psychosocial interventions for patients with co-occurring substance use and severe mental illness. They noted that CM was one of the few interventions with consistent positive effects on reducing drug use in this population, and it also had benefits on other outcome measures as well.

4.1.2 Homeless Populations

Milby and colleagues have studied extensively a program that provides CM in conjunction with an extensive day treatment program for homeless substance abusers. In the first study, Milby et al. (1996) randomized 131 homeless substance abusers to usual care, involving weekly individual and group counseling, or to an enhanced day treatment program that involved a CM component. The day program consisted of group and individual counseling, lunch, and transportation. The reinforcement consisted of the ability to work for pay building homes, along with individual housing, both contingent upon drug abstinence. In the case of a positive sample, the patient was not allowed to work that day, immediately removed from his apartment, and transported to a shelter until abstinence was re-achieved. At the end of the main treatment phase (month two), abstinence rates in the usual care condition averaged 37% versus 70% in the CM condition. By month six, abstinence was 46% in usual care and 62% in the CM condition. Mean days homeless decreased, and days employed increased, in the CM condition as well.

In the second study, Milby et al. (2000) provided the same day treatment described above to 110 patients. The patients were randomized to day treatment alone or day treatment with CM, in which case they were eligible for abstinent contingent housing and work therapy. Again, abstinence rates were significantly higher in the CM relative to non-CM group. In the CM group, average rates of abstinence were 71% and 41% at months two and six, respectively, and for the non-CM group, they were 41% and 15%.

In a subsequent study, Milby, Schumacher, Wallace, Freedman, and Vuchinich (2005) randomized 196 cocaine-dependent homeless patients to day treatment alone, day treatment plus abstinent-contingent housing, or day treatment with housing not contingent upon abstinence. The abstinent contingent group showed the greatest proportion of negative urine samples, but differences between the abstinent contingent and non-contingent group that also received housing did not reach statistical significance. Differences were significant between the housed groups and the non-housed group that received day treatment alone. Mean weeks of continuous abstinence for the non-housed, non-contingently housed, and contingently housed groups were 4.5, 6.6, and 8.3 weeks, respectively. Percent of negative samples submitted between baseline and month two were 41%, 60%, and 69%, and at the end of the six-month treatment they were 18%, 40%, and 46%, respectively. This study demonstrated that housing itself is important for reducing substance use.

Finally, Milby, Schumacher, Vuchinich, Freedman, Kertesz, and Wallace (2008) randomized 206 cocaine-dependent homeless persons to day treatment with CM or CM alone, without the intensive day treatment that included cognitive-behavioral therapy and therapeutic goal management. The CM component was identical in both conditions, and it consisted of abstinence contingent housing and vocational training. Although abstinence did not differ between the groups during the first six months, the day treatment plus CM group maintained greater abstinence during the six-month follow-up phase. The average percent negative samples in months six through twelve was 35% in the CM alone condition versus 49% in the CM plus day treatment condition. These results suggest that including an efficacious psychotherapy along with CM can improve long-term outcomes relative to CM alone, and they parallel results by Higgins et al. (2003) from a general sample of cocaine-dependent outpatients.

Another group has likewise demonstrated the efficacy of CM in reducing drug use among homeless populations, using much less intensive procedures. Tracy et al. (2007) conducted a randomized trial evaluating a brief, four-week, low-cost CM program for 30 individuals in a homeless shelter who had both substance use and psychiatric disorders. Patients assigned to CM earned the opportunity to win prizes for submitting cocaine- and alcohol-negative samples. On average, CM patients received $43 in prizes, and this magnitude of reinforcement was sufficient for significantly reducing cocaine and alcohol use compared to an assessment only condition.

4.1.3 Employment Training

Unemployment is a serious and chronic problem among substance abusers. Silverman and colleagues conducted a number of studies of CM in the context of a therapeutic workplace. They developed a not-for-profit business, in which substance abusers submit urine samples prior to entering the therapeutic workplace. If they test negative, they are allowed to train or work for the day on data entry, and they receive voucher or monetary-based reinforcement for their performance while training or working. In the initial randomized study, Silverman, Svikis, Robles, Stitzer, and Bigelow (2001) assigned 40 pregnant or post-partum drug-abusing women to the therapeutic workplace or to a usual care condition. Throughout the initial six-month treatment period, an average of 45% of the women assigned to the workplace condition attended daily, and abstinence rates were twice as high in these patients relative to those assigned to usual care, with 59% versus 33% abstinent from cocaine and opioids. In a subsequent report, Silverman, Svikis, Wong, Hampton, Stitzer, and Bigelow (2002) evaluated long-term outcomes of these women, who were allowed to continue working in this setting for up to three years. Relative to patients who received standard care, those in the therapeutic workplace maintained greater abstinence for cocaine (54% vs. 28% negative) and opioids (60% vs. 37% negative). Further, reversal designs showed that magnitude of reinforcement (i.e., wages available) are closely linked to performance in the therapeutic workplace setting (Silverman, Chutuape, Bigelow, & Stitzer, 1996; Wong et al., 2003).

Two other studies examined whether the availability of the therapeutic workplace or the contingent nature of the workplace impacts outcomes. DeFulio, Donlin, Wong, and Silverman (2009) randomly assigned 51 substance abusers to a therapeutic workplace contingent condition, in which work (and pay) were contingent upon abstinence, versus the therapeutic workplace alone, in which samples were collected but patients were allowed to work for pay even without testing abstinent. During the one-year period, those in the abstinence-contingent condition provided significantly more cocaine-negative samples than those in the non-contingent condition, 79% versus 51%. In this study, patients in the two conditions attended the workplace at similar rates (>70%). However, in an earlier study with a similar design, Silverman et al. (2007) randomized 56 substance abusers to contingent and non-contingent workplace conditions. In that study, patients in the contingent condition again submitted a greater proportion of cocaine-negative samples (29% vs. 10%) but attended and worked fewer days (38.6% vs. 71.3% of days) than those in the non-contingent workplace condition. In this study, rates of abstinence were much lower overall in both conditions, relative to the DeFulio et al. (2009) study. The reasons for differences in outcomes between these two studies are unclear, but both demonstrate beneficial effects of contingent reinforcement on abstinence, if not attendance, at the workplace.

Another study found somewhat similar yet more pronounced effects with respect to patients' failure to engage when the workplace was contingent upon abstinence alone. Knealing, Wong, Diemer, Hampton, and Silverman (2006) randomized 47 crack cocaine users from methadone maintenance programs to usual care or the therapeutic workplace, in which work was contingent upon abstinence from opioids and cocaine. Only 32% of patients assigned to the workplace condition initiated consistent periods of abstinence and workplace attendance. There were no differences between the groups with respect to abstinence outcomes. Thus, these various studies generally showed positive effects with respect to abstinence outcomes when work was contingent upon abstinence, but not all patients responded to this procedure, perhaps in part related to their baseline levels of drug use. Patients with more severe drug use problems may have greater difficulty in achieving initial abstinence and hence lower engagement in a contingent therapeutic workplace program.

Drebing et al. (2005) integrated CM in the context of a more traditional vocational rehabilitation program for dually diagnosed veterans. Nineteen patients were randomly assigned to a compensated work therapy program or that same program in which they received additional reinforcers for drug-negative urine specimens and for taking steps toward obtaining and maintaining a job. In this condition, they could earn up to $1006 over 16 weeks. Compared to the usual work therapy condition, those in the CM condition submitted more substance-negative samples, engaged in more job-search activities, were more likely to obtain employment, and earned higher wages.

In a larger follow-up study, Drebing et al. (2007) randomly assigned 100 veterans with comorbid psychiatric disorders and substance dependence to standard vocational rehabilitation alone or vocational rehabilitation plus CM. The CM condition provided escalating reinforcement up to $1,170 for submitting negative samples and completing tasks related to sobriety and job search and maintenance. Relative to patients in the standard vocational rehabilitation group, those in CM group had significantly longer periods of abstinence and more intense job searches, and they transitioned to competitive employment faster and at higher rates. For example, the longest period of consecutive abstinence was 11.8 weeks among those in the CM condition versus 9.4 weeks for those in the standard care condition. Of patients in the CM condition, 86% completed a résumé by the end of the initial 16-week treatment period compared with 68% of patients in the standard care condition. Similarly, 78% of those in the CM group submitted their first job application by week 16 versus 50% of those receiving standard care. Fifty percent of the CM group and 28% of the standard care group had entered competitive employment by the end of the nine-month follow-up. These results suggest that employment outcomes may be enhanced by adding CM that directly targets and reinforces achievement of employment-related goals.

4.1.4 Criminal Justice System

Unlike most of the above studies that showed positive effects of CM in dual diagnosis, homeless, and employment training settings, studies of CM in criminal justice populations have found mixed effects. Most likely, the variable findings in this population relate to lack of adherence to CM principles in design of CM conditions or fairly high levels of program compliance and abstinence when the negative consequences of non-compliance are rapid and severe, such as a return to prison. Prendergast, Hall, Roll, and Warda (2008) randomized 163 drug court patients to standard drug court procedures or to those same procedures plus one of three CM conditions. In the CM conditions, patients were reinforced for submission of drug-negative urine samples, completion of goal-related activities, or both. There were no differences in retention across the groups, with 60% to 76% of patients completing the intervention. No group differences emerged in the proportion of negative tests submitted, with over 67% of tests negative. The authors attributed the lack of effect of CM to the strong sanctions imposed by the judge for drug use and treatment non-compliance, and the use of delayed reinforcement in the CM condition, as on-site urinalysis testing was not done. Further, a flat reinforcement schedule was in effect, that did not increase with sustained abstinence or activity completion. Given the importance of immediate reinforcement (Lussier et al., 2006) and escalating reinforcers (Roll et al., 1996; Roll, Reilly, & Johanson, 2000), features of this CM intervention may have hindered its effectiveness.

Marlowe, Festinger, Dugosh, Arabia, and Kirby (2008) also evaluated the effects of CM in the context of a drug court setting. They randomized 269 drug court patients to drug court as usual or to CM interventions that provided up to $390 in gift certificates to a local mall over 12 court hearings that occurred over a 13-month period. In one CM condition, the amounts earned started at $5 and escalated up to $60 if the judge deemed the patient compliant with all court rules in the past month. In the other condition, the same total reinforcement was available, but the amounts started at a higher level ($30 for compliance); after three sessions the reinforcement delivery was less frequent, such that the patient was required to be compliant for two and then three hearings to receive reinforcement. In neither CM condition did resets occur for non-compliance, but unexcused absences resulted in the issuance of bench warrants for arrest and imprisonment. Attendance (78% to 84%) and abstinence (82% to 86%) rates were high overall and did not differ across conditions. The lack of effects may have related to the relatively low reinforcement amounts over a 12-month period, the strong sanctions imposed by the drug court setting itself, and high compliance in the drug court alone condition. In addition, the behavior targeted for reinforcement was not explicitly defined, and it consisted of a number of different behaviors, none of which was consistently or frequently monitored and reinforced (see Chapter 5).

In contrast to the above studies in which no effect of CM was found in drug court settings in which attendance and abstinence rates were generally high, two other studies in court-referred populations find strong benefits of CM. Sinha, Easton, Renee-Aubin, and Carroll (2003) randomly assigned 65 probation-referred marijuana-abusing patients to receive a three-session motivational enhancement treatment (MET) or MET plus CM. In the CM condition, patients could receive up to $120 for attending all three sessions on time. Robust effects of CM occurred, with 65% of patients assigned to MET plus CM completing all three sessions compared to 39% of patients who received MET alone.

Carroll et al. (2006) completed a larger study in which 136 probation-referred, marijuana-dependent young adults were randomized to one of four eight-week conditions: MET with cognitive-behavioral therapy (CBT), MET/CBT with CM, drug counseling, or drug counseling with CM. In the CM conditions, patients earned escalating vouchers for attendance at treatment (up to $340) and for submission of marijuana-negative samples (vouchers started at $50 for the first negative sample and increased by $5 for consecutive negative samples, up to $540 for abstinence and $880 in total). There was a significant beneficial effect of CM on treatment retention (with means of 5.7 sessions vs. 4.5 sessions attended for those in CM and non-CM conditions, respectively) and marijuana-negative samples submitted (with means of 2.1 vs. 1.1 negative samples and 27 vs. 19 days of abstinence, respectively). Further, the combined MET/CBT plus CM condition was most effective, and patients in this condition continued to reduce the frequency of marijuana use throughout a six-month follow-up period. Thus, data from these two studies indicate that when positive reinforcers are provided in manners consistent with CM principles and baseline rates of attendance and abstinence not already at or near ceiling levels, CM can have beneficial effects in criminal justice system populations.

4.1.5 Pregnant Women

CM also has beneficial effects in pregnant substance-abusing women. In the first known study of CM for pregnant women, Elk, Schmitz, Spiga, Rhoades, Andres, and Grabowski (1995) compared cocaine use before and during CM treatment. In the initial non-contingent phase, seven pregnant women were expected to attend the clinic three days per week, one of which was for a prenatal visit and the other two for drug abuse treatment. Attendance expectations were the same during the CM phase, in which they received $10 for a decrease in level of cocaine metabolites and $12 for a cocaine-negative sample; if all three samples in a week met criteria for reduced or no cocaine use, they received an additional $15. Time in treatment depended on gestational week, as all patients remained in treatment until delivery, with a mean of 16 weeks, and the length of baseline was three to six weeks, depending on stage of pregnancy at time of treatment entry. The percentages of cocaine-free samples were numerically higher during the contingent phase in six of the seven patients and statistically significantly higher in three of the patients.

Jones, Haug, Silverman, Stitzer, and Svikis (2001) randomly assigned 80 pregnant cocaine-using methadone maintenance patients to a standard intensive treatment program or that same program with CM. In the first seven days of the program, patients had to attend treatment for the full day to receive reinforcement. In days eight to 14, they had to attend treatment and provide a cocaine-negative urine sample to receive reinforcement. Reinforcement amounts started at $5 the first day and increased by $5 per day, such that by day 14, they could earn $70 for treatment attendance and abstinence. Patients in the CM condition attended an average of 12.1 days of treatment versus 10.6 days for those in the standard care condition. About 77% of urine samples tested negative for cocaine among women assigned to standard care versus about 88% among those assigned to CM, and these differences were significant. Although opioid abstinence was not reinforced, a significant increase in opioid-negative samples was noted as well. Whereas about 82% of samples tested negative for opioids in women receiving standard care, over 90% were negative in women in the CM condition.

However, effects were not as strong in a study that applied lower reinforcement magnitudes. Jones, Haug, Stitzer, and Svikis (2000) randomly assigned substance-abusing pregnant women to a usual care non-CM condition or to a CM condition in which they could receive $5 for attending each treatment sessions plus bonuses for consecutive attendance up to a total maximum of $85 over the entire CM program. This low magnitude reinforcement did not affect attendance in patients from psychosocial (non-methadone clinics), but pregnant methadone-maintained patients who received CM attended more treatment than their counterparts in the non-CM condition.

Svikis, Lee, Haug, and Stitzer (1997) also studied CM for attendance in pregnant women in methadone maintenance and drug-free treatment modalities. They found that patients in drug-free clinics who received higher value reinforcers (i.e., up to $10/day) for attendance increased treatment days attended. However, CM was not effective at lower magnitudes (i.e., $1/day) or with methadone-maintained women who, in this study, attended a majority of treatment days regardless of treatment condition.

In addition to these studies of CM for illicit substance use, several studies have found pronounced benefits of CM for smoking cessation in pregnant women. Higgins et al. (2004) randomized 58 pregnant women who were smoking to a usual care plus smoking monitoring condition in which they received vouchers for attending the visits, or a CM condition in which they received vouchers contingent upon negative CO readings in the first week, followed by vouchers for cotinine-negative urine samples in subsequent weeks. In total, women could earn up to $1,135 in vouchers if they maintained smoking abstinence throughout their pregnancies and the first 12 weeks post-partum. At the end of pregnancy, 37% of those in the CM group were abstinent versus 9% of those in the usual care condition. Twelve weeks post-partum, 33% of those in the CM condition were abstinent compared with 0% of those in the usual care condition. Benefits of CM were maintained throughout a 24-week follow-up period in which no reinforcers were provided. Twenty-seven percent of the women who had earlier received CM remained abstinent versus none of the women in the standard care condition.

In a follow-up study, Heil et al. (2008) randomized 82 smokers initiating prenatal care to similar conditions as in the above study. In addition to measuring smoking outcomes, this study also evaluated fetal growth outcomes. Again, the CM condition significantly increased abstinence at the end of pregnancy relative to the usual care condition (41% vs. 10% abstinent) and at the 12-week post-partum assessment (24% vs. 3% abstinent). Although 24-week post-partum evaluations found no continued benefit of CM in terms of abstinence outcomes in this study (8% vs. 3%), there were benefits to the infants. Serial ultrasound examinations revealed significantly greater growth in fetal weight, femur length, and abdominal circumference among infants in the CM condition. Further, while not statistically significant, 9% of babies born to mothers in the CM condition were born pre-term compared with 23% of babies born to mothers in the standard care condition. These results suggest benefits to both mothers and infants for integrating CM for smoking cessation during pregnancy.

4.1.6 Adolescents

Numerous studies have examined the role of CM for smoking cessation in adolescents. In the first study, Corby et al. (2000) used a reversal design with eight adolescents. A one-week baseline phase was followed by a one-week CM phase, and then another one-week baseline phase occurred. In all phases, CO samples were collected twice daily, before and after school. In the baseline phases, the adolescents were encouraged to use willpower to stop smoking, and they were paid $4 for each sample submitted. In the CM phase, they earned $1 for the first CO-negative reading submitted, and amounts earned increased by $0.50 for each consecutive negative sample submitted, with additional $3.75 bonuses for five consecutive negative samples. In each phase, they could earn up to a total of $40 if they submitted all samples or maintained smoking abstinence. Rates of CO-negative samples were substantially higher in the CM phase compared to the initial baseline phase, with means of 9.6 versus 0.9 negative samples submitted. Rates of negative samples remained high (7.5), even when the contingent reinforcement for abstinence was removed in the second baseline phase.

Subsequent randomized studies have found similar beneficial effects of CM for smoking cessation in adolescents. Roll (2005) randomized 22 adolescents to a condition that reinforced negative CO readings with escalating vouchers or one that reinforced attendance at CO monitoring meetings. Both groups could receive the same amount of reinforcement, and attendance was similar between the groups. In this study, the CM phase was four weeks in duration. Fifty percent of the adolescents in the abstinence reinforcement condition remained continuously abstinent throughout the trial versus 10% of adolescents in the attendance condition, and positive effects were maintained throughout the one-month follow-up period.

Krishnan-Sarin et al. (2006) randomized 28 adolescent smokers to a one-month school-based smoking cessation program involving CBT with or without CM. In the CM condition, adolescents received escalating reinforcement for negative CO readings. At the end of one week and one month of treatment, cotinine-verified abstinence levels were significantly greater in the CM group, with 76.7% of CM adolescents abstinent at one week and 53.0% at one month. In contrast, only 7.2% of adolescents receiving CBT were abstinent at week one and 0% at one month. A follow-up study with 34 adolescents (Cavallo et al., 2007) found similar results.

Reynolds, Dallery, Shroff, Patak, and Leraas (2008) have begun evaluating a web-based CM intervention, in which four adolescent smokers submitted three daily video recordings of themselves providing breath CO readings. Using a reversal design, adolescents could receive reinforcement for negative readings during the CM phase. Over 97% of expected samples were obtained, and all four adolescents achieved prolonged smoking abstinence during the CM phase, which was maintained in three of the four during the second baseline phase. The introduction of web-based procedures obviates the need for frequent (multiple times daily) in-person CO readings, when more traditional methods are used. Together, these studies find strong benefits of CM for reducing smoking in adolescents, and the effects of the CM persist even after the reinforcement is discontinued.

In examining CM for treatment of illicit substance use disorders in adolescents, Kamon, Budney, and Stanger (2005) describe an intervention that combined clinic administered reinforcement for the adolescent's abstinence along with CBT. In this treatment development project, parents also received CM, in that they were reinforced for attending parent training classes that instructed them in directing an additional CM procedure that targeted their child's drug abstinence and conduct. A total of 19 adolescents participated. Average attendance was 10.3 and 10.6 of 14 sessions for adolescents and parents, respectively. Rates of abstinence increased from 37% pre-treatment to 74% post-treatment, and 53% of adolescents remained abstinent at a one-month post-treatment follow-up. In addition, externalizing behavior and negative parenting behaviors decreased significantly pre- to post-treatment.

In a trial examining the efficacy of a similar intervention, Stanger, Budney, Kamon, and Thostensen (2009) randomly assigned 69 marijuana-using adolescents to MET plus CBT alone or in conjunction with CM. In both conditions, the adolescents provided urine samples twice weekly. In the CM condition, they earned increasing vouchers for sustained marijuana abstinence. Parents of adolescents in the CM condition received a weekly behavioral parent training session that involved a parent-delivered, abstinence-based substance monitoring contract. In the non-CM condition, parents were involved in a weekly psychoeducational parent training session. The CM condition had statistically significant benefits relative to MET plus CBT alone. Adolescents in the CM condition achieved an average of 7.6 weeks of continuous abstinence versus 5.1 weeks for those in the non-CM condition, and 50% versus 18% of the adolescents in the two respective conditions achieved 10 or more weeks of continuous abstinence. Reductions in measures of negative parenting were significant predictors of post-treatment abstinence.

In addition to these studies, Henggeler and colleagues have been evaluating the efficacy of a CM intervention for adolescents involved in the juvenile justice system. In the first study, Henggeler, Halliday-Boykins, Cunningham, Randall, Shapiro, and Chapman (2006) randomized 161 juvenile offenders to one of four conditions: usual family court and services, drug court, drug court plus multi-systemic family therapy, or that same condition with CM. Compared to standard care, the CM condition had the greatest benefits on most during and post-treatment drug use outcomes, including self-reports of alcohol and heavy alcohol use and some measures of marijuana and polydrug use, as well as drug-negative urine samples. In addition, the CM condition evidenced benefits relative to standard care in terms of status offenses, crimes against persons, arrests, and reductions in general problem behaviors.

Following this trial, Henggeler et al. (2007, 2008) described the effects of a large-scale training initiative for community-based therapists in CM. The vast majority of public sector agencies (44 of 50, or 88%) supported attendance of their therapists to the training, and 432 of 543 (80%) eligible therapists completed a one-day training in CM. Most non-attendance was due to logistical issues, not philosophical concerns about CM. Of the attendees, Henggeler et al. (2008) reported that 58% adopted and implemented CM with at least one substance-abusing patient within six months of completing the CM training workshop.

Other examples of community adoption of CM for adolescents can also be found. Lott and Jencius (2009) implemented a CM system clinic-wide in a community-based outpatient adolescent treatment program. They compared attendance and urinalysis results in the three months prior to the introduction of CM to rates during the 12-month CM period. The CM consisted of the chance to win prizes for submitting negative urine samples. Draws for negative samples increased for sustained abstinence, and patients could earn one additional draw for perfect attendance for a full week. In total, there were

83 adolescents included in the baseline phase and 253 in the CM phase. The average length of stay increased significantly from 13.0 to 15.0 days between the baseline and CM phases, and the proportion of urine samples that tested negative for cocaine, opioids, and marijuana concurrently increased from 66.7% to 76.6% between the phases. The total cost of the CM intervention was $1,524. The amount billed for clinical services increased significantly from $3,671 per patient before CM to $4,395 per patient during CM. The program was introduced with minimal changes to existing procedures, and it was effective as well as cost-effective.

Thus, a variety of studies have demonstrated benefits of CM across a range of patient populations. Positive effects are noted in tightly controlled randomized studies to reversal designs and clinic-wide implementation projects. Most of these studies reinforced abstinence, either alone or in conjunction with attendance or goal-related activities. Other possibilities of behaviors to reinforce include medication adherence, as described below.

4.2 CM FOR MEDICATION ADHERENCE

Several studies have evaluated the efficacy of CM for enhancing adherence to medication regimens in substance-abusing, as well as non-substance-abusing, populations. The primary issue in this line of research relates to ensuring ingestion of the medication. One of the central tenets of CM is to reinforce objective evidence of behavior change. In the case of medication adherence, different methods have been utilized to monitor ingestion, depending on the patient population. CM has had somewhat mixed effects on improving outcomes of medication compliance, depending on the populations and procedures in place.

Preston, Silverman, Umbricht, DeJesus, Montoya, and Schuster (1999) randomized 58 formerly opioid-dependent patients to one of three treatment conditions: naltrexone treatment alone, naltrexone treatment with vouchers available on an unpredictable schedule not tied to naltrexone ingestion, or escalating vouchers contingent upon naltrexone ingestion in the clinic setting. In the contingent condition, patients could earn up to $1,155 in vouchers over 12 weeks. Retention and naltrexone ingestion differed significantly across the groups. In the contingent naltrexone condition, the mean weeks of retention was 7.4 versus 5.0 in the non-contingent group and 2.3 in the naltrexone alone condition. Mean doses ingested were 21.4 in the contingent condition versus 11.3 and 4.4 in the non-contingent and naltrexone alone conditions, respectively. These data indicate the efficacy of CM for improving adherence to naltrexone.

However, another study failed to find such strong benefits of CM. Carroll, Sinha, Nich, Babuscio, and Rounsaville (2002) randomized 55 detoxified opioid-dependent patients to one of three 12-week treatment conditions: naltrexone alone, naltrexone with CM up to $562, or naltrexone with CM up to $1,152. In all conditions, patients provided urine samples three times per week and consumed naltrexone under the supervision of a clinic nurse. In the two CM conditions, escalating reinforcers were provided for consuming the naltrexone and submitting drug-negative urine samples. Reinforcers were provided on independent schedules for the two separate behaviors, and at equal magnitude for each behavior. The drop-out rate in the study was high, and only 42% of randomized patients completed treatment. CM (regardless of magnitude) had benefits in reducing opioid use during treatment, but effects did not reach significance on other measures, including time in treatment or number of naltrexone doses consumed. The mean number of naltrexone doses consumed was 14.1, 22.4, and 19.7 in the three respective conditions. Although this study included some important features of effective CM approaches and had an excellent method for ensuring medication consumption, the lack of statistically significant benefits on medication adherence may have related to the small sample size and because reinforcement was split between two behaviors (abstinence and naltrexone ingestion).

Several studies have investigated CM for adherence to HIV medications, with much more positive findings. In the first of these, Rigsby et al. (2000) randomized 55 HIV-positive patients receiving antiretroviral medications to one of three conditions: usual medication adherence training, cue-dose training, or cue-dose training plus CM. In the cue-dose training conditions, patients were shown readings from an electronic printout each week that recorded the time they opened their pill boxes, which were programmed with an electronic Medication Event Monitoring System (MEMS) cap that records timing of bottle opening. Therapists queried patients about missed doses and taught them to develop cues to remember appropriate dosing schedules. In the CM condition, patients also received up to $280 for consuming their medications at the appropriate times each day. The amount of reinforcement began at $2 per correct dose and increased up to $10 per correct dose for consecutive adherence. The treatments were in effect for four weeks, and patients were monitored throughout a 12-week follow-up period. Mean adherence at baseline was 70% in all three groups, and adherence remained at about 70% in both non-CM groups throughout the duration of the study. Adherence increased significantly to about 90% in the CM group during all four weeks of the intervention. Although not statistically significant, adherence in the CM group remained numerically higher than the other groups throughout the 12-week follow-up period.

In a subsequent study, Rosen et al. (2007) randomized 56 HIV-positive patients with suboptimal antiretroviral adherence to 16 weeks of supportive therapy with or without prize CM. Again, the CM involved reinforcing appropriate adherence according to MEMS cap readings. Patients could earn up to $800 in prizes for adhering to the medication regime for 16 weeks. Mean adherence at baseline was about 60% in both groups. In the CM condition, adherence rose to 76% throughout the 16-week intervention period, and five patients (18%) achieved 95% adherence throughout the intervention period. No patients in the supportive therapy group achieved this optimal level of adherence, and mean adherence averaged only about 44% throughout the 16-week treatment period in this group. In addition, there was a significant effect of CM on reducing viral loads during the treatment period. During the follow-up period, CM patients remained adherent an average of 61% of the time versus 46% for those in the supportive therapy condition.

Sorensen et al. (2007) randomized 66 HIV-positive patients to medication coaching alone or with CM for 12 weeks. Again, reinforcers were contingent upon opening of MEMS bottles at the appropriate times, and up to $1172 was available. Adherence during a four-week baseline period was about 50% in both groups. Throughout the intervention period, adherence rose significantly in the CM group to 78%, but it remained near baseline rates (55%) for those in the medication coaching alone condition. In the four-week follow-up period, adherence was 53% in the patients who had not received CM earlier, and it was 66% among those who had previously received CM. Thus, all three of these studies find significant benefits of CM for improving medication adherence in HIV patients.

Warfarin is an anticoagulation medication for patients at high risk of stroke, and poor adherence places patients at risk for stroke and bleeding complications. Volpp, Loewenstein, et al. (2008) conducted a pilot study of CM for improving adherence in 20 patients. During the study period, patients earned chances of winning monetary prizes ranging from $10 to $100 for adherence as assessed via a medication monitoring system. In one CM phase, the average daily expected earning was $5, and in the second it was $3. There were no differences between the two monetary amounts in terms of improving outcomes, but both CM phases appeared to increase adherence relative to historical control rates. The mean proportion of correct pills taken during the CM phases was about 98%, compared with an historic mean of 78% in this clinic. Although not a randomized design, the effects of CM seem promising in this population as well, suggesting that CM procedures may have broad beneficial effects in a range of patient populations with adherence concerns. For example, CM procedures may be effective in improving medication adherence among hypertensives, asthmatics, and diabetics.

4.3 OTHER BEHAVIORS

CM interventions are also being adapted and tested in other populations with modifiable health behaviors. Two such areas in which research is ongoing are exercise adherence and weight control. The American College of Sports Medicine (Thompson, Gordon, & Pescatello, 2009) advocates that for optimal health benefits, individuals should exercise at least three to five days per week, for 30 to 60 minutes per day, and include aerobic, resistance, and flexibility exercises. We have a study ongoing in which patients receive CM for participating in exercise activities. They receive a pass to the local YMCA, which has card readers to track workouts and personal fitness goals. If patients complete exercise activities building toward these levels of fitness, they receive reinforcement. Pilot data from the first five patients participating in a CM program revealed that 86.8% of exercise activities selected were done and verified. The most popular activities were attending exercise classes, working out at the Y, and walking using a pedometer to gauge number of steps (working up to 10,000 steps per day). Compared to pre-treatment, this CM intervention appears to be improving physical fitness and medical outcomes. Significant improvements from pre- to post-treatment are noted on a standardized floor transfer test (amount of time needed to go from a sitting to standing position and back) and on a handgrip test. Trends toward reductions in systolic blood pressure are noted as well.

In addition, we have a study ongoing evaluating the efficacy of CM for weight loss. Obese patients are randomly assigned to a standard individual therapy weight loss condition or that same treatment with CM. In the CM condition, patients receive chances to win prizes for completing health-related exercise and nutritional activities and for losing weight. With just the first 20 patients completing treatment, there are already statistically significant benefits of CM. Over a 12-week period, average weight loss was 13 pounds for those receiving CM versus two pounds for those receiving usual care.

Volpp, John, et al. (2008) used a different CM schedule for weight loss. Fifty-seven obese patients were randomly assigned to one of three 16-week conditions: a standard weight loss condition, a condition in which they earned the chance to win money contingent upon losing weight, or a condition in which they earned back deposited funds contingent upon weight loss. In the two CM conditions, average weight loss over 16 weeks was 13 to 14 pounds, and in the non-CM condition it was only four pounds. Thus, both these studies show benefits of CM procedures in encouraging weight loss among obese patients, suggesting potential widespread benefit across a range of patient populations with modifiable health behaviors.

SUMMARY

In conclusion, CM interventions are efficacious in improving outcomes in a variety of substance-abusing and non-substance-abusing populations. Review of the literature shows strong benefits of CM, as long as certain conditions and parameters are carefully considered in the design of CM interventions. The behavior selected for reinforcement must be objectively measured and should not already be occurring at maximal, or near maximal, rates. The reinforcers must be of sufficient magnitude, and they should escalate with sustained behavior change. Finally, reinforcement should be withheld when the targeted behavior does not occur. These three central tenets of CM are important in designing CM interventions, and the next five chapters explicitly take you through steps for developing the best possible CM intervention for your setting.

II

Designing a Contingency Management Intervention

Chapter 5

Selecting a Behavior to Reinforce

The first step in designing a CM intervention is to determine the behavior that you wish to change. Earlier chapters described behaviors that are typically reinforced via CM procedures. In the substance abuse field, they most commonly include abstinence from a specific drug of abuse and attendance at individual or group therapy sessions. Other options are compliance with treatment-related activities. In residential settings, possibilities include completing chores and getting up on time in the mornings. While these are all options, they are not exhaustive. One can design CM approaches to reinforce any behavior that can be objectively determined, meaning that there is a clear and indisputable method for ensuring whether or not the behavior occurred.

CM interventions should be developed to address behaviors with clinical utility. In other words, you want to select a behavior that adversely impacts patients' functioning or one that negatively affects the clinical environment in which they are receiving treatment. Reinforcing steps toward improving employment in a patient who already has a job with which he is happy and functioning well has little benefit. Similarly, reinforcing attendance is unlikely to be useful in a group in which 80% or more patients already attend. Although drug use often occurs at high rates in methadone clinics, drug use is usually low in residential settings in which access to the outside is strictly controlled. In such settings, providing reinforcement for drug abstinence would have little clinical utility.

Some clinicians have an expectation of CM as a magic bullet; they feel that CM could or should solve all the behavioral problems of patients. It is unlikely that any procedure is going to be universally effective for all problem behaviors. The key to successful CM implementation is to take one step at a time. CM interventions should address one problem behavior at a time, whether that problem relates to a single patient, a subset of patients, or a clinic-wide system.

When you design your first CM program, you should consider a number of issues in selecting the behavior to modify: (1) clinical importance, (2) specificity, (3) ability to objectively determine the behavior, (4) frequency with which the behavior occurs naturally, and (5) practicality with respect to monitoring the behavior. This chapter initially describes each of these issues and how and why they are critical to keep in mind when designing a CM program. By the end of the chapter, you will have decided upon a couple of potential behaviors to change with CM.

5.1 ISSUES RELATED TO SELECTING BEHAVIORS TO REINFORCE

In this section, each of the five considerations related to selecting behaviors for CM programs are described. Examples and tables are provided to assist you in choosing behaviors on which to focus your first CM protocol. After completing these exercises, you will be able to narrow your choices down to the most appropriate behaviors.

5.1.1 Clinically Relevant Behaviors

Let's start initially by selecting behaviors of clinical importance. In the worksheet in Table 5.1, list the top 10 clinical issues you are currently facing that may be appropriate targets for a CM intervention. Don't worry about deciding on any one particular behavior at this point. It is better to have a good idea of the many options open to you. As you continue working through this and the remaining worksheets and chapters, you will narrow your preferences down.

In addition, don't limit your thinking to one particular type of behavior. To start with, any behavior is worth considering for change. Be sure to include behaviors of a single patient, those that are applicable to several patients in your clinic, and those that are troublesome for the entire clinic setting. Basically, you are trying to come up with a number of behaviors that you may consider designing a CM intervention to change.

I have listed below a number of potential behaviors. You may draw from these examples, or come up with new ideas on your own. There are no right or wrong answers. This exercise is designed for you to brainstorm about ideas that you may like to change using CM. The only thing you do not want to include are behaviors that have little or no clinical utility or benefits.

At this point, it does not matter if you list the negative behavior (the one you want to decrease in frequency) or the positive behavior (the behavior you want to see more often). As you design your CM intervention, you will match the reinforcers toward the positive behavior, as reinforcement is designed to increase the frequency of a given behavior. The negative behavior is usually the opposite of the desired behavior. By reinforcing the positive behavior, its converse (the negative behavior) should decrease.

Before reading on, try to list at least five, if not 10 or more, behaviors you may want to work on in the bottom section of Table 5.1. Consider a range of

Table 5.1   Brainstorming Clinically Relevant Behaviors

Examples of Behaviors to Change

Reduce drug use

Have more patients come to the initial phases of treatment

Get residential patients to do chores

Get John G to be healthier

Increase adherence to medications

Have people show up on time to groups

Complete relapse prevention homework

Have patients participate positively in groups

Get patients to pay their copays on time

Increase number of patients who transfer to aftercare

Encourage adolescents to do therapeutically appropriate activities at home

Reduce recidivism to jail

Your Initial Ideas of Behaviors to Change

_____

_____

_____

_____

_____

_____

_____

_____

clinically relevant behaviors that may be appropriate to design CM interventions to address. The more behaviors you list, the higher the likelihood that you will narrow your options down to ones that are most useful and apt to change with CM techniques.

5.1.2 Specificity

In the above exercise, you began to think about behaviors that you would like to change. The remainder of the exercises and discussion in this chapter will refer back to the sample behaviors I outlined, as well as the behaviors you included in Table 5.1. You will decide that some behaviors listed are not appropriate for CM interventions, others may be more difficult to change than you originally anticipated, and still others will be good starting points for a CM intervention. You may also add to or alter these behaviors as you move through these exercises.

One area in which it may be necessary to make some changes relates to the ***specificity*** of the behaviors you have chosen. CM interventions work best when they target a specific single behavior, such as attendance *at particular sessions*, abstinence *from a certain drug*, or medication compliance *to an explicit medication regimen*.

Global behaviors, such as "having a good attitude" are not specific. If this behavior were further classified into "displaying a positive attitude throughout a group session," it becomes somewhat more specific. If it is defined as "not swearing in group," it becomes even more specific, and hence more easily adapted to CM approaches.

In addition to specificity, CM interventions work best when they are focused on a single behavior at a time. Getting John to be healthy may entail seeing his physician at least three times annually, filling his prescriptions once a month, taking his medicine twice daily, exercising three times per week, and eating nutritiously. Each of these is a specific health behavior, but they are five different behaviors. Designing a CM intervention to alter five behaviors concurrently is going to be much more challenging than developing a CM intervention to address one of these behaviors. If you have an example that encompasses multiple behaviors, break it down into several categories and/or select the single most clinically relevant behavior.

Go back through your behaviors in Table 5.1 and see if any require further specifications. Specificity may relate to more clearly defining the kinds or numbers of patients, drugs they use, types of behaviors, or actual groups they attend. In Table 5.2 I re-framed the initial responses to be more specific.

After comparing how these examples changed between Tables 5.1 and 5.2, you can take your original examples from Table 5.1 and make them more specific. Include as much detail as possible about the specific behaviors you want to alter in the bottom section of Table 5.2.

Table 5.2   Specifically Defining Potential Target Behaviors

Examples of More Specific Behaviors to Change

Reduce methamphetamine use in the subgroup of patients with methamphetamine dependence

Increase proportion of patients who phone the clinic to attend the intake session and engage in and complete the 10-week initial engagement outpatient treatment program

Get residential patients to finish daily chores (dishwashing, cleaning) without staff reminders

Get John G to exercise three times per week

Increase Tom K's adherence to medications by having him record his medication consumption three times daily

Have people show up on time for the first morning groups: M,T,W,Th,F at 8 am

Help people in the relapse prevention group (Mondays 3 pm) to complete their homework each week prior to coming to group

Encourage positive discussions in weekly aftercare groups on Thursdays at 3 pm

Get patients to pay their weekly copays (range $10 to $100 per week) by Fridays

Increase proportion of patients who transfer to aftercare sessions (Thursday groups) after completing intensive outpatient treatment

Encourage adolescents to complete therapeutically appropriate activities at home (do homework, chores, hobbies)

Reduce % of patients sent back to jail

More Clearly Specify Your Initial Ideas of Behaviors to Change

_____

_____

_____

_____

_____

_____

_____

_____

_____

_____

5.1.3 Objective Determination of Behavior

You can design CM programs to alter any behavior that can be objectively assessed. The ability to impartially determine the behavior is a critical construct. Objective determination refers to clear and indisputable ascertainment of the occurrence or absence of a behavior.

The reason why urine toxicology screens are often used in CM treatments relates to the ability of the tests to objectively determine if the behavior (use of a particular substance) occurred. Toxicology screening does not rely on any judgment call of the clinician, and these tests are greater than 99% accurate in ascertaining if someone used a drug in the recent past. Whether a patient denies or self reports use, it is the outcome of the test that is reinforced.

Similarly, it is easy to determine whether or not a patient attends a session, and therefore, attendance has been another behavior reinforced in a number of CM projects to date (Alessi et al. 2007; Ledgerwood et al., 2008; Rhodes et al., 2003; Sinha et al., 2003). Sometimes, attendance is further specified as "on-time" attendance to ensure that late arrivals to sessions are not reinforced. In any case, showing up at a group or individual session is an objectively measurable behavior.

Contingency management interventions less often focus on behaviors such as medication compliance, in part, because such behaviors are more difficult to objectively verify. Studies do describe successful adoptions of CM for reinforcing medication adherence via mouth checks to ensure ingestion (Carroll et al., 2002; Preston et al., 1999) or MEMS caps readings (Rigsby et al., 2000; Rosen et al., 2007; Sorensen et al., 2007). MEMS caps are electronic devices that record the timing of opening medication bottles. These devices can objectively determine whether one has *opened* the bottle at the appropriate time, but they are unable to provide information about whether the patient actually *consumed* the medication. Hence, this approach is most often used in clinical situations in which patients desire to take their medications, but they fail to do so regularly. A good example of an appropriate population in which to reinforce medication consumption using MEMS caps is patients with hypertension. Most patients with hypertension realize the importance of taking their medications and desire to take them, but remembering when to take them can be challenging. By reinforcing bottle opening, many more patients would be likely to learn to take their medicines as scheduled.

Reinforcing MEMS cap openings would be inappropriate in patient populations with little or limited desire to consume medications, such as some bipolar patients. Bipolar patients who do not want to consume lithium because they enjoy the experiences of the hypomanic phase or they find the side effects troubling would be inappropriate candidates for a CM intervention that reinforces MEMS cap openings. These patients may open the pill bottles at the appropriate time to obtain the reinforcer, yet fail to consume the medication. Thus, objective verification of actual pill consumption (e.g., mouth checks, monitoring of metabolite levels in the blood) would be needed. Similarly, detoxified opioid-dependent patients who are prescribed naltrexone to prevent relapse to opioid use would be unlikely to respond well to a CM program that reinforced MEMS cap openings alone. In contrast, hypertensive patients would be less likely to simply open the cap without consuming the medication to gain reinforcement, although this remains a possibility. If objective verification is not completely possible, then it is important to consider the patient population in designing a CM intervention. Regardless of the population, the more objectively one can verify a behavior the more amenable it will be to CM techniques.

Even more difficult to objectively assess than medication adherence are behaviors such as "good attitudes." A good attitude, while clinically important, is not something that can be easily quantified or objectively determined. Consider a therapy group that is co-led by two therapists. A court-mandated patient, Mike, is often silent in the sessions and spends most of the group time doodling on a notepad. When he is called upon, he often makes a negative remark about how stupid the topic is or why he doesn't want to be in the group. The therapists often avoid calling on him so as not to disrupt the group discussions, and Mike then does not participate at all. One of the therapists may feel that Mike's attitude during such a session is acceptable so long as he doesn't make negative remarks, whereas the other therapist may consider the doodling and lack of participation to be unacceptable. Hence, it would be difficult to objectively quantify Mike's behaviors, unless the therapists more clearly defined what was acceptable or not.

The therapists could decide that in order for Mike's behavior to be considered acceptable he must make some contribution to the group, and it must not be negative in nature. Although this definition is more specific, the therapists may still not agree on the objective determination of the behavior. For example, if Mike responds to a direct question about urges by saying, *"No, I didn't have any urges to use this past week,"* would that be sufficient to constitute appropriate behavior? One therapist may argue yes, while the other may still not consider this contribution of sufficient magnitude, even though it was not negative in nature. What if Mike made this comment, but with what one therapist considered to be a negative tone of voice, such that Mike seemed to be making fun of the concept? The other therapist may not have considered the tone to be mocking and took the comment at face value. How can tone of voice be objectively determined?

If Mike doodled throughout the group, or if he was only doodling during five minutes of group, would that change the decision about classifying his attitude as appropriate? Moreover, a good attitude can quickly change to a bad one, or vice versa, such that determinations of when an attitude is good, versus when it is not, becomes complex.

Table 5.3   Methods for Determining Occurrences of Behaviors and Their Objectivity

Examples	Method for Determining	Objectivity (1–10 scale)
Reduce methamphetamine use in the subgroup of patients with methamphetamine dependence	Urine toxicology results	10
Increase proportion of patients who phone the clinic to attend the intake session and engage in and complete the 10-week outpatient treatment program	Attendance	10
Get residential patients to finish chores (dishwashing, cleaning) without staff reminders	Staff reviews for appropriate completion	7
Get John G to exercise three times per week		
Increase Tom K's adherence to medications by having him record his medication consumption three times daily		
Have people show up on time for first morning groups: M,T,W,Th,F at 8 am		
Help people in the relapse prevention group (Mondays 3 pm) to complete their homework each week prior to coming to group		
Encourage positive discussions in weekly aftercare groups on Thursdays at 3 pm		
Get patients to pay their weekly copays (range $10 to $100 per week) by Fridays		
Increase proportion of patients who transfer to Thursday aftercare sessions after completing intensive outpatient treatment		
Encourage adolescents to complete therapeutically appropriate activities at home (do homework, chores, hobbies)		
Reduce % of patients sent back to jail		

Table 5.3 lists the sample behaviors again. The middle column has space to list potential methods of determining the occurrence of each behavior. In the furthest right column, you can indicate the degree to which each behavior can be objectively verified. Use a "1" to "10" scale, with "1" representing behaviors that are "extremely difficult to objectively define" or those that may lend to a lot of controversy in determining, such as attitudes. A "10" should represent the other end of the spectrum and be recorded for behaviors that have little room for variation in determining their presence or absence. Scores in lower middle ranges would reflect behaviors that are

Table 5.4 Methods for Determining Occurrences of Potential Behaviors for Reinforcement and Objectivity

Your Ideas of Behaviors to Change (from bottom of Table 5.1)	Method for Determining Behavior	Objectivity 1 (low) to 10 (high)

fairly difficult to conclusively monitor, and those in the higher ranges represent behaviors that have good to quite good, albeit not excellent, methods for objective verification.

At this point, do not consider feasibility of implementing the method for objective determination. For example, you may not consider it easy to introduce urine testing procedures into your clinical setting, but urine testing procedures are highly reliable, valid, and objective in determining many forms of drug use, so they should be rated with a high number.

The first three sample behaviors are completed for you. You should then fill in answers for the remaining sample behaviors in Table 5.3.

In completing this exercise, you should have rated group discussions and homework completion behaviors lower than attendance and abstinence behaviors. My ratings of objectivity for each of the above behaviors appear later in the chapter (see Table 5.5). Although you may not rate them exactly as I did, there should be some correlation between your scores and mine. After reviewing them, write down the behaviors you are considering for a CM protocol in Table 5.4 and see which seem most and least appropriate from the standpoint of objective verification. Indicate how you would objectively measure each behavior. If there is no way to objectively monitor a behavior that you originally listed (e.g., "having positive thoughts"), write "none" in the middle column.

Table 5.5 Frequencies of Behaviors and Practically of Assessment

Column A *Examples of Behaviors*	*B* *Objectivity* *(1 to 10)*	*C* *Frequency of* *Behavior*	*D* *Practicality* *(1 = low to 10 = high)*
Reduce methamphetamine use in the subgroup of patients with methamphetamine dependence	10	Most use four to five days per week	
Increase proportion of patients who phone the clinic to attend the intake session and engage in and complete the 10-week outpatient treatment program	10	Once for the intake session, weekly for the outpatient treatment	
Get patients to finish chores (dishwashing, cleaning) without staff reminders	7	One to three times per day, depending on chore	
Get John G to exercise three times per week	4	Up to daily	
Increase Tom K's adherence to medications by having him record his medication consumption three times daily	2	Three times per day, seven days per week	
Have people show up on time for the first morning groups M,T,W,Th,F at 8 am	10	Five times per week	
Help people in the relapse prevention group (on Mon 3 pm) to complete their homework each week prior to coming to group	7	Weekly	
Encourage everyone to discuss and participate in the weekly aftercare group sessions on Thurs at 3 pm	3	Weekly	
Get patients to pay their copays (range $10 to $100 per week) by Fridays	10	Weekly	
Increase the proportion of patients who successfully transfer to Thursday aftercare (AC) sessions after completing intensive outpatient treatment	10	Transfer to AC occurs only once. AC is once weekly.	

Table 5.5 (continued)   Frequencies of Behaviors and Practically of Assessment

Column A	B	C	D
Examples of Behaviors	Objectivity (1 to 10)	Frequency of Behavior	Practicality (1 = low to 10 = high)
Encourage adolescents to complete therapeutically appropriate activities at home (do homework, chores, hobbies)	6	Daily to weekly	
Reduce the proportion of patients who are sent back to jail	10	Occurs up to daily for group as a whole but only once per patient	
Your Ideas of Behaviors to Change	Objectivity (1 to 10)	Frequency of Behavior	Practicality (1 = low to 10 = high)

In the far right column, you can also rate each behavior on a "1" to "10" scale with respect to the degree to which it is objectively verifiable. For behaviors that cannot be objectively verified, you would list a "1" in the right column. In determining the objectivity, consider the perspectives of patients, as well as those of other therapists, in defining each behavior. For example, if you were a patient being reinforced for the behavior outlined, might you have different definitions about how that behavior could be measured so that you could earn reinforcement? If so, the behavior is probably not very objective and should be ranked with a lower score.

Once you have decided upon a method to verify and have rated each of your initial behaviors in terms of their objectivity, consider the rank orderings in the Objectivity column. Are the behaviors rated the lowest ones that are most difficult to objectively confirm, and the ones ranked the highest the most likely to be readily observed and confirmed? If not, you may want to reconsider some of your initial objectivity ratings.

5.1.4 Frequency of the Behavior

For the behaviors that you identified as having a reasonably high likelihood of being objectively verifiable, next consider how often they occur naturally. Some may occur multiple times each day, such as cigarette smoking or medication consumption for twice- or thrice-daily medication regimens. Others occur about one a day on average, and examples may be daily attendance at a methadone clinic or a daily chore at a residential clinic. Still others happen regularly more than once a week (e.g., attendance at a twice-weekly group session), or irregularly but on average a few times a week (e.g., cocaine use). Some behaviors may occur only once a week (e.g., weekly therapy attendance) and others even less often (e.g., occasional use of cocaine in a primary heroin-dependent patient or attendance at a monthly psychiatrist's appointment).

In the top section of Table 5.5, I listed again the sample behaviors along with examples of how frequently they may occur naturally (Column C). For now, leave Column D blank.

Below the sample items, list the behaviors that you are considering targeting for change in order of their ability to be objectively verifiable (from Table 5.4). Then in Column C, list the frequency with which the patient(s) currently exhibits the behavior.

Once you finish writing in the ideal frequencies for the sample behaviors, do the same for the behaviors you initially selected to change. This information can be recorded in the bottom section of Table 5.5. Presumably, some of these will be behaviors that occur very often, whereas others are less frequent.

5.1.5 Practicality

In deciding upon the best behaviors to target for CM interventions, practicality or feasibility must also be considered. Some behaviors, although ideal from a CM perspective, may be unrealistic to reinforce in your particular clinical setting because of cost or time constraints.

In Column D in Table 5.5, rate how practical you think it would be to monitor the behaviors given your clinical setting. In determining practicality, consider the frequency of monitoring and staff time associated with monitoring the behaviors, and any specialized equipment you may need to assess the behaviors and the availability (and costs, if applicable) of such equipment.

For behaviors that are easy to monitor and add little or no cost or staff time (e.g., attendance at that clinic), the rating should be high. Behaviors that would require expensive and unavailable equipment or more staff time than possible would be rated much lower on the scale. Initial abstinence from cigarette smoking, for example, can be objectively monitored using carbon monoxide monitors. However, monitors cost about $1,200, and they can only objectively ascertain smoking abstinence over a brief (roughly four-hour) window (see Chapter 7). To objectively monitor smoking abstinence, one would need to have the monitor and ability to obtain samples from patients several times per day. These considerations would make this behavior a more difficult one to monitor and reinforce from a practicality and feasibility perspective in most settings.

Try rating the sample behaviors at the top of the chart in terms of practicality and feasibility in your own setting. Fill in a rating from "1" to "10" in Column D in Table 5.5, with a "1" representing very low feasibility or practicality (e.g., impossible) to 10 being very easy. Then, rate the practicality of monitoring the behaviors you selected in the lower half of Table 5.5.

5.2 NARROWING DOWN BEHAVIORS TO REINFORCE

Once you feel that the rank orderings are appropriate in terms of feasibility of monitoring the behaviors you outlined in Table 5.5, concurrently consider the objectivity ratings (Column B) and practicality ratings (Column D) to determine the best behaviors to target for reinforcement in your setting. For example, monitoring good attitudes or active participation in groups may be very easy and practical to assess and receive a rating of 10 in Column D, but it is relatively non-objective, with a sample rating of perhaps only 3 in Column B. Conversely, alcohol abstinence is a highly objective behavior to monitor, but if you are in an outpatient setting, this behavior should have received a very low score in terms of practicality (Column D), because it would need to be monitored multiple times per day as breathalyzers can only detect very recent alcohol use (see Chapter 7, Section 7.1.2.1). In outpatient settings, this frequent monitoring is difficult, if not impossible, to do at night or on weekends (when most alcohol use occurs). Thus, neither of these behaviors is likely to be selected as a top behavior for designing a CM technique in most settings.

In Table 5.6, list your four top behaviors for designing a CM intervention. List them according to your current order of preference, after weighing both the objectivity and practicality ratings. If some behaviors tie in terms of objectivity and practicality, then order those by clinical usefulness. If you have decided there are other, more appropriate behaviors, write those down as well, or instead of, the behaviors you listed early in the worksheets. The goal of this section is to have decided upon a couple of behaviors that are objectively

Table 5.6 Top Behaviors for Designing a CM Intervention

1.
2.
3.
4.

verifiable, specific, clinically useful, and can be practically monitored in your clinical setting.

SUMMARY

You have now completed the first step toward designing an effective CM intervention, and you have narrowed down the behaviors on which you would like to focus. In the next chapter, you will pare down this list further by selecting a population with whom you wish to work using CM techniques.

Chapter 6

Choosing a Population

Once you have narrowed down potential behaviors that you may like to change with a CM intervention as you did in Chapter 5, the next step involves selecting a population with whom you want to implement CM. There is one global choice to make for each behavior, and it relates to designing a CM intervention for an entire clinic population or for a subset of the patients in your clinic. A subset may involve as few as one patient to as many as hundreds. The choice relates to a balance between clinical utility and practicality. There is little rationale for introducing a CM intervention to all patients in a clinic if the CM protocol is designed to affect a behavior that is not a concern for all patients. On the other hand, a behavior may be problematic for a large proportion of patients, but practicality in terms of time or resources available may limit the number who can receive the CM intervention.

At first blush, you may be inclined toward integrating CM clinic wide, most likely because of issues related to "fairness." Most patients will want to participate in CM programs. Many clinicians unfamiliar with the technique are concerned that if CM is not available to all patients, those who are not involved with it will be upset, perhaps even to the extent of withdrawing from treatment.

Although concern about equity and fairness is legitimate, CM has been successfully integrated in clinics around the country with only a portion, and usually only a very small portion, of patients enrolled in the clinics. Integration of CM for a specific target behavior can proceed relatively easily once the therapists and administrators are aware of the reasons for partial integration of CM.

This chapter provides case examples of patients and providers who have experienced CM protocols that were integrated among only a portion of clinic patients. It also describes reasons why and cases in which CM may be better introduced to only a subset of patients in a clinic. The chapter includes a brief quiz to assess whether you should be designing a CM program for a subset of patients or for your entire clinic population. It describes rationales for selecting different types of patients with whom to integrate CM, and it discusses the pros and cons of integrating CM on an individual basis with patients versus a group-based approach. It concludes with suggestions for discussing non-eligibility of CM with patients. Once you have completed the readiness quiz and read through the chapter, you will be better informed about how to further narrow down your choice related to which behavior to reinforce with your first CM intervention.

6.1 CASE EXAMPLES

Case 1: Reinforcing group attendance at one group. Substance Abuse Services, a large outpatient treatment provider, learned about CM in a regional conference and thought it would be a good idea to try in its clinic. The director was particularly swayed by discussions at the conference that CM had an impact on retaining patients in treatment longer, especially those in the early stages of recovery. They, therefore, implemented CM for attendance using the Name-in-the-hat procedure for group attendance (see Chapter 14) in their Monday afternoon Early Recovery group. Typically, this group was supposed to contain up to 15 members, but rarely did more than four persons attend. They decided to implement CM for 12 weeks to see how it would work. Once the CM was introduced, the number of attendees began approaching the cap of 15 patients per group in weeks three to 12. New patients were occasionally skeptical when first told that they could win prizes for attending groups, but after their first session and seeing the prizes, most were motivated to return the following week. Previous annual reports from this clinic noted that only about 20% of new patients completed the Early Recovery groups. The proportion of completers rose to 60% during the 12 weeks that CM was introduced. Clinicians informed patients who were already in treatment and not eligible for CM that the CM was a test program for new patients. Although they were not eligible for this round of CM, the clinicians would look for ways to expand CM to other groups at the clinic given its success in helping patients engage in treatment.

Case 2: Reinforcing group attendance at all groups. Clinicians at Apple Recovery were concerned that implementing CM with only a portion of patients may make those not getting the CM feel left out or jealous of those who were getting the reinforcers. They implemented CM in all the groups at the clinic, and there were about 15 groups held weekly. In some groups, patients regularly attended 80% or more of the time, and these groups saw little or no improvement in attendance with CM. Other groups that were usually attended by only 30% to 50% of those enrolled experienced positive benefits, and attendance rates rose to about 70% in those groups. Patient feedback was universally positive about the procedure, and even those who regularly attended reported that they liked receiving prizes for coming to group. The clinicians were pleased with the response to CM, but they ran out of funds for the reinforcers after four months. They petitioned the Chief Financial Officer to provide more resources.

Case 3: Reinforcing cocaine abstinence. Ongoing cocaine use is a problem for about 30% of patients at Recovery Services, a large state-supported provider. Patients who arrive at the clinic having recently used, or who test positive for cocaine during two consecutive random screenings, are discharged from this clinic, and about one or two patients are discharged each week for using cocaine. Clinicians were concerned that if they only implemented CM for cocaine abstinence with patients who tested positive at least once on random testings, more patients would use cocaine in order to become eligible for the CM program. On the other hand, clinicians did not want to conduct cocaine urine sample screens twice weekly on all patients (70% of whom never used cocaine). Therefore, patients were selected for inclusion in the CM program only if they had evidence of cocaine dependence in their initial evaluation. Although word may get out that new patients calling into this program should state they are using cocaine to get offered CM, patients would still be required to attend the clinic regularly and provide cocaine-negative samples to earn the reinforcers. Clinicians also felt they would be able to discern inconsistencies in responses during the baseline evaluation and would not offer CM to patients whom they suspected were trying to get into treatment just to obtain the reinforcement. They also set a limit on the number of patients per month who would be offered CM, using clinical judgment in conjunction with original criteria (cocaine dependence at the intake evaluation) to select the 10 patients per month (no more than two or three new admissions per week) who would be offered CM. The decisions were made in weekly staff meetings, and each clinician was allowed to propose up to two new patients per month who met the inclusion criteria for the CM program and whom they thought would benefit from it. In this manner, clinicians who already had several CM patients and did not feel that they would be able to collect and screen more urine samples could wait before including new patients; clinicians with more time and patients who were likely to benefit could be enrolled in the CM intervention rapidly.

John, a marijuana-dependent patient in the aftercare phase of treatment, heard about the CM program ongoing at this clinic during his eighth week in treatment. He had a good friend who was participating in the CM program and earning reinforcers for cocaine abstinence. John asked his clinician if he could get into the CM program. The clinician informed John that the CM program was a pilot program that was being tested with just a few patients at the clinic. The clinician further stated that if the program worked well, they would look for ways to expand the CM so that more patients could benefit from it. John expressed mild disappointment that he could not participate, but he understood the rationale.

In two of the examples above, clinicians made a decision to implement CM with a subset of patients enrolled in the clinics. Only patients in a specific group or initiating treatment with a particular substance use disorder would be eligible to receive the CM. In both cases, the decisions about who can participate are not arbitrary, but based on pre-defined characteristics: enrolled in a group with poor attendance or beginning treatment with cocaine problems. If ineligible patients request CM treatment, the therapists have a good rationale for explaining ineligibility without encouraging false self-reports to gain access to CM. In case example 2, in contrast, therapists decided to apply CM universally. Although this decision can be appealing, it can also be costly. Because CM was being applied to groups that were already attended at high rates, the Chief Financial Officer may deny the request to continue supporting the CM. When averaged across all patients at the clinic, attendance may have only increased 10%, but if CM were targeted just toward groups with poor attendance, the improvement rate may be 35%, making it highly cost-effective in those groups.

As you review the above examples, you can see that different clinical needs and sites require thoughtful consideration about how to best implement CM. CM need not be introduced with every patient in a clinic, and it can still have excellent results.

6.2 REASONS TO INTRODUCE CM TO A SUBSET OF PATIENTS

There are a number of important reasons why CM should be offered to only a subset of patients in a particular clinic. From a practical standpoint, a primary rationale is that it gives you a chance to get used to CM procedures. Implementing any new type of treatment is not easy, and it requires time and practice. By taking it slowly, you will be better able to concentrate on implementing CM correctly. If you were to introduce it with everyone in your clinic all at once, you would likely feel overwhelmed. Mistakes are more likely to be made in these circumstances. Patients (and therapists) may get upset, and benefits of CM would be less likely to be realized.

A second reason for slow and gradual implementation with only a select sample of patients is that gradual introduction of CM will give you an opportunity to try the procedures and see if they are working as intended. If your monitoring or reinforcement schedule is not ideal (Chapters 8 and 9) and behavioral changes are not occurring as anticipated, then you can make modifications to the system prior to implementing it with the next cohort of patients. If it does work well, then you will have gained important skills and confidence. You can implement CM more easily and perhaps with an even larger cohort in a subsequent round.

Not only will gradual implementation allow you to learn, but it will also provide an important test for other clinicians or administrators who may be skeptical of the approach. Beginning with a test case allows for a more limited investment of time and resources. If all goes as anticipated, you will have experience and outcomes for skeptics to review. If things do not go as planned, you can learn from your mistakes and make revisions.

On a related note, limited implementation has the advantage of costing less than wide-scale implementation. Integrating CM into one group can cost as little as $300 for 12 weeks using the Name-in-the-hat procedure for reinforcing group attendance. To integrate CM into all groups in a clinic would cost $300 multiplied by the number of groups.

Another advantage of a targeted administration of CM is that you can focus on a single issue and a single behavior at a time. As reviewed in Chapter 5, CM works best when it specifically targets one behavior at a time. Not all patients at any clinic are likely to share one particular problem, and there is little point in reinforcing patients for behaviors that are not problematic for them. There is no reason to add CM to a group that is already at or near its maximum attendance, for example.

Finally, an approach that many clinicians use once they have become familiar with CM is to alter the behavior being reinforced or the target population over time so different groups of patients get a chance to experience and benefit from CM. Cocaine abstinence may be targeted initially for three to six months, early morning attendance at alcohol relapse prevention groups may be targeted in the next three to six months, then attendance at parenting groups, and finally attendance at family groups. As with many things, novelty in the application can lead to increased enthusiasm about CM for both the patients and the staff.

6.3 ASSESSMENT OF TARGET POPULATIONS FOR CM PROGRAMS

To assess your readiness to implement CM with relatively few or many patients, take the following survey. Pick the response that best fits your feelings for each of the items in Exhibit 6.1.

If you answered "a" to three or more of the items in Exhibit 6.1, I recommend that you consider implementing CM to only a subset of patients in your setting. There are certainly instances in which it is best to apply CM to all patients, but this typically relates to closed settings such as prisons or residential programs. In these settings, non-monetary-based reinforcers such as clinic privileges can be used, which obviates one of the primary concerns about widespread CM implementation—costs (see Chapter 10). As noted earlier, if CM is implemented clinic wide, it is going to cost substantially more than if it is integrated with only a subset of patients.

EXHIBIT 6.1   READINESS TEST FOR IMPLEMENTING CM WITH SOME OR ALL PATIENTS IN A CLINIC

1. My current goal in implementing CM is to:
   a. try to figure out how well it works with my patients.
   b. fully integrate CM because I know it works.
2. My level of experience with CM is best described as:
   a. I have relatively little experience with this intervention.
   b. I feel very confident in my ability to implement CM correctly.
3. The behavior that I am most interested in addressing with CM:
   a. affects some but not all patients at my clinic.
   b. affects all or most all the patients in my clinic.
4. Funds available for me to use for CM purposes are:
   a. limited.
   b. not a substantial concern.
5. The time clinicians have available to learn about CM is:
   a. limited.
   b. not a substantial concern.
6. The amount of time I and other staff have available to implement CM is:
   a. limited.
   b. not a substantial concern.
7. Staff at my clinic:
   a. have mixed feelings about CM.
   b. all think CM is a great idea.

Starting slowly is usually the best way to approach many situations. Just as you would first practice a new psychotherapy such as motivational interviewing or cognitive-behavioral therapy with only a few patients at a time, so too should you probably introduce CM.

6.4 HOW TO DECIDE HOW MANY AND WHICH PATIENTS GET CM

The group of patients with whom you initially apply CM will depend in large part on the behavior you choose to reinforce. In Chapter 5, you narrowed your choices down to a few behaviors that can be objectively verified and that can be practically monitored. We will now determine how many patients and which ones ought to be offered CM.

6.4.1 Specifying Number of Patients Eligible

Initially, we will review three of the sample behaviors from Chapter 5. If a CM program were designed to reduce methamphetamine use, such a CM program would clearly be applicable only to patients who use methamphetamine. Let's

Table 6.1 Estimating Numbers of Patients for CM Programs

Behavior	Number of Patients	Group or Individual	Best Number to Implement
Sample Behaviors			
Reduce methamphetamine use in the subgroup of patients with methamphetamine dependence	~150		
Increase proportion of patients who phone the clinic to attend the intake session and engage in and complete the 10-week outpatient treatment program	~1,200 annually		
Get residential patients to finish daily chores (dishwashing, cleaning) without staff reminders	~30		
Your Possible Behaviors			

presume there are about 150 methamphetamine users in a large clinic that serves about 600 patients a day. Therefore, "about 150" is written in the second column of Table 6.1 for this example.

Now, consider the second example. It applies to engagement of new patients in treatment. For this example, we will assume it relates to a fairly busy clinic that has 1,200 admissions annually, and about 1,200 annually is included in the second column.

If, in the third example, CM were implemented in a residential program to improve compliance with chores, the CM program would be instituted with all the patients at that residential treatment program (presuming all the patients had assigned chores). Let's assume this is a 30-bed facility, and the program is usually full. We write "about 30" in the second column.

Now write in your behaviors potentially targeted for change in the lower rows. These refer to the behaviors you selected in Table 5.6. In the column next to it, indicate the number of patients currently in your program for whom these particular behaviors are a problem and who may benefit from a CM intervention. The exact number of patients is not important, but indicating a rough estimate is necessary for planning purposes. For now, you will leave the two right-handed columns blank, and we will come back to those later.

6.4.2 Group or Individual CM Administration

CM interventions can be administered in either an individual or a group context. In the original studies, all CM was conducted on an individual basis, but as described in Chapter 3, recent research has moved CM into group administration.

Table 6.2 outlines pros and cons of CM in individual and group formats. The main advantage to administering CM individually is that the monitoring and reinforcement are confidential, and this is particularly important for certain behaviors (e.g., urine toxicology testing or possibly sensitive issues such as medication adherence). Other behaviors, such as group attendance, are by their nature not confidential and may be easily amenable to group reinforcement. When CM is conducted on an individual basis, the alliance between the patient and the clinician can be strengthened as the clinician directly administers the reinforcers and can explain in a personalized manner why reinforcement is not earned when appropriate behaviors do not occur. The therapeutic alliance is associated with outcomes in CM interventions (Petry, Alessi, Ledgerwood, & Sierra, 2010). Specific CM protocols can also be designed for unique patient issues (e.g., medication adherence regimens, parenting concerns) when CM is administered on an individualized basis.

Group-based CM also has a number of advantages. Perhaps most importantly, the overall costs of CM can be reduced (both in terms of administration time and reinforcers) when it is implemented in a group context. Rather than monitoring and reinforcing each individual separately, all the monitoring and reinforcement occur in the group. Typically, group-based reinforcement can be integrated in just five to 10 minutes of a group session, thereby utilizing relatively little overall administration time. In the Name-in-the-hat prize CM procedure for group attendance, described initially in Chapter 3 and outlined

Table 6.2 Pros and Cons of Individual versus Group CM

	Individual CM	*Group CM*
Pros	Confidentiality	Reduces time needed for CM administration
	Can strengthen alliance between individual patients and clinician	Can be less costly
	CM designs can be individually tailored	Group cohesion can occur
Cons	Takes more time to monitor and reinforce patients individually	Retaliation potential if others' behaviors reduce reinforcement for the group
	Usually more costly	Others know what individuals earn
	Patients do not benefit from seeing how appropriate behaviors are reinforced in others	All individuals in the group ought to be eligible for the CM

in detail in Chapter 14, the overall amount of reinforcement provided is quite low. For example, costs of CM can be arranged at about $20 per group per week, which may translate to less than a few dollars per patient; in contrast, each patient is able to earn $20 or more per week in many individually administered CM programs. One reason that the costs can be reduced in a group format without adversely affecting effectiveness is that patients directly observe other patients who have performed the behavior and hence earn reinforcement. Seeing others earn large magnitude reinforcers for sustained behavior change can have positive benefits on new group members who may then strive to emulate those behaviors. Group members can encourage one another to achieve goals and earn reinforcement, and strong group cohesion can occur when patients work together to achieve goals and earn reinforcers.

Group-based CM can also have some disadvantages. If reinforcers are contingent upon all members achieving a goal (e.g., no one gets reinforcement if one member does not attend the group), then patients may retaliate directly or indirectly against group members who are responsible for a lack of reinforcement. Thus, it is important that clinicians are cognizant of these issues in designing group-based CM interventions. The CM protocols outlined in this book describe behaviors and reinforcement schedules that do not result in retaliatory behaviors. Another potential concern about group-based reinforcement is that all patients in attendance will know what others have earned. Patients who earn large magnitude reinforcers may have them stolen. If this is a concern, clinicians may consider delivering large magnitude reinforcers to patients' home, or arranging for a private time for them to pick them up. Another issue that should be considered with group-based reinforcement is that all individuals in the group ought to be eligible to earn the reinforcement. It would not be appropriate to reinforce cocaine users in a group in which only four of the 12 group members were cocaine users and eligible to participate in the CM intervention. The remaining eight group members would feel left out if they were witnessing others receive reinforcement and never had the chance to earn prizes themselves. In such cases, it would be better to conduct the reinforcement individually with the few patients for whom cocaine use was problematic.

Individually administered CM also has some disadvantages, primarily related to staffing and direct reinforcement costs. It takes more time to administer and reinforce patients individually than in groups. Patients who are not earning reinforcement may not fully recognize the value of the reinforcers when CM is administered on an individual basis. If they never receive the reinforcers, they may not understand how many vouchers or prizes they can earn. In contrast, in a group setting, patients can see that patients who exhibit the behaviors earn reinforcement, and they can directly observe the positive benefits of behavior change.

After fully considering the pros and cons of individually based and group-based CM, indicate whether each behavior listed in Table 6.1 is best reinforced on an individual or a group basis. Some behaviors are unique to certain individuals or are personal in nature (e.g., parenting or medication issues) or are troublesome for only one or a few patients in a particular group (e.g., loud outbursts). Others are a concern for most, if not all, patients in a particular group (attendance or on-time attendance, completing homework assigned in group). For the former, these behaviors would probably best be reinforced individually. For the latter, reinforcement in a group context would be appropriate and would have the advantages outlined above.

For the three sample behaviors listed at the top of Table 6.1, the behaviors would be best reinforced in an individual, group, and individual context, respectively. Those answers can be written in for those behaviors in the third column from the right. Next, you can indicate in what context the behaviors you selected would be best reinforced in the lower section of Table 6.1.

6.4.3 Ideal Number of Patients for CM

In the column furthest to the right in Table 6.1, you can indicate the best number of patients with whom to administer the CM protocol. The maximum this number would be is the number of patients impacted by the behavior, that is, the number in the column second to the left. However, you need not implement CM with all the patients for whom it would apply. In monitoring urine toxicology screens, you may want to apply CM to only a small group of the 150 methamphetamine-dependent patients, or 10 to 15 patients to start. This behavior will be reinforced individually and will require collection and testing of at least two samples per week, which would mean 20 samples per week if 10 patients are enrolled in the CM program and 30 samples per week if 15 patients are enrolled. You can easily see why 150 patients should not start such a CM program at once! It would require collection of 300 samples per week. For the second sample behavior, you need not implement the CM will all new patients for a year; implementing it for all new patients over a one-month period should translate to about 100 patients. Because CM is integrated in groups in this context, it may mean it would be instituted in about four or five groups per week. If this seems like too many groups, you could implement CM into just two of the early recovery groups, and this would cut down the number of groups (and patients) impacted even further by about 50%, or down to 40 to 50 patients over a one-month period. For the final sample behavior (completing chores), only 30 patients are affected. In this case, it may be appropriate to implement CM with all the patients in a rather small residential setting.

Once you have considered how the sample behaviors can be administered with a subset of patients, try this exercise with the behaviors you selected.

Of the patients who experience the problem behaviors you identified, indicate the number who could realistically be exposed to CM during your initial attempt at CM delivery in the right-hand column of Table 6.1.

6.4.4 How to Discuss Ineligibility for a CM Program

As mentioned earlier in this chapter, a common concern is that patients who are not participating in the CM program will be upset, perhaps to the point of withdrawing from treatment. I have instituted CM at over 50 clinical programs, each treating hundreds to thousands of patients annually. I have never encountered a single patient who withdrew from standard care because she or he was unable to participate in the CM program.

If non-eligible patients approach you wanting to know how to get into the CM program, simply state, "I'm glad to hear you're interested in this new program. Right now, we are testing it with just a few patients. If it works with them, we hope to get more funds so that we can expand the program to other patients like you." Patients in all types of clinics have accepted and understood explanations such as this.

SUMMARY

By the end of this chapter, you should have further specified your potential behaviors for reinforcement and decided upon the number of patients with whom it is best to administer CM. This process may help you further rank order your preferences in terms of the type of behavior you would most like to reinforce using CM. You may have decided, for example, that you really want to administer CM in a group context rather than individually, and therefore, you can narrow down the target behaviors to only those that best occur in a group context. Alternatively, you may decide that it would be best to administer CM to a smaller subset of patients with a similar problem, rather than coming up with a way to select among a large group of patients with a common concern. At this point, narrow down your choice of behaviors to reinforce to your top choice: _____.

In the next chapter, you will determine the most appropriate behavior monitoring schedule for this behavior. If you decide later to revisit another behavior, you can complete the exercises described in the subsequent chapters with other behaviors.

Chapter 7

Determining a Behavior Monitoring Schedule

Now that you have decided upon a behavior to target and a population with whom to introduce CM, the next step in designing a CM protocol involves choosing a monitoring schedule. To select a schedule, you should consider several issues: (1) the frequency of the behavior in the natural environment, (2) methods for objective and valid verification of the behavior, (3) temporal relationships between the behavior and its monitoring, (4) frequency of monitoring, and (5) duration of monitoring. Previous chapters touched upon some of these issues. This chapter will describe them in more detail, especially as they relate to developing appropriate monitoring schedules. This chapter will also describe and critique examples of monitoring schedules used in practice for some of the most commonly reinforced behaviors. By the end of this chapter, you will have decided upon an optimal monitoring schedule to improve the behavior you want to change using CM.

7.1 DETERMINING MONITORING SCHEDULES

A number of principles should be kept in mind when deciding upon the best schedule to monitor behaviors in CM interventions. Initially, I describe four of these principles as they relate to the most commonly reinforced behaviors.

7.1.1 Frequency of Behavior

In Chapter 5, Table 5.5, you indicated frequencies with which behaviors occur in the natural environment. By this point, you should have narrowed your possible behaviors down to a single behavior on which you wish to focus. For the behavior in which you are designing a CM intervention, ensure that the initial frequency you indicated in Table 5.5 is correct. If you have objective data available to help you confirm the frequency of the selected behavior, you may want to obtain and review those data now. The more accurate these estimates are, the better you will able to assess the effectiveness of your CM intervention.

If you are targeting abstinence from a specific drug, go back to actual patients' charts to ascertain the frequencies with which users of this drug tested negative and positive for this substance. Review intake evaluations with respect to the number of self-reported days of use of this substance. In making these determinations, the more patient information that you use, the more accurate your estimation will be. Our memories are often swayed by unusual cases (e.g., the 10% of patients who use cocaine daily, when the vast majority of patients seeking treatment for cocaine use it a few days per week). You want to be basing the frequency of the behavior on the best estimate, integrating information from as many sources as possible.

If you plan to monitor and reinforce attendance at a particular group, go back and review attendance records at that group for the previous year. If you intend to start a new group and therefore do not have historical records available, examine attendance records from the most similar group(s) that occurred in your clinic in the past year.

Several behaviors are listed in the upper portion of Table 7.1 as examples, along with potential objective information you can utilize to determine their frequencies. In the right-hand column, the usual frequency (in appropriate time units) is noted.

Table 7.1　Natural Frequencies of Behaviors

Behavior	Data Available to Determine Frequency	Frequency Before CM
Reduce methamphetamine use in the subgroup of patients with methamphetamine dependence	Self-reported days in a typical month; random (at least monthly) utoxes Urine toxicology screens (utoxes)	Self-reports = average 12 days per month Utoxes positive = 20% positive each month
Increase proportion of patients who phone the clinic to attend the intake session and engage in and complete the 10-week outpatient treatment program	New caller records in past year; intake evaluations from past year; and treatment completion rates over the past year	2,196 scheduled intakes; 1,122 attended intakes; 221 completed 10 weeks of treatment
Get patients to finish chores (dishwashing, cleaning) without staff reminders	No records, but staff can collect data for two to four weeks before starting CM	TBD—estimated 30% to 50% of chores are completed without staff reminders.
The Behavior You Are Targeting	*Data Available to Determine Frequency*	*Frequency Before CM*

After reviewing the sample behaviors and their frequencies in the Table 7.1, complete the bottom section of the table for the behavior you decided to target for change. In the middle column, list information you can access to ascertain the frequency of that behavior.

It may take you some time to obtain and review this information. Therefore, you may not be able to fill in the right-hand column about actual frequencies until you investigate the behavior. Although it is not necessary to have a completely accurate account of the frequency of the behavior to design a CM intervention, having this information will better allow you to determine whether or not your CM intervention is having an impact on behavior.

If you decide later in this chapter, or at another point, to select a different behavior to modify using CM, you can add that information to a new Table 7.1. Nevertheless, at this point, it is best to focus on developing a CM intervention for one behavior at a time.

7.1.2 Methods for Objective and Valid Verification of the Behavior

As you examine evidence regarding the occurrence of a behavior, you are probably also considering objective evidence that can verify whether or not the behavior occurred. For example, if you looked through old clinical records to ascertain attendance at a group, you reviewed objective records about if patients came to the group sessions or not. If you are considering reinforcing abstinence from a particular substance, you are likely to be examining urine toxicology screens. These are both examples of objective methods to verify whether or not a particular behavior occurred. As noted throughout this book, CM procedures can only be developed for behaviors that can be objectively verified, and Chapter 5 described the need to focus CM procedures on verifiable behaviors. Next, I detail objective verification methods along with some nuances associated with measuring these behaviors.

7.1.2.1 Abstinence

Abstinence is commonly reinforced in CM programs, and there are objective methods to verify abstinence from many substances. Typically, it involves urine toxicology testing. Onsite testing is necessary for CM protocols reinforcing abstinence. If you send a sample offsite, one to three days will elapse between the submission of the sample and receipt of the results, making it impossible for you to closely link the behavior with the reinforcement. Although your clinical setting may utilize offsite testing for reimbursement or legal reasons, you must use onsite testing for CM interventions. Test kits that are highly reliable and valid for assessing use of opioids, stimulants, and marijuana are available. These include EZ-SCREEN® from MedTox (Burlington, NC) and Varian Cupkits (Agilent Technologies, Lake Forest, CA), along with other examples you can find online. Each provides results in as little as one to two minutes at relatively low cost of about $1 to $2 per reagent.

The most common onsite urine toxicology tests can reliably and validly detect use of opioids (including heroin and many commonly prescribed opioid analgesics, such as Percocet, Darvocet, etc.) and stimulants (cocaine, amphetamine, and methamphetamine, although each is measured separately) over a 48- to 72-hour period. When testing for opioids, methadone is detected separately from other opioids, so use of illicit opioids can be distinguished from methadone in methadone-maintained patients. Onsite testing kits generally utilize similar cut-points for ascertaining use or abstinence as laboratories, although manufacturer specifications should be considered. Further, one needs to consider that onsite kits are qualitative in nature. They only distinguish recent use from non-use, not increases or decreases in use from prior days.

Saliva and hair testing is available for some substances, but to date, limited data exist on the reliability and validity of these methods. In addition, time frames over which these methods detect substance use may differ from urine toxicology testing. Manufacturer specifications should be considered in determining their ability to assess use and abstinence from substances. No published CM studies have utilized saliva or hair testing to reinforce abstinence, so the current recommendation is to use the more conventional method of urine testing.

Although reinforcing urine specimen results is a relatively straightforward procedure, testing urine samples suffers from some practical difficulties. First, onsite testing systems are often not reimbursable costs. You may therefore need to add urine toxicology testing to your budget for designing a CM intervention. See Chapter 10 for more details on determining costs.

Second, when contingencies on urine toxicology results are in place, some patients will try to leave fake samples. Therefore, submission of specimens should be observed by staff to ensure validity. Checking temperature, dilution, and pH can also address issues related to the validity of samples, and commercially available products are available for all of these, but they add to the costs. AdultaCheck® (Sciteck, Inc., Arden, NC) is a commercially available test strip (http://www.onsitedrugtesting.com/drugtest/adcheck.htm) that detects common methods of urine adulteration. It does this by indicating whether the sample shows normal ranges for creatinine, pH, glutaraldehyde, and nitrates. If the test indicates that the urine is outside normal range on any of these features, it can be counted as invalid, as outlined in Chapter 13.

Third, some technical issues need to be considered in CM protocols. Many types of benzodiazepines exist, making it difficult to detect all forms of sedative use, and the onsite testing kits do not screen for every form of sedative. Some substances, like methadone and benzodiazepines, can be prescribed as well as taken illicitly. Differentiating licit from illicit use can be difficult, if not impossible, for patients with legitimate prescriptions for these medications. Although you can readily differentiate other opioid (heroin, Percocet, Darvocet) use from methadone use in methadone maintenance patients, you will not be able to distinguish clinic-prescribed methadone use from illicit methadone use. Further, many intravenous drug users and heavy alcohol drinkers have liver disease. Liver diseases may result in a longer delay (e.g., three to five days rather than one to two days) between abstinence and samples reading negative.

In chronic marijuana users, up to four weeks of abstinence may need to be achieved before samples test negative. Patients can find this delay between the behavior (abstinence) and the reinforcer discouraging. The goal of a CM intervention is to frequently and immediately reinforce patients for abstaining. For chronic marijuana users, it is not possible to reinforce initial attempts at abstinence with currently available onsite technology. Hence, in many CM protocols reinforcing marijuana abstinence, patients are reinforced for attendance in the first one to three weeks, with reinforcement becoming contingent on negative marijuana readings starting in week three or four. (Although it may take up to three or four weeks for a sample to read negative after chronic use, marijuana use following a period of abstinence should result in the sample testing positive for two or three days, and it would not test positive for another three or four weeks unless use was persisting.)

If CM procedures are designed to reinforce alcohol or nicotine abstinence, the detection window is very short in duration. Breathalyzers detect alcohol use over only brief intervals of three to six hours, and ideally, breath samples would need to be screened several times a day to detect any use of alcohol. Such a testing schedule, however, is impractical in most non-residential treatment settings. Urine and blood tests are available for assessing alcohol use, but they do not measure back much further than breath tests. Similarly, carbon monoxide readings must be taken several times daily to detect all instances of smoking during initial stages of smoking cessation. Thus, technological limitations present some complications for developing CM procedures for certain drugs of abuse.

If you are considering a CM intervention to reinforce abstinence from alcohol, nicotine, or benzodiazepines, you may wish to select another behavior at this time. Once you gain experience with CM for reinforcing abstinence from a drug that is more amenable to monitoring, you may be better prepared to make modifications for these relatively more difficult-to-monitor behaviors. Onsite technology for detecting opioid, stimulant, and marijuana abstinence is available at fairly low cost. Guidelines for using urine toxicology for CM have been developed, and substantive evidence indicates these procedures are effective in reducing use of these drugs. Chapter 13 provides details on implementing CM to reinforce abstinence for these substances.

7.1.2.2 Attendance

Attendance is an easy behavior to objectively verify, because either a patient showed up for a session or she did not. Although simple on the surface, reinforcing attendance has one common complication, and that relates to *excused absences*. There may be times in which patients cannot attend sessions. These may include a medical or legal appointment, an illness, a family emergency, a death in the family, or transportation difficulties. These potential reasons for missing treatment may or may not be considered legitimate, depending on the population with which you are working and your setting. Criminal justice settings are usually less flexible than outpatient settings in allowing for excused absences.

You should consider existing guidelines in your clinic to determine whether or not each of these scenarios would be considered a legitimate reason to miss treatment. If your clinic has a policy that personal or family illnesses or transportation difficulties are not considered acceptable reasons to miss a session, then you should incorporate those policies in your CM protocol. In such cases, non-attendance because of family illness would result in no credit for attendance (and a reset in reinforcement magnitude, see Chapter 9). In contrast, if your clinic has a fairly liberal policy on missed sessions, you may consider each of the cases above to constitute an excused absence when designing your monitoring schedule.

If you intend to reinforce attendance, you will also be monitoring excused and unexcused absences, and therefore these also should be assessed objectively. If a patient made a phone call to the therapist in advance of the missed session, an excused absence may be granted in some cases. In others cases, an indicator of the reason for missing the session may be required along with objective verification for the absence (e.g., a doctor, lawyer, or probationer officer's note, or a car repair bill). No matter how you decide to handle excused and unexcused absences, the rules as they apply to earning and losing reinforcement must be considered carefully and addressed explicitly prior to implementing CM.

In addition to the issue of excused and unexcused absences, you should also consider how you will handle late attendance at a session. Does the patient need to arrive within five to 10 minutes of the start time to receive credit for attending, or would attending even a half hour late constitute full attendance? Again, there are no correct or incorrect answers to this question, but consideration of the possibilities and defining rules in terms of how they will apply to reinforcement earned or lost is necessary.

7.1.2.3 Other Therapeutically Appropriate Behaviors

Substance abusers can also be reinforced for other objective behaviors, such as completing chores in residential settings as outlined in the sample exercises. In addition, because substance abusers tend to experience a wide variety of psychosocial difficulties, including unemployment and unsafe housing, outpatients can be reinforced for making progress related to these treatment goals. In research studies reinforcing activity compliance, patients usually

Table 7.2 Activity Contract

Activity	Goal Area	Ideal Time	Potential Problems	Verification	Done (Yes or No)
1. Write letter to sister	Family relations	Monday evening	Don't feel like it	Bring letter	
2. Attend AA meeting	Sobriety	Friday 2 pm	Transportation	Signed slip with phone number of leader	
3. Find potential jobs in Sunday paper	Employment	Sunday afternoon	Don't buy paper	Bring in paper with at least five jobs circled	

decide upon two or three discrete activities each week related to their treatment goal(s). Examples of the former are attending a medical appointment if the goal is to improve health, going to the library with their child if the goal is to improve parenting, or filling out a job application if the goal is to obtain employment (Petry, Tedford, & Martin, 2001). If patients successfully complete these activities and provide objective verification of engaging in them, they receive reinforcers. Typically, verification consists of receipts or letters or business cards from agencies that are signed by an official (and contain phone numbers for further verification). An example of an activity contract that includes acceptable forms of verification appears in Table 7.2.

As noted in Table 7.2, each specific activity is listed along with the therapeutic goal area to which it is related. By focusing activities on specific goal areas, the therapist can ensure that small steps toward important goal areas (in this case, family relations, sobriety, and employment) are being made. The two middle columns indicate the anticipated date and time that the activity ought to occur, to assist patients in better planning their weekly schedules. Typically, patients need not complete the activity at the ideal time to earn reinforcement; rather, these are suggested dates and times. So long as the activity is completed and verified by the next session, reinforcement would be provided. Potential problems that the patient may encounter in accomplishing the activity are then listed. The rationale for this column is so the therapist and patient can brainstorm about methods to overcome the problems to ensure activity completion and reinforcement. If a patient doesn't feel like writing a letter to his sister, the therapist may suggest the patient write a list of reminders about why he wants to improve his relationship with his sister. If transportation is a concern, the therapist may assist the patient in determining people to call for a ride. If the patient forgets to buy the Sunday paper, the therapist may remind him that he may be able to get a copy from a coffee shop or the library, or get the job want-ads online at the library. Finally, the exact acceptable verification of activity completion is detailed. The next week, the final column is checked as to whether or not the activity was completed and verified. Note that two copies of the activity contract are necessary—one for the patient and one for the therapist.

If your CM protocol reinforces activity completion, it is critical to assign only activities that can be objectively verified and to closely monitor the verification process. If the activity is done onsite as is the case with chore completion, you may need to have a staff member witness the completion of the chore or evaluate its completion soon after it is done. For activities that occur offsite, you need to be sure that verification is not forged, as patients may attempt to falsify verifications in order to obtain reinforcement. Completing daily CBT (cognitive-behavioral therapy) homework exercises may be a goal of a CM intervention, but patients may cursorily complete the exercises immediately before group. If there is no method to ensure the exercises are completed on a daily basis, then monitoring will be difficult. Medication adherence suffers from similar problems because pill counts or daily records of consumption may be altered in attempts to obtain reinforcement.

If you are monitoring compliance with therapeutic behaviors, be sure you consider carefully what is appropriate objective verification. Bear in mind potentially ambiguous behaviors and monitoring practices and how you will handle them. It is probably best to write out extensive lists of potential behaviors and methods for verifying them, ensuring that the methods will be valid, prior to embarking on such a CM protocol. A non-exhaustive example of such a list appears in Table 7.3, adapted from Petry, Tedford, et al. (2001). Lists of activities assigned for adolescents are available in Godley, Godley, Wright, Funk, and Petry (2008).

7.1.3 Temporal Relationships between the Behavior and Its Monitoring

Once you decide how often the behavior occurs and an objective method to verify it, you want to consider how often to monitor the behavior in practice. Ideally, you want to monitor (and reinforce) a behavior in close proximity to when it occurs. Behavior modification procedures work best when as little time as possible elapses between a behavior and its consequence.

An ideal method to reduce drug use would be to reinforce a patient immediately after she declines an offer to use or does not seek out drugs when urges occur. This practice, however, would require following a patient in her environment and reading her mind about urges. Such a monitoring schedule is not possible (nor does it use objective measures in the case of urges). Instead, most CM

Table 7.3   Examples of Specific Activities and Verifications across Different Treatment Goal Areas

Goal Area	Activity	Verification
Further education	Go to GED appointment or class	Get info about exams, course notes
	Computer course or use computer at library	Receipt, library slip, print out
	Study	Homework
	Finish class	Diploma
Employment	Get job	Contract, letter
	Get info about jobs from newspaper ads	Make lists, circle ads in newspaper, call from office
	Work on resume	Bring in resume
	Submit applications	Business card, application
	Go to job fair or employment services	Business card, application
	Keep job	Time cards, release of info to boss
	Start job, or go to work	
	Volunteer	Signed form
Family		
Parenting	Research, sign up for, or go to parenting classes	Info about classes
	Read parenting book	Buy book; complete exercises or write about sections
	Homework with child	Bring in homework copy
	Call for or get information about events for children	Information or receipts
	Specific outings with child (ice cream, plays)	Receipts or programs
Relationships with other relatives	Family counseling	Appointment cards
	Send cards or letters to relatives	Bring in cards/letters, post office receipts

(continued on next page)

Table 7.3 (continued)   Examples of Specific Activities and Verifications across Different Treatment Goal Areas

Goal Area	Activity	Verification
Health/Psychiatric	Make doctor, dentist, eye appointment	Appointment slip, or call from office
	Attend doctor, dentist, eye appointment	Receipt, business card
	Get needed info from doctor (refill a prescription, results from tests, info about disease)	Prescription, informational brochure
	Find out about or attend an alternative health program (acupuncture, massage, vitamin therapy)	Brochure, receipt
	Attend community health education class or event	Brochure, receipt, forms
Housing	Make or attend a caseworker appointment	Brochure, receipt, forms
	Medication compliance	Diary of days/times
	Find out about programs	Brochure, receipt, forms
	Meet with housing counselor, case manager	Call from office, pamphlets, forms, business cards
	Circle appropriate apartments in newspaper	Circled ads
	Look at apartments	List pros/cons and prices
	Call landlord, lawyer, or health inspector	Paperwork, call from center
	Make repairs, pay utilities	Before/after photos, receipts
	Put deposit down on new apartment, pay rent	Receipt or contract
Legal	Find out info about legal problems	Call from office, paperwork
	File legal paperwork	Paperwork
	Legal aid appointment	Business card
	Go to court, parole officer appointment	Paperwork, signed/dated business card

Table 7.3 (continued)   Examples of Specific Activities and Verifications across Different Treatment Goal Areas

Goal Area	Activity	Verification
Personal Improvement		
Communication	Counseling session	Attend session
	Talk to more people at clinic, eat lunch w others	Verify at center
	Lists, worksheets, books	Completed lists, receipts
Grooming	Get haircut, shave, bathe	By sight, receipts
Financial	Complete budget sheets	
	SSI appointment	
	File income taxes	Completed forms, sheets
Sobriety	Attend one to five AA/NA meetings in upcoming week	Signed/dated pamphlet with phone number
	Chair a meeting	Discuss
	Read Big Book	Write impressions
	Get a sponsor	First name, phone #
Social/ Recreational	Go to church	Dated bulletin
	Go to specific events (sport events, museums, movies, out to eat, etc.)	Receipts, brochures
	Library	Take out books
Transportation	Get info about license	Information
	Study for driver's test	Practice tests
	Get insurance, registration	Receipts, forms
	Get car fixed	Receipt
	Get bus pass	Bring in pass/receipt
	Arrange for medcab transportation	Call from office

studies reinforcing drug abstinence consider the temporal relationships between drug use and the technological specifications of the testing equipment. Onsite toxicology tests for most substances can determine use or abstinence over a two- to four-day period. Therefore, successful CM protocols monitor use of these substances two or three times per week, with two to four days between tests. There is little point in monitoring use of these drugs more frequently (e.g., daily) because you would be capturing many of the same abstinence (or using) intervals. When measuring alcohol or nicotine use, the monitoring intervals should be in the range of hours not days. CM protocols that reinforce abstinence from these substances will require testing multiple times daily.

If you are monitoring attendance, it is usually best to do so at each session or day. If your CM protocol is monitoring therapeutic activities or chores in a residential setting, it is best to arrange monitoring and reinforcement in as close proximity to the completion of the activity as possible and practical. In a residential setting, the monitoring should occur at least daily for applicable chores, and more frequently if chores need to be done several times during the day. In outpatient settings, patients may not attend the clinic daily to report upon their completion of activities, but activity completion ought to be monitored regularly and not less than weekly.

7.1.4 Frequency of Monitoring

A general rule of thumb is that a behavior that cannot be monitored at least once a week is probably not appropriate for a CM intervention. CM techniques are best able to impact behaviors that occur regularly and can be reinforced often.

Groups that occur only monthly are less likely to be impacted by CM procedures than groups that occur weekly or those that are held several times each week. Similarly, it is necessary to monitor substance use and abstinence frequently if you are reinforcing abstinence. Empirical data support the notion that more frequent assessment and reinforcement of abstinence is associated with better outcomes with CM (Lussier et al., 2006). Because monitoring schedules need to capture all instances of substance use, CM interventions that monitor stimulant, opioid, or marijuana use infrequently (once a week or less) are less effective than those that monitor it two or three times weekly. In the case of activity monitoring, frequency is likewise important, and compliance with activities should be assessed and reinforced at least once a week.

The minimal frequency for monitoring a behavior is usually once a week, and the maximum depends upon the behavior being monitored and temporal relationships between the behavior and your ability to assess it. For drug abstinence, the frequency of monitoring should be a balance between the ability of the test to detect use of the drug and practicality in the clinical setting. Urine toxicology screens usually detect use over a two- to four-day window, and erring on the conservative end of the window would result in monitoring every other day. One excellent testing schedule would be Monday-Wednesday-Friday-Sunday-Tuesday-Thursday-Saturday over each two-week period. However, because most clinics are not open on weekends, most CM protocols do not utilize such a testing schedule. Instead, a Monday-Wednesday-Friday testing schedule is often used. For patients who only attend clinics twice a week, twice-weekly schedules are arranged (Monday-Thursday, Monday-Friday, or Tuesday-Friday).

If nicotine abstinence is monitored via carbon monoxide (CO) readings, the testing schedule is usually at least two times per day for CM to be effective. In some cases, frequency of monitoring can be reduced after success is achieved with more frequent monitoring. For example, you can initially reinforce CO negative readings two or three times daily; once the patient has achieved abstinence on these frequent CO tests, you can move to monitoring cotinine abstinence via urine tests that detect smoking over a three- to four-day period (Heil et al., 2008; Higgins et al., 2004). Cotinine tests are not ideal for *engendering* initial smoking abstinence, as smoking is a behavior that naturally occurs about 20 times per day. Cotinine tests would require a long interval between achieving initial smoking abstinence and the ability of the test to ascertain abstinence (i.e., abstaining 20 times daily for four days, or 80 times to test negative). Once abstinence is achieved, a less frequent monitoring and reinforcement schedule—using cotinine testing—may be suitable.

For attendance, most likely you will want to monitor (and reinforce) each session attended, but there may be instances in which such a reinforcement schedule would become too dense or costly. An example is an intensive outpatient program in which attendance at the first session of the day is highly associated with attendance at all sessions that day. In this case, you may monitor attendance at each of the two to five sessions per day, but only provide reinforcement at the first session of the day.

For chores or activities done daily in a residential setting, monitoring should be at least daily, and even more frequently for chores that ought to be completed more than once a day (e.g., thrice daily if washing dishes after each meal is a chore). In monitoring compliance with treatment goals in outpatient settings, monitoring occurs at least weekly, and often twice weekly, during initial stages of treatment. Once patients become used to the procedures and are successfully completing activities, monitoring frequency can be decreased. Initially, monitoring may occur twice weekly and then reduce to weekly after four weeks. Such tapering schedules are often consistent with reductions in the frequency of care over time as well.

The key to a successful CM protocol is to monitor most behaviors no less than weekly, and monitor drug use and abstinence behaviors more frequently (not less than twice weekly for most illicit substances). These monitoring schedules relate back to the key principles of CM: Frequently monitor the behavior intended for change, so that you can frequently reinforce that behavior whenever it occurs.

7.2 CRITIQUING MONITORING SCHEDULES

Now, let's consider two possible monitoring schedules. Read each example below, and create a list of the strengths and weaknesses of the monitoring approaches.

Sample Case 1: Monitoring Outpatient Group Attendance

Betsy wants to reinforce patients for attending an early recovery program. Groups meet twice a week for 12 weeks. To graduate from the program, patients must attend at least 20 of 24 sessions. On average about five of the 10 to 12 patients enrolled in the early recovery program attend each group, and rate of successful completion is only 20%. Two different counselors lead the groups. Betsy runs the Monday group, and Amy leads the Thursday groups. Although Betsy feels CM may be the ideal approach to improve attendance and graduation rates, Amy is skeptical of the approach and does not want to commit the time to learning and implementing a new treatment. Betsy therefore decides to institute a CM program in just her Monday groups.

Betsy takes attendance at the start of each of her groups, and patients earn reinforcers that increase in magnitude for each successive Monday group that they attend. Betsy also includes an extra, larger reinforcer for patients who successfully complete the entire program.

The patients love the CM, and attendance at Betsy's groups increases up to an average of eight or nine patients per week. However, graduation rates from the early recovery program still remain below 35%. Amy and the clinical director therefore feel the CM was not really useful.

Before reading on, list what you think is good about Betsy's CM approach, and areas in which the CM approach could be improved, in Table 7.4.

Table 7.4 Positive and Negative Features of Sample Case 1	
Positive Features	*Negative Features*

Some of the positive features of Betsy's CM intervention include that it (a) was designed around an objectively verifiable behavior (attendance), (b) the monitoring schedule was fairly frequent (weekly), and (c) escalating reinforcement was provided for successive attendance (an issue that will be further detailed in Chapter 9). Betsy also had data regarding pre-CM attendance rates (the frequency of the behavior naturally), and these rates were low so that CM had a reasonable chance of improving them. Indeed, Betsy was able to show an improvement in attendance rates at the groups in which the CM was introduced.

However, this CM protocol was not successful in increasing graduation rates. Attendance at the Thursday groups remained low, and few patients attended the requisite number of sessions to successfully complete the program. The primary problem with Betsy's CM intervention is that although it targeted one objectively verifiable behavior (attendance at Monday groups), it did not monitor or reinforce attendance at the other group that was equally necessary for graduation.

Betsy included a bonus reinforcer for graduating from the program, but this reinforcer is delayed in time. Patients could not receive this bonus unless they attended 20 groups for an entire 24-week period, so each instance of the target behavior (attendance) was not reinforced. Although many therapists feel that a bonus reinforcer (or a single reinforcement at the end of some period) is a good idea, there is no evidence that a one-time reinforcer is useful in shaping patient behavior. Betsy felt she could not insist that Amy also implement CM, and she thought the bonus reinforcement might be a good compromise. However, attendance at Amy's group was not directly tied to the primary weekly reinforcers, and a one-time bonus reinforcer is unlikely to influence behavior. The time and frequencies between the behaviors (twice-weekly attendance) and bonus reinforcer (a one-time reinforcer available 12 weeks later) violates CM principles.

A better alternative might have been to make some aspect of the reinforcement delivered during Betsy's group contingent on attendance at Amy's group. Betsy could have provided some reinforcement for attending each Monday group, with escalating reinforcement for successive attendance at both Monday and Thursday groups. In this manner, increasing reinforcement would be contingent upon the ultimate behavior desired—twice-weekly attendance for 12 weeks. This monitoring schedule would still not be as good as monitoring and providing reinforcement twice per week in more direct proximity to each attendance behavior, but it would have been a practical compromise given this situation. Amy would not have had to provide any reinforcement herself, and Betsy could have reviewed Amy's attendance records and directly linked each patient's escalating reinforcement to their attendance the prior Thursday and each Monday.

Sample Case 2: Monitoring Compliance with Job Seeking in a Criminal Justice Population

Dylan is a probation officer. He has about 15 unemployed patients on his caseload, and as a condition of their probation, all patients are supposed to obtain employment. They are expected to attend a weekly group that focuses on job skills and weekly individual sessions with him. Attendance at both types of sessions is fairly good because patients are sent back to jail if they do not attend them. Nevertheless, Dylan notices that most patients fail to take steps recommended between sessions. He decides to implement a CM protocol to improve this situation.

Dylan wants to implement CM into his weekly employment groups. At the end of each of these group sessions, Dylan assigns homework tied to the content of the group. These homework exercises include completing an employment interest survey, taking an abilities test, writing and refining a résumé, and obtaining and completing employment applications. The behavior he targets for change is adherence to these vocational exercises.

Dylan begins monitoring completion of the homework exercises. Typically, only two or three group members complete the exercises. Dylan thinks CM can increase the proportion of patients who complete these exercises, which in turn may lead to a greater rate of job acquisition.

In terms of the monitoring schedule, Dylan decides to assess homework completion weekly. At the start of group, patients show their homework to him and the group. If completed, they receive reinforcement, and amounts escalate with successive weeks of completion.

The number of patients who bring in the homework assignments increases markedly when the CM protocol is introduced. About 10 to 12 of the 15 patients bring in the homework each week. However, Dylan soon notices that the quality of homework completion is poor, and some patients are cursorily filling in the forms in the waiting room, right before group occurs. None of the patients are getting job interviews, and none are employed after 10 weeks of CM.

Critique this CM protocol. What are its positive and negative features, and what could Dylan do to ensure that not only do the patients thoughtfully complete the exercises but also obtain employment interviews and hopefully actual jobs? List your critiques in Table 7.5.

The positive features of this CM protocol are that it (a) was designed around an objectively verifiable behavior (homework completion), (b) the monitoring schedule was fairly frequent (weekly), and (c) escalating reinforcement was provided for successive homework completion (see also Chapter 9). Dylan gathered data regarding pre-CM homework completion rates, and these rates were low, so CM could improve upon them.

Table 7.5 Positive and Negative Features of Sample Case 2

Positive Features	Negative Features

There are, however, a couple of concerns about this CM protocol. First, Dylan was monitoring assignment completion once a week, and he did not specify the period during which it was supposed to be completed. By allowing the patients a full week to complete the assignment and not assessing completion throughout the week, patients could (and did) save the homework until immediately before the session. One way to get around such an issue would be to have patients complete the homework earlier in the week, and have them mail it in or drop it off prior to the group session occurring, if this is feasible. If the homework was something that was supposed to be completed daily, the first three of the seven days could be monitored during the individual session that occurs between the group sessions. This practice would increase the monitoring schedule to twice weekly, and more frequent monitoring is usually desirable. In this scenario, the twice-weekly monitoring may increase the probability that at least some thought was put into the assignment during the week, rather than just waiting until the end of the week.

The second issue is that the quality of the work was not specified with respect to monitoring. It is much more difficult to objectively monitor quality of work than whether or not the assignment was done. In order to monitor quality, Dylan may need to specify the exact number of words that need to be written on an assignment, and this may vary from assignment to assignment. He may also need to reconsider the appropriateness of some of the homework assignments to ensure that a quality indicator can be readily and objectively determined. Once homework that has objective quality standards is designed, Dylan may decide to only consider homework completion that meets the standards to qualify for reinforcement.

Finally, Dylan desired to increase not only weekly homework assignments but also job attainment. All of the monitoring and reinforcement were provided around the weekly assignments, which did not lead naturally, or with a high correlation, to job attainment. In this manner, this sample CM protocol is dissimilar to the earlier one by Betsy; in that situation, attendance was directly linked with graduation rates. In this case, Dylan may want to introduce some additional reinforcers for completion of activities that are more directly tied to job acquisition. For example, in addition to the reinforcement earned for completing the pen-and-paper homework assignments, patients could earn escalating bonus reinforcers for each job interview they attend. In this manner, patients may be more likely to seek out interviews, and the only way to get hired is to attend interviews. This CM protocol is an example of one in which monitoring and reinforcing of two independent, yet related, behaviors may be best.

7.3 DECIDING UPON THE BEST MONITORING SCHEDULE FOR YOUR CM PROTOCOL

Now that you have evaluated a couple of monitoring schedules, it is time to consider the best monitoring schedule for your CM protocol. In Table 7.6, list the behavior in the left column and the objective method to verify it in the next column. In the third column consider special issues, such as excused absences for attendance, or in the case of monitoring marijuana abstinence the need to monitor for several weeks without expecting the sample to test negative. In the final column, list the frequency with which you wish to monitor the behavior, after considering the temporal relationship between the behavior and your ability to monitor it, along with practical issues in your setting.

The three examples from earlier in the chapter are outlined in the upper section of the table. Your CM program may have issues similar to one or more of these sample behaviors. There may also be unique concerns to address in deciding upon the best monitoring schedule.

7.4 DURATION OF CM INTERVENTIONS

A final issue to consider related to monitoring is the duration that the CM intervention is in effect. In determining the duration of the intervention, you should consider it from the patient's perspective as well as from the therapist's and clinic's perspectives. A CM intervention that reinforces attendance at a specific group may occur for 12 weeks for any given patient, but you may want to test the intervention on at least 30 new patients. Because 30 patients are unlikely to start or be at a particular group during the first week you introduce CM, you may implement it for a total of 24 weeks, or until 30 patients are enrolled in the program.

By implementing CM in this manner, you will have a better sense of whether or not the CM program works than if you only institute it with a very small

Table 7.6 Determining Monitoring Schedules

Behavior	Objective Method to Verify	Special Considerations	Frequency of Monitoring
Reduce methamphetamine use in the subgroup of patients with methamphetamine dependence	Urine toxicology screens	If excused absence, sample must be submitted next day; observed samples	Two times per week (MTh, MF or TF)
Increase proportion of patients who phone the clinic to attend the intake session and engage in and complete the 10-week outpatient treatment program	Attendance	Excused absences for verifiable and pre-approved medical or legal appointments	Initial assessment is once, then weekly
Get patients to finish daily chores (dishwashing, cleaning) without staff reminders	Assigned staff to examine	Train staff about what constitutes acceptable completion; staff has to stop reminding patients to do chores. Patients should not be penalized in terms of reinforcement if no chore is assigned one day.	Thrice daily seven days a week
The Behavior You Are Targeting	Objective Method to Verify	Special Considerations	Frequency of Monitoring

cohort of patients. If you were to try CM with just the four to six patients attending the group at any one particular point in time, there might be something unique about this cohort that could impact their response to CM. They may have already formed a negative (or positive) group dynamic, or they may all be impacted by a new copayment regulation that independently impacts attendance. Further, reaction to the CM may be very positive during the first few weeks but then stabilize over time. CM should be implemented for a long enough period to engender behavioral changes; for any behavior to change, it must be given time to change. On the other hand, you don't want to commit to a long-lasting CM program if it is not working as intended.

For most CM protocols, a good rule of thumb is to keep CM in effect for a minimum of eight weeks and a maximum of 24 weeks. CM interventions that reinforce a behavior fewer than eight times are unlikely to engender much behavioral change, as change is something that needs to repeatedly occur. If patients only have the opportunity to receive reinforcement a few times (e.g., fewer than eight weeks), the behavior is not going to become ingrained.

On the other extreme, arranging reinforcement for more than 24 weeks is going to get expensive (see Chapter 10). The longer CM is in effect, the more it will cost. Once behavior successfully changes, you may no longer need to provide continued external reinforcers.

Most CM studies employ the intervention for 12 weeks for each patient, which is usually a good duration. In order for each patient to receive CM for 12 weeks, the CM protocol as a whole may need to be in effect for 16 weeks or longer, because most likely not all patients exposed to the CM intervention will start it at the exact same time. So that you can gain practice with CM, it is probably best to start with just a few patients or groups at a time and keep the intervention in effect until a reasonable number of patients are exposed to it.

In Table 7.7, consider again the three sample behaviors. For the first (abstinence), the optimal duration of the CM intervention would be about 12 weeks for each patient. For the second, the intervention would be in effect for 10 weeks for each individual patient, as it is a 10-week treatment period that is being targeted. Finally, in encouraging residents to complete chores, you would probably want to keep the CM in effect about 12 weeks. Because some patients may leave the residential setting during the intervention (and new ones may enter), not all will receive the CM for the full 12 weeks, so "up to 12 weeks" is recorded. After reviewing these issues for the sample behaviors, complete the two middle columns for your CM protocol. The right-hand column will be filled in later.

Next, consider how long the entire CM intervention ought to be kept in place. This decision will depend in part upon how many patients will be exposed to CM, an issue that was considered extensively in Chapter 6. In the case of monitoring abstinence among 10 patients, it is unlikely that all 10 would start the CM program in the same week. More often, CM initiation would be staggered such that four patients may begin in the first week, two more patients initiate CM the next week, two the following week, and two a week later. In order for the 10th patient to finish the 12-week CM program, the CM would be in place for a total of about 16 weeks.

The second sample CM program relates to a clinic-wide program for all new patients initiating treatment. Assuming that about 100 new patients enter treatment monthly, the initiation of CM would continue for about a four-week period until 100 are enrolled. The time the last of these 100 patients completes his or her 10-week CM program would be 10 weeks after week four, or about 14 weeks of CM in total.

Table 7.7 Determining the Duration of a CM Program

Behavior	CM Duration for Patients	Number of Patients to Receive CM (Table 6.1 right column)	Overall Expected Duration of CM Protocol
Reduce methamphetamine use in the subgroup of patients with methamphetamine dependence	12 weeks	10 patients total	~16 weeks (assuming all 10 will not start CM the same week)
Increase proportion of patients who phone the clinic to attend the intake session and engage in and complete the 10-week outpatient treatment program	10 weeks	About 100 patients	Implement CM for about 14 weeks total
Get patients to finish daily chores (dishwashing, cleaning), without staff reminders	Up to 12 weeks	~30 (and about two patients per month start or leave the program)	12 weeks
The Behavior for Your CM Program	CM Duration for Patients	Number of Patients to Receive CM	Overall Expected Duration of CM Protocol

For the last sample behavior outlined, the CM will be implemented in week one among all patients currently enrolled in the facility. With an average of two patients per month coming or going, up to about 36 patients may be exposed to the CM if it is in place for 12 weeks. The few patients who leave treatment soon after CM starts will only have a fairly brief exposure to the CM, as will the few who begin residential treatment in the last few weeks of the CM program.

Once you consider your sample behavior, the number of patients you want to expose to CM, and the manner in which patients will begin and end the CM protocol, indicate how long your CM protocol will be in place in the bottom of Table 7.7. Ideally, this duration will be between eight and 24 weeks. This amount of time will give you sufficient experience to implement the procedures and see how well they are working in practice. At the same time, it will not be too long of a period, so that if you subsequently wanted to make changes to the procedure you could do so, without being overly committed to a particular approach.

SUMMARY

By now, you should have determined the behavior you want to reinforce, the patient groups with whom you want to implement CM, and the methods, frequency, and duration you want to monitor the behavior. The frequency of reinforcement should directly match the frequency and duration of monitoring, an issue that will be described further in Chapter 9. The next step in developing a CM protocol is to determine which reinforcement strategy you will use. The different types of reinforcers available and their pros and cons are outlined in Chapter 8.

Chapter 8

Reinforcers to Use

Once the behavior, population, and monitoring schedules are determined, the next step is to decide upon the most appropriate and feasible reinforcer. This chapter will review the four most commonly applied reinforcers: clinic privileges, vouchers, prizes, and Name-in-the-hat prize CM for group attendance. It will outline methods for implementing these reinforcers and review their advantages and disadvantages. The chapter will also describe variations on these approaches. Some clinics intermix non-monetary-based privileges with monetary-based reinforcers as potential prizes, and some provide cash as reinforcers rather than vouchers or prizes. Others use rebates of copays or deposits as reinforcers.

Throughout this chapter, caution will be drawn to procedures that are unlikely to have the desired effect of altering patient behavior. Clinicians implementing CM for the first time often limit the options or substantially reduce the costs of reinforcers. These approaches will diminish effectiveness, and CM will not have its desired benefits. This chapter will emphasize achieving a balance between the magnitude of reinforcers provided and the behavior changes desired. In some cases, it is possible to alter behavior substantively, with fairly minimal costs.

8.1 DIFFERENT REINFORCERS

In this section, I describe the most popular reinforcers in CM protocols and their advantages and disadvantages. I also outline other approaches that have been used successfully in some settings.

8.1.1 Clinic Privileges

Clinic privileges were among the earliest reinforcers applied in CM treatment. Using privileges as reinforcers is certainly possible in methadone maintenance and residential settings.

In maintenance clinics, a take-home dose of methadone is a highly desirable reinforcer. Take-home doses do not cost the clinic anything, and patients never satiate on take-home doses so the value of this reinforcer does not diminish. In many ways, take-home doses are an ideal reinforcer for CM purposes. However, U.S. laws limit the ability to provide take-home doses. As reviewed in Chapter 2, patients have to attend clinic and provide negative samples for at least a three-month period before becoming eligible for take-home doses. Because this reinforcer is not available for many patients, other reinforcers may require consideration. They may include access to a rapid dosing window in which waiting time is short or nonexistent. A rapid line for urine testing is another option, as is a reduction in the weekly copay or a special parking spot.

In residential settings, there are a multitude of highly desirable privileges that are available at low or no cost. These include phone calls, evening passes, weekend passes, visitor hours, having a choice in chores (e.g., making dinner rather than cleaning bathrooms), getting out of chores for a day or a week, having earlier or later eating times, getting to sleep late, viewing television or movies, missing a group, having outdoor breaks, accessing exercise equipment, and so forth.

Some of these privileges are more highly valued than others. For example, a weekend pass is more appealing than a one-night pass. Some patients will desire particular reinforcers but not others. For example, only patients who have friends or family members whom they want to see will be interested in visiting hours, and not everyone likes to sleep late or exercise.

If you are considering using clinic privileges as reinforcers, it is imperative that you have a sufficient selection of reinforcers so that **all** patients can identify highly desirable reinforcers among your possibilities. If the reinforcers you select are not attractive, patients will not change their behavior to attain them. There are very large individual differences in what patients consider preferred and worth working toward.

When patients earn clinic privileges in the context of a CM program, they should be able to earn a privilege (if even a small one) each time they exhibit the target behavior. This is a basic principle of CM and was the situation in the early CM programs using take-home doses to reinforce drug abstinence in methadone-maintained patients. If a multitude of clinic privileges are available from which patients can choose, then often a system of exchange rates is created, such that patients earn points exchangeable for various privileges. They can choose between relatively modest and more substantial privileges, based on the points they have accumulated.

The primary advantage of privileges is that they are very low or no cost. The main disadvantage, however, is that they have limited applicability. Privileges are usually inappropriate as reinforcers in most outpatient settings because patients are only in the clinic setting relatively briefly, making most clinic-specific reinforcers of minimal value.

8.1.2 Vouchers

In contrast to clinic privileges, vouchers are applicable to all settings. Vouchers are similar to money, but money is not handed directly to the patient. Instead, the patient is given a voucher, worth a particular monetary amount, that accumulates in a clinic-managed bank account. When the patient has earned enough vouchers to purchase an item he desires, he makes a formal request for voucher spending. Clinicians can approve an item if it is in concert with treatment goals, or not approve requests deemed likely to result in relapse or non-therapeutic activities. For example, requests for a rock concert ticket may not be considered appropriate.

A typical voucher schedule employed in 12-week CM studies is depicted in Table 8.1. Urine samples are tested thrice weekly, and patients earn a minimum of $2.50 for each negative sample submitted. The amount earned increases by $1.25 for each consecutive negative sample submitted, and patients also earn a $10 bonus each week in which all their samples test negative for the targeted drug. The "Cumulative" column shows the overall amounts earned if abstinence is maintained throughout the full 12 weeks. In total, patients can earn nearly $1,000 in vouchers.

In a voucher CM program, the clinician hands the patient a voucher that indicates the amount of money he earned that day. The clinician should provide this voucher immediately after the urine sample tests negative or the patient exhibits whatever behavior is being reinforced. The voucher should state not only the amount earned that day but also the next time he is eligible for reinforcement and how much he will earn if the appropriate behavior (e.g., cocaine abstinence) occurs. The total amount of money the patient has earned thus far throughout the program, and the amount remaining in his account, should also be included. The difference between these numbers reflects the amount the patient has "spent." In the case presented in the sample voucher that appears in Exhibit 8.1, the patient has spent $60.75 on items.

If the target behavior does not occur, the voucher value resets to the originally low amount. Therefore, if a patient failed to attend the clinic or provide a positive sample, he would earn no reinforcement that day. The next time he provided a negative sample, he would earn only $2.50 in vouchers.

The primary benefit of vouchers is that patients find them highly desirable. Vouchers have many similarities to money, clearly a highly desirable and universal reinforcer. Because voucher spending is personalized, all patients

---

EXHIBIT 8.1   SAMPLE VOUCHER REMINDER SLIP

You tested *negative* today and earned *$18.75*.
Your next testing session is *Friday, April 21*.
You can earn *$20.00, plus a $10.00 bonus* if you test negative then.
In total, you have earned *$188.75* in vouchers.
You currently have *$128.00* available in your account.
Keep up the good work!

Table 8.1 A Typical Voucher Reinforcement Schedule

Week	Day	Voucher	Bonus	Cumulative	Week	Day	Voucher	Bonus	Cumulative
1	M	$2.50		$2.50	7	M	$25.00		$321.25
	W	$3.75		$6.25		W	$26.25		$347.50
	F	$5.00	$10	$21.25		F	$27.50	$10	$385.00
2	M	$6.25		$27.50	8	M	$28.75		$413.75
	W	$7.50		$35.00		W	$30.00		$443.75
	F	$8.75	$10	$53.75		F	$31.25	$10	$485.00
3	M	$10.00		$63.75	9	M	$32.50		$517.50
	W	$11.25		$75.00		W	$33.75		$551.25
	F	$12.50	$10	$97.50		F	$35.00	$10	$596.25
4	M	$13.75		$111.25	10	M	$36.25		$632.50
	W	$15.00		$126.25		W	$37.50		$670.00
	F	$16.25	$10	$152.50		F	$38.75	$10	$718.75
5	M	$17.50		$170.00	11	M	$40.00		$758.75
	W	$18.75		$188.75		W	$41.25		$800.00
	F	$20.00	$10	$218.75		F	$42.50	$10	$852.50
6	M	$21.25		$240.00	12	M	$43.75		$896.25
	W	$22.50		$262.50		W	$45.00		$941.25
	F	$23.75	$10	$296.25		F	$46.25	$10	$997.50

will be able to identify items they wish to earn. Using the schedule above, there is also a high magnitude of reinforcement possible, and most patients would be interested in earning $1,000 of goods or services during a treatment episode. The voucher procedure also has a great deal of scientific evidence demonstrating its efficacy when implemented in the manner described above. Chapter 3 described these studies in detail.

Although vouchers have many advantages, they also have some disadvantages. The primary concern about vouchers relates to cost. Few clinics have $1,000 to make available for every patient. Even if CM were administered on a rather small scale, the amounts needed add up quickly. Exposing 10 patients to 12 weeks of voucher CM could cost up to $10,000. Not only must the direct costs of the vouchers be considered, but so must the administrative costs associated with tracking the vouchers earned and spent and the personnel time associated with shopping for voucher requests. Ideally, items requested by patients should be provided to them at their next clinic visit to minimize the time between earning the reinforcer and its receipt. This practice requires shopping on a regular basis. Because voucher requests are personalized, voucher purchasing may entail going to different stores for all patients in the voucher program. Cost-effectiveness analyses of voucher CM estimate the costs of managing the voucher program to be two to three times higher than the actual costs of the vouchers themselves (Olmstead & Petry, 2009; Olmstead, Sindelar, Easton, & Carroll, 2007).

In attempts to reduce the costs of these procedures, some researchers decreased the amount of vouchers available. One can reduce voucher amounts by decreasing the initial voucher value, lowering the manner in which vouchers escalate, or reducing the duration of time in which CM is in effect. However, studies that have empirically evaluated lower voucher magnitudes generally find that they decrease efficacy (Dallery et al., 2001; Lussier et al., 2006). Thus, caution should be extended in CM protocols that substantially decrease voucher amounts.

A method to decrease administrative costs of the voucher system is to eliminate personalized shopping requests. Some clinicians provide only gift certificates or electronically available gift cards (i.e., computerized shopping on the Internet). Although this may seem like a good idea, some patients do not have transportation and will be unable to use gift cards to many stores. Others do not like or are unaccustomed to shopping online and prefer to see items. Thus, caution is suggested in using these approaches exclusively.

A clinic "store" can also be arranged, and all voucher requests can be made from the available clinic merchandise, which may include (but should not be limited to) a variety of gift cards, along with other commonly desired merchandise. So long as sufficient variety of desirable items is available, this modification of the typical voucher procedure is likely to be effective. In some ways, a clinic store has the potential of reducing one of the concerns about voucher CM, which is that there is an inherent delay between earning a reinforcer and obtaining the item. With a clinic store, patients will receive the items sooner, and clinicians will have fewer burdens associated with shopping. Shopping could be done as infrequently as monthly, rather than several times per week. The key to success with the voucher CM approach is to ensure a wide selection of items across a variety of prices, so that all patients will be able to identify personally desirable items.

Most effective voucher CM programs arrange for $1,000 or more in vouchers per patient (Higgins et al., 2003, 2007; Higgins, Wong, et al., 2000; Silverman et al., 1999; Silverman, Higgins, et al., 1996), and lower voucher amounts are not as effective (Lussier et al., 2006). A modification of voucher CM is the prize or fishbowl reinforcement system. This system was designed specifically to reduce the costs of voucher CM, without reducing effectiveness.

8.1.3 Prizes

A store-based CM approach has some advantages in terms of reducing the need for personalized shopping, but it still requires availability of large voucher amounts. In the prize CM system, patients earn the opportunity to draw from a prize bowl each time they exhibit the target behavior, and each draw is associated with the possibility of winning prizes of varying magnitudes. There are typically 500 slips of paper in the prize bowl, and half of them are associated with a prize. The other half say "good job!" but do not result in a prize. Among the winning slips, most of them (e.g., 209 of the 500 slips, or about 40%) state "small" prize, a relatively small proportion state "large," and one is a "jumbo" prize. Small prizes are things like bus tokens, $1 gift certificates to fast food restaurants, snack or drink items, toiletries, and so on. Large items include sweatshirts, handheld CD players, watches, and gift certificates to stores or restaurants, and they usually cost up to about $20. The jumbo prize is worth up to $100, and popular jumbos are televisions, stereos, or PlayStations®. Each time a patient draws a winning slip (small, large, or jumbo), she gets to choose from a wide variety of prizes in that category.

Chances of winning prizes are inversely related to the prizes' magnitudes. Because not every draw results in a prize, the cost of the system can be reduced (see Chapter 10). In prize CM, just like voucher CM, sustained behavior change results in increasing reinforcement. The first negative sample (or attendance at group or completion of a goal-related activity) results in one draw, the second behavior earns two draws, the third results in three draws, and so forth. In this system, draws are usually capped at a maximum of eight so that patients never earn too many draws on any given day. As shown in Table 8.2, patients can earn up to a maximum of 260 draws in total if they exhibit the desired behavior throughout a 12-week CM protocol.

EXHIBIT 8.2   SAMPLE PRIZE REMINDER SLIP

You tested *negative* today and earned *6* draws.
Your next testing session is *Friday, April 21.*
You can earn *7* draws if you test negative then.
Remember, the more draws you earn,
the greater your chances of winning large and jumbo prizes!
You can do it!

Similar to the voucher CM system, a lapse in the behavior (a positive sample, or failure to submit a sample or attend group, etc.) resets the number of draws earned. The patient would earn no draws that day, and the amount earned resets to one draw the next time the target behavior occurs. It would take about three and a half weeks to resume to the maximum reinforcement amount of eight draws if a lapse occurred.

In prize CM, you should provide patients with a slip of paper reminding them about the contingencies and directly linking their behavior to its consequence. A sample slip for a CM program reinforcing cocaine-negative samples is shown in Exhibit 8.2.

The main advantage of the prize CM system over the voucher CM system is that it reduces costs without compromising efficacy. Prize CM is considered a type of escalating reinforcement variable ratio schedule because not every occurrence of the target behavior (negative sample) is followed by tangible reinforcement (a prize). Still, the escalating component of the reinforcement system increases the probability that some tangible reinforcement will be earned as the behavior increases in frequency. If 50% of the slips are winning, most patients will have earned a prize by the second time they exhibit the behavior. As shown in Table 8.2, patients will have earned a total of three draws by their second negative sample, and most will win a prize by this time.

The voucher system, in contrast, may be described as an escalating reinforcement fixed ratio schedule because every occurrence of a target behavior is followed by receipt of a voucher. All other things being equal, variable ratio schedules generate higher rates of sustained behavior relative to fixed ratio schedules. By capitalizing on this characteristic of variable ratio schedules, the prize system can sustain high rates of behavior at reduced costs.

Further, overweighing small probabilities when making decisions leads to the attractiveness of gambling (Kahneman & Treversky, 1979). Inclusion of a jumbo prize in the prize bowl system appears to make this approach efficacious at relatively low costs. As you can imagine, patients are very excited about the possibility of winning $100 prizes, even though few actually win them. The inclusion of the jumbo prize adds little to the overall costs of the prize bowl CM approach (Chapter 10).

Table 8.2   A Sample Prize Draw Reinforcement Schedule

Week	Day	Draws	Cumulative	Week	Day	Draws	Cumulative
1	M	1	1	7	M	8	124
	W	2	3		W	8	132
	F	3	6		F	8	140
2	M	4	10	8	M	8	148
	W	5	15		W	8	156
	F	6	21		F	8	164
3	M	7	28	9	M	8	172
	W	8	36		W	8	180
	F	8	44		F	8	188
4	M	8	52	10	M	8	196
	W	8	60		W	8	204
	F	8	68		F	8	212
5	M	8	76	11	M	8	220
	W	8	84		W	8	228
	F	8	92		F	8	236
6	M	8	100	12	M	8	244
	W	8	108		W	8	252
	F	8	116		F	8	260

Another advantage of the prize CM system is that administrative costs are reduced compared to voucher CM. Olmstead and Petry (2009), Olmstead, Sindelar, and Petry (2007), Sindelar, Elbel, and Petry (2007), and Sindelar, Olmstead, and Peirce (2007) estimated costs of staff management ranged from $90 to $136 per patient in 12-week prize CM trials, while staff management costs of voucher CM were $422 to $516 per patient in a shorter eight-week trial (Olmstead, Sindelar, Easton, et al., 2007). Thus, management costs above and beyond costs of reinforcers are about two to five times higher in voucher CM than prize CM. Most of these higher costs are attributed to the increased shopping with voucher CM. With prize CM, therapists usually only shop for prizes about once a month, and they can maintain a fully stocked prize cabinet with a lot of options in each category of prizes. Chapter 12 further details commonly desired prizes in each of the prize categories.

A potential concern about prize CM is that the system is somewhat analogous to a lottery system. Chances of winning vary from person to person and over time. Substance abusers have high rates of pathological gambling (Petry,

2005), and this system may be inappropriate for patients "in recovery" from pathological gambling as it may instigate gambling relapse. However, substantive evidence shows that exposure to prize CM does not lead to gambling problems. Petry and Alessi (2010) and Petry, Kolodner, Li, Peirce, Roll, and Stitzer (2006) measured gambling before, during, and after treatment in over 1,000 substance abusers randomized to prize CM or standard care without CM. There was no indication that prize CM led to increased gambling or gambling problems. Not a single individual exposed to prize CM developed gambling problems. Thus, prize CM is considered safe.

An issue with prize CM is that its efficacy, just like voucher CM, is magnitude dependent. If you substantially reduce the amount of prizes available, the procedure will not be as effective (Petry et al., 2004). About $300 to $400 in prizes is recommended if the behavior you are trying to change is substance use. However, if you are targeting group attendance behaviors, there is a modification to the prize bowl CM approach called the "Name-in-the-hat" prize approach. This version of prize CM appears effective in increasing attendance at groups at costs as low as about $20 per week per group of patients.

8.1.4 Name-in-the-Hat Prize CM for Group Attendance

Most substance abuse treatment is provided in the context of groups, yet each of the CM approaches described above was developed and tested for use in an individualized format. There is an adaptation of the prize CM approach that is applicable for reinforcing group attendance. It is called the Name-in-the-hat prize approach for group attendance, and its main advantage is that it substantially reduces costs. Rather than each patient earning an escalating number of draws from a prize bowl for sustained behavior change, each patient increases his chance of getting a draw from a prize bowl for behavior change. Individual patients do not earn hundreds of draws, but each patient's chances of getting a draw increase with successive attendance. Patients also observe one another's winning prizes (and earning greater chances of winning prizes for sustained attendance). Furthermore, large magnitude prizes are won in the groups, and this winning enhances excitement. By not awarding as many overall draws, costs can be substantially reduced, yet the approach generates a great deal of enthusiasm among patients as well as clinicians.

In this CM system, which is further detailed in Chapter 14, each time a patient attends group, his name goes into a "hat." The number of times his name goes in the hat increases with sustained attendance. Patients who have attended only one time have their name placed in the hat once, and those who have attended twice in a row get their names in the hat twice. Those who have attended three times in a row have their name placed in the hat three times, and so forth.

During group, a particular number of names are drawn from the hat (e.g., five names are drawn if 10 people attend). Each of the five people whose names are drawn from the hat gets to draw for a prize from a prize bowl. In this case, all the slips in the bowl are winning slips, and no "good job" slips are present. The reason for this modification is so that each person whose name is drawn is guaranteed to win a prize, but only about half the people in the group win a prize each week. The costs for each draw are typically arranged to be about $4. So, if five names are drawn, the entire cost of the system each week is $20. This $20 in reinforcement is spread among all the patients who attend the group each week. To implement this Name-in-the-hat prize CM system for group attendance for eight weeks among 10 patients costs about $160 in total, or an average of $16 per patient.

In Table 8.3, I depict eight weeks of this procedure with 10 patients. The number of times each patient's name went in the hat is shown in the middle row for each patient across the eight weeks. This number starts at one the first week the patient attended and increases by one for each successive week of attendance. If ever the patient did not attend group, his name did not go in the hat that week, and the next week of attendance resulted in his name being placed in the hat only one time. The first patient (AK) attended group all eight weeks in a row, and his name went in the hat eight times in week eight. KC did not attend at week one, so his name was not in the hat that week. He attended in weeks two and three, and his name went in the hat one and two times, respectively, those weeks. He failed to attend in week four, so in week five, the times his name went in the hat reset to one.

Each week, the therapist drew **half** as many names from the hat as people attended group. In week one, six people attended group, and therefore three names were drawn. As depicted in the lower row and in italicized font for each patient, three patients had their names drawn in week one: JM, TS, and NF. These three patients received one prize each.

In week two, seven patients attended group and had their names placed in the hat at least once. The number of patients who attended is denoted by those whose names went in the hat one or more times in the column labeled week two: AK, KC, TS, LS, NF, TR, LF. Four names were drawn from the hat (because the number of names drawn is rounded up if an odd number of people attend group). Four prizes were awarded that week to patients AK, LF, and TS (who received two prizes, as her name was drawn twice).

As noted in the furthest right columns, the more times patients attended group the greater was the likelihood of their winning prizes. MP only attended once and won no prizes, whereas AK had the best attendance and won the most prizes. Some patients with similar attendance are "luckier" than others. TS, NF, and TR attended seven times, but TS won the most prizes (five) and TR the fewest (three). Still, greater attendance results in greater likelihood of having one's name drawn and winning prizes.

Table 8.3 Sample Attendance Logs and Draws for the Name-in-the-Hat Prize CM Procedure

		Week								Times Attended Group	Total Prizes Won
Patient		1	2	3	4	5	6	7	8		
AK	Attended (N = no; Y = yes)	Y	Y	Y	Y	Y	Y	Y	Y	8	
	Times name in hat	1	2	3	4	5	6	7	8		
	Times name drawn	*0*	*1*	*0*	*1*	*0*	*1*	*2*	*2*		*7*
KC	Attended (N = no; Y = yes)	N	Y	Y	N	Y	Y	Y	N	5	
	Times name in hat	0	1	2	0	1	2	3	0		
	Times name drawn	*0*	*0*	*1*	*0*	*0*	*0*	*1*	*0*		*2*
JM	Attended (N = no; Y = yes)	Y	N	Y	Y	N	Y	Y	Y	6	
	Times name in hat	1	0	1	2	0	1	2	3		
	Times name drawn	*1*	*0*	*0*	*0*	*0*	*1*	*0*	*0*		*2*
TS	Attended (N = no; Y = yes)	Y	Y	Y	Y	Y	N	Y	Y	7	
	Times name in hat	1	2	3	4	5	0	1	2		
	Times name drawn	*1*	*2*	*1*	*0*	*1*	*0*	*0*	*0*		*5*
LS	Attended (N = no; Y = yes)	N	Y	Y	Y	Y	Y	Y	N	6	
	Times name in hat	0	1	2	3	4	5	6	0		
	Times name drawn	*0*	*0*	*1*	*1*	*0*	*1*	*1*	*0*		*4*

(continued on next page)

Table 8.3 (continued)   Sample Attendance Logs and Draws for the Name-in-the-Hat Prize CM Procedure

						Week					Times Attended Group	Total Prizes Won
Patient		1	2	3	4	5	6	7	8			
MP	Attended (N = no; Y = yes)	N	N	N	N	Y	N	N	N	1		
	Times name in hat	0	0	0	0	1	0	0	0			
	Times name drawn	*0*	*0*	*0*	*0*	*0*	*0*	*0*	*0*			*0*
NF	Attended (N = no; Y = yes)	Y	Y	Y	N	Y	Y	Y	Y	7		
	Times name in hat	1	2	3	0	1	2	3	4			
	Times name drawn	*1*	*0*	*1*	*0*	*1*	*0*	*0*	*1*			*4*
TR	Attended (N = no; Y = yes)	Y	Y	Y	Y	Y	N	Y	Y	7		
	Times name in hat	1	2	3	4	5	0	1	2			
	Times name drawn	*0*	*0*	*0*	*1*	*2*	*0*	*0*	*0*			*3*
LF	Attended (N = no; Y = yes)	Y	Y	N	Y	N	N	Y	N	4		
	Times name in hat	1	2	0	1	0	0	1	0			
	Times name drawn	*0*	*1*	*0*	*0*	*0*	*0*	*0*	*0*			*1*
BR	Attended (N = no; Y = yes)	N	N	N	Y	N	N	N	Y	2		
	Times name in hat	0	0	0	1	0	0	0	1			
	Times name drawn	*0*	*0*	*0*	*1*	*0*	*0*	*0*	*0*			*1*
People	in group each week	6	7	7	7	7	5	8	6	TOTAL		
Names	drawn each week	3	4	4	4	4	3	4	3	PRIZES		28

Chapter 14 details complete implementation guidelines for the Name-in-the-hat prize CM procedure. The main advantage of this system is that it reduces cost. Using the prize categories and probabilities outlined in Chapter 14, the system will cost about $20 per week to implement and $160 in total over eight weeks, or $240 over 12 weeks, if an average of 10 patients attend group each week. Another advantage is that the CM procedure can be conducted in a group format, whereas the others are administered individually.

This Name-in-the-hat prize CM system has an additional benefit of getting patients to group on time; if patients are late, they miss the drawings. Clinicians report that it enhances the quality of groups, as patients attend more regularly and bond together over the excitement of winning. According to group leaders who have implemented this approach in over 20 different clinics, patients whose names are drawn occasionally give prizes to other patients whom they feel deserving. Such generosity has greatly enhanced patient interactions and group processes.

The Name-in-the-hat approach has been integrated into many types of groups, including early recovery, aftercare, cognitive-behavioral, educational, 12-step, smoking cessation, adolescent, and dual diagnosis. Any type of group is appropriate for the Name-in-the-hat prize CM system. The system is easily amenable to rolling group admissions and closed group formats. Rolling groups are most common in practice and may particularly benefit from this CM approach; patients who are new to the group observe others earn increased chances of winning for sustained attendance. The patients with committed attendance also seem to enjoy encouraging new patients to come to groups; their own chances of winning increase when more patients attend.

The only issue that needs to be considered in integrating this procedure is that patients in recovery from pathological gambling should not be included. The implementation guidelines in Chapter 14 should be followed carefully. As with other CM approaches, you don't want to reduce the magnitude of the reinforcement or the procedure is less likely to be effective.

8.1.5 Alternative Reinforcement Approaches

Some clinics have implemented modifications of these CM approaches with success. Several possible adaptations are described here and can be considered for specific settings.

8.1.5.1 Mixing Privileges and Prizes

It is possible to intermix the prize CM approach with clinic privileges. If you want to reduce costs of prize CM or cannot come up with sufficient types of privileges to interest all patients, you may want to have a mixture of monetary-based and non-monetary-based prizes (i.e., privileges) available. Patients could earn escalating draws for sustained behaviors, and when they win a small prize, they could choose among monetary-based items worth $1 (bus tokens, food items, toiletries) and modest privileges (such as a five-minute phone call, or a "late to group" pass). If patients draw a large prize, they could select among $20 monetary-based prizes (gift certificates, CD players, etc.) and moderately valued clinic privileges (e.g., a one-week special parking space, a "miss group" with no penalty pass). This type of system could reduce the overall costs of prize CM, as a portion of the prizes will not cost anything. It has an additional advantage of increasing the options available to patients. The main issue to be cautious of in employing this approach is to ensure sufficient selections in each prize category. As with all CM protocols, patients should not satiate on the options, and all patients should be able to identify items they are working toward in each category.

Alternatively, you could also design a CM program in which patients earn points for each targeted behavior they exhibit. Patients could then exchange their accumulated points for a variety of privileges or prizes. As in the above example, the value of each privilege would need to be calibrated with monetary-based reinforcers.

8.1.5.2 Deposits

Early research in CM employed deposit systems, in which patients put forth a deposit at the start of treatment. If they successfully completed the target behavior, they earned back their deposit. For consistency with CM principles, the deposit amount would need to be divided into many small portions so that each instance of the target behavior would result in reinforcement. For example, if your clinic collected a $200 deposit from each patient for an eight-week treatment episode, the average weekly payout in reinforcement would be $25.

An advantage of deposits is that the reinforcers do not cost the clinic any money, but a disadvantage is that this system is unattractive to many substance abusers with limited incomes. The approach could be modified by using monies deposited by family members or via portions of patients' entitlements if they have a representative payee and are receiving disability payments (Ries et al., 2004). However, such approaches are only applicable to certain subsets of patients.

1.5.3 Cash

Cash has some advantages over vouchers and prizes, and it has been effectively implemented in some CM programs (Drebing et al., 2007; Vandrey,

Bigelow, & Stitzer, 2007). The primary benefit of cash is that it is perhaps the most highly valued reinforcer. Everyone likes to receive money. Moreover, cash reinforcement is easier to implement than vouchers or prizes, both of which require staff time for shopping.

Some have argued that cash is inappropriate to provide to substance abusers, although others note that substance abusers regularly have access to cash and learning how to spend it appropriately may be therapeutic. Further, if patients were to spend cash on drugs, they would test positive at their next session, reinforcement would be withheld, and the value of subsequent reinforcement would reset. If cash were used to reinforce behaviors other than abstinence, there remains a possibility it could be utilized for drugs. In such situations, it would be important to have clinic regulations in place for handling drug use among patients.

8.1.5.4 Copayments

Another reinforcement approach involves the Name-in-the-hat prize procedure for group attendance, in which the prize each week is a portion of copayments collected from each attendee. If each group member is expected to contribute $10 weekly as a copay and five persons attend, the clinic collects a total of $50 in copayments. If 20% of the copayments collected are redistributed back to one randomly selected attendee, the person whose name was drawn would receive $10. If more persons attended, the amount of earnings would increase such that $20 could be won if 10 people attended. Patients encourage one another to attend so that the pot of earnings is higher. The costs of this system are pre-determined, and if it increased attendance by only one or two persons per week, it would likely be cost-effective to implement. The only potential disadvantage of this approach is that just one person "wins" each week, and if copays and proportions redistributed are similar to those outlined above, the overall rate and frequency of tangible reinforcement for each individual attendee is low. Nevertheless, a clinic in Maine has been implementing this system for several years, with excellent results.

8.1.5.5 Social Reinforcers

Social reinforcers may include positive statements ("You're doing a great job!" or "I'm really proud of you!"), social recognition (clapping when one achieves a milestone), or special status (becoming a group leader). All of these are excellent examples of positive reinforcement that should be integrated into CM protocols that also utilize monetary-based reinforcement (see Chapters 13, 14, and 15).

Many clinicians are inclined to utilize only social reinforcers in CM programs because these reinforcers do not involve any associated costs. CM programs based entirely on social reinforcers have not been empirically tested.

Thus, the evidence basis of purely social reinforcement is unknown. Because magnitude of reinforcement is so closely and directly linked with efficacy of CM (Lussier et al., 2006), purely social reinforcers are substantially less effective than monetary ones. In fact, social reinforcement is included in the condition to which monetary-based reinforcers are compared in CM studies, and these conditions fare worse than those in which monetary-based reinforcement is provided.

If no other options are available, there is no harm in designing a CM protocol around social reinforcers. The difficulty lies in integrating basic behavioral principles in a CM system that relies entirely on social reinforcers. In other words, you need to come up with sufficient social reinforcers that patients find genuine and do not satiate upon. Stating "You're doing a great job!" every time a patient attends treatment or leaves a cocaine-negative sample may make a patient feel proud the first few times he hears such praise, but it may become less appreciated with time. It is also difficult to envision how social reinforcers can escalate with sustained behavior change, and escalating reinforcers are critical for continued behavior change (see Chapter 9).

There may be creative ways in which social reinforcers can be included contingently into treatment programs. A residential adolescent program, for example, placed sticky notes in group rooms every day whenever they were cleaned up, thanking the adolescents for keeping the rooms in good order. The content of the note varied, and adolescents soon began rushing into the room to see when the note was left and what it said. A week of cleaned rooms daily led to a special pizza dinner, and residents encouraged one another to keep rooms cleaned. If you are inclined toward using only social reinforcers, try to come up with creative approaches toward applying such reinforcers that integrate important behavioral parameters as you review the next sections.

After considering these options and weighing their pros and cons, you may think of additional possibilities of potential reinforcers. So long as appropriate behavioral principles are included in your CM design, many reinforcers can alter behaviors, although all else being equal, monetary-based reinforcers are more efficacious.

8.2 SELECTING THE BEST REINFORCEMENT APPROACH FOR YOUR PROTOCOL

The decision of the best reinforcer for your CM program depends on several factors. These include the behavior you are targeting for change, the population and setting in which you are implementing CM, and the resources you have available.

Behaviors that are more difficult to change require higher magnitude reinforcers to alter. Reinforcing abstinence necessitates both submission of a negative sample and clinic attendance (a patient cannot earn reinforcement for abstinence unless he also comes to the clinic). Thus, reinforcing abstinence generally requires greater reinforcement magnitude than reinforcing attendance alone. You would not want to implement a CM system that only provides very small returns of a portion of a copayment to patients for achieving and maintaining cocaine abstinence. On the other hand, small returns of copayments may work well for improving attendance at groups in methadone patients, who are attending the clinic to receive their methadone doses.

Some types of reinforcers are limited to specific populations and settings. Clinic privileges are highly desirable in residential settings, but their use is restricted in other settings. The Name-in-the-hat prize CM procedure can be readily integrated into any group setting, but it is probably inappropriate for reinforcing abstinence behaviors, as results of drug testing are usual kept confidential. If the goal of your CM intervention is to reduce drug use in an outpatient setting, you will be better off with an individualized voucher or prize approach.

Finally, available resources must be considered. Although $1,000 per patient for vouchers or $300 per patient in prizes is likely to be effective in changing many behaviors across a range of settings, you may not have the funds to implement CM in this manner. You may consider $300 prize CM in conjunction with making available non-clinic privileges or using proportions of copayments to subsidize the system. If CM improves attendance and therefore increases revenue to the clinic, the system may be cost-beneficial to your program (see Chapter 10).

Returning to the three sample behaviors from the previous chapters, we can now decide upon reinforcers for each. The left column in Table 8.4 reminds us of the behaviors targeted for change. The next columns describe a good reinforcement system for each behavior, along with its potential pros and cons. After reviewing these for the sample behaviors, add the behavior you are targeting for change and your decision about the most appropriate reinforcement approach.

SUMMARY

Vouchers, prizes, and Name-in-the-hat prize CM for group attendance are the most commonly applied and researched reinforcers, and each has demonstrated evidence of efficacy. The least costly of these approaches is Name-in-the-hat prize CM, but it can only be implemented in the context of groups, and it may only be effective for improving attendance behaviors. If that is the behavior you are targeting for change, general guidelines for purchasing prizes are presented in Chapter 12, and Chapter 14 provides detailed instructions about administering the Name-in-the-hat prize CM approach. You can

Table 8.4 Reinforcement Systems for Various Behaviors

Behavior	Reinforcement System	Pros	Cons
Reduce methamphetamine use in the group of patients with methamphetamine dependence	Prize CM	Lots of evidence of efficacy Lower costs than vouchers	Need funds (up to $300/patient) Not appropriate for pathological gamblers in recovery
Increase proportion of patients who phone the clinic to attend the intake session and engage in and complete the 10-week outpatient treatment program	Name-in-the-hat prize CM	Low cost Costs may be offset by greater reimbursement Can do in group May improve morale and on-time attendance	Need to come up with needed funds Some patients may not win many prizes
Get patients to finish daily chores (dishwashing, cleaning), without staff reminders	Clinic privileges	Almost no costs	Need to come up with lots of potential reinforcers
The Behavior You Are Targeting	*Reinforcement System*	*Pros*	*Cons*

move to those chapters now if you will be implementing this approach once a week in groups. If you want to utilize that approach, but you are targeting groups that occur more than once weekly, you should read Chapter 9 before moving to Chapters 12 and 14, as you will need to slightly tailor the reinforcement system to accommodate more than weekly attendance.

In the event that you plan to utilize another reinforcer described in this chapter, you will need to consider the relationship between your monitoring system and your reinforcement system. These procedures are outlined in the next chapter—Chapter 9. If you are utilizing anything other than clinic privileges or social reinforcers alone, you will also need to consider costs, and Chapter 10 describes methods for estimating costs of the CM system you design. Chapter 11 outlines methods for finding or raising funds to support CM programs.

Designing a Reinforcement Schedule

Now that you have decided upon the behavior you want to target, the population with whom you will implement CM, the monitoring schedule, and the reinforcers, the next step in designing a CM protocol relates to determining the reinforcement schedule. Generally, the reinforcement schedule should be consistent with the monitoring schedule, such that each instance of the appropriate behavior is reinforced. In addition, you should consider specific behavioral principles in designing the reinforcement schedule to ensure frequent and immediate reinforcers, along with variety in reinforcers. Escalating reinforcers that reset when the desired behavior does not occur are also important for engendering sustained behavior change.

This chapter details typical voucher and prize reinforcement schedules, with worksheets and examples provided. It also discusses variants on the usual approaches to accommodate clinical needs, while retaining use of appropriate behavioral principles. The chapter will depict examples of less than ideal reinforcement schedules so that you can critique them and ultimately devise a CM plan that is most likely to impact the behavior you are trying to change.

9.1 BRIEF REVIEW

First, let's briefly review decisions you have made so far regarding your CM plan. In the bottom section of Table 9.1, list the behavior you are targeting, the population with whom you will be working, the monitoring schedule, and the type of reinforcement you will be using. This information should be similar to what you noted in the tables listed at the top of each column, and the information can be transcribed from those tables to Table 9.1. I provide this information for the three sample behaviors I have been describing throughout the book.

9.2 BEHAVIORAL PRINCIPLES

There are some important behavioral principles to keep in mind when designing reinforcement schedules. After completing this

Table 9.1   Review of CM Schedules

Behavior Targeted (From Table 8.4)	Number of Patients (From Table 6.1)	Frequency of Monitoring (From Table 7.6)	CM Duration for Patients (From Table 7.7)	Reinforcement System (From Table 8.4)
Reduce methamphetamine use in a subgroup of patients with methamphetamine dependence	10	Two times per week (MTh, MF or TF)	12 weeks	Prize CM
Increase proportion of patients who phone the clinic to attend the intake and engage in and complete the 10-week outpatient treatment program	100	Initial assessment is once, then once a week for 10 weeks	10 weeks	Name-in-the-hat prize CM
Get patients to finish chores (dishwashing, cleaning) without staff reminders	~30	Thrice per day	12 weeks	Clinic privileges
Your CM Intervention	*Number of Patients*	*Frequency of Monitoring*	*CM Duration for Patients*	*Reinforcement System*

section, you will have created a reinforcement system for the behavior you are planning to change.

9.2.1 Priming

Priming refers to providing a reinforcer even when patients have not exhibited the behavior targeted for change. The purpose behind priming is to ensure that patients have some experience with the reinforcer. By arranging priming reinforcers, patients realize the value of the reinforcer, and they gain some direct exposure to it. A voucher may be an abstract concept to patients until they have some personal experience with the items they can buy with vouchers. The prize system may also seem foreign until patients actually draw slips and win a prize. Typically, priming occurs very early in treatment—at the initial CM session.

In voucher CM systems, priming vouchers are provided (Higgins et al., 1993, 1994). Patients receive their choice of a movie theater or restaurant gift certificate during the first therapy session. In this manner, patients learn that they can receive desired items by participating in treatment. In prize CM studies (e.g., Petry et al., 2000), all patients receive a drawing on the first day of treatment, and they can draw until they win a prize. Patients are further encouraged to "practice" drawing from the prize bowl until they draw a large prize slip. Although a large prize is rarely awarded the first session, drawing until a large slip is pulled allows patients some direct experience with the probabilities of winning slips in the prize bowl.

In the Name-in-the-hat prize CM system for group attendance, all patients have their name placed in the hat at each session they attend. Although not all receive tangible reinforcement, patients observe others winning in the group. Patients find direct observation useful for understanding the reinforcement system. In both the individual prize CM and Name-in-the-hat approaches, it is important to allow patients to directly observe (and even handle) the prizes that can be won, while ensuring that desirable prizes exist in each prize category for every patient. It is important that patients gain direct exposure to the tangible reinforcers.

Take a moment and think about how you might integrate priming in your CM protocol. An example of priming is listed for each of the three sample CM protocols in Table 9.2.

9.2.2 Immediacy

Learning occurs best when each time the target behavior occurs, it is followed by its consequence without delay (e.g., Ferster & Skinner, 1957). Voucher programs use this behavioral principle by providing vouchers immediately upon submission of a negative specimen. Samples are screened within minutes of collection, and as noted in Chapter 7, onsite testing systems are necessary for CM interventions that reinforce abstinence. Draws from the prize bowl, or exchange of vouchers for retail items, should occur with minimal delay. Meta-analyses demonstrate that immediacy of reinforcement is linked to effect sizes in CM studies (Lussier et al., 2006). Thus, in designing your CM protocol, be sure that the reinforcers will be provided as quickly as possible after the behavior is monitored.

In Table 9.3, list the frequency with which you plan to assess the target behavior and methods with which you can ensure the reinforcer will follow behavior monitoring with as minimal delay as possible. Sample schedules are outlined, along with reinforcement frequencies.

Table 9.2 Examples of Priming Reinforcers

Behavior to be Reinforced	Example of How Priming Can Be Integrated
Reduce methamphetamine use in the subgroup of patients with methamphetamine dependence	Patients draw until they win a prize for submitting first sample (regardless of results).
Increase proportion of patients who phone the clinic to attend the intake session and engage in and complete the 10-week outpatient treatment program	Patients are informed at intake scheduling that they will receive a $1 to $100 prize if they attend the intake evaluation.
Get patients to finish daily chores (dishwashing, cleaning) without staff reminders	All patients get a letter stating that beginning on 11/15 (first day of CM) they will earn a small reinforcer (choice of a five-minute outdoor pass, one-minute phone call, or 15-minute stay-up-late or oversleep pass) at the group meeting describing CM for chore completion.

Your CM intervention

Behavior to be Reinforced	How Priming Can Be Integrated

9.2.3 Escalating and Reset Features

Including an escalating schedule of reinforcement is essential for engendering sustained behavior change. As patients achieve longer periods of abstinence or attendance, the amount of the vouchers or number of draws increases. By the end of the 12-week treatment period in successful voucher studies (Higgins et al., 1994, 2003; Higgins, Wong, et al., 2000), patients can earn over $40 for each negative urine specimen submitted. Similarly, in the prize CM procedure, patients can usually earn up to eight draws. With the Name-in-the-hat prize approach, the number of times one's name goes into the hat (directly proportional to one's chance of winning prizes) increases for successive attendance.

If the behavior does not occur, then the value of the next earned reinforcer is reset to an originally low amount. Thus, if abstinence is reinforced and a sample tests positive, is refused, or missed due to an unexcused absence, the next negative sample results in a reset to $2.50 in vouchers or one draw. If attendance is reinforced, an unexcused absence results in draws earned (or times one's name goes into the hat) dropping to one the next time the patient attends

Table 9.3   Methods to Ensure Immediate Reinforcement

Behavior	Monitoring Schedule	Immediacy of Reinforcement
Reduce methamphetamine use in the subgroup of patients with methamphetamine dependence	Two times per week (MTh, MF, or TF, depending on patient schedule)	Immediately after testing sample, give draws and have patients select prizes.
Increase proportion of patients who phone the clinic to attend the intake session and engage in and complete the 10-week outpatient treatment program	Initial assessment is once, then once a week for 10 weeks	When patients arrive for intake evaluation, provide priming reinforcer; then at beginning of each group attended, names go in hat; draw names and award prizes at start of group.
Get patients to finish daily chores (dishwashing, cleaning) without staff reminders	Three times per day 9 am, 1 pm, and 6 pm	Slip will be placed in residents' mailboxes after chore checks, indicating points earned. Patients can exchange points any time after they are earned.
Your Behavior	Your Monitoring Schedule	How Immediately Can You Provide Reinforcement?

a session. After a reset occurs, patients can then escalate reinforcement for sustained behavior change in the same manner as occurred before the reset.

Table 9.4 highlights an escalating system for each of the three sample behaviors. After reviewing those, you then can indicate how escalating reinforcers will be integrated into your CM protocol and in what circumstances resets will occur.

9.2.4 Magnitude

Magnitude of reinforcement clearly affects outcomes in CM interventions. One must consider the magnitude of reinforcement for each individual behavior, as well as the overall magnitude of reinforcement possible throughout the CM intervention.

Clearly, the greater the reinforcement is the more likely it is to alter behavior, but a balance must be achieved between reinforcement magnitude and

Table 9.4 Circumstances for Reinforcement Resets

Behavior	Monitoring Schedule	Escalating Reinforcement	Resets
Reduce methamphetamine use in the subgroup of patients with methamphetamine dependence	Two times per week (MTh, MF, or TF)	Draws increase by one for each consecutive negative sample submitted (up to a maximum of eight draws per sample).	No draws if positive, refuse a sample, or have an unexcused absence on a testing day. Draws reset to one for next negative sample.
Increase proportion of patients who phone the clinic to attend the intake session and engage in and complete the 10-week outpatient treatment program	Initial assessment is once, then weekly for 10 weeks	Times name goes in the hat increases by one for each consecutive session attended.	Times name goes in the hat resets to one for next attendance if ever an unexcused absence occurs or if patient leaves group before it ends.
Get patients to finish daily chores (dishwashing, cleaning), without staff reminders	Three times per day 9 am, 1 pm, and 6 pm	More points for sustained chore completion: one per chore; five bonus points for a week of perfect chore completion, and bonuses increase by five for each full week of chore completion, e.g., 5, 10, 15, 20. Cap at 20.	No bonus points that week if fail to complete a chore. Bonuses reset to five for the next full week of chore completion (and then escalate again).
Your Behavior	Your Monitoring Schedule	Escalating Reinforcement	Resets

practicality concerns. Few clinics will be able to provide voucher reinforcement (as outlined in Higgins et al., 1994, 2003, 2007; Higgins, Wong, et al., 2000). The prize CM approach is an alternative to voucher CM, but even with prize CM, it will not be efficacious in reducing drug use if the amount of prizes offered gets too low (e.g., less than $300 per patient over 12 weeks). In reinforcing group attendance, the Name-in-the-hat approach can improve attendance at costs as low as $20 per week per group.

Let's consider how each reinforcement schedule relates to individual behaviors, and then to the maximal overall reinforcement for each patient. For **standard voucher CM**, the values possible were outlined in Chapter 8, Table 8.1. The initial voucher amount is $2.50 for the first negative sample, so this is the lowest reinforcer value. The cumulative amount of reinforcement available is $960, plus the $20 priming reinforcer described in Section 9.2.1 of this chapter, for a total of $980. This is clearly a high magnitude reinforcement schedule.

With **prize CM**, the reinforcer magnitudes were described in Chapter 8, Table 8.2. For each behavior, the minimal number of draws is one, and up to 260 draws can be earned during a 12-week treatment period in which samples are monitored three times per week. As will be described in Chapter 10, each draw translates to a cost of about $2 in the typical approach, so the average total maximum reinforcement would be about $520 for a thrice-weekly testing regimen (260 draws × $2/draw). For twice-weekly monitoring, the total number of draws is 164, with an average maximum reinforcement cost of $328 (164 draws × $2/draw). These magnitudes of reinforcement are effective in altering drug-using behavior (Pierce et al., 2006; Petry, Alessi, et al., 2005; Petry, Martin, et al., 2005; Petry, Peirce, et al., 2005; Petry, Alessi, et al., 2006).

With **Name-in-the-hat prize CM for group attendance**, the reinforcement potential for each behavior and overall reinforcement is much lower. Using the approach detailed in Chapter 14, each day of attendance results in about a 50% chance of winning a prize, as each patient in the group usually has about a 50% chance of having his or her name drawn. Over a 10-week period, patients could expect to receive about five draws and five prizes if they attended all sessions. Average cost per draw is about $4 (as this system awards a prize with each draw). Therefore, this system results in an average of about $20 in reinforcement per patient over a 10-week period.

In Table 9.5 I outline a reinforcement schedule for a 10-week Name-in-the-hat CM program. Two sample patients are outlined; on the left is a schedule for a patient with perfect attendance who earns the maximum reinforcement, and on the right is one for a patient who has less than perfect attendance. Note that the manner in which the name goes in the hat increases by one for each successive week of attendance for both patients. The patient with perfect attendance gets his name in the hat more often, and wins more prizes, than the patient without perfect attendance. There is no capping in this schedule, because 10 is the maximum number of times one's name can go into the hat, and the number of times one's name goes in the hat adds nothing to the costs of the procedure. It is the number of patients whose names are drawn, and the number of prize draws awarded, that impacts costs (see Chapter 10).

In the last two columns, I estimate the number of times each patient's name gets drawn from the hat, which could range from zero to up to the maximum number of times his name went into the hat at that session. The probabilities of how often one's name is drawn relative to the times the name is placed in

Table 9.5 Reinforcement Schedules for Name-in-the-Hat Prize CM for Group Attendance

	Patient with Perfect Attendance				Patient Who Misses Treatment in Weeks Three and Nine		
Week	Times Name in the Hat	Times Name Drawn	Est. Earnings	Week	Times Name in the Hat	Times Name Drawn	Est. Earnings
Intake		Priming	$4	Intake		Priming	$4
1	1	0	0	1	1	0	0
2	2	1	$4	2	2	1	$4
3	3	0	0	3	0	0	0
4	4	0	0	4	1	0	0
5	5	2	$8	5	2	1	$4
6	6	1	$4	6	3	0	0
7	7	1	$4	7	4	0	0
8	8	2	$8	8	5	2	$8
9	9	2	$8	9	0	0	0
10	10	3	$12	10	1	0	0
Total	55	12	$52	Total	19	4	$20

the hat depends on luck as well as the overall total number of names in the hat at that session, which is directly related to other patients' attendance.

Assuming that the costs (or earnings) related to each draw are about $4 (the magnitude recommended for the Name-in-the-hat approach; see Chapters 10 and 14), the patient on the left will receive, on average, 12 draws from the prize bowl throughout the program multiplied by $4 in prizes per draw, for a total of about $48 worth of prizes. In addition, for attending the intake evaluation, each patient earns one prize draw, again estimated at $4, for a total of about $52 in prizes over the 10-week program. The amounts are about less than half for a patient with missed sessions.

9.2.5 Optional Section: Reinforcing Chore Completion with Clinic Privileges

The third sample CM protocol from Table 9.1 is a 12-week program that monitors and reinforces chore completion in a residential setting up to three times daily. Whereas chore completion is monitored and reinforced three times each day for the clinic as a whole, let's presume each resident usually has only one chore a day. For example, one resident may be assigned to wash dishes after breakfast, another after lunch, and another after dinner. Still another will clean the living area in the morning and another in the evening. Someone else is assigned to clean one bathroom, and yet another person another bathroom. Each of these residents will earn their points in close proximity to when their chore was checked, either in the morning, afternoon, or evening.

The reinforcers are points exchangeable for clinic privileges. Patients earn one point for every chore completed and five bonus points that escalate in increments of five for each consecutive week of chore completion, up to a maximum of 20. Hence, points possible are one for each day in which the target behavior occurs, and 84 in total over the 12-week period (one per day × seven days per week × 12 weeks = 84 draws). The number of bonus points possible in week one is five, 10 in week two, 15 in week three, and up to 20 each in weeks four to 24, resulting in up to 210 points from bonuses. Combining the total daily points (84) with the weekly bonus points (210) results in an overall maximum of 294 points per patient, as outlined in Table 9.6. Note that patients who enter the facility after the 12-week CM program has begun will not be able to earn this full reinforcement amount. Someone beginning treatment one month after CM starts could earn up to about 186 points (56 points for eight weeks of daily chore completion and 130 points in bonuses).

This CM protocol is flexible enough to allow for differences in chore frequencies that may occur. If, for example, a patient who completes a relatively more difficult chore of cleaning bathrooms for three days is not assigned additional chores for the remainder of the week, the protocol would not penalize such patients with respect to bonus point earnings, which constitutes the bulk of the reinforcement (210 of the 294 points). For simplicity sake, each chore completed could result in one point as described earlier, and any days off from chores (because of more difficult chores or because one was excused from chores) would not reset bonuses, which are proportionally more valuable. Thus, such a patient may earn one point on Friday for cleaning the bathrooms, one point on Saturday, and one on Sunday. Because he has no more chores for the rest of the week, he earns no more daily points, but on Sunday he would get bonus points due (between five and 20 points, depending on how many weeks in a row he completed all assigned chores).

Similarly, if some patients were assigned two chores on some days, they could earn two points that day, but their bonus that week would still be contingent on completion of all assigned chores over the seven-day period. Hence, a patient with twice-daily chores for an entire week could earn 14 points that week for individual chores, but the bonus points (up to 210 over 12 weeks) would be the same as a patient with one chore per day (or even fewer) would earn.

Knowing the total amount of reinforcement possible (even if actual schedules may vary slightly given extra or fewer chores in a given week), a clinician desiring to use this schedule would now have to translate points to privileges.

Table 9.6   Sample Maximum Reinforcement Schedule for Reinforcing Chore Completion

Week	Day	Points per Chore	Bonus Points (Full Week of Chores)	Week	Day	Points per Chore	Bonus Points (Full Week of Chores)
1	M	1		7	M	1	
	T	1			T	1	
	W	1			W	1	
	Th	1			Th	1	
	F	1			F	1	
	S	1			S	1	
	S	1	5		S	1	20
2	M	1		8	M	1	
	T	1			T	1	
	W	1			W	1	
	Th	1			Th	1	
	F	1			F	1	
	S	1			S	1	
	S	1	10		S	1	20
3	M	1		9	M	1	
	T	1			T	1	
	W	1			W	1	
	Th	1			Th	1	
	F	1			F	1	
	S	1			S	1	
	S	1	15		S	1	20
4	M	1		10	M	1	
	T	1			T	1	
	W	1			W	1	
	Th	1			Th	1	
	F	1			F	1	
	S	1			S	1	
	S	1	20		S	1	20

Table 9.6 (continued)   Sample Maximum Reinforcement Schedule for Reinforcing Chore Completion

Week	Day	Points per Chore	Bonus Points (Full Week of Chores)	Week	Day	Points per Chore	Bonus Points (Full Week of Chores)
5	M	1		11	M	1	
	T	1			T	1	
	W	1			W	1	
	Th	1			Th	1	
	F	1			F	1	
	S	1			S	1	
	S	1	20		S	1	20
6	M	1		12	M	1	
	T	1			T	1	
	W	1			W	1	
	Th	1			Th	1	
	F	1			F	1	
	S	1			S	1	
	S	1	20		S	1	20
					Totals	84	210
					Grand total		294

One point needs to be exchangeable for something, but it must be a low valued privilege. Higher point values would be assigned to more valuable privileges. Choice and variety are important in each "cost" category.

A possible menu of reinforcers and their "costs" in terms of points may be similar to those shown in Table 9.7. In determining options, be sure that all reinforcers in a category have a roughly equal magnitude. The best way to determine this is to survey patients about how desirable they would rate each item on a one to 10 scale. You can then lump items rated the lowest in the smallest cost (one-point) category and those consistently rated the most desirable at the highest cost category. Options outlined in Table 9.7 are one example, and may or may not have similar values in your clinical setting.

Given the reinforcement schedule above, a patient could earn an overnight pass after about three weeks of perfect chore completion according to reinforcer "costs" outlined below. If this (or another privilege) is not appropriate for your setting, you would not include it as an option. Note also that these levels of reinforcers are likely to be reinforcing even among patients who start

Table 9.7 Possible Privileges Available at Different Point Costs

1 Point	5 Points	10 Points	20 Points	50 Points
1 min phone call	10 min phone call	Get out of chores for one day	Extra meal choice	Overnight pass
1 min late to group pass	10 min late to group pass	1 hr of use of exercise room	Get out of chores for 2 days (with no reset in bonus)	No chores for a week (with no reset in bonus)
Coffee or tea	Can of soda	1 hr stay up late pass	3 hr stay up late pass	
Extra helping of a food at a meal	Small bag of chips	1 hr visitor pass	Evening pass (leave for 4 hrs)	
Stamp	Granola bar	1 hr sleep late	Miss a group pass	
Pen, paper, small office supply	Exchange a daily chore	1 hr outside pass		
	20 min on computer	30 min phone call		
		1 hr on computer		

the CM program late (i.e., after it has been in effect for several weeks). Patients who are eligible to earn only 78 or 156 points (with four or eight weeks of CM participation, respectively) can still achieve meaningful reinforcers.

9.3 DETERMINING YOUR MONITORING AND REINFORCEMENT SCHEDULE

If you are reinforcing a behavior individually with a patient, in Table 9.8, detail your monitoring and reinforcement schedule, including your priming reinforcer and escalating reinforcers. You should already have an idea about what the minimal reinforcement amount is for the first occurrence of the behavior. In Table 9.4 you outlined how your reinforcers will escalate with sustained behavior change. Consider the amount of reinforcement possible for a patient with optimal behavior by plotting out how reinforcers accumulate with perfect behavior throughout the duration of your CM intervention. The template should fit most schedules, and extra columns could be added, which you can label if needed. You can also use an Excel spreadsheet version to calculate sums over the entire period.

Table 9.8   Your Monitoring and Reinforcement Schedule for an Individually Reinforced Behavior

Week	Day(s) Monitoring	Reinforcement Possible	Bonus Reinforcers (If Applicable)	Cumulative Reinforcement
Cumulative total				

Table 9.9   Your Reinforcement Schedule for Group-Based Reinforcement

Week	Groups Reinforced per Week	Maximum Patients per Group	Maximum Draws per Group[a]

Total number of groups in which reinforcement occurs:_____

Cumulative total draws:_____

[a] Maximum number of draws per group is usually half the number of attendees.

If you are reinforcing group attendance behavior, different parameters need to be outlined. With group reinforcement procedures, you should consider the weeks that the reinforcement system will be in place, the number of group sessions per week that will be reinforced, the maximal number of patients who will attend each group, and maximum draws per group. This information can be placed in Table 9.9.

9.4 CRITIQUING REINFORCEMENT SCHEDULES

Now that you have settled upon a reinforcement schedule, make sure that it (a) includes a priming reinforcer, (b) arranges reinforcement as immediately as possible to the target behavior, (c) allows for escalating reinforcement, and (d) provides sufficient reinforcement magnitude so that your patients will want to work toward earning the reinforcers. If your schedule appears to violate any of these principles, you may want to make some adjustments.

You will also want to consider reinforcement schedules that clinicians have designed so that you can better critique your own schedule. Below, I outline some reinforcement approaches. Describe their strengths and weaknesses, and also try to consider your own schedule within these contexts. If the schedule you designed in Tables 9.8 or 9.9 contains flaws identified in the reinforcement schedules outlined in the next sections, you may want to reassess aspects of your schedule to better conform with CM principles.

Case 1: Reinforcing Abstinence Using Prize CM

Anna is working in an outpatient clinic in which many patients have problems with methamphetamine. She has some funds available to start a CM approach but not the $300 recommended per patient. She creates a reinforcement schedule that tries to address many of the issues outlined in this chapter, while containing costs. In her protocol, patients leave samples twice a week, and they get a priming draw for the first sample submitted, regardless of results. Number of draws earned increases by one per negative sample and caps at four. The total number of draws possible during the 12-week intervention is 91, considerably less than the 260 draws in Table 8.2. Table 9.10 outlines this approach. Critique its strengths and weaknesses.

This schedule contains many positive features. It includes twice-weekly monitoring and reinforcement (the minimum recommended) and a 12-week duration. A priming reinforcer is provided in week one, and the reinforcers escalate for sustained abstinence.

The only potential concern with this schedule is that there is a cap of four draws for each negative sample submitted. One needs to achieve only two weeks of abstinence to be at the maximal reinforcement level. This also means that a reset for a missed or positive sample may be of relatively low

Table 9.10 Sample Prize CM Reinforcement Schedule for Abstinence

Week	Day	Draws	Week	Day	Draws
1	M	1+prime	7	M	4
	Th	2		Th	4
2	M	3	8	M	4
	Th	4		Th	4
3	M	4	9	M	4
	Th	4		Th	4
4	M	4	10	M	4
	Th	4		Th	4
5	M	4	11	M	4
	Th	4		Th	4
6	M	4	12	M	4
	Th	4		Th	4
			Cumulative total		91

salience. Patients who relapse or fail to submit a sample would drop from four draws to one draw for their next negative sample. Thus, this schedule may not engender sustained behavior change as well as a schedule that provides a greater maximum rate of reinforcement (e.g., six or eight draws) and for which a reset is more substantial.

Case 2: Name-in-the-Hat Prize CM When Patients Attend Different Numbers of Groups Each Week

Mary works in an outpatient program that holds dual diagnosis groups on Mondays, Wednesdays, and Fridays. About 20 patients are enrolled in the program at a given time. Not every patient is scheduled to attend all the groups. Some patients come to just one or two of the groups, and some attend all three. Mary wants to implement CM to boost attendance but does not want to limit CM to just one of the groups because then some patients would get CM for some of the sessions but not all.

Mary modifies the Name-in-the-hat approach so that for each group attended, the patient gets to put his name in the hat once. Names go into the hat at the start of each group session. At the patients' last group of the week, Mary puts their names in the hat a bonus number of times. The bonuses start at one and escalate by one for each week in a row in which patients attended all scheduled sessions.

Table 9.11   Critique of a Sample Name-in-the-Hat Reinforcement Schedule

Positive Features	Negative Features

Rather than draw names for prizes at every group session, Mary decides to draw all the winning names at the end of the week, during the Friday group. Mary will draw 10 names from the hat at the Friday group. Those who are present can select from prizes then. For patients who are not scheduled for Friday groups, Mary will inform them the following week if they get to draw from the prize bowl for a prize.

Before reading further, what are the good features and potential pitfalls of this approach? List them in Table 9.11 before reading further.

The positive features are that each instance of the behavior results in a reinforcer: the chance to possibly have one's name drawn to win a prize. The behavior is objective and measured frequently (up to three times per week, and at least once a week for each patient). There is escalating reinforcement for sustained behavior with the bonus chances.

However, there are some notable concerns with this schedule. Primary among them is that the reinforcement is only provided once a week, and for some patients it is not provided in group but on an individual basis, and those patients will not observe others winning prizes. In fact, patients who are not scheduled for Friday groups could go weeks without winning (or seeing any other patient) win prizes. They may then begin to suspect whether or not anyone is actually winning and if drawings are rigged.

In addition, the reinforcers are not being provided in close temporal proximity to the behavior. Patients need to wait up to the end of the week or longer to know whether or not they will actually win a prize.

There is an escalating and reset feature in terms of the bonus chances. However, the number of bonus chances is relatively low for patients who are scheduled to attend three sessions per week. These patients' names go in the hat three times for each of three sessions attended, and an additional one time for attending all three groups in a week, for four times total. This is a low bonus proportionally (25%). In contrast, the patient who is assigned to attend one group a week has a higher proportional bonus.

One better approach would be to arrange some reinforcement at each group session (e.g., draw names at each of the three weekly sessions). In that manner, each group would be associated with some prize winnings. Each patient could earn escalating bonuses, starting at three and increasing by one per week, based on the number of weeks in a row in which he attended all his scheduled sessions. These bonus name slips would be earned for a full week of consecutive attendance, such that the bonus slips would be presented on Wednesdays for those who only came on Wednesdays and on Fridays for those who made it to their first full week of attendance on a Friday, or on Monday, if Monday constituted the first full week of attendance. In that manner, any given patient's chances of having his name drawn may vary by group and week, depending on how many other attendees were present and when his and others' bonuses were earned, but this natural variation would likely stabilize over time. At each group attended, each patient would have some chance of winning a prize and observing others win prizes.

SUMMARY

You should now have a good handle on the reinforcement schedule you want to implement. Go back to the reinforcement schedule you outlined in Table 9.8, and make any modifications to it necessary to guard against the problems outlined in these sample schedules. In the next chapter, I review methods for calculating the costs of reinforcement schedules.

Chapter 10

Calculating Costs

For CM programs that use only clinic privileges as reinforcers, the upfront expenses may be negligible. In these cases, the only costs of CM relate to administrative time costs for setting up and implementing CM. Administrative costs are outlined in the final section (Section 10.3) of this chapter, and if you are not using voucher or prize CM, you can move to that section now.

Voucher and prize CM systems will clearly incur costs, and this chapter details methods for calculating their expected costs. It initially describes approaches for determining per-person and overall costs for individually administered voucher and prize CM procedures. Choice points for altering CM protocols are also described with the goal of deciding upon a realistic CM program to implement in your clinical setting. Then, techniques are suggested for estimating costs associated with biological testing (if applicable).

The second part of the chapter outlines cost expectations for the Name-in-the-hat prize CM procedure for reinforcing group attendance. If you are implementing this procedure, you can go directly to Section 10.2.

Regardless of the CM system being employed, there are indirect administrative costs associated with implementing CM. They relate to the time required for learning about, setting up, and instituting CM, as well as for supervision or review of CM implementation. Methods for determining these time estimations are outlined in Section 10.3.

10.1 DETERMINING COSTS FOR CM PROCEDURES THAT REINFORCE PATIENTS INDIVIDUALLY

10.1.1 Per-Person Reinforcement Costs

10.1.1.1 Voucher CM

In Chapter 9, you outlined your reinforcement schedule. You created a schedule that tallied up the total amount of reinforcement possible for each patient over the duration of the CM intervention in Table 9.8. If your reinforcement system relates to vouchers, you should know exactly how much voucher reinforcement a patient could earn. If the amount seems too high, you can modify it by (a) decreasing the initial voucher amount (e.g., from $2.50 to $1.00); (b) reducing the manner in which vouchers escalate (e.g., from $1.25 per consecutive behavior to $0.50 per consecutive behavior); (c) capping maximal earnings (e.g., instead of increasing by $1.25 for every negative sample over the entire duration of the CM intervention, stop escalating once a patient reaches some amount); (d) reducing the duration of the intervention (e.g., from 12 to eight weeks); (e) decreasing the frequency of reinforcement (e.g., from three times weekly to twice weekly); or (f) eliminating bonuses.

In Table 10.1, I show a modified voucher schedule that integrates all six of these changes relative to the standard voucher schedule outlined in Table 8.1. This table represents each of the above options for illustrative purposes only. You need not integrate all of these changes, but instead you should modify your schedule based on fiscal realities in conjunction with your knowledge of behavioral principles and your clinical population and setting.

As shown, integrating all these cost-saving modifications substantially reduced the costs of the CM from $997.50 per patient in Table 8.1 to $62 per patient in Table 10.1. Although these changes reduce costs, they may also

Table 10.1   A Non-Ideal Voucher Schedule That Greatly Reduces Magnitudes of Vouchers Available

Week	Day	Voucher Amount	Notes	Cumulative
1	M	$1.00	Voucher value starts at $1 rather than $2.50	$1.00
	F	$1.50	Values escalate by $0.50 rather than $1.25	$2.50
2	M	$2.00	Twice rather than thrice weekly testing	$4.50
	F	$2.50	No extra $10 bonuses earned	$7.00
3	M	$3.00		$10.00
	F	$3.50		$13.50
4	M	$4.00		$17.50
	F	$4.50		$22.00
5	M	$5.00	Voucher amounts cap at $5.00	$27.00
	F	$5.00		$32.00
6	M	$5.00		$37.00
	F	$5.00		$42.00
7	M	$5.00		$47.00
	F	$5.00		$52.00
8	M	$5.00		$57.00
	F	$5.00	Eight rather than 12 weeks of CM	$62.00

impact effectiveness. As noted earlier, frequency and duration of reinforcement, as well as escalating reinforcers and magnitude of reinforcement, impact effectiveness. You need to achieve a balance between integrating appropriate behavioral principles and feasibility with respect to costs. There is no evidence in the literature that $62 in vouchers per patient will be sufficient to reduce drug use. In fact, studies investigating voucher reinforcement magnitude generally find that less than $500 in voucher reinforcement is ineffective in changing drug use behaviors (Dallery et al., 2001; Lussier et al., 2006; Silverman et al., 1999).

A better compromise may be to try to determine which modifications you can make without adversely impacting the behavior you are trying to alter. For example, you may think that few, if any, patients will find it worthwhile to abstain from cocaine to earn a $1 voucher, so you may wish to start at an initial $2 voucher value. You may elect to keep the testing frequency at twice per week, because your clinic is not open on Wednesdays. You may cap the voucher values after patients achieve a solid eight-week period of consecutive abstinence, but you may keep the CM in effect for 12 weeks, as eight weeks seems rather short. A $1 escalating reinforcement value may be more effective than $0.50, which would result in a very slow proportional rate of escalation. Such a schedule would look as outlined in Table 10.2.

The schedule in Table 10.2 provides a maximum of $334 in vouchers per patient and is still much lower than that utilized in efficacious research protocols with voucher CM (usually about $1,000 per patient). Nevertheless, it is probably more likely to engender the desired effects than the leaner schedule outlined in Table 10.1, and it retains many of the behavioral principles central to the efficacy of CM, as described in Chapter 9.

If you are utilizing voucher CM, indicate here your overall maximal amount of vouchers available for a patient with perfect behavior over the entire CM intervention: $_____. This amount should be calculated in Table 9.8, but you may want to modify your CM protocol from that originally outlined based on the information above. If you make changes to the monitoring and reinforcement schedule, do so now in a modified Table 9.8 and include the final maximum value of vouchers above. If you are using voucher CM, you can move to Section 10.1.2 now.

10.1.1.2 Prize CM That Reinforces Behavior Individually

If you are using individualized prize CM, you should have determined the maximum number of draws per patient throughout your CM protocol in Table 9.8. However, you have not yet estimated overall costs of the CM intervention for each patient, because prize-based CM requires an additional calculation to determine the average dollar amount per draw. In individual prize CM, a draw is typically worth an average of about $2. This amount is estimated when the

Table 10.2   Sample Voucher Schedule Altering Some Parameters

Week	Day	Voucher Amount	Notes	Cumulative
1	M	$2	Voucher value starts at $2	$2
	F	$3	Voucher values escalate by $1	$5
2	M	$4	Twice rather than thrice weekly testing	$9
	F	$5	No extra $10 bonuses earned	$14
3	M	$6		$20
	F	$7		$27
4	M	$8		$35
	F	$9		$44
5	M	$10		$54
	F	$12		$66
6	M	$14		$80
	F	$16		$96
7	M	$18		$114
	F	$20	Amount caps at $20 after two months of abstinence	$134
8	M	$20		$154
	F	$20		$174
9	M	$20		$194
	F	$20		$214
10	M	$20		$234
	F	$20		$254
11	M	$20		$274
	F	$20		$294
12	M	$20		$314
	F	$20	Retain 12 weeks of CM	
			Total	$334

prize bowl from which patients draw contains the breakdown of slips noted in Table 10.3.

The typical prize bowl contains 500 slips. As outlined in Table 10.3, half the slips in the bowl are not associated with a prize, and these "good job!" slips add nothing to the costs of CM. About 42% (209 of 500 slips) are small prizes

Table 10.3 Typical Prize Ratio for Individual Prize CM Reinforcement Schedules

Number of Slips	Type of Slip	Maximum Value of Prize	Average Value of Prize	Probability of Drawing[a]	Cost per Draw[b]
250	Good jobs	0	0	0.5	$0.00
209	Smalls	$1	$0.80	0.418	$0.33
40	Larges	$20	$18	0.08	$1.44
1	Jumbo	$100	$80	0.002	$0.16
Total					
500 slips					$1.93

[a] Probability of drawing each slip equals "Number of Slips" divided by "Total Slips" in the bowl.

[b] Cost per draw is "Probability of Drawing" times "Average Value of Prize" in that category.

that are worth an average of about $0.80 in value. Multiplying $0.80 (average cost of a small prize) times 0.418 (probability of drawing a small prize) results in the small prizes adding $0.33 to the cost of each draw. The maximum value of a small prize is $1, so any item from a "dollar store" would constitute a small prize. Other small prize items can be purchased at supermarkets and Walmart or Kmart type stores, and can include toiletries. Some items can be purchased in bulk (e.g., pack of 12 socks) and then divided into smaller quantities as individual small items. They key is not to exceed $1 in value for small prizes, or the costs of your CM protocol will increase relative to those outlined above. In Table 10.3, the expectation is that the overall average cost of each small prize will be $0.80.

Large prizes should average $18 in value and not exceed $20. Examples are $20 gift cards to various stores as well as handheld CD players, kitchen and tool items, and clothing items. Items can often be purchased on sale for significantly less than $20 to reduce the overall costs. Eight percent (40 of 500) of slips are large prizes, and each adds about $1.44 to the cost of each draw so long as the overall average cost of large prizes is about $18.

Finally, the jumbo prize can usually be purchased for far less than $100 in value, as televisions, stereos, window air conditioners, microwaves, and so forth, may cost as little as $60 on sale. Using a generous average cost of $80 per jumbo prize estimates that the availability of one jumbo prize in the bowl (1 of 500 slips) adds $0.16 to the cost of each draw. Often, clinicians presume that eliminating the jumbo prize (or decreasing its value to $50) will reduce costs of the prize CM system. However, as outlined above, *the jumbo prize adds the least of any prize category to the overall costs of the system.* Patients are greatly excited about the concept of winning jumbo prizes—especially

$100 jumbo prizes. Therefore, it is highly recommended that the jumbo category be retained as outlined above.

If you take the overall number of draws possible in your CM system that you detailed in Table 9.8 (_____) and multiply that number by the average cost of a draw from Table 10.3 ($1.93), you will derive the average maximum cost per patient with the above system: _____.

If you wish to decrease the overall costs of the prize CM system, you can utilize some of the same strategies outlined in Section 10.1.1.1. Most likely, your prize draws start at one draw and increase by one draw for each successive behavior. If not, this is something you can change, but in the case of prize draws (unlike voucher amounts), you cannot start at less than one draw. Further, increments with respect to prize draws can only be in whole numbers, as there is no such thing as a half a draw. Review your schedule and see if it makes sense to begin at one draw and increase by one for each successive behavior if you do not currently have these features included.

One thing you can do to reduce the overall amount of draws, and also the costs, is to cap the maximal number of draws at some amount such as eight draws. So, instead of starting at one draw and going up to 24 or 36 draws for eight or 12 weeks of successful behavior change, the draws could stop escalating once the patient achieves a maximum of eight draws. If you are monitoring behaviors twice a week, this cap of eight draws would occur after a month of successful behavior change. This procedure was described earlier and also outlined in Chapter 8.

Reducing the duration of the intervention (e.g., from 12 to eight weeks) or the frequency of reinforcement (e.g., from thrice to twice weekly) will also decrease the number of draws possible. Decreasing the number of draws has a direct impact on the costs of CM, as described below.

Table 10.4 shows a modification of the prize schedule outlined in Table 8.2 in which 240 draws were possible. In Table 8.2, patients could earn draws up to three times per week for 12 weeks. In Table 10.4, patients are now tested and reinforced twice per week. This change reduces the average maximum cost from $499.20 (260 draws × $1.93/draw) to $316.52 (164 draws × $1.93/draw). These are the average maximum per patient costs of the sample CM protocol I am detailing throughout this book that reinforces methamphetamine abstinence twice weekly for 12 weeks. Prize CM schedules arranging for $300 to $400 in average maximum prize earnings are efficacious in reducing drug use (Peirce et al., 2006; Petry et al., 2000, 2007; Petry, Alessi, et al., 2005; Petry, Martin, et al., 2005; Petry, Peirce, et al., 2005; Petry, Martin, et al., 2006).

There is no need to further alter the reinforcement parameters if these costs appear reasonable. If you reduced the duration of the CM intervention to eight weeks, patients would earn a maximum of 100 draws, resulting in an average maximal cost of $192 per patient. Alternative methods to reduce costs are addressed below.

Table 10.4   Draw Schedule for Sample CM Protocol

Week	Day	Draws	Cumulative Draws	Week	Day	Draws	Cumulative Draws
1	T	1	1	7	T	8	76
	F	2	3		F	8	84
2	T	3	6	8	T	8	92
	F	4	10		F	8	100
3	T	5	15	9	T	8	108
	F	6	21		F	8	116
4	T	7	28	10	T	8	124
	F	8	36		F	8	132
5	T	8	44	11	T	8	140
	F	8	52		F	8	148
6	T	8	60	12	T	8	156
	F	8	68		F	8	164

10.1.1.3 Advanced Optional Topic: Modifying the Prize Bowl to Decrease Costs per Draw

With prize CM, there are options for altering the magnitude of reinforcement by modifying parameters of the prize bowl. You can retain the maximal number of draws (e.g., 164) but decrease the costs per draw by changing (a) the overall number of slips in the bowl, (b) the prize categories available, (c) the proportions of slips representing each prize category, and/or (d) the costs of prizes within each category.

Let's assume you wish to retain a 12-week intervention with twice-weekly testing so that the total number of draws available per patient is 164 draws, as outlined in Table 10.4. Let's also assume that you want to decrease the average maximal costs from $1.93 per draw, outlined in Table 10.3, to about $1 per draw so that on average a patient with perfect outcomes would earn about $164 rather than $315 in prizes. Table 10.5 shows an example of a prize bowl configuration that results in a cost of only about $1 per draw.

In comparing Tables 10.5 and 10.3, you can see that the number of "good job!" slips (and the probability of drawing a "good job" slip) has increased substantially in this configuration. Rather than a 50% chance of drawing a "good job" slip, the above prize bowl contains an eight out of 10 chance (or 80%) of not winning a prize with each draw earned. Proportions of small and large prizes are also reduced.

Table 10.5 Example of a Non-Ideal, Very Low-Cost Prize Bowl

Number of Slips	Type of Slip	Maximum Value of Prize	Average Value of Prize	Probability of Drawing	Cost per Draw
400	Good jobs	0	0	0.8	$0.00
79	Smalls	$1	$0.80	0.158	$0.13
20	Larges	$20	$18.00	0.04	$0.72
1	Jumbo	$100	$80.00	0.002	$0.16
Total					
500					$1.01

Although this prize bowl is demonstrated for illustrative purposes, you should carefully consider its likelihood of success in altering patient behavior prior to implementing it. According to the draw schedule, patients would need to exhibit the desired behavior for about a week and a half prior to winning their first prize, which in the greatest likelihood would be a small $1 item. In other words, it would take 1.5 weeks (three consecutive negative samples) to earn enough draws (1 + 2 + 3 = 6 draws), on average, to receive a single prize (as five draws, on average, are needed before winning a prize when the overall probability of winning is 0.2).

Once patients have achieved four consecutive weeks of perfect behavior, they will be earning eight draws per negative sample, so on average, they would only be winning one or two $1 prizes even after long-term sustained behavior. This level of reinforcement may be too lean to encourage and sustain changes in drug use behaviors. It only allows for a 4% (one out of 25) chance of winning a prize worth more than a dollar in value, so patients will be earning, on average, a highly valued prize about every other week even after achieving perfect performance.

Table 10.6 outlines an alternative configuration. It provides a similar cost per draw ($1), but the probability of winning a prize with each draw increases from 20% to about 40%, which is just a little less than the probability noted in the usual prize bowl configuration in Table 10.4—50% winning slips. Further, the probability of winning prizes worth greater than $1 in value is doubled from 4.2% to 8.5% in this configuration compared to the low-cost example in Table 10.5. These increases in winning prizes are balanced by lowering the probabilities of winning large and jumbo prizes. A medium prize category of $5 prizes is also included. As noted below, the overall number of slips in this bowl is 1000 slips.

Chances of winning a jumbo prize are much lower in this prize bowl compared to the others. In Tables 10.3 and 10.5, a patient who earns 164 draws over a 12-week period has a 164/500 chance of winning a jumbo prize (32.8%), or almost a one-in-three chance. However, in Table 10.6, a patient

Table 10.6   Alternate Low-Cost Prize Bowl Configuration

Number of Slips	Type of Slip	Maximum Value of Prize	Average Value of Prize	Probability of Drawing	Cost per Draw
595	Good jobs	0	0	0.595	$0.00
320	Smalls	$1	$0.80	0.32	$0.26
60	Mediums	$5	$4.00	0.06	$0.24
24	Larges	$20	$18.00	0.024	$0.43
1	Jumbo	$100	$80.00	0.001	$0.08
Total					
1000					$1.01

utilizing this prize bowl has only a 164/1000 (16%) chance of winning a jumbo prize. Nevertheless, this patient's chances of winning any prize are about 40% with each draw.

Research has yet to fully explore how probabilities of winning various types of prizes impacts outcomes. However, we know from lottery systems that very small chances of winning large magnitude prizes impact behavior substantially, so long as small wins are fairly plentiful (e.g., the $1 and $5 wins on scratch tickets). To maximize benefits of the prize CM system while minimizing costs, you ought to retain reasonable probabilities of winning prizes across a range of values. Tables 10.3 and 10.6 provide two possibilities of reasonable methods to set up prize bowls, while Table 10.5 outlines a suboptimal configuration. You can likewise test other probabilities to ascertain moderate, or even denser, magnitudes. In Table 10.7, I include a spreadsheet

Table 10.7   Formula for Adjusting Prize Bowls to Alter Costs

Column or Row	A	B	C	D	E	F
1	Number of Slips	Type of Slip	Maximum Value of Prize	Average Value of Prize	Probability of Drawing	Cost per Draw
2	595	Good jobs	0	0	=A2/A8	=D2 × E2
3	320	Smalls	$1	$0.80	=A3/A8	=D3 × E3
4	60	Mediums	$5	$4.00	=A4/A8	=D4 × E4
5	24	Larges	$20	$18	=A5/A8	=D5 × E5
6	1	Jumbo	$100	$80	=A6/A8	=D6 × E6
7	Total Slips					Total Cost
8	=sum(A2:A6)				=sum(E2:E6)	=sum(F2:F6)

in which you can enter different numbers of slips, and the program (available on the accompanying CD) will automatically calculate for you the costs of each draw. In the spreadsheet, you can type new numbers into any cell that is denoted by gray font, and the remaining cells will recalculate the probabilities and costs.

From your draw schedule, indicate the total number of draws possible for a patient with perfect performance: _____. Using $1.93 per draw or another amount from a prize bowl you've designed in Table 10.7, indicate the cost per draw:_____. Now, multiply these numbers: _____ × _____ = _____. This value is the average maximal cost in prizes per patient.

10.1.2 Total Reinforcement Costs (For Individualized Voucher and Prize CM Approaches)

Once you determine the maximal cost per patient, the next step in calculating costs of a CM protocol is straightforward. You simply multiply the maximal cost per patient by the number of patients you wish to treat with CM. This step is identical whether you are utilizing voucher or prize CM.

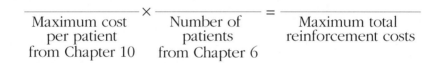

The program cost you calculated above is the maximum program cost if every single one of the patients you treated with CM were to achieve *perfect* performance. Clearly, not all the patients will achieve perfect performance or earn maximum reinforcement.

In most CM studies to date, patients earn about half the maximum amounts. This rule of thumb relates to the fact that some patients never exhibit the target behavior; a proportion will drop out of treatment right away or never become abstinent. They earn no reinforcement and do not add anything to the direct costs of the CM program. Another group of patients (the bulk of them) will perform in an intermediary manner. Some earn only modest reinforcement, others will earn about half the maximum, and still others will earn near but not the full amount possible. Finally, a group of patients whom you treat with CM will earn the maximum reinforcement possible. These are the top performers. This group usually represents between 10% and 35% of the patients you treat. The exact proportions of patients who fall into these three categories will depend on a number of factors. They include your clinical setting, the behavior you are targeting for change, unique characteristics of your patient population, and how well your CM protocol integrates behavioral principles.

Given the CM research to date, a safe and conservative estimate of the actual direct programmatic costs will be half the maximal program costs. So, below indicate this estimate:

$$\frac{\rule{4cm}{0.4pt}}{\substack{\text{Maximum total}\\ \text{reinforcement costs}\\ \text{for the program}}} \div 2 = \frac{\rule{4cm}{0.4pt}}{\substack{\text{Expected}\\ \text{actual total}}}$$

If this expected actual cost is too high, you can return to the earlier section in this chapter to come up with methods for lowering the cost per patient. Alternatively, you can reduce the number of patients you plan to treat with CM. For example, if you initially intended to treat 30 patients with CM, and the maximal total reinforcement costs are $316.52 per patient, this results in $9,495 in maximal total program reinforcement costs. This cost is divided by 2, for an expected actual cost of $4,748. If this amount is too high, a method for reducing it is to treat only 10 patients with CM your first round, similar to the protocol I am outlining throughout this book. If you decrease the number of patients you plan to treat via CM by two-thirds (from 30 down to 10), the overall expected actual total costs of reinforcement would be $316.52 ÷ 2 × 10 = $1,582. This option may be better than weakening behavioral parameters to lower per-person costs. If appropriate behavioral principles are not adapted, the intervention is going to be less likely to impact behavior. It is more worthwhile to implement CM in an appropriate manner with a smaller number of patients than to implement a weak version of CM with a greater number of patients (and have few respond). Methods for raising funds for CM are detailed in Chapter 11.

10.1.3 Biological Testing Costs

In addition to the direct costs of the reinforcers, CM protocols that reinforce abstinence have other costs associated with biological testing. To obtain a full picture of the costs of a CM protocol, these costs ought to be considered. If onsite urine toxicology testing can be charged to insurers and these costs are fully reimbursable, the additional biological testing costs to your CM program will be modest, if any. If your CM protocol does not reinforce abstinence, there probably will be no such additional costs. For CM protocols reinforcing attendance, activity completion, or other such behaviors and that require no equipment purchasing, you can move directly to Section 3 in this chapter: Administrative Time. On the other hand, if you are reinforcing abstinence and cannot recover these costs via insurance or other reimbursement procedures, methods for estimating biological testing costs are outlined below.

10.1.3.1 Estimating Costs for Urine Toxicology Testing

If you are monitoring and reinforcing abstinence from a single drug as recommended in Chapter 5, you should be testing for that substance using onsite testing procedures. For the most commonly reinforced substances in CM protocols (stimulants, opioids, or THC [marijuana]), onsite testing kits are available for under $2 per reagent. You should check various websites to ascertain the exact costs of onsite testing kits you want to use as these costs vary over time. Compare various sites and different products until you find ones that have features you desire at the lowest costs.

Buying kits in bulk can substantially reduce costs. On the other hand, test kits also expire after about a year from the purchase date, so you do not want to purchase more than you will use. Some possible sites to check are noted in Table 10.8, but you should also explore other options, as new companies and pricing may emerge over time. After exploring the options on the Internet and/or via phone, use Table 10.8 to weigh the pros and cons of various test kits. You will also want to ascertain the exact cost per test of your top choice(s).

After determining the cost per test of the system you desire, you should consider ancillary costs. These may include costs of gloves, collection cups, and adulterant and temperature strips if you wish to use them. Costs of gloves and collection cups may just add $0.10 or so to the cost of each test, but assessing for temperature and adulterants may add $1 or more to the cost of each test. Provide your best estimate of the costs for ancillary testing materials. Possible items you may wish to include are listed in Table 10.9, and you should consult current price guides to accurately gauge costs. If you do not wish to include some of these optional items, just indicate $0 in the cost sections for those items.

10.1.3.2 Estimating Costs for Alcohol and Nicotine Screening

If you are reinforcing abstinence from other substances that involve testing beyond urinalysis (e.g., nicotine or alcohol), there may be costs associated with equipment. For reinforcing initial nicotine abstinence, you will need at least one carbon monoxide reader, and more if you plan to have multiple therapists involved in the CM protocol and sharing equipment would not be practical. The costs of such equipment will vary, and searching on the Internet can probably find you the most competitive prices. An example is a PiCO+™ Smokerlyzer® CO monitor (Bedfont Scientific Ltd., Kent, England). Its current price is about $600, and a calibrator and D-piece to reduce cross-infections and contamination are about $195 and $50, respectively. Breath tubes for each testing are $56 for a package of 200.

In most smoking cessation protocols, abstinence is initially detected by negative CO readings using equipment similar to that outlined above. Once initial

Table 10.8 Determining Costs of Testing Kits

Website or Company (Phone # and Contact Person)	Date Accessed/ Date of Call	Pros of Test	Cons of Test	Cost/Box (Tests/Box)	Cost per Test
http://expomed.com/Merchant5/merchant. mvc?Screen=PROD&Store_Code=ODT&Product_ Code=COC308-10&Category_Code=UDAT	9/30/2010	FDA approved Standard 300 ng/ml cut off	Relatively expensive Dipstick rather than cup	$31.87 per box; 10 tests per box	$3.19/test
http://www.americanbiomedica.com/products/ rapidone.html	10/12/2010	Uses SAMHSA cut-off levels FDA approved	Dipstick rather than cup Difficult to read results line	$57.50 for 50 tests	$1.14/test

Note: FDA, Food and Drug Administration; SAMHSA, Substance Abuse and Mental Health Services Administration.

Table 10.9 Additional Items for Urine Testing

Possible Items	Necessary or Not; Notes	Websites or Companies; Date Accessed; Contact Person, if Applicable	Price per Unit and Number in Unit (e.g., $10 for 50)	Cost per Test (e.g., $10/50 = $0.20 each)
Gloves	Mandatory			
Collection cups	Necessary for dipstick tests but not for test cups			
Temperature strips	Not necessary Some test cups contain temp. strips			
Adulterant strips	Not necessary Can test for pH, creatinine, glutaraldehyde, and/or nitrates			
Total cost per sample collected	Sum the cost per test column =			

abstinence is achieved, urine toxicology testing for cotinine can be used, which detects any smoking over longer, three- to four-day, intervals. The cost of urine cotinine testing typically runs about $9 per sample (e.g., Accutest NicAlert™, JANT Pharmacal Corporation, Encino, CA).

Similarly, alcohol monitoring will require at least one or more breathalyzers. There are many commercially available alcohol monitors that range vastly in price. Intoximeters (Intoximeters, Inc., St. Louis, MO) is a brand often used by law enforcement agencies, and a calibrator should also be purchased. The price for a high-quality breath alcohol monitor is about $500, and calibrators range from $30 to $150. With breathalyzer monitoring, the only other associated cost relates to breath tubes. These typically cost about $0.22 each.

In Table 10.10, indicate any such costs your program will require.

10.1.3.3 Overall Costs for Biological Testing

To come to an overall cost for sample monitoring in your CM protocol, you next will determine the total number of tests per patient. This number should be apparent in your CM protocol. For example, to reinforce cocaine abstinence twice weekly for a 12-week protocol would entail 24 tests per patient. If you were testing and reinforcing abstinence thrice weekly for 12 weeks, this schedule would require a maximum of 36 tests per patient. You then need to multiple the total number of tests by the number of patients by the cost of each test.

Table 10.10 Other Equipment Needed for a CM Program

Equipment	Website and Date Accessed	Notes (Pros)	Notes (Cons)	Cost per Unit and # In Unit (if applicable)	Costs per Equipment (or per test)

Sum of other equipment
and testing costs

Table 10.11 outlines steps to determine the overall costs of testing for a CM protocol. A sample is outlined when the cost of a single test is $1.14 and ancillary costs of gloves and collection cups are $0.20 per test, for a total of $1.34 per test. In this sample protocol, we are planning 24 tests per patient with 10 patients. This totals to an overall cost of $321.60 over the 12-week CM protocol.

Not all patients will submit the full 24 tests scheduled, so it is likely that the overall costs will be lower than what you are estimating. You can review current attendance and drop-out rates from patients similar to those you are planning on treating with CM. If current attendance rates are high (e.g., in some methadone or criminal justice mandated populations), you will probably need to budget the full costs of testing. If 12-week program completion rates in your population are low prior to implementing CM (e.g., 30%), you might safely estimate a 70% completion rate with the addition of CM. Thus, you could expect that your total costs in Table 10.11, Column G, would be reduced by about 30%. In the sample description reinforcing abstinence via urine testing, the estimated costs of biological testing could be as low as $321.60 × 0.70 = $225, assuming that, on average, patients submitted only about 16 or 17 of the total 24 urine samples for testing.

Once you have completed your estimation of the costs for biological testing over the course of your CM protocol, you can add those costs to the overall costs of the reinforcement. Remember that if you are not conducting biological testing or if the costs of biological testing are fully reimbursable, these costs will be $0.

$$\$\underline{\hspace{3cm}} + \$\underline{\hspace{3cm}} = \$\underline{\hspace{3cm}}$$

Overall cost of biological testing (Table 10.11, Column H)   Expected actual total reinforcement costs (bottom Section 10.1.2)   Total direct costs

For the sample CM protocol I am describing, the total direct costs of the CM program would be $1,904 ($321.60 for overall cost of biological testing + $1,582

Table 10.11 Steps to Determining Overall Monitoring Costs

Column	A	B	C	D	E	F	G	H
	Cost of One Test	Ancillary Costs per Test (Cup, Gloves)	Total Cost/Test (Column A + B)	# Tests/Patient (Table 9.8)	# Patients (Table 6.1)	Column C × D × E	Equipment (Table 10.10)	Total Cost (Column F + G)
Sample:								
Utox	$1.14	$0.20	$1.34	24	10	$321.60	$0	$321.60
Your CM program								

for expected actual total reinforcement costs). This is a full and probably conservative (or over-) estimate of how much money it would cost to implement prize CM with 10 methamphetamine-dependent patients.

Table 10.12 provides a review of all direct costs associated with the reinforcement system. In the top shaded section, I outline what the total costs would be for thrice-weekly methamphetamine testing for a 12-week period with 10 patients, assuming the usual voucher reinforcement system outlined in Table 8.1. After adjusting for 50% non-perfect performance, I would expect this system would award nearly $5,000 in vouchers across 10 patients. An additional $482 would be spent on urinalysis testing (assuming these costs are non-reimbursable). Thus, the total costs of usual voucher CM would be about $5,470. In contrast, a prize CM approach that treats the same number of patients for the same duration of time (but with a lower frequency of urinalysis testing) will cost less than half this amount.

If the amount you derived for your CM program seems reasonable, you can move to Section 3 in this chapter now. Alternatively, you can lower the costs by utilizing any of the methods described earlier. You can also consider reviewing Chapter 11, which gives examples related to generating funds for CM programs.

10.2 ESTIMATING COSTS FOR NAME-IN-THE-HAT PRIZE CM THAT REINFORCES GROUP ATTENDANCE

In estimating costs of the Name-in-the-hat prize CM procedure that reinforces group attendance, you will not estimate individual patient costs, but rather overall group costs because all reinforcement is conducted in a group setting. These costs will depend upon several features of your CM protocol: (1) the number of sessions in which prize draws occur, (2) the number of prize draws awarded per session, and (3) the cost per draw.

1. The easiest of these to determine is the number of sessions in which prizes will be awarded. This number should be stated in Table 9.9, in the bottom of the second column from the left. Indicate the number of group sessions in which you are planning on providing reinforcement here:_____.

   In the sample CM program I am outlining throughout the book, 100 patients will be exposed to prize CM across five different CM groups, each containing up to 20 persons. Each of the five groups meets 10 times, for a total of 50 CM sessions. (Note that if the CM were being done in only one group of 20 patients, this number would be substantially lower—10 CM sessions.)

2. If you are using the "typical" Name-in-the-hat prize CM procedure, you will award half as many prizes as there are persons in the group at

Table 10.12 Summary of Cost Estimates for Individually Reinforced CM Protocols

Column A	Column B	Column C	Column D	Column E	Column F	Column G	Column H
Maximum Reinforcement/ Patient	Cost/Draw (if applicable; blank if NA)	Number of Patients	Maximum Reinforcement Costs	Adjust for Non-Performance	Expected Total Cost	Total Cost of Testing and Equipment (if applicable)	Total Cost
Instruction: From Table 9.8, Cumulative Reinforcement	($1.93 or see Table 10.7)	Table 6.1	(Column A × B × C)	÷ 2	Column D ÷ E	Table 10.11 Column H	Column F + G
Voucher CM sample: $997.50	n.a.	10	$9,975.00	÷ 2	$4,987.50	$482.40	$5,469.90
Prize CM sample: 164 draws	$1.93	10	$3,165.20	÷ 2	$1,582.60	$321.60	$1,904.20
Your CM protocol:							

each session. Because you will not know attendance until you start the CM program, you will have to estimate it. In our sample program, we plan to allow up to 20 patients into each CM group, so the maximum number of attendees in group any given session will be 20, and half that many prizes will be awarded: 20 ÷ 2 = 10 prizes. If you are using this procedure, indicate the maximum number of patients in the CM group (which should be denoted in Table 9.9): _____ and divide by 2 = _____. (This number should be the same as the maximum draws per group noted in the right column of Table 9.9; however, it is not the cumulative total of that column.)

If you have decided to alter this typical procedure by awarding more (or fewer) prizes each week, then include the maximum number of patients in the group _____ (from Table 9.9) and multiply that number by the proportion of names you intend to draw. If you want to award as many prizes as there are persons in attendance (100%), you would multiply your maximum number of attendees by 1.0, which is the same as the number of attendees. If you want to award prizes to 70% as many patients as attended group, you should multiply the maximum number of attendees by 0.7. Alternatively, if you are awarding a set number of prize draws each session (regardless of level of attendance), then indicate that number here: _____. Now, indicate the number of prize draws that will be awarded at each CM session: _____.

Multiply the numbers derived from Section 10.2 items noted #1 and #2 to determine the total number of prize draws that will occur throughout your CM program.

_____ × _____ = _____
Number of sessions   Number of   Total number
in which prize draws   prize draws   of prize draws
will be awarded   per session

The total number of prize draws over the course of your CM intervention should be the same number as the cumulative total number of draws you derived at the bottom of the last right column in Table 9.9.

For our sample CM protocol, we have 50 CM sessions in which prize draws will be awarded × 10 prize draws per session, for a total of 500 prize draws for the 100 patients to be included. (Note that if we were implementing CM with only one group of patients, instead of in five different groups, the total number of prize draws would be one-fifth of 500, or 100.)

3. Finally, you need to determine the average cost for each prize draw. The system I am recommending is one in which 100 prize slips are present in the prize bowl. The breakdown of slips is as follows: 69 smalls,

Table 10.13   Typical Ratios of Prizes for Name-in-the-Hat Prize CM for Group Attendance

Number of Slips	Type of Slip	Maximum Value of Prize	Average Value of Prize	Probability of Drawing	Cost per Draw
69	Smalls	$1	$0.80	0.69	$0.55
20	Mediums	$5	$4.00	0.2	$0.80
10	Larges	$20	$18.00	0.1	$1.80
1	Jumbo	$100	$80.00	0.01	$0.80
Total					
100					$3.95

20 mediums, 10 larges, and one jumbo. The maximum cost for each respective type of prize should be $1, $5, $20, and $100. Although these are the suggested maximum costs, actual prices paid for items should average slightly lower than the maximum by purchasing items on sale or in bulk. The cost of the typical prize bowl for the Name-in-the-hat prize CM approach is as outlined in Table 10.13. Each draw costs, on average, $3.95.

Note that in this prize bowl, relative to the one described when behaviors are reinforced individually, there are no "good job" slips. The rationale for not including "good job" slips in prize bowls for the Name-in-the-hat prize CM approach is that not everyone wins a prize each session. If one's name gets drawn (which occurs only about half the time), that person then is guaranteed to win some sort of a prize. If a patient's name were drawn every other session, and that patient whose name was drawn had only had a one-in-two chance of winning a prize, the reinforcement schedule would be very lean indeed (a one-in-four chance of winning a prize).

In the Name-in-the-hat prize CM procedure I am recommending, proportions of winning slips, and especially the more valued items, are increased relative to the individual prize bowls outlined earlier. Remember that, on average, patients will have the chance of winning any sort of prize every other week in this system. In contrast, in individual CM systems, patients receive prizes on average every week, and after several weeks, they receive multiple prizes each week.

Table 10.12 describes the recommended prize bowl configuration, which results in an average cost of $3.95 per prize draw. If you take your total number of prize draws determined above and multiply that number by $3.95, you would determine the total costs of the procedure.

$$\frac{\text{Total number}}{\text{of prize draws}} \times \frac{\text{Cost per draw}}{\text{(e.g., \$3.95)}} = \frac{\text{Total}}{\text{program costs}}$$

For our sample CM protocol reinforcing group attendance, we have 500 prize draws in total × $3.95 per draw for a total program reinforcement cost of $1,975 to implement prize CM with 100 patients. Again, if we are using this same Name-in-the-hat prize CM procedure to reinforce group attendance in a much smaller group of patients, for example, for 20 patients instead of 100, the cost for CM implementation for 20 patients over a 10-week period would be $395.

If the number you derive seems too high, you can adjust the cost of each draw by altering the total number of slips in the bowl and/or the probabilities and average costs of each prize category. Caution should be extended in terms of eliminating the jumbo prize, because as noted earlier (Section 10.1.2), large valued items, even if at very low probabilities, are highly desired by patients. They also add relatively little to the costs. If $3.95 per draw is completely impractical for your CM program, consider increasing the total number of slips in the bowl, for example, to 500, so that the probability of winning a jumbo is reduced to 0.02% and the costs decreased to $0.16 per draw. Other prize categories could also be altered, but try not to make the large prizes available at very low frequencies. If all patients ever observe and experience is winning small prizes, your system is unlikely to be effective. Table 10.14 provides an alternate configuration of a prize bowl with lower costs per draw. You can type into the gray-shaded cells in the Excel version of this table to try to determine a reasonable cost per draw.

After you determine the cost per draw and multiply it by the total number of draws, you have a very good estimate (and likely a high estimate) of overall costs required. The reason why this estimate is higher than you will actually need to run the CM program is because you considered perfect attendance in determining the total number of draws awarded. If you estimated drawing

Table 10.14 Alternative Configuration of a Prize Bowl for Name-in-the-Hat Prize CM

Number of Slips	Type of Slip	Maximum Value of Prize	Average Value of Prize	Probability of Drawing	Cost per Draw
369	Smalls	$1	$0.80	0.738	$0.59
85	Mediums	$5	$4.00	0.17	$0.68
45	Larges	$20	$18.00	0.09	$1.62
1	Jumbo	$100	$80.00	0.002	$0.16
Total					
500					$3.05

Table 10.15 Summary of Cost Estimates for Name-in-the-Hat Prize CM for Group Attendance

Column A	Column B	Column C	Column D	Column E	Column F
Number of CM Groups per Week	# Weeks CM is in Effect	# Names Drawn/ CM Session	Total Prizes Awarded	Cost per Draw	Total Costs
(Table 9.9)	(Table 9.9)	(usually half of attendees; see Table 9.9)	= Columns A × B × C	From Table 10.13 or 10.14	= Column D × E
Sample protocol: 5	10	10	500	$3.95	$1,975
Your CM protocol					

10 names per week, you assumed 20 people per week attended. In reality, fewer than 20 people will attend each week, so you will draw fewer than 10 names and award fewer than 10 prizes. Thus, your overall total reinforcement cost estimate should be somewhat lower than the amount you calculated.

Table 10.15 provides a summary of how to determine cost estimates for Name-in-the-hat prize CM for reinforcing group attendance. You may want to double check your math by putting all the information into the same table to ensure you are deriving cost estimates appropriately.

If this amount seems too high, you may want to move to Chapter 11 to consider options for raising funds for CM programs. Although you can alter parameters of the reinforcement schedule to decrease costs, you may also consider some creative approaches to finance these programs, which ought to be fairly low if you are implementing the procedures outlined above.

10.3 ADMINISTRATIVE TIME FOR CM DELIVERY

In addition to the costs of reinforcement and biological testing (if applicable), the other "costs" associated with your CM protocol will entail personnel time. There will be time associated with learning and setting up CM and time for administering it. The time expectations will be greatest when you first implement CM, but they will eventually decrease and taper once you and the patients become familiar with it.

10.3.1 Administrative Time Estimates for the Name-in-the-Hat Prize CM Procedure for Reinforcing Group Attendance

The time associated with learning and setting up a CM program depends upon your familiarity with behavioral therapy and the complexity of your

CM protocol. A relatively simple CM protocol, such as the Name-in-the-hat prize CM procedure to reinforce group attendance, will probably require three to four hours for carefully reviewing Chapters 12, 14, and 15, and possibly another two to three hours in setting up the forms to suit your clinic's group structure if you are making any changes to the usual system. Prior to the first CM group, you should do a practice group with other clinicians (or your family members or friends). This will take about an hour, and it will take about an hour before the practice session to set up the prize bowl. Immediately before your first CM group with patients, you will spend about 30 minutes reviewing the tracking forms and preparing the name slips, and several hours shopping for prizes and stocking and inventorying the prizes.

Delivery of the CM occurs in a group, so CM administration with the patients adds no additional time. However, prior to each CM group, you will spend about 30 minutes to an hour preparing the envelopes and completing the pre-group attendance tracking form (see Chapter 15). Once you have had about three weeks' experience with the CM, the time necessary for preparation should decrease to less than 30 minutes per group. After each CM group, you will need to spend about 30 minutes to an hour reviewing your forms for accuracy and determining what, if anything, could have been done differently; this time may also include CM supervision (see Chapter 15). Shopping trips ought to occur about once a month, so long as you are purchasing sufficient quantities of desirable prizes. Thus, the overall time associated with Name-in-the-hat prize CM approach probably tapers to about four hours per month or less (one hour per week), with an additional two to three hours per month for shopping. These estimates were derived from informal discussions and estimates from 16 clinical programs that instituted the Name-in-the-hat procedure. A sample format for summing these overall costs is as shown in Table 10.16.

If you are utilizing the Name-in-the-hat prize CM procedure to reinforce group attendance, indicate your administrative time effort in hours per month in the lower portion of Table 10.16. You can use the estimates from the upper sample if they appear appropriate for your CM protocol and setting. If you are reinforcing attendance in a group that occurs more than weekly, then the estimate in the middle rows may need to increase accordingly.

10.3.2 Administrative Estimates for Individualized CM Protocols

Administrative time is going to be higher for individualized CM protocols than for group-based CM protocols. If you are meeting one-on-one with patients to monitor a behavior and reinforce it, this will require at least weekly meetings and up to twice- or thrice-daily meetings (e.g., for alcohol or initial nicotine abstinence). Such time commitments may be readily subsumed into your daily schedule if you are already meeting with patients with the same degree of

Table 10.16   Estimating Time for Name-in-the-Hat Prize CM for Group Attendance Administration

Time Estimate (Convert to Hrs/Month)	Activity	Notes
Sample: Name-in-the-hat CM		
0 hrs/month	Patient meetings for monitoring and reinforcement purposes	Meetings and reinforcement all occur in existing groups, so CM adds no additional time
2 hrs/month	Reinforcement preparation	Preparing name slips and tracking forms before groups (30 min/group, weekly groups)
2 hrs/month	Review of reinforcement delivery and supervision	Review how well reinforcement was administered (audiotapes, self-reflection) and supervision (30 min/week)
4 hrs/month	Shopping for prizes	After initial shopping, can restock monthly
8 hrs/month	TOTAL	Sum of three values in left column (0+2+2+4 = 8 hrs/month)
Your CM program	Activity	
	Patient meetings for monitoring and reinforcement purposes	
	Reinforcement preparation	
	Review reinforcement delivery, supervision	
	Shopping for prizes	
	Other(s): _____	
	_____	
	TOTAL	

regularity that you planned for your CM protocol. In such cases, CM will add no to negligible time costs.

On the other hand, CM may add fairly substantially to patient contact time if the CM visits represent additional meetings with patients, above and beyond what you are already doing. Although an individual CM meeting may only last 5 to 10 minutes, it needs to occur on a specified schedule, and such meetings can break up other activities and may be difficult to accomplish given competing demands on your time and the patient's time. If you or the patient is late for the CM meeting, rescheduling can become problematic (and may also impact reinforcement escalation). Further, CM visits can be difficult to accommodate if patients are in the clinic only briefly (e.g., in the case of methadone visits), and you are meeting with other patients when a CM patient arrives. In some clinics that have reinforced abstinence, a nurse or other staff member is dedicated to collecting biological specimens. But, you also want to be sure to deliver reinforcement as quickly as possible to the behavior. In this sense, meeting with one person to submit a sample and another to receive the reinforcement is not optimal, because of the inherent delays (and the need to meet with two individuals per monitoring session rather than one).

Although coordinating the meetings may be challenging, sample collection and awarding voucher or prize reinforcers usually takes only about 10 minutes, once both parties become familiar with the procedures. If you are testing and reinforcing abstinence twice weekly with five patients at a time, this totals 100 minutes of time per week. Such a time estimate may be over and above your current responsibilities, or it may be concurrent with non-CM responsibilities if you are already collecting samples twice a week.

Given your CM protocol and consideration of whether the meetings are in concert with, or in addition to, usual-care meetings, estimate your additional time expectations in Table 10.17.

In Row A, Column B, indicate the number of extra minutes you expect to meet with each CM patient each week. This is likely to be about 10 minutes per CM session, and if there are two CM sessions in a week, the time per week per patient would be $10 \times 2 = 20$ minutes per week. In our sample CM protocol, let's presume one of the CM sessions occurs concurrently with an individual therapy session and therefore does not add any extra time in terms of CM, but the second CM session each week is additional time spent for urine collection and reinforcement. In such a case, the overall number of minutes per week per patient is 10. (If all CM meetings are concurrent with existing patient meetings, this number will be 0.) Then, in Row A, Column C, divide that number by 60 to get an estimate in hours per week you will spend with each CM patient.

In Row B, Column C, indicate the number of CM patients you anticipate meeting with each week. Multiply the number of CM patients you plan to meet with each week by the hours per week you will spend in CM sessions to derive the total time in hours that CM administration will take each week. Remember, this number will be 0 if your CM meetings are concurrent with existing time you are already spending with patients. You will only have a time estimate greater than 0 if the CM adds new meeting times with patients. In the sample protocol, there are 10 CM patients per week × 0.167 additional hours per week for CM specific sessions, so the total per week for CM administration time is 1.67 hours, as noted in Row B, Column C.

You will also want to consider dedicating some time to keeping track of reinforcement, reviewing forms, and receiving supervision (Chapter 15). This

Table 10.17 Time Expectations for Administering Individualized CM

Row	Column A Sample Protocol	Column B Minutes/Week/Patient	Column C Hours/Week/Patient (/60)
A	Time per week for additional CM sessions with each CM patient	10 minutes/week with each CM patient	0.167 hours/week with each CM patient
B	Number of CM patients to meet with in a week	—	10 CM patients per week
C		Multiply Column C/Row A x Column C/Row B	Total time for CM administration: 1.67 hours/week
D	Time for review of CM delivery and supervision	—	0.5 hours/week for review and supervision
E	Shopping time	—	1 hours/week for shopping
F		Total weekly CM time:	3.17 total hours/week

Your CM protocol

Row	Column A Sample Protocol	Column B Minutes/Week/Patient	Column C Hours/Week/Patient (/60)
A	Time per week for additional CM sessions with each CM patient	_____ minutes/week with each CM patient	_____ hours/week with each CM patient
B	Number of CM patients to meet with in a week	—	_____ CM patients per week
C		Multiply Column C/Row A x Column C/Row B	Total time for CM administration: _____ hours/week for CM
D	Time for review of CM delivery and supervision	—	_____ hours/week for review and supervision
E	Shopping time	—	_____ hours/week for shopping
F		Total weekly CM time:	_____ total hours/week

estimate may be up to 1.5 hours a week if you have many CM patients, or as low as 0.5 hours per week if only a few CM patients will be participating at a time. Indicate in Row D, Column C, your estimate of time for managing forms and supervision in hours per week.

Shopping time should also be considered. The time needed for shopping depends in part on how many patients are enrolled in the CM protocol. If there are only a few CM patients participating at a time, shopping for prize CM should be only once a month. In prize CM, most items can be obtained at one to three shops (e.g., Walmart, fast food stores, and the local transit authority). In these cases, you would take the usual estimate of four hours per month (and adjust upward or downward if needed for very busy or small CM protocols, respectively) and derive a weekly estimate by dividing by four (i.e., one hour per week). Shopping estimates should be two or three hours per week (or more) if vouchers are used. For voucher CM, shopping would probably need to be done weekly, as it is more individually tailored. Due to personalized requests, voucher shopping may be substantively more extensive as it involves going to stores of patients' choices.

Finally, add up the values in Column C, Rows C + D + E, and put this number in Column C, Row F. This is the total amount of time per week CM should take. In our sample protocol, it is 3.17 hours per week. Remember that if you are using prize CM and shopping only once a month on average, most weeks you will require less than this amount of time, but about one week per month, you may need to dedicate a few hours exclusively to shopping. Also, if your CM meetings are concurrent with other patient meetings, this number ought to be fairly low, as only CM review/supervision and shopping estimates should factor into the time estimates.

If the amount of time estimated seems high, given your other clinical responsibilities, you may wish to reconsider the number of patients with whom you implement CM or other parameters associated with your CM protocol. Remember, you do not want to take on anything too onerous all at once, and you do not want to try to implement a novel approach that will increase stress. The best chance of success is if you design and implement a CM protocol that follows appropriate behavioral principles and that complements your existing clinical structure.

Chapter 11

Raising Funds to Support Contingency Management Interventions

As highlighted in this book, a concern about CM programs is the cost. In Chapter 10, you estimated the overall direct costs for reinforcers in your CM protocol, as well as the amount of time it will take you to initiate and manage CM once the program is up and running. These costs and time estimates may exceed available resources. If so, you can either scale back on your CM protocol and/or try to come up with unique methods to finance the program.

This chapter will detail options for raising funds for CM, along with advantages and disadvantages of each approach. It will include possibilities such as (a) soliciting donations (and with which populations this process may be best received); (b) writing for pilot, demonstration, or grant funding; (c) supporting initial CM costs with the expectations that increased reimbursement for attendance will occur; and (d) using fee rebates or having patients pay a deposit. These are not all the possible options, and you may come up with additional possibilities. The ultimate goal is to develop a CM protocol that is feasible given your financial and time resources.

11.1 SOLICITING DONATIONS FOR CM

There are real world examples of successful solicitations for donations to support CM programs. Some relevant experiences are described in this section.

In Spain, García-Rodríguez, Secades-Villa, Higgins, Fernández-Hermida, and Carballo (2008) evaluated the potential of soliciting donations for CM. They first surveyed patients about desired items and then developed lists of local vendors that sold those items. A coordinator contacted 136 companies. Initially, the coordinator telephoned managers, provided a brief explanation of the CM project, and requested specific goods or services (e.g., gift cards, items, or services). The coordinator followed up with a formal request by letter, fax, or e-mail, describing the project in more detail and the specified services. Two weeks later, a second telephone request was made, asking for a verbal commitment to donate. When the response was positive, a personal appointment was arranged, at which time the requested items were collected. In exchange for donations, local newspapers published notices of thanks. Copies of such announcements were sent to the companies along with a personalized thank-you letter. Of the 136 companies contacted, 52 (38%) provided donations. A total of $20,371 of goods and services were donated over a six-month period, and costs for soliciting the donations (staff time, fax, mailings) was estimated at $4,854. The mean value of a donation was $417. The minimum donation was about $50, and the maximum was $2,600.

Differences emerged in terms of the types of companies or institutions that were willing to help. Those that offered newspapers or magazines subscriptions were the most likely to offer services, and two of two (100%) such companies that were contacted donated. Other companies with a high donation rate included public transportation offices (three of four contacted, 75%) and leisure service businesses, such as museums, sport events, gyms, adventure sports, and travel companies; a total of 27 of 44 (67%) such businesses donated items or services. Lower participation rates were noted for companies that provided training courses (8 of 19 contacted, 42%), individual shops (eight of 26 contacted, 30%), restaurants (two of seven contacted, 28%), and beauty salons (two of eight contacted, 25%). No service stations (zero of eight asked) were willing to donate gasoline gift cards.

The company size was also related to donation rates. Smaller-sized businesses (family or local businesses) were more likely to contribute, with a participation rate of 50%. In contrast, 33 large organizations (franchises or institutions with more than 50 employees) were contacted for donations, and the proportion that cooperated was only 30%.

In addition, the time between contact and response was associated with donation rates. Among companies that took under a month to provide a definitive verbal response, 82% collaborated, whereas only 19% of those that took two to three months to decide eventually donated. A mean of four telephone calls (range two to 12) was made to the organizations, and no differences in the number of calls occurred between those who eventually donated and those who did not.

This experience suggests that businesses are willing to donate items, and the donations received were sufficient to finance a voucher CM program for 15 patients, in which patients could earn up to about $2,000 each in vouchers. With lower-cost prize procedures, this amount of donations would readily finance a very large-scale CM program. The Spanish experience may be somewhat unique in that this program was instituted in a small region of the country in which solicitations for donations were considered uncommon. In such venues, organizations may be more receptive. Nevertheless, these experiences also indicate that efforts may be best expended toward soliciting donations from smaller and mid-sized companies and businesses, rather than large businesses. Further, if favorable responses are not received fairly readily, it may be fruitful to move to other companies rather than to continue spending time with a company that is noncommittal about donating. Interestingly, in addition to the over $20,000 of donations received initially, a number of companies agreed to supply additional donations as items were selected by patients during the course of the CM program. Thus, subsequent donations may be easier to obtain, once an organization has been willing to provide goods or services.

In North America, the response rate to solicitation requests may be lower than it is in Spain, but it is still possible to finance CM programs via donations. Amass and Kamien (2004) describe attempts in two cities—Toronto and Los Angeles—to solicit donations for pregnant substance-abusing women. The procedures were similar to those described in Spain. Steps included (a) determining appropriate goods and services, (b) identifying potential sources of community sponsorship, (c) locating the correct person within an organization to approach for a donation, (d) constructing a donation solicitation package, (e) following up with phone calls and other contacts, and (f) sending thank-you notes to donors. In Toronto, 38 of 198 (19%) businesses contacted over a two-month period collectively donated $8,000 worth of goods and services. In Los Angeles, 95 of 369 (26%) contacts over a 34-month period yielded $161,000 of goods and services. In Toronto, 53% of donations were from manufacturers, 34% from local attractions/restaurants, and 13% from local retailers. In Los Angeles, donors were corporations (42%), individuals (17%), charitable groups (12%), local retailers (12%), theaters and cinemas (7%), local attractions (2%), restaurants (2%), and others (6%). Thus, some regional differences do exist, but across locations, acquisition of donations for CM programs is certainly possible.

The circumstances in which donations are most readily obtained occur when someone affiliated with the clinic has experiences with fundraising or has a direct connection with a fundraising or philanthropic organization. For example, if someone at your clinic or on your board of directors has a direct personal connection with a local business bureau, that business bureau may be readily willing and able to make a $2,000 or greater contribution to your clinic. Such funds can sustain a group-based prize CM protocol for a year or longer, depending on the number of patients to whom CM is being applied.

Without direct connections to such organizations, soliciting donations will be more challenging logistically. Phoning businesses or individuals for donations is possible, but it may take more hours than most people or clinics have available. If your clinic is non-profit, individuals will probably be more likely to donate than if it is for profit. The patient populations for which it will be easier to generate support are those with public health issues and concerns. For example, it may be easier to solicit donations for adolescents or mothers with children than for adult substance abusers. Obtaining donations for patients with chronic medical conditions such as HIV or hepatitis or for patients with severe psychiatric illnesses may be easier than for general substance-abusing populations or criminal justice system populations. Regardless of the population with whom you are working, soliciting donations is certainly possible to fully or at least partially offset reinforcement costs.

11.2 GRANT WRITING

Another possibility for soliciting funding for CM protocols involves writing local, state, or national grants for implementing innovative and evidence-based treatments. Local opportunities vary, but some websites that describe national funding opportunities, and search engines for regional grants at the time of this writing are noted in Table 11.1. As you search the web, you may be able to locate additional resources for grant funding.

Through the exercises in this book, you have determined the overall costs necessary, and you have explicitly specified the intervention and the target population. Via these efforts, you have already completed the beginnings of a grant proposal by specifying exactly what you plan to do. After reviewing specific grant requirements, you should readily be able to adapt your CM protocol into a grant proposal, which if successful, may cover costs associated with your CM protocol and possibly bring new resources to your clinic as well.

11.3 SELF-SUSTAINING CM

Depending on the population, clinical context, and reinforcers utilized, CM protocols can be self-sustaining. The most straightforward example is the Name-in-the-hat prize CM procedure for group attendance. If attendance increases by 20% to 40% and this increase results in higher rates of reimbursement, the CM protocol has the potential for generating resources. Some clinics have reported greater rates of reimbursement with higher retention and lower rates of unexcused absences, as well as improved transitions to lower level of care, after implementing CM.

To make a successful business case that your CM protocol may be cost neutral or even resource generating, you will need good records of attendance and financial reimbursement records before initiation of CM. Integration of CM on a relatively small scale (e.g., with two cohorts of patients) should provide reasonable projections for changes in attendance and reimbursement. The amount of funding necessary for one or two rounds of CM should be fairly low. Before requesting these start-up funds, you could determine the rate of increased attendance needed to offset the costs of the CM.

Table 11.1   Possible Sources of Grant Funding

Brief Description	Website
This is a government site with information about U.S. Department of Health & Human Services and selected other federal grant programs. It contains a helpful list of Frequently Asked Questions.	http://www.hhs.gov/asrt/og/ aboutog/grantsnet.html
The Foundation Center is an independent non-profit information clearinghouse. The Center's mission is to foster the collection, organization, analysis, and dissemination of information on foundations, corporate giving, and related subjects. This site allows foundation searches by state.	http://foundationcenter.org
Join Together is a project of the National Center on Addiction and Substance Abuse at Columbia University, and it is sponsored by the Robert Wood Johnson Foundation. It contains information about foundations that fund community projects, and you can search grant opportunities by state.	http://www.jointogether.org/news/ funding
ScanGrants is designed to facilitate the search for funding sources to enhance individual and community health. The funding sources listed are of interest to the health field: social workers, nurses, students, community-based health educators, and others. Funding sources include private foundations, corporations, businesses, and not-for-profit organizations. Finding and listing less traditional funding opportunities is a priority. Federal and state funding sources are typically not included on ScanGrants because they are readily available on other sites.	http://www.scangrants.com
This site offers information about grant writing, fundraising, and non-profit news services. It focuses on issues related to mental health and substance abuse programs, child and youth advocacy, Native American issues, and community health services. It provides examples of winning proposals, but registration is necessary to access some services.	www.grantsandfunding.net
The American Medical Association provides seed grants for grassroots public health projects that target the issue of healthy lifestyles, including alcohol, substance abuse, and smoking prevention. Over the years, the fund has provided over 200 grants totaling nearly $300,000 to projects throughout the United States.	http://www.ama-assn.org

(continued on next page)

Table 11.1 (continued) Possible Sources of Grant Funding	
Brief Description	*Website*
The Charles A. Frueauff Foundation's mission is to address pressing issues facing America by serving those who are diligently working to aid those who are less fortunate. It is about assisting those who are developing new ways of dealing with complex issues, including AIDS, poverty, and health care. The Foundation has provided grants in excess of $112,000,000 to more than 600 agencies and institutions, with an average grant size of $25,000. (Due to the weak economy, the Frueauff Foundation did not consider new proposals from first-time grant seekers in 2008 to 2009. Check for details related to funding possibilities after 2010.)	http://www.frueauff.org

Consider a clinic that receives an average of $15 for each patient who attends a group session. If there are 10 patients enrolled in the group, but average attendance is only four, the clinic is receiving an average of $60 per group session. A conservative estimate for improvement with the introduction of CM is six attendees. With six attendees, the average rate of reimbursement would be $90 per group. Over a 12-week period, this would be a total of $90/group × 12 groups = $1,080, which is an increase over the usual pre-CM expectation of reimbursement ($60/group × 12 groups = $720) of $360 ($1,080 − $720 = $360). The average expected costs of prizes awarded using Name-in-the-hat CM for once-weekly groups is $4/draw × three draws/week (if six people attend) × 12 weeks = $144. Subtracting expected overall costs from the increase in revenue translates to $360 in expected extra revenue minus the $144 used for reinforcers, or a net benefit of $216. Even after factoring in administrative costs, the program may still be cost neutral or produce modest cost savings, especially if introduced on a larger scale in which administrative costs are lower. Thus, CM appears to have the potential of being resource generating and likely worth the investment, especially if it improves patient outcomes. If these proportions can be extended to larger groups of patients, your chief financial officer may be swayed to provide more resources for CM in subsequent iterations.

11.4 UTILIZING FEE REBATES OR DEPOSITS

As discussed in earlier chapters, some CM protocols have successfully utilized fee rebate or deposit structures to finance CM protocols. These options are best tailored toward patient populations with greater economic resources, and they are rarely implemented in traditional substance abuse treatment settings with indigent or low-income groups. Patients who are on a sliding-fee scale or whose treatment is covered entirely by entitlements may not have the funds (or possibly the inclination) to invest their limited resources into a CM program, in which they would get small portions of the funds they contributed back as reinforcers. In such cases, these reinforcers would not be practical or feasible.

In contrast, this option may be well suited for middle-class and professional populations (recovering physicians, lawyers, airline pilots, etc.), and for others who are partially or fully mandated to treatment or who already pay fees for services (driver re-education, methadone maintenance, criminal justice, etc.). In these populations and settings, portions of fee rebates or deposit systems can be utilized to partially or fully cover the costs of the reinforcers.

To determine the feasibility of fee rebates in your population, you may want to start by investigating amounts patients currently pay. Review of financial records may reveal a $10 to $80 payment per session. If attendance rates appear fairly low (< 65%), it is possible that CM could improve attendance and hence reimbursement rates. Using the same logic as described in Section 11.3, on self-sustaining CM, consider reimbursement rates given current rates of attendance, and determine how these reimbursement rates may increase if CM improved attendance by 20% or more. If the costs of the CM are less than the projected improvements, the CM should be beneficial in your setting.

If you are considering utilizing funds from a deposit system, you may want to evaluate patients' responses to a questionnaire. A questionnaire similar to that in Exhibit 11.1 could be designed to address whether and how much of a deposit your patients would be willing to consider. I put in italicized font a sample behavior, which you may change depending on the behavior targeted for your change in your CM protocol. In this example, I show how non-returned deposits could be donated to charities disliked by the patients. Other options included pooling unearned deposits for use by the clinic itself (to upgrade the waiting room) or to use for reinforcement for other patients.

After tallying the responses from patients (ideally at least 20 or more), you can determine the point at which 50% would no longer agree to the deposit amount. Such an amount would probably be too high for patients to buy into, but lower values (to which over half the respondents indicated they "Maybe" or "Yes" would be interested in paying) may be appropriate for the deposit system.

Presume that 50 patients were surveyed, and 25 of them reported "Yes" they would or "Maybe" they would be willing to pay a $200 deposit or less. In this case, you would target your initial CM values per patient to be about $150 to $200. This would then be the maximum amount of funds available per patient

---

**EXHIBIT 11.1   SAMPLE PATIENT QUESTIONNAIRE
FOR A DEPOSIT CM SYSTEM**

Dear Patients,

We are considering a system in which individuals would put forth a monetary deposit to assist them with *staying abstinent from cocaine.* Such systems have been found effective for encouraging *abstinence.* Please indicate below your willingness to provide the amounts listed if you could get back the full amount of your deposit by *providing cocaine-negative samples throughout a four-month period.* In the event that you did not *provide cocaine-negative samples,* forfeited portions of your deposit would be *donated to a charity that you dislike (e.g., the opposite political party).*

I would be willing to pay a $15 deposit toward such a system.	No	Maybe	Yes
I would be willing to pay a $25 deposit toward such a system.	No	Maybe	Yes
I would be willing to pay a $50 deposit toward such a system.	No	Maybe	Yes
I would be willing to pay a $75 deposit toward such a system.	No	Maybe	Yes
I would be willing to pay a $100 deposit toward such a system.	No	Maybe	Yes
I would be willing to pay a $150 deposit toward such a system.	No	Maybe	Yes
I would be willing to pay a $200 deposit toward such a system.	No	Maybe	Yes
I would be willing to pay a $250 deposit toward such a system.	No	Maybe	Yes
I would be willing to pay a $300 deposit toward such a system.	No	Maybe	Yes
I would be willing to pay a $400 deposit toward such a system.	No	Maybe	Yes
I would be willing to pay a $500 deposit toward such a system.	No	Maybe	Yes
I would be willing to pay a $600 deposit toward such a system.	No	Maybe	Yes
I would be willing to pay a $750 deposit toward such a system.	No	Maybe	Yes
I would be willing to pay a $1,000 deposit toward such a system.	No	Maybe	Yes
I would be willing to pay a $1,250 deposit toward such a system.	No	Maybe	Yes
I would be willing to pay a $1,500 deposit toward such a system.	No	Maybe	Yes
I would be willing to pay a $2,000 deposit toward such a system.	No	Maybe	Yes
I would be willing to pay a $5,000 deposit toward such a system.	No	Maybe	Yes

for your CM protocol. If it fits within the budgeted amount you outlined in Chapter 10, your CM program should be self-sustaining. If it is too low, you would need to either alter your maximum reinforcement amount or come up with methods to subsidize the deposit system (i.e., with grant funding or other resources).

SUMMARY

Many clinicians and programs struggle with methods to fund CM programs, and it is one of the biggest challenges and obstacles to CM implementation. Although all situations are unique in some regards, there are reasonable options to fund CM, especially when utilizing low-cost approaches such as the individual prize CM approach and the Name-in-the-hat prize system for group attendance. With a little creativity (and sometimes a lot of perseverance), CM programs can be successfully implemented in community settings. Once the funds have been identified, the next steps relate to some practical issues in CM implementation, as outlined in the Chapter 12.

III

Implementing Contingency Management in Practice

Chapter 12

Getting Started

Stocking a Prize Cabinet and Obtaining Other Needed Supplies

Once your CM schedule is developed and costs of the CM program are determined and deemed appropriate, the actual process of CM implementation can begin. The first part of this chapter outlines items that are needed beyond the prizes themselves. Then, specific issues related to how to start a prize cabinet and maintain prize inventories are described. In terms of patient-specific issues, the chapter also outlines how to talk with eligible patients about participating in a CM program, how to explain non-participation to ineligible patients, and how to address common staff concerns. From this point forward in this book, I focus on two CM protocols: prize CM that reinforces abstinence individually and Name-in-the-hat prize CM that reinforces group attendance. CM protocols that utilize other reinforcement systems or reinforce other behaviors can adapt the relevant materials outlined below to address similar issues.

12.1 CM RELATED ITEMS

A number of items need to be obtained or created to start a CM program, beyond just the prizes themselves. These include a prize bowl, a lockable cabinet, and urine testing supplies (if applicable). I recommend you purchase the cabinet prior to obtaining the prizes, because you need a cabinet in which to store the prizes.

12.1.1 Prize Bowl

You can purchase a plastic fishbowl from a department or pet store. It should cost under $10 and be sufficiently large that you can put your (or a large) fist into it. You will also need 500 square (three-inch by three-inch) sticky pad pieces of paper (assuming your fishbowl contains 500 slips; see Chapter 10). All pieces of paper in your bowl should be of the same color (preferably a dark color so that the paper is opaque and you cannot see the writing through the other side of the paper). There is a reason to use only one color of paper in your bowl. If patients find out that the jumbo prize is on a pink slip of paper but there are also blue slips in the bowl, they will preferentially select pink slips.

You can either purchase a stamp set or simply write "small" on the appropriate number of these pieces of paper, given your probability configurations determined in Chapter 10. For the example reinforcing abstinence on an individual basis, you would write "small" on 209 of the 500 slips. You should write on the "sticky" side of the paper, so that you can then fold the sticky side together twice. The final piece of paper that goes in the bowl is one-fourth its original size and should be a perfect square.

You will also write or stamp the appropriate number of slips with the word "large." In our example, 40 slips are designated as large prizes. One slip has the word "jumbo."

The remaining slips (in this case, 250) state, "good job!" Although some therapists have wanted to include inspirational sayings on non-winning slips, you can see that it would require a great deal of imagination to come up with 250 inspirational sayings. It may also be difficult to fit sayings onto slips without being able to tell that some slips contained more writing than others.

For the example related to reinforcing group attendance using the Name-in-the-hat prize CM procedure, you would need only 100 square sticky pad pieces of paper for the prize bowl. You would write "small" on 69 of them, "medium" on 20, "large" on 10, and "jumbo" on one.

Some therapists have elected to print out slips of paper, rather than using the sticky pad method outlined above. If you choose to print out papers, it may actually end up being more complicated than writing them out by hand on sticky pads. It would be essential that all slips that you printed out were the exact same size and that you could not see the writing through the slips of paper. A cautionary tale comes from one clinic. They prepared regular white paper with letters G, S, L, and J printed on them. They put the 500 slips in a prize bowl, and within two weeks of initiating the CM program, patients were drawing larges over 50% of the time! The L symbol could be seen and distinguished from the Gs and Ss, even when the slips were folded. Hence, the patients quickly learned the contingencies—pick a slip that looks like it has an L on the inside.

Another cautionary note is to use the same colored pen (and handwriting or stamp) on each slip. As will be described later, in a section about how to prevent "cheating," the ink and handwriting can be utilized to identify any inappropriate picking behaviors (see Exhibit 12.3).

12.1.2 Other Stationery Supplies Needed for Name-in-the-Hat Prize CM

For Name-in-the-hat prize CM that reinforces group attendance, you will need additional sticky pad pieces of paper on which to write patients' names. As patients' names may go into the "hat" up to 1+2+3+4+5+6+7+8+9+10 = 55 times (for perfect attendance over a 10-week period), you may need up to 55 × 20 (1,100) slips if there are 20 patients to be enrolled in the CM program. For the name slips, I recommend using different colors every week (with some repeats in colors over time). You need to use the same color slips for every patient each week (otherwise, patients who draw the names from the hat may look for their own colored slips). However, you also ought to vary the color slips on a random basis so that patients do not know what color slip will be used on a given week (and try to insert additional name slips of their own; see Exhibit 12.3 later in this chapter on how to prevent inappropriate picking behaviors). Thus, you should purchase about five to 10 different colored sticky pads.

For this system, you will also need envelopes in which to place the patients' name slips and their reminder slips. You will need up to 10 envelopes per patient × 20 patients = 200 envelopes if it is a 10-week protocol with about 20 patients participating.

Finally, you will also need a "hat" into which you will place the name slips each week. Although technically you need not purchase a hat and can use any container, buying a plastic hat that can stand upside down (has a flat top) makes the program's name true to form. You can find plastic hats of this shape at a party store or online. A baseball cap may also work.

12.1.3 Lockable Prize Cabinet

Regardless of the form of prize CM you are instituting, you will need a fairly large cabinet that can house all your prizes, including the jumbo items that are often bulky (e.g., television, stereo). Preferably, the cabinet should have doors that open out and contain four or five shelves. It must be lockable. Examples of prize cabinets are shown in Figure 12.1.

The prize cabinet should be housed in a room that also gets locked. Ideally, it will be stored in a location in which only limited access is allowed or one that is so busy that any tampering would be readily noticed. You will probably not want to place a prize cabinet in an individual therapist's office, unless that is the only therapist using the cabinet. Otherwise, that therapist will be constantly interrupted each time a patient comes in to select prizes. Ideal locations are often areas near restrooms, in photocopy rooms, in group rooms, or in a lockable hallway closet or small office that is rarely used. In determining the location for the prize cabinet, one needs to consider ease of access in terms of prize selections for the patients immediately after having their results tested, along with considerations about the potential for theft. You certainly would not want to place a prize cabinet in the outside entryway of a clinic or in an area that cannot be well secured at night.

In setting up your prize cabinet, you will store all the small prizes on the top one to two shelves, mediums (if applicable) on another shelf, larges on

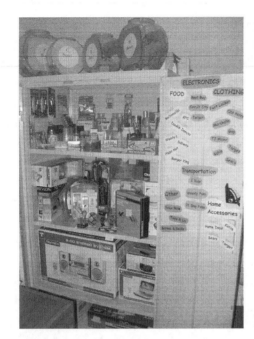 

FIGURE 12.1 Sample prize cabinets.

yet another shelf, and the jumbos on the bottom shelf. The prize cabinet should always be locked, and opened only during CM sessions. The prize bowl should also be locked inside the prize cabinet, when not in use, to prevent tampering.

12.1.4 Urine Testing Supplies

Before starting a CM program that reinforces abstinence, you may also need to purchase urine testing supplies. You will want to determine which onsite testing system to use. Some states, insurers, or clinics may have regulations about the use of urine testing procedures, and these should be consulted as necessary. In addition, costs can vary quite substantially across manufacturers. If you are planning on purchasing large numbers of urine tests, you may be able to get a reduced price. These issues were discussed in Chapter 10.

In addition to testing kits, you will need ancillary supplies: cups to collect the samples (unless you are using a test cup, as opposed to a test stick); gloves; and tamper devices you may choose to use, such as temperature strips, pH meters, or adulterant checks. Some test cups have temperature strips included on them, and temperature strips can also be purchased separately. AdultaCheck® (Scitech, Inc., Arden, NC) is a commercially available test strip that detects some common methods of urine adulteration. It does this by indicating whether the urine sample shows normal ranges for creatinine, pH, glutaraldehyde, and nitrates. If the test indicates that the urine is outside normal range on any of these features, it can be counted as invalid, as outlined later in Chapter 13.

12.2 STARTING A PRIZE CABINET

To begin the process of buying prizes for your prize cabinet, you must become familiar with your clinic's regulations on purchasing, and you need to decide what prizes to purchase. You will have to purchase the items, and you will need to initiate a system to keep track of your purchases. These steps are outlined below.

12.2.1 Clinic Regulations on Purchasing

Some clinics will have a credit card that you can use to directly purchase the items you want. In other cases, there may be a petty cash account, and you can obtain the desired amount of cash and purchase prizes. In still other situations, you need to buy items with your own funds and then submit a request for reimbursement. If this later situation arises, you will want to be sure you are aware of the time it takes to process reimbursements (often six to eight weeks). If you are implementing prize CM, staring a prize cabinet will cost about $400. If your clinic has no other mechanisms than to reimburse you, you may be carrying a $400 debt for up to two months. You may also want to be sure you receive something in writing that states that expenses will be reimbursable to ensure that you do not end up being responsible for the costs of some or all of the prizes.

No matter what the situation is in your clinic, you want to be sure to retain legible receipts for CM purchases. It is always a good idea to make a photocopy of the receipts for your own records in case the originals get lost. When shopping, you should not intermix personal shopping with CM shopping. Most clinics will look unfavorably on splitting items on a receipt. If you pick up something for yourself while shopping for prizes, just pay for it separately, so that your own items are not rung up on the same receipt as the CM prizes. If your clinic is not-for-profit, be sure to get a copy of its tax-exempt number so that you need not pay taxes on the prize purchases.

12.2.2 Determining Initial Prizes

As noted in earlier chapters, most prize bowls contain small ($1), large ($20), and jumbo ($100) items. Thus, you will need an ample selection of prizes in each category. There are two ways you can go about deciding upon prizes, and these two methods are not mutually exclusive. You can survey patients in your clinic (ideally those patients who would be eligible for your prize CM program; see Chapter 6) about two weeks before you begin the CM procedure. You can ask them to rank their top five favorite small prizes, top two or three favorite large prizes, and their favorite jumbo from the list in Exhibit

12.1. You can also ask patients to indicate other desirable options in each prize range.

Purchase those items that are checked by the greatest number of patients. This exercise may also get the patients excited about CM right before it begins. If you decide to survey patients, be sure everything else is ready to go with respect to the CM program before you conduct the survey. Patients will get discouraged if they are told prizes are on their way, and then they end up having to wait months before the CM program actually begins. Because many clinicians have experienced problems with respect to purchasing prizes and other CM supplies, it is imperative that everything but the prizes be ready to go before you survey patients about desired prizes. A second method, which can be combined with the survey method outlined in Exhibit 12.1, is to simply utilize the prize suggestions in Table 12.1 along with your and other clinician's judgment about what will be desired items. The items listed in Table 12.1 have been popular in a variety of clinics, and therefore, should be desired in your setting as well, although you can certainly substitute some items outlined in Exhibit 12.1 with those suggested in Table 12.1. In particular, the gift cards to restaurants and stores should be from nearby businesses.

It will cost about $400 to start a prize cabinet for about 15 patients. If the number of CM patients is substantially greater than 15, then the costs (and number of items purchased) should be adjusted upward. Prizes should be purchased in the categories described in Exhibit 12.1 and Table 12.1 and as outlined further below.

12.2.2.1 Small Prizes

Purchase at least 25 *different types* of small prizes, ranging from $0.50 to $1 in value. In total, spend about $40 on small prizes, such that you have 40 to 50 small items from which patients can choose. Include a large variety of selections (at least 25 different items with one to three prizes of each item). Don't buy more than a few of any one item. Once you know what the most popular items are, you can buy them in larger volume. Note that packs of socks or batteries can be broken into individual items and then may be purchased at fairly low costs. Examples of popular small items are toiletries (soaps, shampoos, ChapStick, toothbrushes, etc.), non-perishable food items, pens, stamps, candles, $1 gift cards to nearby fast food restaurants, and bus tokens.

12.2.2.2 Medium Prizes (Optional)

Although many prize bowls do not contain medium prizes per se, having some items valued at about $5 is helpful once patients begin earning multiple draws. These are referred to as "trade-up" prizes. If a patient selects five small prizes in one day, or between two and three different CM sessions, they can

EXHIBIT 12.1   SURVEY OF DESIRED PRIZES

Dear Patients,

We will be starting an incentive program shortly, in which patients can win prizes for _____ *(insert reinforced behavior)*. We are interested in finding out the prizes people most want. Please check your favorite choices from the lists below.

Small prizes: Please check your top 5 favorite items from the list below. You don't need to rank order them. Put a √ by the 5 items you like best.

____$1 gift cards to Dunkin' Donuts®
____$1 gift cards to McDonald's®
____$1 gift cards to Burger King®
____$1 gift cards to KFC®
____soaps
____shampoo
____conditioner
____tooth paste
____tooth brush
____dental floss
____comb
____bubble bath
____razors
____shaving gel
____barrettes
____hair clips
____candles
____pens
____pads of paper
____notebooks
____small calendars
____nail polish
____make-up
____chips
____rice boxes
____pasta boxes
____ChapStick®
____juice
____candies, indicate preferred types:_____
____socks
____note cards
____key rings
____coffee mugs
____kitchen items (spatulas, dish soap, sponges, etc.)
____tissue paper

(continued on next page)

____batteries
____light bulbs
____liquid hand soap
____mouthwash
____laundry detergent

Optional: Medium prizes. Please check (√) your top 3 favorite items from the list below.

____$5 gift cards to local movie theater
____$5 gift card to SUBWAY® or other food store (list favorites
here: _____)
____$5 gift card to local record/bookstore (list favorites
here: _____)
____$5 phone card
____round-trip subway/bus pass
____T-shirt
____address book
____make-up
____jewelry
____tools (hammer, screwdriver)
____nice notebooks, cards, stationery sets
____picture frame
____photo book
____board games
____popular kid's toys (list favorites here: _____)

Large prizes. Please check (√) your top 3 favorite items from the list below.

____$20 gift card to local movie theater (list favorites here: _____)
____$20 gift card to local restaurant (list favorites here: _____)
____$20 gift card to local record/bookstore (list favorites here: _____)
____$20 gift card to local home store or clothing store (list favorites here:
_____)
____$20 gift card to local department store (list favorites here: _____)
____$20 gift card to children's toy/clothing store (list favorites here:
_____)
____$20 in bus/subway tokens
____$20 phone calling card
____track-phone (that you buy pre-paid minutes for)
____cordless phone
____handheld CD player
____camera
____watch
____took kit
____electric drill
____pot and pan set
____dishes set

____teeth whitener set
____silverware set
____window fan
____coffee maker
____food processor
____hair dryer
____hair cutting kit
____curling iron
____alarm clock
____rice cooker
____sheet set
____towel set
____air mattress
____back massager
____lamp
____electric skillet
____toaster
____iron
____electric can opener

Jumbo prizes. Please check (√) your top two favorite items from the list below.

____television
____radio/stereo/boom box
____DVD player
____window air conditioner
____microwave
____PlayStation®
____iPod®

Please list any other items you would like to win as a prize: _____

_____

_____

choose something more valuable rather than five smalls. Because many stores will not sell gift cards in denominations under $5, and in some cities only round-trip bus/subway tokens are possible to purchase and cost well more than $1, it can be helpful to allow patients the flexibility of selecting between a small prize on the day they won it, or waiting until five smalls are won and then obtaining an item worth about $5 in value. If you decide to purchase $5 items, I recommend you purchase about five or 10 to start your cabinet, which ought to cost $25 to $50, depending on the number you purchase. Remember to not exceed $5 per prize. Also remember that patients must fully earn or draw five small slips prior to obtaining a medium prize.

Table 12.1 How to Start a Prize Cabinet

Small Prizes	Medium Prizes	Large Prizes	Jumbo Prizes
Buy 25 *different types* and at least 50 in total; do not exceed $1.20 per item	(Optional) 5 to 10 types; do not exceed $5 per item	Buy 8 to 12 items; do not exceed $20/item	Buy two items; average $60 to $80 each
10 $1 gift cards to Dunkin' Donuts	1 $5 gift card to Blockbuster™	4 $5 gift cards to a nearby movie theater	1 television
10 $1 gift cards to McDonald's	1 $5 gift card to Subway	4 $5 gift card to Home Depot®	1 radio/stereo system
5 $1 gift cards to KFC	1 $5 gift card to record or bookstore	4 $5 gift cards to JCPenney	
5 $1 gift cards to local stores that provide this denomination	1 $5 gift card to CVS (or other pharmacy) or nearby drug store	4 $5 gift cards Toys"R"Us®	
20 $1 bus tokens (if tokens cost >$2 in your area, do not use as small prizes, as you will go over budget)	1 $5 phone card		
1 soap	1 T-shirt	1 handheld CD player	
1 toothbrush	1 pair earrings	1 camera	
1 razor pack	1 hammer	1 tool kit	
1 candle	1 coffee mug	1 watch	
1 small calendar	1 photo album	1 pot and pan set	
1 box of Band-Aid® bandages		1 coffee pot	
2 Kleenex® boxes			
1 dental floss			
1 ChapStick			
1 lotion			
1 pen set			
1 notepad			
1 bubble bath			
1 nail clippers			
1 rice or pasta box			

Table 12.1 (continued)   How to Start a Prize Cabinet

Small Prizes

1 large bag of chips

4 men's socks

4 women's socks

1 candy bar

1 liquid hand soap

1 set of batteries

1 set of stamps

1 pack envelopes

1 light bulb package

12.2.2.3 Large Prizes

Purchase at least eight large prizes to start your prize cabinet. Do not exceed $160 for eight large prizes, and you should be able to purchase 10 large prizes for about $160. Have a mixture of gift cards and tangible items (e.g., no more than two to four gift cards to start). Buy only one of each type of large prize until you learn which large prizes are popular at your site. Do not exceed $20 in value for each large, although you should be able to get some desirable items worth $20 in value on sale for $10 to $15 or so. Examples of popular large items are gift cards to movie theaters, JCPenney, Marshalls, or other discount retail stores; tool kits; kitchen sets (pots and pens or dish or silverware sets); cameras; phone cards; and portable CD players. (I suggest purchasing four $5 gift cards rather than one $20 gift card so that they can be intermixed across the categories, especially if you are using medium prizes. Having smaller denomination gift cards also allows patients the flexibility of choosing two $5 movie theater cards and two $5 store cards when they draw a "large" slip.)

12.2.2.4 Jumbo Prizes

Purchase at least two jumbos to start your cabinet. You can buy them on sale and perhaps even get nice ones for $60, so you will be spending about $120 to $150 on jumbo prizes initially. Popular items are televisions and stereo systems. Other options are noted in Exhibit 12.1.

I recommend that you create a shopping list so that appropriate numbers of items in each category are obtained. Although you can certainly vary from your list once you are at a store (and perhaps something new sparks your interest or is on sale), a list will help guide selections.

You will probably be able to purchase the vast majority of items (everything other than specific gift cards) at one or two stores. Usually, a store like Target, Walmart, or Kmart will carry many of the items outlined above. For gift card purchases, an online company Stored Value Marketing (SVM), http://www. svmcards.com/home/?CFID=8796400&CFTOKEN=82344493, sells gift cards to a large selection of individual stores at a fairly nominal processing charge.

12.2.3 Issues Related to Prizes

As you develop your shopping list, there are some issues to consider. These are outlined in Exhibit 12.2.

12.2.4 Preventing Cheating During Draws

It is possible that a patient will try to beat the prize selection procedure. Typically, cheating involves palming the large and jumbo slips at one CM session and then trying to pass those slips off at the next session. It can also involve the patients creating their own prize slips (or name slips) and introducing them into the bowl when the therapist is not watching. Less direct forms of cheating involve seeing through the prize slips to determine the winning category or somehow demarking (crinkling or folding corners of) large and jumbo slips in the bowl so they can be recognized and drawn in the future. Although any one patient may just be very lucky, repeated winning of large and jumbo prizes by a single individual (e.g., for three sessions in a row) may suggest that the patient is somehow beating the system.

Prevention of cheating requires that the therapist set up and maintain the prize bowl appropriately so that slip categories cannot be distinguished and so that probabilities of winning remain at the set levels over time. It is also important to be vigilant always in observing and controlling draws. Ideally, you should check the number of prize slips at least monthly. The guidelines outlined in Exhibit 12.3 are suggested to ensure patients do not receive more large and jumbo prizes than the CM schedule calls for.

If you are implementing the guidelines presented in Exhibit 12.3 and still suspect cheating because a patient has been drawing multiple larges three or more sessions in a row, you can create a new prize bowl. In the new prize bowl, use the same colored slips, but alter the color of ink used to denote the prize category on the inside. For example, if your original bowl used yellow slips and the inside writing was blue, create a new bowl with yellow slips in which the inside writing is in red ink. In that manner, if a patient were passing bogus slips into the bowl, he would be used to yellow slips with blue writing. If at the next session, he drew yet another "large" and the ink color was blue, you would be certain he somehow cheated the system. You could inform him that you switched the bowl, and all the valid slips are now in red ink.

EXHIBIT 12.2   IMPORTANT NOTES ABOUT PRIZES

a. Avoid purchasing gift cards to stores that sell liquor, cigarettes, or weapons. Walmart sells weapons, and many restaurants and some grocery stores (and in some states, gasoline stations) sell liquor. Do not purchase gift cards to such stores, as patients may then purchase inappropriate items. You should also be cautious about purchasing general gift cards that are good at all stores in a mall or a geographical region. Many malls may have stores that sell drug paraphernalia or weapons.

b. Don't purchase only gift cards for your prize cabinet. Some patients prefer tangible items, and not all patients have transportation (or desire) to shop for themselves. Although it may appear to be simpler to purchase only gift cards as prizes, feedback from patients is that they like having choices (and wide choices) between actual items and gift cards. Similarly, don't only allow for online computer shopping as prize options as many patients are unfamiliar with (or untrusting of) online shopping. Online shopping also adds a delay to receipt of items.

c. Be cautious of expiration dates. Some gift cards may have expiration dates, or the card may lose value after a period of time of inactivity. Some stores go bankrupt. Thus, be careful that you do not buy too many gift certificates of one type, as they may not be selected or get used in time.

d. Consider food items carefully. Some clinics may not look favorably on patients consuming food and drink items in the clinic. If this is the case, don't buy candy bars, sodas, or other food items. Even if you do purchase food items, buy in small quantities, as food items expire.

e. Remove price stickers from items. Remove price stickers from purchased products after you log the items in your inventory (see Section 12.3). With price stickers on, patients may try to bargain with you or select the most expensive item and complain when less costly items are available. For example, a patient may want to combine a $15 large prize with five $1 prizes, or say, "It isn't fair Amy got an $18 pan set, and this one is only $12.99, so I should get seven smalls, too." With price stickers attached, they also may be able to return items to a store (e.g., and exchange it for cigarettes). To avoid these problems, it is simply easier to remove the tags.

A manner of handling cheating when you catch it is to be playful. For example,

> Ah, Sam, you've been getting me for a while, but now I got you! I changed the bowl this morning. All the slips in THIS bowl have red writing. Look. [Open 10 to 15 slips.] So, tell me how you pulled this over on me without my seeing? Don't worry, I'm not going to try to take away prizes you've already won. I just want to prevent someone else from doing this sort of thing in the future.

EXHIBIT 12.3   PREVENTING CHEATING DURING PRIZE DRAWS

1. Allow only one patient at a time to touch the prize bowl.
2. Be alert to any attempts at distraction, and maintain control of the prize bowl at all times (i.e., do not leave it unattended, and lock it in the prize cabinet when you are not using it).
3. Have the patient remove outer clothing with long sleeves and/or roll up long shirt sleeves on the arm he will use to pick slips with.
4. Have the patient open the palm of his hands toward you before and after selecting slips from the bowl.
5. Have the patient place the slip on the table right after picking it, and unfold it immediately (i.e., do not allow the patient to pick multiple slips then put some back in the bowl before opening them).
6. Put your hand in the bowl and mix up all the slips prior to each patient drawing. This process will ensure that probabilities remain random. (If a "large" slip is selected and then put back on the top of the slips, it will have a greater chance of being selected the next time.)
7. Inventory the prize slips at least once per month and preferably more often, especially if multiple therapists have been having patients draw from the same bowl.

In this case, the patient is unlikely to get defensive or argumentative, and you are likely to keep him engaged in treatment while at the same time addressing and stopping his (and possibly other patients') inappropriate behaviors.

12.3   KEEPING TRACK OF PRIZES

Once you purchase prizes, you want to institute a system to keep track of them. You need to be fiscally responsible for the prizes and make sure they are being used as intended to avoid potential problems if your clinic or the CM system were ever audited. Below are guidelines for keeping track of prizes.

12.3.1 Responsibilities of the CM Shopper(s)

As soon as prizes are purchased, the purchaser should enter all items into a Prize Inventory Log. These logs can be kept in hard copy format or electronically. Separate forms or databases are best for each category of prizes purchased (e.g., small, medium, large, and jumbo). For each item, the purchaser should enter a brief description, the date of purchase, the price (from the receipt, with any discounts applied), and SKU number (found on its packaging). Thus, each prize has its own line in the Prize Inventory Log, such that if five $1 McDonald's coupons are purchased, each of those five coupons is entered onto its own line. A sample Prize Inventory Log for small prizes is shown in Table 12.2. Similar forms should be created and used for other prize categories (medium, if applicable; large; and jumbo).

Table 12.2 Small Prize Inventory Log

Small Prize Description	Purchase Price	Record Control #	Purchase Date	Date Selected[a]	Therapist Responsible[b]	Audits						Any Problem Reports?
						Date[c]	Date[c]	Date[c]	Date[c]	Date[c]	Date[c]	

Note: Each prize, even every gift card, is entered on its own line. Continue on multiple sheets.

a   If not completed, the prize should be in the prize cabinet (see *** below).

b   Prize Release Forms for each therapist should be reconciled with each item delivered (i.e., check patient Prize Sign Out Sheets for each therapist to ensure the prize was taken; once verified, put date of verification in the Audit box for that item).

c   Audit dates: Dates the cabinet was checked to see that the item remains in cabinet if not selected, or that the item was delivered to a patient as noted on a Prize Release Form. (Once verified as delivered, no more audit date boxes will be checked for the item as it was appropriately delivered, and "NA" will be written in remaining audit date boxes.)

Items that are packaged together and separated (i.e., batteries, socks) should be listed separately in the Prize Inventory Log, one on each line in the appropriate category. For example, if a six-pack of socks were purchased for $4.98 and broken into six pairs for six small items, each pair of socks would be entered onto its own line in the Prize Inventory Log. For the column in which the inventory control number is to be listed, the purchaser would list the SKU number from the package of socks, and add a,b,c,d,e,f to the end of the SKU number to denote how many divisions of the package occurred—in this case, six. Any items that do not have an identifying SKU number should have a SKU number assigned. For example, if a box of candy bars is purchased, SKU numbers, such as #111a, #111b, #111c, and #111d, can be made up for use for the four candy bars (a,b,c, and d) in that box (designated #111). The purchaser will need to add control numbers to each candy bar, so they can be tracked in the cabinet as well. Finally, the adjusted and actual cost of each item should be entered on each row, so that the $4.98 package of six socks would result in a cost of $4.98 ÷ 6 = $0.83 each. For a four-pack of candy bars that costs $2, each bar would be listed at $0.50. This Prize Inventory Log should be used throughout the duration of the CM project, constantly being updated and monitored as outlined below.

12.3.2 Responsibilities of the CM Therapist(s)

After logging inventory into the Prize Inventory Log, the CM therapist should keep all prizes in a secure, locked cabinet. Each time a prize is taken by a patient, there should be two separate written records of the transaction: (1) the Tracking Form (detailed in Chapter 15, indicating number of draws earned and outcomes in terms of prize categories, i.e., small, large, or jumbo), and (2) the Prize Release Form (Table 12.3) outlined below. The Tracking Form contains outcomes of the draws, not the actual prizes selected, which is what the Prize Release Form is designed to monitor.

The Prize Release Form includes items that have been taken, SKU numbers of items, handwritten initials (by both patient and therapist), and the date the patient accepted the item. In individual CM protocols (i.e., that reinforce abstinence), each patient has his or her own Prize Release Form to maintain confidentiality so that patients do not see what other patients received in terms of prizes (which correlates with abstinence achieved). In group-based CM protocols (i.e., that reinforce attendance), each group could have a Prize Release Form, as confidentiality cannot be maintained in such situations.

The CM therapist uses the Prize Release Forms to update the Prize Inventory Log after each prize is awarded. Thus, after having the patient initial for each item received on the Prize Release Form, the therapist should immediately document the removal of that item in the Prize Inventory Log (Table 12.2). In the middle columns of the Prize Inventory Log, the therapist should indicate

Table 12.3 Prize Release Form

Patient: _____

By my initials below, I indicate that I received the following prizes:

Prize Category	Specific Item	Record #	Date Received	Patient Initials	Therapist Initials	Date Therapist Recorded on PIL	Date Supervisor Checked (PIL/Tracking)	Problems?

PIL = Prize Inventory Log.

the date the item was taken by a patient, and the therapist should initial the Prize Inventory Log.

12.3.3 Responsibilities of the CM Supervisor

I recommend that one individual (other than the person doing the shopping and the CM administration) be in charge of prize inventory oversight. The reason for a separation of responsibilities is to ensure that if the clinic were audited, there would be appropriate documentation of how CM funds were being spent.

This supervisor should check the accuracy of the Prize Inventory Log (Table 12.2) against the purchase receipt for the items. The supervisor should also file a copy of original receipts in a binder. Most likely, original receipts will be required so that the shopper can be reimbursed. Even if the clinic has a credit card for purchasing, it is still important to retain original receipts.

The supervisor should also conduct at least quarterly audits (and as frequently as weekly during initial stages of CM implementation to quickly correct any problems) of the purchasing protocol. In the audit, the supervisor should check the contents of the prize cabinet against the Prize Inventory Log (Table 12.2) and the Prize Release Forms (Table 12.3), which in turn should be checked against patients' Tracking Forms (see Chapter 15).

Specifically, any item not indicated as having been selected on the Prize Inventory Log should be in the prize cabinet. Any item recorded as having been selected should be double checked with that therapist's patients' Prize Release Forms. This process entails matching the item description and SKU number and date awarded. Information on a patient's Prize Release Form should also be back checked with the Tracking Form to ensure that a patient who received a prize on a day was awarded prize draws on that day. (Note that to maintain confidentiality, the actual patients who selected specific prizes are not listed on the Prize Inventory Log.)

A correctly accounted for selected item on the Prize Inventory Log would include the description of the item, its SKU, date of selection of that item, and the therapist's name who gave that prize to a patient. A correctly completed Prize Release Form must include date, item name, SKU, type of prize (i.e., small, large, or jumbo), initials of the patient receiving the prize, and therapist's initials. Further, for items selected on a given date on the Prize Release Form, the Tracking Form for that patient on that date should be checked; the patient should have earned at least as many draws as prizes were selected that day, and outcomes of draws on the Tracking Form ought to match the prize categories awarded on the Prize Release Form for that day.

All items that remain in the prize cabinet should be listed on the Prize Inventory Form and noted as still available by virtue of not having been signed out. If items are in the prize cabinet that do not appear in the Prize Inventory

Log, that scenario would suggest someone purchased prizes without logging them into the system.

Conversely, any items that are no longer in the prize cabinet but are not indicated as selected on the Prize Inventory Log are most likely items that a therapist forgot to log out. These cases should be noted in the Prize Inventory Log (highlight and comment on the cell of the missing item). The supervisor can go back to Prize Release Forms to see if any contain the missing item, and discuss with the CM therapist that each item awarded to a patient needs to be signed out in the Prize Inventory Log as well. Clearly, tracking down unaccounted-for merchandise will be more difficult when more therapists are involved in the CM program. In some cases, the supervisor may be unable to account for a missing item, but if records are checked diligently, this should be a rare event. Typically, less than 1% to 2% of the inventory should be unaccounted for, unless there was a theft of merchandise. If theft does occur or is suspected, police should be notified and reports filed accordingly.

The supervisor should record dates of each audit on the Prize Inventory log, with each item dated as checked. Note that once an item is selected by a patient, and the supervisor double checks this information with the Prize Release Forms and Tracking Forms, the item need not be checked again in the future. At that point, the reconciliation of that item is considered completed.

After each audit, the supervisor should create a written audit report, citing any protocol-associated problems. The resolution (if possible) for each issue should be stated, and corrective actions should be discussed with CM therapists who make errors in terms of logging prizes into or out of the system. If audits are conducted diligently and frequently (e.g., weekly in the beginning, followed by monthly and then quarterly) during initial stages of CM implementation, problems can be quickly addressed and corrected. When feedback is consistent, therapists will get into good habits regarding the tracking of prizes, and then audits can occur as infrequently as quarterly if issues are not arising during more frequent audits.

If CM therapists are appropriately logging in and out prizes, full audits may be eventually forgone in favor of random audits. In random audits, a supervisor would simply check a portion of the inventory that was purchased (e.g., select 20 random items from different sales receipts) and ensure that each of those items is either still in the cabinet or was appropriately awarded to patients. So long as no problems are uncovered during random audits, the clinic directors may feel comfortable that theft of merchandise is not occurring.

12.4 BEGINNING A CM PROGRAM

After you have prepared everything for your CM protocol, you will begin identifying appropriate patients and presenting CM to them. In Chapter 6, you reviewed your clinic records to get a sense of the number of patients who meet criteria for your CM protocol. Once the program is finalized and all the materials are ready, you can begin discussing CM with them.

I recommend NOT discussing CM with patients until all set-up work is completed. If you describe a CM program to patients, they will get excited about it. If it then takes four weeks for the urine toxicology test kits to arrive, or if you have difficulty accessing clinic funds to purchase prizes, the excitement will wear off. Patients will be disappointed if it takes too long to get the program up and running. Once you are actually ready to start, patients you may have approached earlier may have completed or dropped out of treatment. Thus, do not begin discussing the CM with patients until everything is in place and ready to go.

12.4.1 Describing CM to Eligible Patients

Once you have settled on your CM protocol, you should write up a brief description of it. This description should be about one page in length, with the goal of explaining the system in an easily understandable manner. A sample description is below (Exhibit 12.4) for a CM protocol that applies the prize CM system for reinforcing abstinence from methamphetamine. For an example related to reinforcing attendance in a group setting, see Chapter 14.

The description given in Exhibit 12.4 would need to be adjusted to accommodate differences in target behaviors, reinforcers, durations and frequencies of monitoring, and so forth. Nevertheless, this example provides a structured method for describing CM to patients.

You should review your CM description with patients and answer any questions they have. Unless CM is being implemented clinic wide, you would allow patients the option of participating or not participating in the program as described in the next section. If more than 10% of the patients you identify for CM decline participation, you should reconsider how you are describing the program. The vast majority of eligible patients should want to participate in a CM program. Only if the program is presented in a negative light, or if patients perceive it as somehow interfering with other needs (e.g., if they worry that CM urine sample results may be shared with the legal system), should they decline participation. With CM, patients only have a chance of gaining something—prizes and improved recovery! It is in this light that you should present CM to patients.

12.4.2 Describing CM to Ineligible Patients

Unless your CM program is being implemented clinic wide, patients (perhaps the vast majority) will not be eligible for your initial CM program. The ones who are participating are likely to discuss it with others. It is important to be prepared about how to handle non-participation. Below are guidelines and examples about how to explain ineligibility.

EXHIBIT 12.4   CM DESCRIPTION REINFORCING ABSTINENCE

Dear _____,

We are beginning a program that provides the chance to win prizes for achieving and maintaining abstinence from methamphetamine. Twice a week, you will provide urine samples, which may be observed by a same-sex staff member and which will be tested for methamphetamine.

Each time your urine sample tests negative for methamphetamine, you will receive at least one draw from a prize bowl, with a 50% chance of winning a prize. The prizes you can win range in value from $1 to $100. Prizes include such things as gift cards to fast food restaurants, bus tokens, kitchen sets, clothing items, tools, TVs, and stereos. Each time you win a prize, you can select from options in the category (small, large, or jumbo). We also encourage you to make suggestions for other prizes you would like to win.

For your first negative sample, you will get one draw from the prize bowl. If the next sample tests negative, you will get two draws that day. If three samples test negative three times in a row, you will get three draws. The number of draws earned increases by one for each sample in a row that tests negative until you reach a maximum of eight draws (after four full weeks of abstinence).

If ever you fail to provide a valid sample on a scheduled testing day or a sample tests positive for methamphetamine, you will get no draws that day. The next day you test negative, the number of draws you earn resets to one. You can then start earning increasing draws for each negative sample in a row, up to a maximum of eight draws.

Absences on scheduled testing days reset draws. If you cannot come to the clinic on a scheduled testing day, you must obtain permission for the absence by calling at least 24 hours in advance and providing written documentation for a valid absence (a doctor's or lawyer's note).

If all 24 of your scheduled samples (two per week) test negative for methamphetamine over the next 12 weeks, you can earn up to 164 draws. You would have an average likelihood of winning about $316 worth of prizes.

To try out the system, you will get to draw until you win a prize the first day you provide a sample, regardless of its results. If your first sample tests negative, you will earn your first abstinence draw that day as well. The more negative samples you give, the greater your chances are of winning prizes and the better your recovery will be. We hope you are interested in participating in this program!

---

1. Do not indicate why a patient is ineligible (otherwise, patients may learn the eligibility criteria and attempt to portray themselves in a manner consistent with those criteria).
2. Make decisions about CM participation global rather than specific or person based.
3. Inform ineligible patients that they may have an opportunity to participate in the future.

A sample manner of discussing ineligibility for a CM program is as follows:

Patient: I want to get into that new program here—that one where you win prizes.

Therapist: That is becoming a very popular program. A lot of people want to be involved in it. But, unfortunately, we only have funding to use it with a small number of patients right now. If it works with them, we're hoping to expand it to more patients in the future.

Patient: Why can't I be in it now? John is in it. Why can he do it, and I can't?

Therapist: No one person makes decisions about who joins the program. It's based on a lot of factors, and your friend might have just gotten lucky in terms of being chosen this time around. I'm glad you are interested in it, though. I'm going to tell the supervisor of the program about all the demand, in hopes we can get more money to expand it.

In this dialogue, you can see that the therapist did not get defensive with the patient. She maintained her ground but did not reveal the inclusion criteria for the CM program. Instead, she made it appear as though it related to a committee decision and to luck. She also validated the patient's desires to participate. It is likely that the patient was satisfied with this response and did not feel singled out or discriminated against in terms of eligibility.

12.4.3 Describing CM to Staff

You may have designed a CM protocol that only one clinician (you!) will implement. Alternatively, you may have developed one in which multiple clinicians are involved. All clinicians at your site may have jointly participated in the CM development process, or only a portion of the clinicians. Unless all have been involved from the outset, you are likely to encounter questions and concerns about CM by other staff.

For staff who are not participating in the CM protocol, you may want to present the program and its rationale at a staff meeting a few weeks before implementation. At such a meeting, you would want to describe the rationale for CM using material described in Chapters 2 through 4, along with describing the specific CM protocol you will be implementing. For this latter section, you can show staff the same overview letter you will use with the patients.

You will also want to be prepared for questions. Some commonly voiced questions and concerns are outlined in Exhibit 12.5, along with responses to them.

When you first describe CM to the staff at your clinic, you are likely to encounter some, if not all, of the concerns outlined. Having responses to issues as they are raised is one way to open dialogue about concerns and increase

EXHIBIT 12.5 COMMONLY VOICED CONCERNS ABOUT CM

1. Isn't it unethical to be paying people to do what they should be doing anyway?

Ethics is a branch of philosophy that relates to the study of what is right and wrong or moral and immoral. Whereas some people may argue that it is "wrong" to provide prizes or other reinforcers to substance abusers who submit negative urine samples or who come to treatment, it may also be considered "wrong" or "immoral" to withhold an efficacious intervention from patients. CM has been repeatedly demonstrated efficacious in treating substance-abusing patients. In fact, a meta-analysis of psychosocial interventions finds CM to be the *most* efficacious treatment for substance abusers (Dutra et al., 2008). In other areas of medicine and health care, "unethical" is a term rarely (if ever) applied to efficacious interventions, and it is unclear why efficacious interventions should be withheld or considered inappropriate for patients who abuse substances.

2. Isn't prize CM like gambling?

Although prize CM contains an element of chance, it is not gambling. By definition, gambling entails risking something of value. With prize CM, patients risk nothing. No evidence indicates gambling problems develop with prize CM. Researchers have followed thousands of patients in CM projects and assessed gambling before, during, and after participating in CM. There have been no cases of pathological gambling developing in any CM-treated patients (Alessi & Petry, 2010; Petry, Kolodner, et al. 2006). Although no data suggest that prize CM is harmful, patients in recovery from pathological gambling should not be included in prize CM programs, as it has not been studied in these patients.

3. Won't use of other, non-reinforced substances increase?

If a CM program reinforces attendance (or abstinence from one drug), then attendance (or abstinence from that drug) should increase. Although (other) drug use could persist when patients are earning prizes for attendance (or abstinence from one substance), this rarely happens. Most patients' drug use will decrease when they are engaging in positive behaviors like coming to groups (or abstaining from another drug). In addition, no CM studies have reported increases in other drug use when abstinence from any one drug is reinforced (Kadden, Litt, Kabela-Cormier, & Petry, 2009). If use of the most problematic drug decreases, other drug use is likely to decrease or remain constant. Further, usual clinic practices will apply to all CM patients. If a patient arrives intoxicated, standard procedures will be in place, such as calling police or emergency services and not allowing access to clinic services (including CM). If patients test positive for other substances on clinic urine testing procedures, use of those substances should be handled clinically, in the usual fashion.

(continued on next page)

4. Won't patients just sell the reinforcers and buy drugs?

If patients buy drugs with their reinforcers, they would test positive at their next CM session and be ineligible for additional reinforcement if an abstinence-based reinforcement procedure was in place. In addition, the amount of reinforcement they would be eligible for at the next CM session in which they tested negative would reset to a low value. Exchanging reinforcers for drugs is therefore an uncommon event in CM programs that reinforce abstinence. If a patient were participating in a CM program that reinforced attendance, it is unlikely that he would attend group after recently having used. If he did, usual clinic policies related to intoxication and substance use would apply; an intoxicated patient would be asked to leave the group and would be ineligible for reinforcement that day, which in turn would reset subsequent reinforcement magnitudes. Patients with high levels of continued drug use should be referred to higher levels of care (which may not involve CM). Studies have demonstrated that drug use is rare after patients receive research incentives, even when such incentives are provided in cash and are of large magnitudes (e.g., Festinger et al., 2005). If you do suspect a patient is selling reinforcers, you should discuss it with him and encourage selection of prizes that he desires to keep.

5. I/Others didn't get prizes for not using. Why should they?

Some people may feel that substance abusers do not deserve special treatment, in the form of opportunities to earn prizes. Although some patients with drug use disorders do cease using without CM treatments, many do not. Outcomes of substance-abusing patients are marred by high rates of attrition and frequent relapse. CM is an efficacious intervention for improving outcomes of substance-abusing patients. By implementing CM, more patients should have better outcomes, which is the ultimate goal of all treatments. CM is an adjunct to other forms of care, and it can be applied in conjunction with virtually any form of therapy to improve outcomes.

6. Won't external reinforcers like prizes reduce internal motivation to change?

External reinforcers foster behavior change. After being paired with prizes or vouchers, attendance at groups (or abstinence from drugs) may become reinforcing in its own right. Many patients state they initially attend (stop using) only for the prizes. Once they begin attending treatment regularly and cease using drugs, these become meaningful behaviors, and the prizes are no longer as salient. Researchers have measured internal motivation to change in response to standard care and standard care plus CM. CM had no adverse impact on motivation to change (Ledgerwood & Petry, 2006).

7. What happens after CM ends?

Many clinicians express concern that when CM ends, patients will drop out of treatment or relapse. This is not typically what happens. Most patients prepare for the ending of CM, and a strong predictor of long-term abstinence is the longest duration of abstinence achieved during treatment (Higgins, Badger, et al., 2000; Petry, Alessi, et al., 2005; Petry, Martin, et al., 2005; Petry, Peirce, et al., 2005; Petry et al., 2007). In CM programs reinforcing attendance, many former CM patients continue attending CM groups, even when they are no longer eligible for prizes. They act as mentors to new CM patients. In all CM programs, patients should be reminded about, and prepared for, the ending of CM (see Chapters 13 and 14). Providing certificates on the last day of CM is a good way to celebrate successful completion of a CM program (see Chapters 13 and 14 for examples). Petry, Kelley, Brennan, and Sierra (2008) provide a description of case examples of how patients handled the ending of a CM program and maintained long-term abstinence.

buy-in from your colleagues, who will make their opinions known to patients, subtly or overtly, once CM begins. Many of the initially most vocal opponents of CM can become some of the strongest supporters of CM once it is implemented and they observe directly patients responding favorably. However, in order for patients to respond positively, the CM program must be designed in a manner consistent with behavioral principles and implemented with appropriate adherence and competence, as outlined in the next chapters.

Implementation Guide for Reinforcing Abstinence Using Prize Contingency Management

In this chapter, I provide detailed instructions on how to implement a prize CM program that reinforces abstinence. The guidelines are adapted from an unpublished manual from the NIDA CTN trials (Petry & Stitzer, 2003). I describe a 12-week CM protocol that reinforces abstinence from methamphetamine, with twice-weekly urine testing. If you are reinforcing abstinence from another substance, instituting a different duration of reinforcement (e.g., 16 weeks), or implementing a system that monitors samples more frequently (e.g., Monday-Wednesday-Friday), you will need to make minor modifications to the procedures described.

The guidelines are written under the assumption that you understand the rationale behind the details of the CM program. Thus, earlier chapters should be consulted as necessary if you are unclear about the reason for reinforcing abstinence from a single substance; instituting CM for a 12-week period, including escalating prize draws with reset features; or utilizing the stated numbers and probabilities of slips in the prize bowl.

13.1 GENERAL OVERVIEW

In CM sessions, patients who test negative for the targeted substance—in this case, methamphetamine—earn draws from a prize bowl. The number of draws increases by one for each successive negative sample submitted up to a maximum of eight draws per negative sample. Patients are tested twice weekly for methamphetamine, using an onsite testing system, and they receive reinforcement (the chance to draw for a prize) immediately upon testing negative for the targeted substance. Missed, invalid, or refused samples result in no draws that day and a reset to one draw for the next methamphetamine-negative sample submitted. The system is in place for 12 weeks, after which time the patients are no longer eligible to receive reinforcement.

With this prize CM system, the longer a patient remains abstinent, the more likely it is that she will receive prizes. Because draws escalate with successive negative samples, the probability of winning prizes increases each time a negative sample is submitted. Throughout CM treatment, it is important that you continuously remind patients how much they have to gain by staying abstinent—better recovery, enhanced self-esteem, improved functioning in other life areas (e.g., family, work, health), and increased chances of winning prizes. Although one clear focus of CM treatment is on tangible prizes, emphasizing other positive changes associated with abstinence is also important.

Some general guidelines related to CM sessions are useful, and a manual by Ledgerwood and Petry (2010) available at http://contingencymanagement.uchc.edu/index.html provides extensive instructions for administering CM sessions competently (see also Chapter 15). Typically, CM sessions are short (five to 10 minutes). They involve collection of a urine specimen, reading results with the patient, and describing consequences of the results with respect to draws. Sample CM sessions are outlined in this chapter.

13.1.1 How to Integrate CM with Other Treatment

The CM can be done as a brief stand-alone session, or it can occur in the beginning of a more typical counseling session. I do not recommend conducting the CM component at the end of a lengthier (e.g., 30 or 50 minutes) session, because throughout the session, patients will be thinking about the prizes they may win. Patients are less likely to focus on the other important non-CM components of the session if the CM is withheld until the end.

Whether CM sessions are brief or more extended, maintaining an upbeat and positive attitude is important. You should give the patients praise for coming to treatment and for keeping their appointments, even if they have recently used, or even if they are late for the appointment. CM is all about positive reinforcement for positive behaviors, no matter how seemingly small the appropriate steps a patient may be taking are. In each CM session in which a patient tests negative for a targeted substance, the patient should be told that he or she is doing a great job remaining abstinent (if applicable). If the patient does not test negative, you should encourage and congratulate him or her for coming into treatment, because attending treatment is an important aspect of recovery as well. The CM therapist should also be supportive for any other positive activities that a patient may report (e.g., going on a job interview, improving health, etc.).

Counselors or other staff, such as nurses, technicians, interns, or other trained personnel, can conduct CM sessions. If CM is separate from standard therapy, a staff member other than the primary counselor can administer all aspects of the CM. In such cases, the CM therapist should avoid talking extensively about patients' difficulties. Although brief casual conversions are fine, if patients are utilizing a brief CM session to talk about crises and other life difficulties, the CM counselor can listen empathetically and express sympathy, but keep the conversation to a minimum—just a few minutes. The main goal in these cases is to focus CM sessions on CM issues, and other counseling should occur in its usual way. When patients bring up difficulties to a CM therapist, the CM therapist is advised to encourage the patients to make an appointment with their primary counselor to discuss the issue, raise the concern at their next group counseling session, or, in urgent circumstances (e.g., danger to oneself or others), escort the patients to the primary counselor's office for further discussions.

On the other hand, if CM is integrated during individual counseling sessions, then therapists would be conducting CM during the course of usual care sessions. Any non-CM-related issues that arise would be dealt with in the standard way. Because the CM should only take five to 10 minutes once the therapist and patient are accustomed to it, there should be plenty of time for other aspects of standard counseling (e.g., cognitive-behavioral therapy, 12-step treatment, daily planning, etc.). If individual counseling occurs only once per week, but the CM occurs twice weekly, one weekly appointment can be short (10 minutes) and the other more extended. If non-critical issues arose during the CM-only appointment, the therapist would indicate that she would be happy to discuss that issue in more detail at the next lengthier appointment. The CM should not detract from the standard care component of treatment; instead, it should enhance usual care because patients should be more likely to attend scheduled sessions and participate actively in them, especially if they are maintaining abstinence and receiving positive reinforcement for doing so.

13.1.2 Potentially Troublesome Interactions

Although most CM sessions go smoothly and patients know what to expect, some patients may become argumentative or demanding, especially if things do not go their way. It is important that the CM therapist be as supportive and nonconfrontational as possible, while maintaining the principles of CM. Flexibility is encouraged, so long as the CM therapist does not violate basic features of CM: monitoring the target behavior at the appropriate frequency, reinforcing objective evidence of behavior change at the specified magnitude and frequency, and withholding reinforcement when the target behavior does not occur.

Typically, if patients do not like what is happening with CM (or other aspects of treatment), they will simply leave. In the case of CM, absenteeism can be particularly troubling because it results in immediate loss of reinforcement and resetting of future reinforcement. As noted earlier, CM is designed to positively reinforce behavior change, so if a patient does not earn tangible reinforcers (i.e., draws), it is critically important that the CM therapist provide social reinforcement for any other positive behavior exhibited. The CM therapist should always keep in mind that coming to treatment is a very positive behavior that ought to be encouraged.

Throughout this chapter, I provide examples of potentially troublesome interactions that have actually occurred with CM patients and ways to handle them. Please refer back to this chapter for pointers after you encounter difficult situations with patients. Although you may have to "act on the spot" when a patient is present, you may be able to think of new ways to handle similar difficult situations in the future. Reviewing this chapter and discussing the interaction with another clinician familiar with CM may be helpful as well.

13.2 IMPLEMENTING CM: DISCUSSIONS WITH PATIENTS

13.2.1 Talking with Patients about CM before the First CM Session

In Chapter 6, you considered the number of patients for your first CM protocol. You may have also reviewed your clinic records to ascertain the availability of patients for the CM program you designed. Not all patients whom you originally thought would benefit from CM may be involved in treatment when you are ready to initiate your CM program. In addition, some patients who are eligible for CM may not want to participate because of scheduling conflicts, skepticism, or concerns that CM will be "too much work" or that they are "too busy."

The more aligned your standard clinical operations are with CM procedures, the less likely it is that patients will not desire to participate. For example, if all patients at your clinic are expected to provide urine samples twice a week as part of standard care, patients will be unlikely to consider the urine sample testing requirements to be an additional burden. In contrast, in a clinic that rarely or only once a month collects urine samples, patients may consider the increased urine testing to be onerous and perhaps even adverse, especially if they suspect the results could be shared with a legal organization (courts, probation/parole officers, children's protection agencies) or employer. In these cases, you may need to consider offering CM to more patients to obtain the number necessary for your first round of CM implementation. Alternatively, and if possible in your setting, increasing the frequency of standard urine testing procedures would diminish differential expectations between CM and non-CM procedures.

Once you identify a patient who may be suitable for your CM protocol, you will want to review his records to ensure appropriateness for the CM program. For example, if you are planning to use CM only with patients who began outpatient treatment within 30 days and who self-report methamphetamine use at least three days in the past month before treatment, you would want to ensure the potential patient meets these criteria before discussing CM with him.

If your standard intake procedures assess pathological gambling, you would want to check the patient's responses to such questions. Patients in recovery from pathological gambling should be excluded from prize CM programs, as discussed in Chapter 12. If your usual procedures do not address gambling, you would have a conversation with the patient similar to this:

> We are starting a new program, and you might be eligible for it. I need to ask you a couple of questions to find out if the program is right for you. Tell me about your drug use in the month before you started treatment here. What drugs did you use, and how often? … Now, I want to ask you a little about gambling. By gambling I mean lottery, scratch ticket, bingo, sports betting, slots, horse racing, and anything like that. How often do you gamble? Are you in recovery from a gambling problem? That is, have you stopped gambling because you had serious problems with it in the past? (Or, Do you want to stop gambling [if the patient indicated recent heavy gambling]?)

Patients who appear appropriate for the CM protocol because they meet the criteria designed (in this case, the appropriate drug use histories and are not in recovery from, or desire to stop, pathological gambling) would be eligible for the CM program. Those found ineligible would be thanked for their time and interest and referred for other treatment if appropriate.

An example of speaking with an ineligible patient is the following:

> Thanks for meeting with me and telling me a bit about yourself. Only a small number of patients actually qualify for this program so we end up asking these questions to a lot of people. It doesn't seem that my program would be right for you, but I'm sure the services you are receiving at the clinic will be helpful for you as you work on your recovery from alcohol problems. We'll all be here to help you any way we can. I think your next group starts in about 15 minutes. Do you want me to show you how to get back to the meeting room?

In the case of ineligibility for CM because of gambling problems that a patient is currently struggling with, you may say something like this:

> I'm glad you told me about the struggle you are having with gambling. While this clinic doesn't have any specific groups for gambling, I urge you to discuss your gambling with your primary

counselor. Linda can help you with that, and in addition, I have this brochure that describes a private gambling treatment clinic if you are interested.

Note that in the cases of ineligibility outlined above, the CM therapist did not indicate why the patient was ineligible for the new CM program. If word got out that only individuals with methamphetamine use, or only those who are not in recovery from gambling problems, get the opportunity to win prizes, then patients may alter their self-reports to fit into the CM program. In addition, in neither of these cases are the prizes themselves mentioned to the patients until the patients are deemed appropriate for participation.

For eligible patients, you would explain the CM program to them in more detail. You should have a one-page handout available to hand to them, similar to that outlined in Chapter 12, Exhibit 12.4.

As noted in the dialogue below, you should show the prizes displayed in the cabinet. Be sure the patient looks at and handles prizes in it. Explain that there are small, large, and jumbo prizes, and that they will get to win them by providing methamphetamine-negative urine samples. Ask the patient what he sees in the cabinet right now that he would like. The reason for having the patient identify a desired prize is to demonstrate concretely the type of items he can obtain in the CM program. The discussion may go something like this:

> Tom, I have a new program for a select number of patients at this clinic, and you qualify for it. Let me tell you a little about it, because I think it may really help you with your recovery. The program involves contingency management therapy, which basically means I will be providing you with the chance to win prizes every time you test negative for methamphetamine. Prizes include such things as $1 gift cards to fast food restaurants, bus tokens, socks, food items, and toiletry items like shaving cream, shampoos, and soaps. These are small prizes in this program. You would also have the chance to win large items like tool kits, CD players, sweatshirts, fans, cameras, coffee makers, and $20 gift cards to a variety of stores. One prize that you could win is a jumbo prize; it is your choice of a TV, iPod, or air conditioner. Let me show you some of these prizes I have available.

Show the prize cabinet to Tom, and encourage him to handle items in it. Answer questions about the items that arise.

> To win these prizes, what you'll need to do is provide methamphetamine-negative urine samples over the next 12 weeks.

If you are interested in this program, I will collect urine samples from you twice a week on Tuesdays, when you are already scheduled to come in for groups, and on Fridays, when you usually meet with me. Each time you give a sample that tests negative for methamphetamine, you will get to draw from this fishbowl (show bowl) and you will have a 50/50 chance of winning a prize. In addition, the more often you test negative for methamphetamine, the greater your chances of winning prizes will be. For every sample in a row you leave that tests negative for methamphetamine, you get increasing draws from the bowl. So, if you test negative today, which is Tuesday, you get one draw, and if you are negative again on Friday, you get two draws on that day. The week after that, if you are negative on Tuesday, you'd get three draws, and then four draws that Friday, and so on. You can get up to eight draws at a time.

We think this system is very useful for helping patients with drug problems. Many research studies have shown this system to be very effective in decreasing drug use, so it should help you with your recovery. If this sounds like something you are interested in, I can tell you a little more about the program.

If the patient appears interested in the program and wants to hear more about it, you would continue the conversation similarly to that outlined below.

Great. I'm glad this sounds like something you are interested in. Let me tell you a bit more about it. I have this sheet here that details the program, and I'm going to go over it with you. You can ask any questions you have.

13.2.2 The First CM Session/Priming Reinforcement

Providing a reinforcer in the first CM session (see also Chapter 9, "Priming Reinforcers") can help garner patients' interest in CM and provide them experience with the reinforcers. If the patient desires to participate in the CM program, you can start CM with him or her right away. You can state something to the effect of the following:

Therapist: Great. We can start today. I'll take a urine sample from you, and if it is negative for methamphetamine, you will earn one draw. In addition, the very first day you leave a sample—so this happens just today—you get free draws until you win your first prize. If the first winning slip you draw says "small," you'll get to choose whichever small prize you like. If it states "large," you'll select a large prize, and then you can get that camera that you wanted. And, if you're really lucky, you may even draw a jumbo prize your first time, and can leave with the TV that you like. You get to "draw until you win" just once, and after that, you'll need to test negative from methamphetamine to earn draws. So, if you test negative for methamphetamine today, you'll get to draw until you win, plus get an additional draw. Sound good? Let's have you do your first "draw until you win" draw now. Pick one slip from my fishbowl here.

Patient: I have one slip. It says "good job" on it.

Therapist: Half of the slips in the bowl say you are doing a good job, but they don't result in a prize. Because you get to draw until you win your first day, you get to select another slip. Here you go, make another selection from the bowl.

Patient: This one says, "small." Does that mean I won a prize?

Therapist: It sure does! You won a small prize. Let's go back over to the prize cabinet and you can select a small prize. All these things on the top two shelves are small prizes. Take another look, and see what you'd like most for today. There's no rush here. Go ahead and take your time to decide.

Patient: Hmmm. There are lots of things to choose from. But, I think I want a McDonald's coupon. I like that new coffee they have, and I think I can even get it for a dollar.

Therapist: That sounds good. Here you go. I just need you to sign out for the prizes you take on this sheet. It will also help remind you of all the great things you've won over time.

After the patient has selected his first prize from the "draw until you win" primer draw, the therapist instructs him to sign for it on the Prize Release Form (Table 12.6). Then, the therapist may move onto the collection and screening of the urine sample. An example of how this dialogue may go is the following:

Therapist: So you've gotten your first prize, and you'll have a chance to draw once more if your urine sample tests negative for methamphetamine today. Let's go into the restroom, and I'll collect a urine sample from you, okay?

Patient: All right.

Therapist: This is the testing system we use for the reward program. When I put the test stick into your sample, it will read either negative or positive for methamphetamine. It only takes about 30 seconds. Here it is. The strip says you are negative for methamphetamine. Excellent! That means you get another draw today. Let's go back to my office, and you can draw again. Then, I'll review with you how you can win even more prizes.

Patient: Okay, one more draw. Great. I got another small.

Therapist: Good. What else on those top two shelves would you like to have?

After the patient selects another prize from the appropriate category, the therapist would again have him sign for it. If the patient had drawn a "good job" slip, the therapist would have reminded him that not every pick results in a prize, but half of them do. In either case, the therapist should then explain that if the patient tests negative for methamphetamine on the next day he is due in for urine testing, he will get two draws and have a 50% chance of winning a prize every time he draws. In addition, the therapist should ask the patient what prizes he sees that he would like to work for next. For example,

Therapist: If you remain abstinent and test negative for methamphetamine on Friday, you will earn two draws, which means you'll have a pretty good chance of winning another prize then. Remember how I told you draws go up for each day in the row you test negative? So, you earned one draw today, and you'll get two on Friday if you test negative for methamphetamine. Other than the TV, what is something else you see in the prize cabinet you'd like to work for?

After the patient has decided upon a prize he wants to work toward, you should remind him of a few key points about the CM. As noted above, he will earn increasing draws for sustained abstinence. On the other hand, missed samples or positive samples break the string of escalating draws. In the first session, it is often best to simply mention these issues briefly and then bring them up again at the next session. An example is the following:

Therapist: I'm glad you see a lot of prizes that you'd like to have. Let me just remind you of how you can increase your chances of winning them. As I mentioned earlier, your draws will increase every time you provide negative samples in a row, and you can earn up to eight draws at a time once you've provided about a month's worth of methamphetamine-negative samples. That would mean you'd have a good chance of winning a large prize every week once you get up to 16 draws in a week. But, to get that many draws, you need to come in and see me each time you are scheduled for a sample, and give me a negative sample each time. If you ever provided a positive sample, or if you ever didn't come to clinic one day that you were supposed to give me a sample, that would mean you get no draws that day, and the number of draws possible would drop back down to one draw the next time you tested negative for methamphetamine. So, it's really important that you come in and see me each time you are supposed to leave a sample, every Tuesday and Friday. If there is ever a reason you can't be here on a scheduled testing day, you have to let me know ahead of time. If you have a doctor's appointment or something like that, you need to tell me ahead of time so we can arrange alternate testing so that your draws don't drop back to one. Sound fair?

The preceding dialogue is relevant when the patient tests negative for methamphetamine the first testing session. If the patient tests positive for the targeted substance, review the results with him as before, and encourage him to refrain from using methamphetamine between now and his next scheduled testing day so that he can get a draw at the next session. A sample dialogue is the following:

Therapist: I know you said you haven't used since Saturday, but unfortunately, as you can see here by the marking, your sample today is not negative for methamphetamine, so it hasn't cleared out of your system yet. Therefore, I can't give you any more draws today. However, if you don't use between now and Friday, you should test negative for methamphetamine then. The first time you test negative for methamphetamine, you'll earn one draw from the prize bowl, and if the next sample is negative, draws will go to two, and then three, and then so on up to eight. You have 12 weeks in this program, so there are lots of opportunities to win the camera and the other prizes you were looking at.

At the end of each CM session, it is important to congratulate patients for being abstinent, if applicable, and for coming to treatment if they are not yet abstinent or if they have recently slipped and used. You should also remind patients when they are next due for urine sample testing and the number of draws they can have at that time if they are abstinent. A reminder form should also be provided to patients at each CM visit. An example appears below in Exhibit 13.1. (The exact substance from which abstinence is being reinforced

---

EXHIBIT 13.1   REINFORCEMENT REMINDER FORM

You earned ____ chances of winning a prize today
for providing negative samples _____ times in a row.
If you provide a negative sample on _____,
you will earn ____ chances of winning a prize.
You can do it!

---

is purposefully not mentioned on the slip to maintain confidentiality in case someone found the slip in the patient's wallet or purse. Nevertheless, you should clearly state the substance for which reinforcement is contingent when delivering the slip.)

The first CM session may end with a discussion such as the following:

Therapist: I'm really glad I'm going to be working with you in this program for the next 12 weeks. Here is your reminder form indicating that you can earn two draws on Friday if you test negative for methamphetamine then. I look forward to seeing you Friday at 11:00.

13.2.3 The Second CM Session

When the patient arrives at their next CM session, you should welcome him and inquire briefly about how he has been. Casual conversation in the context of a CM session is good. On the other hand, CM sessions are designed to be short, so the meeting should be fairly directed. There are eight things you should cover in every CM session:

1. Collect the sample.
2. Test the sample.
3. Show the patient the results of the sample.
4. State the number of draws earned at that session.
5. Inquire about desired prizes.
6. Discuss any drug use or urges to use.
7. Remind the patient of the next CM session.
8. State the number of draws possible at the next CM session.

In addition to the eight issues that should be covered in every CM session, you will also have the patient draw and select and sign out any prizes if she tested negative for the target substance. A sample CM dialogue in the second CM session may go something like this:

Therapist: Kim, I'm glad to see you again. How have you been doing?
Patient: Oh, I'm good.
Therapist: I'm glad to hear it. What we'll do today is just like we did on Tuesday. I'll collect an observed urine sample from you, we'll test it together, and then you'll get two draws if the sample tests negative for methamphetamine. Are you able to provide a sample now?
Patient: Yeah, sure.

After accompanying Kim to the restroom and observing the sample submission process (see Section 13.3.1, this chapter), you may test the sample in the restroom with Kim or in another appropriate area (e.g., laboratory testing area), disposing materials immediately after the testing.

Therapist: As you can see here, your sample today again tests negative for methamphetamine. That is great news! I know you are working really hard on your recovery, and this shows how well you're doing. A negative sample also means you'll earn two draws today. Let's go back to my office and see what you win.

   Here is the fishbowl—the same bowl from before. Each time before you draw, I am going to ask you to roll up your sleeves and show me the palm of your hand. It's just a rule we have about drawing slips (see Exhibit 12.3). Okay, great. Now, go ahead and make your two draws. Hopefully, you'll draw some winning slips today.

Patient: I got a "good job," darn. And, a "small."

Therapist: A small is good! Here again are the two shelves with small prizes on them. Take a look, and let me know what you'd like to have today. There is no rush to decide.

Patient: I already know what I want. I'll take this toothpaste.

Therapist: Toothpaste, that sounds good.

Patient: Yeah, my tube at home is running out. I guess this is good timing.

Therapist: Sure is. And, what about other prizes? Are there other things you see you'd like to work for? Or other suggestions for prizes I may not have in there yet?

Patient: Well, that watch is nice, and the silverware set.

Therapist: Yes, those are large prizes, and as you earn more draws you'll increase your chances of winning large prizes. Let me review the program with you. You earned two draws today and got some toothpaste for your prize. Next Tuesday, when you are due to see me again, you can earn three draws so long as you test negative for methamphetamine. And, on Friday next week, you could get up to four draws. The draws will keep going up and up until you get to the maximum of eight, and at that time you'd be drawing 16 times a week—eight on Tuesdays and eight on Fridays. With 16 draws, you'll have a very good chance of winning large prizes.

Patient: Yeah, I remember that part.

Therapist: And, just as a reminder, now that you are earning more draws, it's really important that if ever you can't make it in on a scheduled testing day—a Tuesday or Friday—you need to let me know ahead of time. Otherwise, a missing sample will be considered positive with respect to the draws, and you'd go back down to one draw.

Patient: I remember you told me that last time. I'll be here again next Tuesday.

Therapist: Great, because I want you to get as many draws as possible. How many draws will you get on Tuesday if you test negative for methamphetamine?

Patient: Three, right?

Therapist: Yes, that is correct. And, you've already been abstinent for a week, which is a great accomplishment. How has it been for you? Have you had any urges or temptations to use since you started this program?

Patient: No, I've been keeping busy. Haven't used a thing. Not even a drop of alcohol.

Therapist: That is good to hear. You know if you ever are having urges, it's important that you talk with someone about them. You can do that in group here, or call your sponsor.

Patient: I know. Look I have to get to group in a couple minutes.

Therapist: Sure, we are just about done here. All I need for you to do is to sign for the toothpaste. And, I'll see you Tuesday at 10:00, and you can get three draws if you test negative for methamphetamine, as it says here on your reminder card.

The preceding example addressed all of the eight issues outlined for an ideal CM session. The entire interaction took less than 10 minutes. The therapist was focused, yet engaged, and enthusiastic and supportive of the patient.

The interaction would be similar, minus draws and prize awarding aspects, if the patient had tested positive for methamphetamine. Below, a CM session is outlined for a positive sample.

Therapist: Hi, Amy. I'm glad you are here and right on time. How are things going?

Patient: Okay, I guess. I'm here.

Therapist: You are here, and that's great. Coming to treatment is the first step of recovery. Let's go to the restroom, and I'll get a urine sample from you, just like we did last time.

Once the sample is collected, the therapist would screen it immediately and inform the patient about the results and the consequences in terms of draws.

Therapist: Amy, from our test, you can see here that your sample isn't negative for methamphetamine today. This means I can't give you any draws today. Do you want to tell me what happened?

Patient: I ran into an old friend of mine over the weekend. She had some meth. We used. That was all.

Therapist: Thanks for being honest about your use. I know that can be hard to do. Coming back to treatment after using is really a big step, so I think it shows good progress that you came here today. I think you should talk a bit about your use in group today. The other group members should be able to give you some advice on how to handle old using friends. Do you think you'll be able to talk about this in group this morning?

Patient: I guess so. That's why I'm here.

Therapist: I'm glad you want to work on your recovery. And, I will see you again on Friday this week, same time—10:00. If you don't use between now and then, you should test negative for methamphetamine and earn a draw at that time. I got some new prizes over the weekend. Do you want to take a look and see if anything catches your eye?

Patient: I don't really feel like it right now. I got to get to group.

Therapist: I understand. I think it was the digital camera and MP3 player you were interested in, right?

Patient: Yeah, those would be good.

Therapist: If you test negative on Friday, you'll have a chance of earning those and other great prizes. Here is your reminder form, and I'll see you Friday at 10:00.

The preceding example describes an interchange between a therapist and a patient who tested positive and appeared somewhat depressed over her use. The therapist was supportive about positive behaviors that the patient had made (coming to treatment) and encouraged the patient to discuss her recent use in group. The conversation about self-reported drug use was brief, but the therapist acknowledged the use in an appropriate manner.

When offered to identify desired prizes, the patient declined. The therapist did not push the issue, but reminded the patient of items she expressed interest in the prior session. In this manner, the therapist addressed the issue of desire for prizes in an appropriate fashion given the circumstances. If patients continuously test positive and do not earn draws for several sessions, they may no longer see the prizes as salient. Thus, it is important to remind patients of prizes and regenerate interest in them, ideally at every session, with this being one such example.

The two examples outlined earlier address the two possible situations that could occur in the second CM session—a patient testing negative and a patient testing positive. In each case, the therapist adeptly addressed all eight issues identified as important for CM sessions. As patients move further into a CM program, other possibilities exist such as excused and unexcused absences, and breaks in a string of negative samples. The next section describes these scenarios.

13.2.4 CM Sessions Three to 22

In this section, I provide sample CM sessions for the most common situations that arise during CM interventions: (a) a patient who has achieved a series of negative samples and continues to test negative for the targeted substance,

(b) a patient who provides a positive sample after having a long duration of abstinence, (c) a patient who returns after having an unexcused or missed sample, and (d) a patient who returns after an excused absence.

13.2.4.1 Continued Negative Samples

As patients come in and consistently provide samples negative for the targeted substance, CM sessions would proceed as outlined in CM session 2. For each consecutive negative sample provided, the therapist continues addressing the eight aspects outlined earlier. An example of a session in which a patient has achieved the maximum number of draws is outlined below.

Therapist: Hi, Mike, how is it going today?
Patient: Pretty good. I'm up to eight draws today, aren't I?
Therapist: If your sample is negative for methamphetamine, you sure are! Can you give a sample now?
Patient: Not a problem.

After collecting the sample, the dialogue may proceed as follows:

Therapist: Yes, we can see from this line that your sample is negative for methamphetamine. This makes a whole month of abstinence! Great job, Mike. Let's go back to my office and get you eight draws.
Patient: It's my lucky day! I got two larges!
Therapist: Two larges and a small. What do you see in the cabinet that you'd like now? Tell me what else you'd like next week, too, because I can tell you're going to clean me out!
Patient: I'll take this gift card to Best Buy, and those work gloves, because mine all have holes in them. And, a $1 card to Dunkin' Donuts.
Therapist: Sounds good, just sign for them here. What about future prizes? Any special requests now that you're up to the maximum number of draws? You know, you'll get 16 draws next week—eight on Tuesday if you test negative for methamphetamine, and another eight on Friday.
Patient: I'd like a cordless drill. And, maybe a stepstool for my garage. Can you get something like that?
Therapist: I don't see why not. I'll look for those things on my next shopping trip. Let me just remind you that since you're up to the maximum number of draws, it's really important that you keep coming to all our scheduled sessions. If you were to miss a session, your draws would drop back down to one, because we count missed samples just like positive samples, like we talked about earlier.
Patient: Yeah, I remember that. Come to think of it, I think I am going to have a court date on a Tuesday. I think it's in about two weeks from now.
Therapist: Is it on the 14th?

Patient: Yeah.

Therapist: I'm glad we're talking about that now, then. Can we reschedule your testing for Monday that week, on the 13th?

Patient: That's not good for me. I work on Mondays, you know.

Therapist: Could we do Wednesday of that week?

Patient: I work on Mondays, Wednesdays, and Thursdays. I really can't come in any day other than Tuesdays and Fridays.

Therapist: What time is your court appointment on Tuesday? Maybe we could meet before or after it?

Patient: I have to go to court in the city. It's going to take me half a day to get there and back, and they're never on time. My time is supposed to be at 1:00, but you never know.

Therapist: Because we are talking about this ahead of time, I can grant you an exception for that day. That week, you can come in on Friday only, and I'll count Tuesday as an excused absence. That way, your draws will not reset so long as you test negative for methamphetamine before and after the absence. You will have to bring me a slip from the court, stating you were there. Sound okay?

Patient: Sure. But, next week is Tuesday and Friday as usual, right?

Therapist: Yes, that's right. Next week I'll see you Tuesday and Friday for urine testing and draws. As this reminder slip states, you'll keep getting eight draws for methamphetamine-negative samples. But, before you leave, let's just talk a minute about your court date. Are you worried about court, or had any urges or temptations to use? I just want to make sure all is okay.

Patient: No urges or anything. And, I'm not worried about court. It's just a child support hearing. It's been a long time coming, and my lawyer says I don't have anything to be worried about.

Therapist: Okay, then. I'm glad it's all under control. Just remember, if it doesn't work out as planned, we're here for you, to help you in any way we can.

Patient: Yeah, I know. Thanks. I'll see you next Tuesday.

As noted above, the therapist granted a pre-approval for a missing sample because the patient had a legitimate reason for non-attendance, and rescheduling was clearly burdensome. Later in this chapter, dialogue from a session in which an excused absence occurred is provided.

13.2.4.2 A Positive Sample

When patients provide samples positive for the targeted substance, the CM therapist must handle the situation delicately. In most cases, the patient who has used will self-disclose use of the substance prior to the testing. However, sometimes patients do not offer the information about recent use, and still other times patients deny use after testing positive. Methods for handling all three of these situations are described below.

13.2.4.2.1 Self-Disclosure of Use

Typically, when patients use the targeted substance, they will inform the CM therapist about their use before submitting a sample. Often, patients will tell the therapist that they don't really want to leave a sample because they know it will test positive and they know they are not going to get any draws that day. Even in these cases, it is important that the therapist encourage patients to provide the sample and discuss what will happen with respect to the contingencies in effect. For example,

Patient: I just want to tell you that I used last night. So, I don't really feel like leaving a sample. It's going to be positive, and I know I won't get any draws today.

Therapist: Thanks, John, for telling me that you used methamphetamine last night. I really admire you for coming in after you used. I know that is hard to do, and it shows you have a real commitment to trying to stop using. I also encourage you to talk about this lapse in group later today. The group members can help you process what happened, and maybe give you some ideas about how to handle situations that come up in the future. Do you think you can bring up your use in group this afternoon?

Patient: I can try.

Therapist: I think it'll help you to talk about it with others. It happens to a lot of people who are trying to stay off drugs, like you are, and it's nothing to be ashamed of. I also think it's important for you to leave a sample, like you do every time we meet, and once we test it, I'll describe how you will again be eligible for draws, hopefully by Friday.

Notice how in the preceding example the therapist was congratulatory for the positive behaviors the patient was making (attending treatment, being honest about use) and encouraged further discussion of the lapse in another setting. Thus, the discussions about self-reported use need not be extensive in CM, although they certainly could be more involved if CM is being paired with a more involved psychotherapy such as cognitive-behavioral therapy in an individual session. After the preceding dialogue, the remainder of the CM session should proceed as usual, with the therapist addressing other issues important to CM sessions, as outlined in CM session 2.

⸱ Another example of a discussion of self-reported drug use when the sample tests positive, thus confirming the patient's disclosure of drug use, is outlined below.

Therapist: Hello, Sally. How was your week?

Patient: Not great. I tried really hard, but I used on Saturday.

Therapist: That's too bad. Tell me what happened.

Patient: I went to this party, and there was a lot of rock there. I just couldn't handle it.

Therapist: I'm glad you came in today and told me about it. It's not easy getting through this addiction, especially when you are surrounded by the stuff. That's why we're here for you. Let's go and collect your urine sample, and then I'll describe to you what happens and how we can get you back on track. ... As expected, your urine drug screen is not negative for methamphetamine, so you won't get any draws today. But, you are working hard, and I know you can do this. If you don't use between now and Friday, you should test negative then and get one draw.

Patient: I think I might need more help, though.

Therapist: Here's what I suggest. You have group later this afternoon, right?

Patient: Yeah.

Therapist: I encourage you to talk about your use in group and see if you can get some advice from other members who have been through this before. How does that sound?

Patient: Not easy. It's embarrassing. I was doing really well, but I guess I can try.

Therapist: Good. I have no doubt that you want to stop using. I know it's hard, but I also know you can do this. I'll see you in three days. Keep focused on your goals. If you test negative for methamphetamine on Friday, you will earn a draw then. Once you get back on track, I know you can get that watch and other things you were looking forward to winning.

Patient: I do want that watch. I might be able to think about it if I get tempted.

Therapist: That is a great idea. Take a look in the prize cabinet now, and get some pictures in your mind of things you want to earn.

Patient: I am going to think about that watch, and maybe that nice bedspread you've got down there.

Therapist: Excellent. Keep your focus and remember what is important to you. There is the watch, along with all the other positive things in your life that can happen when you're not using. Like the better relationship I know you've been having with your daughter.

In this example, the therapist was understanding and supportive. At the same time, she was directive in terms of sticking to the guidelines and purpose of CM sessions. You could easily see how self-reports of use in such a situation could lead to a longer therapeutic session, but in the context of a stand-alone CM session, such discussions are not necessary. Therapists can be supportive and offer advice in the context of CM, and do so in a focused manner, directing patients to other clinical resources as needed. In this context, the CM therapist's role does not get intertwined with other clinical issues. On the other hand, if the CM were integrated in the context of a lengthier cognitive-behavioral session, the preceding exchange may have been very similar, but the therapist may have gone on to conduct a functional analysis of drug use. In both cases, the CM component of the session should still be focused as previously outlined. The session would end in the usual fashion, with the therapist presenting the patient with the reinforcement reminder slip and discussing the date and time of the next testing session.

13.2.4.2.2 No Disclosure of Use Until After the Sample Tests Positive

Some patients will be much less forthright about their drug use. As a CM therapist, you will never know whether or not the urine sample will test negative for the targeted substance until after it is collected and screened. Therefore, is important that you not be too presumptive of a negative sample, even among patients who have achieved long durations of abstinence. Consider the following exchange, and how it would have been inappropriate if the therapist had assumed ahead of time that the patient was going to test negative.

Therapist: Hi, Melissa, how are you today?

Patient: I'm doing well. Can't complain. Hoping to win that towel set today.

Therapist: Yeah, that is a nice one. Hopefully, it will be your day to draw a large. Let's head down to the restroom and get your sample.

Therapist: Melissa, as you can see here, your sample is not negative for methamphetamine today. Do you want to talk a little about that?

Patient: Not really.

Therapist: Maybe it would be a good idea to bring this up in group today. Or, if you don't want to talk in group, perhaps you can schedule a time with your other counselor to talk about it one-on-one.

Patient: I don't know. What happens with my draws?

Therapist: As we discussed earlier, if your sample is not negative for methamphetamine, I can't give you any draws that day. But, if you don't use between now and next Tuesday, you should test negative then, and you can earn one draw then, and two next Friday.

Patient: But, I was up to eight draws!

Therapist: Yes, you were. And, the good news is that you can get back up to eight draws. I know that you want to stop using, and I also know you can do it, because you did it before. We just need to get you back on track, so you can win that towel set and the other things you were looking forward to. Do you think you can talk about this in group today?

In this example, the therapist is supportive but does not force or push the patient when she is not ready to talk about her use. As in the other examples, the therapist directs the patient to other available resources and reminds the patient how she can again become eligible for draws.

Note that in this example, and others, when a patient tests positive for the substance from which abstinence is being reinforced, the therapist never states the patient is "positive." Instead, the therapist uses the phrase "not negative." The "not negative" phrase sounds less harsh and is less likely to bring about a defensive reaction in the patient.

The remainder of the session should proceed as usual. It should address the other issues relevant to a CM session as outlined in CM session 2.

13.2.4.2.3 Denial of Use With a Positive Sample

In perhaps the most difficult of the situations to handle, a patient may test positive for the targeted substance but deny its use. An example appears below.

Therapist: Tom, unfortunately, as you can see here, your sample was not negative for methamphetamine today. Can you tell me what happened?

Patient: No way! I didn't use. Your test is wrong!

Therapist: Tom, like we talked about earlier, we have to go by what the test results say in this program. So, today I can't give you a draw. But, you've shown that you can get draws. If you don't use between now and Tuesday, you should test negative then, and you can draw again then.

Patient: I haven't been using! I was in a car last night where another guy was smoking crack. Maybe I got some second-hand smoke from him.

Therapist: I know it's hard to stop using, and being around other people who use puts you in a tough spot. I encourage you to talk about this in group today. Can you do that?

Patient: I guess so.

Therapist: You'll have another chance to earn a draw on Tuesday. What is it that you want to work for in the prize cabinet?

In this example, the patient denied use and brought up the potential of an invalid test result. Rather than arguing with the patient or offering to re-test the patient, the therapist instead brought up the program rules—that all draws are based on the onsite test results. The therapist also brought the conversation back to how draws and prizes can be won in the future, rather than focusing on the loss of reinforcement or the patient's denial of use.

13.2.4.3 Unexcused Absences

Another difficult situation can arise when a patient fails to provide a scheduled sample on a testing day. In some such situations, the patients realize that their draws will reset, especially if they have been reminded several times throughout the CM program that missed samples will result in resets. In other cases, patients may deny knowledge of the reset criterion for missed samples, or try to argue for an exception to the rule. Responses to these situations are as follows.

13.2.4.3.1 Patient Knows Reset Will Occur

An example of a dialogue that may occur when an unexcused absence occurs but the patient is prepared for a reset in reinforcement is outlined below.

Therapist: Hi, Mike. Good to see you today. I missed you on Friday.

Patient: Yeah, I know. I was supposed to come in, but I overslept.

Therapist: I see. I'm glad you made it back in, though. Sometimes it's hard to come to treatment after missing a day.

Patient: No, I just overslept that day. I'm not dropping out. This program is doing too much for me.

Therapist: I'm glad to hear it. Any cravings or temptations to use since I last saw you?

Patient: No. I'm good.

Therapist: Let's test your urine result, and then we can talk about what will happen. … I'm happy to report that your sample is negative for methamphetamine, as you can see here.

Patient: Yeah, I knew it would be.

Therapist: That is great that you are staying off drugs. But, because you missed a sample on Friday, I do have to reset your draws back down to one today.

Patient: Yeah, you told me about that.

Therapist: Had you given me a call on Friday when you woke up, I could have rescheduled your appointment for a little later in the day. Then, you would not have needed to reset.

Patient: I guess I just knew I blew it, and I didn't feel like coming on Friday anyway.

Therapist: Just keep that in mind for the future. If you know you're going to miss an appointment, at least give me a call, and I'll see what I can do to help you out. The good news is that you get one draw today, and if you test negative for methamphetamine again on Friday, you'll get two draws then. Let's have you roll up your sleeves and see what you get!

Patient: Hey, at least I got a small.

Therapist: And, what do you see that you'd like in the cabinet?

Patient: Well, I'm still hoping for that TV, but today, I'll take one of these candy bars.

Therapist: Sounds good. Let's just have you sign for it here. Before we wrap up here, tell me, have you had any cravings or urges to use since I saw you last?

Patient: No, none at all. I'm good.

Therapist: Okay, great. I'll see you again on Friday at 9:30. Here's your reminder slip, and you can get two draws on Friday if you test negative for methamphetamine then.

As noted in the preceding example, the patient was not surprised or upset about draws resetting. When patients are adequately informed of the reset contingencies, they will be less likely to contest them when they occur. However, some patients may still get upset when resets occur, as noted in the following example.

13.2.4.3.2 Patient Denies Knowledge of Reset Criteria and Tries to Argue for an Exception

One of the most difficult aspects of CM sessions is when patients are upset about the rules and try to ask for exceptions. This situation can get tricky related to unexcused absences especially if the rules are gray. Thus, it is highly recommended that you try to outline potential situations that could arise and how these situations ought to be handled prior to beginning your CM program. If the rules are known ahead of time, it is much easier to refer an unhappy patient toward them. At the same time, remind the patient that the rules were designed for a reason. You have to follow them, but at the same time you want to do everything you can to help the patient so that they can get all the reinforcement possible.

Therapist: Hi, Angel, how are you today?

Patient: Oh, pretty good, I think.

Therapist: That is good to hear. I missed you earlier this week. What happened?

Patient: My car broke down—on the way in here.

Therapist: Really? That's too bad. Did you get it fixed?

Patient: Yeah, it was just some belt. My buddy fixed it yesterday.

Therapist: That's good, but I wish you had called me to let me know. I was expecting you.

Patient: My cell got cut off a few months ago, and I don't have a phone. It's hard to call.

Therapist: I see, but without calling in or my knowing anything about your whereabouts, I have to count that as a missed sample.

Patient: What does that mean?

Therapist: Like we talked about earlier in the program, if you need to miss an appointment for any reason, you need to let me know. A missed sample resets your draws. So, we can get a sample today, and if it tests negative for methamphetamine, you will get a draw. And later this week, your draws will start increasing again.

Patient: You gotta be kidding me! My car breaks down and now you're making me go back to one draw when I've been at eight for weeks! That's not fair.

Therapist: I know it might not seem fair to you right now, but we did talk about this, and it's also written on the handout about the program I gave you when you started. That same handout that I have hung here on my wall. We really need you to come in for all your scheduled samples for you to stay at the high number of draws.

Patient: Forget this. This is ridiculous. I'm just going to quit this program then.

Therapist: I know you are upset, and I know this isn't good news. But, quitting the program probably isn't in your best interests either. You are already here, and if you test negative for methamphetamine, you will earn one draw. That is certainly better than no draws. And, in a few weeks, you can be right back up to where you were in terms of draws.

Patient: Can't you make an exception? Jeez. I haven't missed a single other appointment.

Therapist: I know you haven't, and I know how well you are doing. I also know you can continue to do well. Why don't we go ahead and get that sample? If you test negative for methamphetamine, I'll be hoping that you draw that jumbo today.

Patient: Yeah, right. Like that's going to happen.

Therapist: It can happen. And, like I said, one draw is better than no draws, right?

Patient: I suppose so.

After the therapist collects and tests the sample, the conversation may proceed as follows.

Therapist: Good news, you can see here that your sample is negative for methamphetamine today, just like you said it would be. Let's go back to my office, and you can do your draw. How about any cravings or urges to use? Did the car breakdown upset you to the point of wanting to use?

Patient: No. It was no big deal.

Therapist: Well, looks like you got a "good job" slip today. Sorry about that, but it is true—you are doing a great job here. Let's have you take a look at the prize cabinet and see what interests you for Friday. See anything you want to work for next?

Patient: I would like more of those Dunkin' Donut cards. And, maybe a prepaid cell phone. Do you still have any of those?

Therapist: I think I do—right here. I'll pick up another, because those are very popular. And, as I mentioned earlier, if you provide a methamphetamine-negative sample on Friday, you'll earn two draws, which means a pretty good chance of winning a prize. Here's your reminder slip, and I look forward to seeing you on Friday.

In the preceding example, the therapist was delicate in terms of her discussion of approaching the missed appointment, the reset, and the request for an exception. If the patient continued to push the concept of an exception, the therapist could have responded something to the effect of the following:

I know how unfair it seems. But, just imagine if we let everybody have exceptions. We would no longer have any rules, and this whole program would be meaningless.

Or …

Let's try to focus on the positive parts. You have won a lot of good prizes already, and if I remember, you also got a large the very first time you drew from the bowl. So, there is no saying you might not win some good prizes as you're working your way back up to eight draws.

13.2.4.4 Excused Absences

There are times when patients have legitimate reasons for not coming to the clinic and providing a scheduled sample for CM. If the patient were negative prior to the absence, samples during the excused absence are considered to continue (i.e., not break) the string of abstinence and will not reset the patient to the original low number of picks. Thus, when the patient returns from an excused absence, he will essentially return to the level of draws where he left off with no penalty. (However, patients do not continue to escalate during the excused absence such that if they were receiving three draws on Tuesday and had an excused absence on Friday, they would get four draws the following Tuesday if they test negative, not five draws.)

The best example of an excused absence is when a patient is in a controlled environment such as a jail or hospital. Sometimes, patients must travel out of town for a legitimate reason (e.g., a funeral), and other times they will have an important appointment on their scheduled visit day. The best way to handle an excused absence is to try to reschedule the CM visit the day before (if the situation is known in advance) or the following day, but this will not always be possible, especially in clinics when patients are not expected to attend daily. The principle in dealing with excused absences is to remain flexible and supportive, but at the same time ensure that the patient is not avoiding urine testing when he has recently used.

In the beginning of CM programs and occasionally throughout the duration of the CM program, you want to impress on your patients that if they cannot meet with you for a scheduled appointment, they need to let you know. A telephone call may suffice. As long as the patient calls, he or she may be excused for appointments, court dates, or even child care problems. Similarly, when there is a holiday on a scheduled urine testing day, and the patient has no other reason for coming into the clinic that week, he or she may provide only one sample that week, without penalties for the escalating picks. The decisions about what constitutes an excused absence need to be considered, in conjunction with clinic rules and regulations, before initiating a CM program. Patients need to know what to expect if they fail to provide a scheduled sample.

If the absence involves some sort of appointment, you should encourage patients to bring in documentation that the appointment was kept. You may need to exert clinical judgment and consult with others (primary therapists, supervisors, etc.) in some cases. If multiple therapists at your clinic are implementing CM, it is imperative that all make decisions in the same manner.

What follows is an example of how to handle a single missed sample due to an excused absence. In this situation, Tom was up to five draws prior to the absence.

Therapist: Hi, Mike. Good to see you today. How did things go in court on Tuesday?

Patient: Oh, okay, guess. I have to pay a little more in child support, but I expected that.

Therapist: I see. Well, thanks for letting me know about the court date ahead of time, so that we could excuse your missed sample on Tuesday. As you know, if you ever can't be here it's important to let me know ahead of time so that we don't have to reset your draws. You're up to a high number of draws now, so you have a lot to gain by coming to all your appointments. Are you ready now?

Patient: Yeah, I can go now.

Therapist: You can see here that your sample tested negative for methamphetamine, which is great news. So, you will get you six draws today, one more than you got last Friday. Let's go back to my office and we can do the drawings there.

They return to the office, and the patient rolls up his sleeve and shows his palm prior to drawing.

Patient: Good job. Good job. Small. Small. Good job. And a large!

Therapist: That's great! You drew a large and two smalls today. What do you see in the prize cabinet?

Patient: A drill set and two bus tokens, please.

Therapist: Perfect. Let me have you sign for those here. What did you want to work for next? I know you've been eyeing that drill for a couple weeks now?

Patient: I think that other tool set looks good, too. And, I wouldn't mind one of those toy store gift cards, because it's my son's birthday soon.

Therapist: Yeah, you could certainly get him something nice with that. Let me just remind you that when you come in on Tuesday next week, if you test negative for methamphetamine then, you'll get seven draws and have a really good chance of winning those things next week as well. You're doing really well in this program. How about any urges or cravings to use before or after the court date? Was that a problem for you?

Patient: No, not really. I'm just glad it's finally over.

Therapist: That's good that you put it all in perspective. Being able to stay off drugs during stressful times is hard, but you are showing me how well you can handle things. I'll see you Tuesday at 10:00. Here is your reminder card.

The preceding dialogue related to a single missed testing session. In the event that a patient must be away for a prolonged time (e.g., because of a hospitalization), you can make the decision that (a) missed samples during a prolonged excused absence will result in the patient earning no reinforcement during the time he is unable to provide samples, but the patient can continue in the CM program where he left off when he returns; (b) time in the CM program will be suspended until the patient returns; or (c) a certain duration of non-attendance would terminate a patient from the CM program, regardless of the reason for the absence.

In the first situation, a three-week absence during the CM program would shorten the CM program by three weeks for that patient. For example, if a patient were hospitalized in weeks four to six of a 12-week CM program, he would earn reinforcement until his hospitalization occurred in week four, then be absent for weeks four through six, and pick up in week seven where he left off in terms of the draw schedule. However, he would only have six weeks of CM remaining. Alternatively, in the second option, if a patient missed three weeks of a 12-week CM protocol because of hospitalization (e.g., in weeks four through six), the patient could re-enter the CM program when he returned to the clinic in week seven, and have another nine weeks of CM treatment remaining. You could also decide (the third scenario) that anyone who failed to provide two (or four) consecutive weeks of samples for any reason would be terminated from the CM program. These decisions ought to be made prior to implementing CM so that they can be applied consistently across patients when issues arise.

13.3 OTHER ISSUES

13.3.1 Sample Collection and Validation

Ideally, a same-sex observer should witness submission of all urine samples. The observer should ask the patient to remove bulky outer clothing so that she or he is able to visualize the urine stream leaving the body (i.e., don't just stand in the bathroom with the patient). Because negative samples result in tangible reinforcers, some patients will be motivated to try to pass bogus samples. Therefore, it is imperative that you try to ensure valid collection of samples. If patients see you being observant, they will be less likely to try to leave fake samples.

Nevertheless, direct observation will not always be possible due to gender differences between CM therapists and their patients, staff shortages, busy clinics, and other factors. To the extent you can arrange for at least a portion of samples to be observed, the lower the likelihood will be of patients submitting fake samples. It is most important to observe samples early in the CM program (to ward off the possibility of patients considering providing fake samples), when patients are earning large numbers of prize draws at a time (e.g., after three or more weeks of abstinence), and whenever you suspect a patient may be leaving fake samples.

Patients who are suspected of leaving a fake sample (or whose sample does not pass temperature or other validity checks) should be encouraged to drink a cup of water and give a second sample in 30 to 60 minutes, or later, that same day. If they decline, the sample should be counted as missing and therefore positive for purposes of reinforcement. You want to be sure you obtain the second sample the same day, because a 24-hour or longer period between tests may be sufficient for drug use to be no longer detectable.

Patients may be upset and argumentative if their test results comes up as invalid, or if you request a second sample in a single day. A negative reaction can occur whether or not they actually tried to give a fake sample. The following is an example of how an invalid contested urine sample can be handled.

Jody leaves a urine sample after having tested negative for three weeks in a row. The therapist thinks he overheard Jody talking with another patient outside the clinic about getting a sample from her earlier that morning. After Jody leaves her sample, the therapist tells her he spilled it, and he asks her to leave a second sample. She becomes irate and tells the therapist she's only leaving one sample a day, and if he messes it up it's his fault. The therapist apologizes and tells her that sometimes we all make mistakes, but in order for him to give her draws, he really needs to get another sample from her. Jody becomes even angrier, wanting to know what he is accusing her of. The therapist assures Jody that he isn't accusing her of anything, and he just needs another sample. He offers to buy her some coffee or a soda, and encourages her to provide another sample either before or after group.

Jody says she can't go again. The therapist sees she is still angry with him, so he lets her go to group without further discussion. At the end of the group, the therapist again asks Jody if she might be able to go now. She says that she already told him that she went once today.

Therapist: Yes, I know, and I am sorry about that. But, if you think you can go again, and if the test is negative for methamphetamine, then you can get your draws. You're due for seven draws today if your sample reads negative. I want you to get all the draws you can.

Patient: Of course it's negative (still in a hostile tone).

Therapist: Well, you're here still for two more hours, right? Why don't you stop by when you have to go to the bathroom, and we'll see if we can get you those draws then. If you really don't want to go again today, I'd still like for you to come back on Friday.

When the therapist checks in with Jody two hours later, Jody still refuses to leave another sample. On Friday, Jody leaves a sample, which the therapist has a female therapist observe very closely. The sample tests positive for methamphetamine.

Often, but not always, when patients refuse to give a second sample, it is because they have used. Note that in this case, the CM therapist was not at all accusatory toward the patient. The therapist gave Jody several chances to leave a second sample, while reminding her of all she had to gain by trying again. On Friday, the therapist would say something to the effect of the following:

> Jody, I know you were angry about what happened a couple days ago, and I'm really glad you came in again today. Your urine sample doesn't read negative today, as this line shows, but coming in tells me that you are really trying hard to stay off of methamphetamine. Maybe you can discuss in group today how you're feeling, and the group can help you out. I really hope you'll come back again next Tuesday. If you don't use between now and then, you should test negative and will be eligible for a draw again on Tuesday. I know there are a lot of prizes in the cabinet you've been working toward, especially that coffee maker. Thanks for coming in today.

13.3.2 Unable to Urinate

You want to encourage patients to provide samples on every scheduled testing day. Some patients will not want to give a sample on a scheduled testing day when they know they will be positive, and they will want to wait a day or two to let the drug clear from their system so they are not penalized with respect to draws. If a patient avoids you on a scheduled urine testing day or states that she absolutely CANNOT go to the bathroom that day, the therapist may state,

> Sometimes, we all have problems going. Our policy is that you need to give a sample on all scheduled days. But, if you really cannot go today and you need to leave right now for a doctor's appointment, what I can do is schedule an additional test for you tomorrow morning at 8 am. If you come in and test negative for methamphetamine early tomorrow morning, I'll count that as today's sample, and I won't reset your draws. You'll still have to give a urine sample on Friday this week too, though. Does that sound fair?

If the patient shows up the next morning, the therapist may say,

> I really made an exception for you yesterday, and I don't mind doing it one time. But, you know, I really can't do that again. I know you couldn't go yesterday and you needed to leave right away, but some people try to delay their test to try to leave more time for drugs to clear from their systems. In the future, I really need you to give urine samples on the scheduled days for you to keeping getting the increased draws, okay?

13.3.3 Coordination with Clinical Urine Testing

Some clinics have policies in place for conducting urine screening, in which they may send the samples to an outside laboratory for testing. CM should not interfere with standard clinic procedures. If the clinic tests urine samples randomly once a month using an outside laboratory, they should continue to do so. You may split a urine sample in half and give half to the clinic for its own testing, after you have finished testing for CM purposes. That way, patients will not have to give two samples on the same day.

On very rare occasions, the outside laboratory tests may read differently than onsite tests. This discrepancy may be related to different cut-off values for classifying a sample as positive versus negative. In other words, some tests are more or less sensitive. Different tests may also screen for different metabolites of drugs, and a patient positive for any one of the metabolites may test positive in a global manner. A discrepancy may also occur if samples are collected on different days and patients used on the intervening day.

Because different testing procedures may produce different results, it is important that the patient and the CM therapist understand that for the purposes of CM, the results from the onsite test only are used. For other clinical purposes (e.g., informing probation or parole or testing for other nontargeted substances), results of the outside lab testing will generally be applied. However, these outside test results will not be considered for CM purposes.

Note that if outside testing is conducted for substances other than those being targeted for reinforcement as part of the CM protocol, positive results for nontargeted substances should not impact reinforcement in the CM program. Clinically, it is a good idea to discuss positive results for nontargeted substances with patients, as it is to discuss self-reports of supplementary drug use. The connection should be made that use of any substance is likely to lead to use of the targeted substance, which in turn would impact reinforcement.

An example of how to handle a clinic-collected sample that tests positive for heroin, when a patient is being reinforced for methamphetamine abstinence, is outlined below. Note that the entire CM session is not described, just the sections relevant to the issue of clinical urine testing for supplemental drugs.

Therapist: Carol, as you can see here, you tested negative for methamphetamine today, which is great. So, you are up to eight draws, which is really excellent. Let's go back to my office and see what you win today.

Carol rolls up her sleeves, shows the palm or her hand, and draws eight slips.

Patient: Three smalls and a large! I got a large!
Therapist: Good for you. Before you select your prizes, let's talk a minute about any cravings or urges to use drugs you may have had in the last week or so.
Patient: None. I've been staying off meth, and it's been pretty easy for me.
Therapist: I'm glad to hear that. How about other drugs? Like heroin? I know you mentioned some issues with that in the past.
Patient: Well, yeah … I had problems with that, but not lately.
Therapist: I noticed that your clinic urine sample came back from last week. Although you've been negative for methamphetamine, which is great, your sample tested positive for heroin.
Patient: Yeah, that … I thought it would have cleared before the test, but I guess not.
Therapist: As you know, Carol, all your draws are related to testing negative for methamphetamine. But, I am worried that if you're using heroin— even a little—heroin use might lead you back to methamphetamine. Have you spoken at all in group about your heroin use last week?
Patient: No. I didn't want to bring it up. It was just once. I didn't think anyone would notice.

Therapist: Even if it didn't come up on your test, I think it's really important that you talk about any slips you've been having in group. The group members can give you some ideas about how to handle slips and cravings. Can you talk about what happened last week in group today?

Patient: I guess so.

Therapist: I think it's going to be really important that you find ways to say no to heroin, the same way you've been doing with methamphetamine. You're up to eight draws now, and a lapse to methamphetamine use would drop you way back down in terms of draws.

Patient: I know. I guess you're right. Heroin use may make me be more tempted to use meth. I was lucky that night that no one had any meth.

The therapist in the preceding example very adeptly raised the issue of a positive sample for a supplemental substance. Although the patient was not forthright about her heroin use, she was willing to discuss it when gently prodded. By connecting heroin use to the potential of methamphetamine use and loss of reinforcement, the therapist may have helped the patient prevent not only a lapse or relapse to methamphetamine use but also future use of heroin.

13.3.4 Handling Contested Urine Sample Results

In general, when dealing with contested urine sample results, you will do best for yourself and the patient if you stay calm and focused on the CM protocol in place. You can sympathize and say that the patient may very well be correct about not using drugs. Unfortunately, right now, you have to go with what the onsite test says.

One thing that works well is to never say that a patient is "positive." When a test indicates drug use that a patient did not admit to upfront, you can say,

> Sharon, your sample does not test negative for methamphetamine today. Maybe you can discuss what happened today in group. You can draw again as soon as Friday, if your sample reads negative then.

Note that the phrase "does not test negative today" sounds less harsh than "is positive."

Sometimes patients may use an outside laboratory test result as grounds to contest a CM sample result. Following is an example of a contested CM sample, when clinic urine samples have been negative.

Chuck leaves a urine sample that reads positive for methamphetamine. You say,

Therapist: Chuck, I'm sorry, but your sample today doesn't read negative for methamphetamine, as you can see here. Although you can't draw today, I'm glad you came in, because it shows you are working hard on your recovery. Maybe you can discuss what happened in group today, and if your sample is negative on Friday, you can draw again then.

Patient: This is bullshit! I've been clean for four weeks! All my clinic urines are clean. I've never been dirty.

Therapist: I know you've always left negative urine samples with me before, and that's great. You're doing really well in treatment. I want you to keep doing well. If you tell me you didn't use, I believe you. Really, I do believe you. But, you have to understand that I have to go by the results of this onsite test for the draws. If you didn't use, then your sample should test negative on Friday, right? If it's negative Friday, you can draw again then.

Patient: My clinic urines are always clean. I'm going to have them check because you're wrong.

Therapist: You can certainly ask your group counselor to get a second urine test, if you want. But, remember that for the purposes of CM, we have to go by our onsite tests. Sometimes the labs test for different drugs than we do, and sometimes they have different cut-off values. That means that our tests might be more sensitive than theirs. We can detect just a tiny bit of drug, while they may set their test only to detect lots of a drug. You can ask your group counselor to order another test, if that's what you want. But, my hands are tied here. I have to go by the result I got on the onsite test. Why don't we just focus on your having a negative test for Friday?

Note that the CM therapist did not get accusatory or defensive. She encouraged Chuck's choice to complain to his group counselor and order a clinic test. At the same time, she was firm in her stance that the draws and the CM program rely solely on the onsite testing system.

The CM therapist in this situation, if she really believed Chuck didn't use, could pour the urine sample into a second testcup (or use another dipstick) to reassure both herself and the patient that the result was not due to anything wrong with the particular cup or dipstick employed. However, it is not a good idea to get into the habit of testing every positive urine sample twice.

Had Chuck gone to the group counselor, the counselor would have reiterated the CM therapist's decision and confirmed that reinforcement decisions are made based on the onsite tests. The counselor may or may not have ordered another test, but this counselor would need to emphasize (as would you) that the outside test is for clinical purposes only and not for CM.

If a clinical test were ordered and came back negative, the discussion of different cut-off values may have taken place again, with a continued conversation of how the CM has to go by the onsite test results. Note that most offsite testing will take one to three days to get the result. During this time, the patient may have time to calm down. Reaffirming belief in the patient, and stating something to the effect of one of the statements below can also be helpful.

You know if you used or not, and that's what's really important, right?

Or

Sometimes, mistakes do happen, but we have to go by the results of the onsite test, like I mentioned in the beginning of this program. Just think about how crazy this place would be if we had to get two tests every day on every patient! Everybody would be wanting multiple tests, and then what would we do?

Or

I think it's much more important for you to stay abstinent no matter what the results of this test. I also think that your being able to calmly discuss this with me when I know you think I'm totally wrong is a really positive thing.

13.3.5 Handling Positive Urine Samples due to Prescription Medication Usage

Some patients may have a legitimate prescription for opioids (e.g., Percocet, Darvocet, codeine) or may be using over-the-counter medications for colds and flus that contain stimulants detected by the onsite testing system. Some amphetamine-based hallucinogens (e.g., methylenedioxyamphetamine [MDA], or methylenedioxymethamphetamine [MDMA, more commonly known as ecstasy]) may also test as positive for stimulants. However, most CM protocols do not allow for prescribed medications to function as excuses for positive samples. If a patient tests positive and vehemently denies using the targeted substance, you can question him or her about other drugs or medications that he or she might be using. Situations that involve prescribed medications should be discussed with a supervisor and/or with the manufacturer of your onsite testing kits. If the patient needs a prescribed medication that renders him ineligible for reinforcement, he may withdraw from the CM program. If at all possible, efforts should be made to help the patient find an alternative medication that will not interfere with testing for the targeted substance.

13.3.6 Urine Testing Summary

What is important in the previously presented examples is that sample testing represents one of the most sensitive areas of interaction in CM programs that reinforce abstinence. Urine testing provides the opportunity to be supportive and encouraging of the patient's abstinence. It is also fertile ground for contested results and carries a potential for argumentative interactions. In general, when dealing with contested results, you will do best for yourself and the patient if you can keep calm, stick to the protocol, and use your best professionalism. You can sympathize and say that the patient may very well be correct about not using drugs. Unfortunately, right now, you have to go by what the onsite testing system says, so the patient will not be able to draw that day. A positive sample can be especially discouraging after a long string of negative samples. In this case, you may want to remind patients that any draws are better than no draws and that they can return quickly to receiving draws and prizes by coming in with a negative sample at the next scheduled CM session. You know they can do that because they have already shown that they can stay drug free, and you'll be rooting for them.

13.4 PREPARING FOR THE END OF A CM PROGRAM

As noted throughout this book, participation in most CM programs is time limited. Some patients will be somber about CM ending. For many, CM is a significant positive aspect of their lives, and it is now ending. You should inform patients a couple weeks before the last session that CM termination is approaching in order to provide patients with the opportunity to reflect and express any feelings or thoughts regarding the upcoming transition. In the sample case I am describing here, CM is in place for 12 weeks. Therefore, in about week 10, and no later than week 11, you should discuss the ending of the CM program. An example follows:

Therapist: Sam, you've been doing really well in this program, and I know how hard you've been working to stay off of methamphetamine. You're in your 10th week now, so we only have about a week and a half left of prizes. You'll continue earning draws for negative samples, just as you have been, until March 16, but that will be the last day I'll be meeting with you as part of this program. Do you want to take a little time to talk about how you feel about this prize program ending?

Patient: Yeah, I knew it was coming to an end. I thought I had three weeks left, though.

Therapist: You started before the holidays, so March 16 makes it 12 weeks exactly. I guess it's coming a little sooner than you thought.

Patient: It is, but I can keep on going to my regular groups, right?

Therapist: Absolutely, the ending of the prize program won't affect your usual treatment in any way. Your relapse prevention groups will keep going on, and I'm hoping you'll still want to go to them.

Patient: Sure, I wouldn't want to stop both at once.

Therapist: I wouldn't think that would be a very good idea either. Prizes often keep people involved and interested in treatment in the beginning. But, once they achieve a long period of abstinence—as you have—they see the benefits of treatment and no longer need the prizes so much.

Patient: I'm going to keep up with the relapse prevention group. I'm also going to start the aftercare group next week. I'm switching my second relapse prevention group for that one, because it's a little earlier in the day, which is better with my work schedule, and the counselor says I'm ready for it now.

Therapist: That is good to hear. I know that is a great group, and I'm happy to hear you are progressing in your treatment plan.

At the final CM session with patients, you should recap their experiences with the CM program, inquire about any feedback they may have, encourage them to continue with usual care treatment and their recovery, and express congratulations for their accomplishments. Often, patients enjoy receiving a certificate of completion, which can be created especially for your program and handed to the patient in the last CM session. A sample appears in Figure 13.1. Many patients have actually framed their certificates, and frames can be good prizes for the prize cabinet as well.

After reviewing the final urine toxicology result in a CM program, award the patient his or her final draws from the prize bowl and any prizes earned. Then, you may want to briefly discuss the patient's experiences with CM and establish goals for the future. This process may help the patient see changes made since the start of CM. You can review periods of drug abstinence, reflect on any slips, and encourage a better understanding of the patient's progress during the CM period. The following questions may provide a guide.

Drug Abstinence

Were there any periods of abstinence? How long? If they were able to stay abstinent for a period of time, what helped? What changes did they notice because of being abstinent? Were they enjoyable? What made it easy to stay abstinent? What made it difficult? What are their plans to stay abstinent? What did they learn about themselves during CM treatment?

CM Program

What did they think of this program before they started? How did their thoughts change over time? What influenced any changes in perception of the program? What did they like best about the program? What did they like least? Would they recommend it to others? What helped them the most? Why?

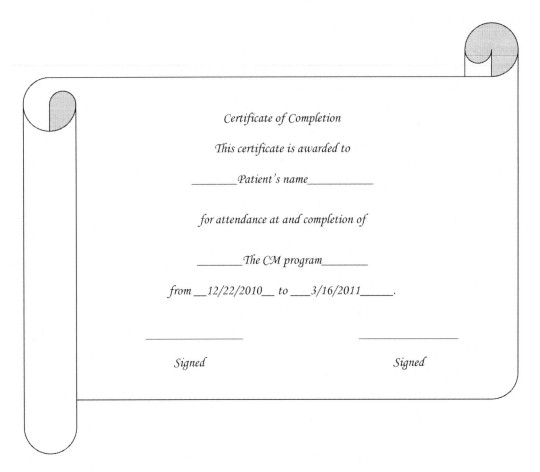

Certificate of Completion

This certificate is awarded to

_____Patient's name_____

for attendance at and completion of

_____The CM program_____

from ___12/22/2010___ to ____3/16/2011_____.

_____   _____

Signed   Signed

FIGURE 13.1   Certificate of completion.

Some patients may attribute success they have had to the wisdom, concern, or thoughtfulness of the therapist. For example, a patient may say, "You've helped me so much, I really can't thank you enough." However reaffirming these remarks may be, these remarks implicitly deny the role and actions taken by the patient during treatment and prevent the patient from acknowledging responsibility for progress made. Although a CM therapist cannot stop a patient from expressing gratitude, the therapist should be sure to reframe the patient's accomplishments in a way that empowers him to see the change and see himself as the agent of change. This can be done by simply indicating the patient's own contributions to treatment.

Patient: Thank you so much for all you've done for me. If it weren't for you, I would never have done so well. You really helped me.

Therapist: Thank you, Jimmy, but really you were the one putting in all the hard work. The good things that are happening now in your life are the result of your efforts.

You can then present the certificate of completion to the patient.

Therapist: I do have something for you on your last day of the program. This is a certificate of completion, signed by our clinic director and me, stating that you successfully completed this program. I hope you will remember this and all you did to achieve your goals as you move forward with your recovery. I also hope you'll keep going to your aftercare groups and remain involved with Cocaine Anonymous. I know that those programs have helped you along the way, and they can be sources of support in the future as well. I wish you the best.

SUMMARY

The examples in this chapter detail methods for handling most every situation that will arise in a CM protocol that reinforces abstinence. In the next chapter, I describe similar implementation guidelines for the Name-in-the-hat prize CM procedure for reinforcing group attendance. Chapter 15 describes methods to keep track of how draws are earned and how to ensure high degrees of adherence to, and competence in, the CM protocol you have developed.

Chapter 14

Implementation Guide for Name-in-the-Hat Prize CM for Reinforcing Group Attendance

This chapter provides a step-by-step guide to implementing the Name-in-the-hat prize CM procedure. It presumes that you have already decided upon using CM to enhance group attendance and that you understand the rationales for using the Name-in-the-hat procedure, which are detailed in Chapter 8. Note that the Name-in-the-hat procedure can ONLY be applied in a group context.

Groups can either be formed de novo at the start of the CM program (ideally with a minimum of eight and maximum of 25 patients), or the CM can be integrated into an existing group (again with between eight and 25 patients). In either case, group members should be informed of the CM procedure before its initiation, as described in this chapter. For an initial implementation period, at least eight weeks (and a maximum of 24 weeks) of CM is recommended, as outlined in Chapter 7. If you are utilizing an open group format (i.e., new patients can enroll in the CM program at any time during the project), be sure that any new attendees begin the CM group no later than week four of an eight-week CM program, or week 20 of a 24-week cycle. In this manner, each patient is able to attend CM groups for at least a four-week period. As detailed in Chapter 7, the period of monitoring and reinforcement should not be too short. New patients starting treatment in week 23 of a 24-week cycle, for example, would only be exposed to CM for one week. Clearly, behavior is not likely to change in a one-week period. Thus, you need to consider timing of monitoring and reinforcement carefully for patients in the group in which you are instituting CM.

Pragmatic information related to starting a prize cabinet and monitoring attendance is provided in Chapters 12 and 15, respectively. Exhibit 14.1 is a quick guide to what you need to start this CM procedure, but earlier chapters should be reviewed for more explicit instructions, especially Chapter 12 for information on purchasing and Chapter 15 for instructions on tracking patient attendance. This

EXHIBIT 14.1 WHAT YOU NEED (BESIDES PRIZES) TO START A NAME-IN-THE-HAT PRIZE CM PROGRAM

1. For the Name-in-the-hat draws:
   - Envelopes (a couple hundred)
   - Different colored 3″ × 3″ sticky pads to write names on (use different colors each week)
   - Different colored ink pens (use one color each week)
   - A hat or other container in which to place all the slips with names each week
   - Attendance record sheets (see Chapter 15, Exhibit 15.3)
   - An envelope containing correct number of name slips and a reminder slip (see Exhibit 14.3 later in this chapter) to be prepared for each patient before each group
2. For the prize bowl:
   - A plastic fishbowl
   - Assuming you are using the regular configuration of prize slips (see Chapter 10, Table 10.13), 100 3″ × 3″ sticky pad pieces of paper all of the same dark color (so they're opaque)
   - Write small on 69 of these pieces of paper—write on the sticky side of the paper
   - Write medium on 20 of these pieces of paper—write on the sticky side of the paper
   - Write large on 10 of these pieces of paper—write on the sticky side of the paper
   - Write jumbo on one of these pieces of paper—write on the sticky side of the paper
   - Fold each piece of paper twice (so that it becomes a small square one-quarter the size of the original piece, folding the sticky side inward, so that it sticks together)
3. Prize Release Form for all prizes selected (see Chapter 12, Table 12.3)
4. Prize Inventory Log for all prizes purchased (see Chapter 12, Table 12.2)
5. Lockable prize cabinet:
   - Preferably a large cabinet with doors that open out; must be lockable (see Exhibit 12.2)
   - Store it in a room that also gets locked, and to which only limited access is allowed.
   - Store all the small prizes on one to two shelves, mediums on another, larges on yet another shelf, and the jumbos on the bottom shelf.
   - Lock the fishbowl in the prize cabinet when not in use.
6. Practice:
   - Practice hosting your first CM group.
   - Get together with at least five colleagues.
   - Do the entire CM procedure with them as mock patients until you feel comfortable.

chapter focuses on how to describe and engage patients in a CM group using the Name-in-the-hat prize procedure.

The procedures described herein are similar whether you are reinforcing attendance at groups designed for general populations of substance-abusing patients or for specific subgroups or subpopulations, such as adolescents, patients with severe and persistent mental health disorders, or pregnant women. The only differences that would arise may relate to the non-CM content of the groups and the types of prizes made available. For example, adolescents will request and desire different prizes than adults, and more disenfranchised populations (e.g., dual diagnosis or methadone patients) tend to prefer basic sustenance prizes such as food items (rice or pasta boxes, canned foods) more so than other populations. Higher income populations (with jobs and transportation) tend to prefer gift cards more so than lower income populations.

In this chapter, I outline specific implementation guidelines as would pertain to a 10-week CM protocol with a closed-group design. Using the example highlighted throughout the book, new patients initiating treatment would receive a draw for attending the intake evaluation, and their names then go in a hat for group attendance at each of 10 weekly group treatment sessions. Again, these procedures need be modified only slightly to accommodate variations in the types of groups in which the procedure is implemented.

14.1 GENERAL OVERVIEW

There are two linked reinforcement systems in the Name-in-the-hat prize CM approach for reinforcing group attendance. Patients who attend group get an increasing number of **name slips** based on consecutive group attendance. The more name slips they earn, the greater their chances are of having their names drawn so that they can **draw from a prize bowl** and win a prize. Both aspects of this reinforcement system are outlined in this section.

14.1.1 Escalating Name Slips for Consecutive Attendance

Patients who attend a CM group (and arrive within one or two minutes of the start time) will have their names written on at least one slip of paper. These slips will be placed into a "hat" at the beginning of the group session. Conducting the CM at the beginning, rather than the end, of a group session ensures that people arrive on time. Moreover, as you will discover when you implement CM, the entire process will take only about five to 10 minutes once you and the patients become familiar with it. Clinicians have found that integrating CM at the end of group becomes disruptive. If CM occurs at the end of the session, patients will fail to focus on the content of the group therapy and spend the bulk of the session thinking about the CM and when it will happen. (If you are concerned about patients leaving group early right after the drawings occur, you can stipulate that escalating draws for subsequent weeks are contingent upon staying throughout the group session.)

The number of times each patient's name goes into the "hat" (i.e., the number of name slips) will *increase by one for each consecutive week that the patient attends the CM group*. Thus, patients who attend the group for the first time, and those who attended previously but missed the week(s) before (or left the last group early), will have their names placed in the hat one time. Patients who attended two weeks in a row will have their names placed in the hat two times. Patients who have attended group three weeks in a row will have their names placed in the hat three times, and so forth. A patient who has attended 10 times in a row would place her name in the hat 10 times the 10th week of consecutive attendance.

Circumstances that impact the number of name slips that a patient may receive include (a) excused absences and (b) unexcused absences. Methods for handling absences are outlined next.

14.1.1.1 Excused Absences

Excused absences (physician-documented sickness, court appearances, etc.) that are approved by the counselor generally will **not** reset the number of times one's name goes in the hat for the next week of attendance. Consider a patient who came to group four weeks in a row (and had placed his name in the hat four times in the fourth week). He then missed a session due to a scheduled and approved doctor's appointment and did not have his name placed in the hat that week of his excused absence. If he attended group the next week, his name would go in the hat five times that week, and hence he would not be penalized for the excused absence in terms of name slips dropping back down to one. (Note that his name does not go in the hat six times the week he returns to group.)

If a patient attends group **late** (after the drawings occur), her name does not go into the hat that week. However, the number of times a late patient's name goes in the hat the following week will continue to increase by one slip. Consider a patient who attended group five times in a row and was up to five slips. If she arrived late in week six (after the drawings were over), she would get no slips to add to the hat that week, even though she would have received six slips if she had arrived on time. In week seven, she would get seven slips. Thus, lateness results in no chance of winning a prize during the session in which she was late, but lateness did not penalize the patient with respect to successive increases in slips the next time she attended. You wouldn't want to punish a patient twice for being late—both that week and the next! And, lateness should not punish a patient as significantly as an unexcused absence.

14.1.1.2 An Unexcused Absence

An unexcused absence will result in a reset to one slip for attendance the next week the patient attends group. Once a patient has reset to one slip, he can then resume the number of slips received at the next session (e.g., up to two, then three, etc.) for consecutive attendance at group. Consider a patient who attended group three times in a row and had received three slips that week. If he missed group in week four, his name did not go into the hat at all that week. The next week he came, he received one slip. If he again attended group the following week, he would receive two slips with his name for attending two consecutive weeks, and so on.

14.1.1.3 Optional Variation on Handling Absences

Each patient could be provided one "missed session" that will not reset the number of times his name goes in the hat for the next attendance. They can use this pass only one time, for any reason, during their CM treatment period. If you elect this option, then excused and unexcused absences become irrelevant. Each patient is allowed one miss only, and more than that (even if for a valid reason) would reset to one slip.

14.1.2 How Name Slips Are Distributed

The CM therapist should **prepare an envelope** for each patient, containing the appropriate number of slips and with patients' names written in the group leader's own handwriting, prior to the group. Thus, an envelope containing the appropriate number of slips will be handed to each patient upon entering the group room. Any patient who failed to attend group would not have his slips placed into the hat that day (and at the next group session, his envelope would contain only one slip if the absence was unexcused the week before).

The group leader should vary the colors of name slips used from week to week (using different colored sticky pad slips) and also vary the ink used to write names. Variation in colors and ink is necessary so that patients do not create their own additional slips and introduce them into the hat, thereby increasing their chances of having their names drawn. Any inappropriately colored slips would be readily recognized by this method and would invalidate the drawing.

Preparing these slips should take no more than 20 minutes once you become familiar with the procedures. It should be done when the group leader has uninterrupted and dedicated time to review attendance records from the previous week. It can be done at any point between CM group sessions—either imme-diately after a CM group ends, to anytime up to an hour or two before the next CM group session. It is imperative the correct number of slips is distributed to patients, depending on their previous attendance. It is a good idea to have one clinician prepare the envelopes and slips and another to check them for accuracy, especially if you are implementing CM for the first time (see Chapter 15 for more information related to supervision).

14.1.3 Prize Bowl Drawings

14.1.3.1 Determining Number of Patients Who Get to Draw for Prizes

The number of times one's name goes into the "hat" is related to the chance of winning prizes. Each group session, a certain number of names will be drawn from the hat. Each person whose name is drawn from the hat gets the chance to draw from a prize bowl and win a prize.

You can decide how many people each week you want to win prizes. The decision should be based in part on costs (see Chapter 10), as the more names that are drawn, the greater the costs of the CM will be. The decision should also be based on behavioral principles. You don't want so few patients winning prizes that the chances of winning are so low that the procedure is not reinforcing.

As a rule of thumb, the number of names drawn should be equivalent to at least half the number of group attendees. Most typically, clinicians draw x/2 names, with x being the total number of people who attended group that day. For example, you would only draw two names if four people attended group. If 16 people showed up for group, you would draw eight names. If an odd number of people attended group, you would draw one extra name (e.g., draw nine names if 17 people attended). Thus, the number of patients who win prizes is likely to vary from week to week. The more people who attend group, the more patients will win prizes.

You could also choose to draw as many names from the hat as there are people in group for a CM session. Some clinicians have felt this is a fairer approach and a way to ensure that more patients receive a prize. This is cer-tainly possible to do, but it will double the cost relative to the version in which half the patients who attend draw (see Chapter 10). Further, not all patients will necessarily win a prize each week. If eight people attended group, and four of them placed their name in the hat five times because they had attended group five weeks in a row, those four people would be more likely to have their names drawn twice than a person who had only come once to group. Thus, drawing more names may still result in some patients not earning tangible reinforcement. In general, patients do not mind not winning every week so long as they know they have a chance of winning, and the chance of winning increases with sustained attendance.

14.1.3.2 Selecting Names from the Hat

Either the therapist or randomly selected group members can pull out the appropriate number of names from the hat at the beginning of each group session. Each patient whose name is drawn from the hat will earn **one draw from a prize bowl**. Note that the same individual may earn more than one draw from the prize bowl if his name is placed in the bowl more than once and it is drawn more than one time.

After the appropriate number of names is drawn from the hat, the therapist should collect the hat full of names. These name slips should all be discarded at the end of the group session. Each CM session should begin with an empty hat. (If you left in name slips week after week and let them accumulate over time, you may end up drawing names of people from the hat who were not in group that day.)

14.1.3.3 Draws from the Prize Bowl

Once the names are drawn from the hat, those patients whose names were drawn get to select from a prize bowl, and each of them will win a prize. The prize bowl I am recommending contains 100 slips of paper (see Chapter 10 for other configurations). All of the slips need to be of same color and size, and you should ensure that you cannot see any writing through the slips.

Sixty-nine of the 100 slips in the prize bowl state "small," 20 state "medium," 10 state "large," and one states "jumbo." Small prizes are things worth up to but not exceeding $1. Medium prizes are items worth about $5 in value. Large prizes are worth up to but not exceeding $20, and jumbo prizes do not exceed $100 in value (see Chapter 12 and Exhibit 14.1 for instructions about How to Create a Prize Bowl and Table 12.1 for How to Start a Prize Cabinet).

The slips from the prize bowl should be RETURNED to the prize bowl after each drawing so that the probabilities of winning prizes remain constant. Thus, it is possible that two patients could win a jumbo prize in the same CM session. However, to prevent increased chances of the same slip being selected by patients, you should shake up the prize bowl between each draw.

Prior to drawing from the prize bowl, patients should roll up their sleeves (if applicable), and show the palms of their hands. This procedure is used to prevent cheating (palming "large" or "jumbo" slips and passing them off as won). Exhibit 12.3 contains more information on how to prevent cheating from the prize bowl.

You should check the prize bowl to ensure that it continues to contain 100 slips every month or so. You want to be sure that some slips do not disappear and that the proportion of winning slips remains as intended.

14.1.3.4 How Number of Prizes Impacts Costs of the CM System

As described in detail in Chapter 10, using 100 slips with the probabilities outlined above, each draw from the prize bowl will cost an average of $3.95. Therefore, if 10 people attend group each week and you draw five names each week, these five patients will draw from the prize bowl, which will result in an overall programmatic cost of about $19.76 in prizes. Over a 10-week period of CM, this will result in about $198 of prizes being awarded ($19.76 per week × 10 weeks = $198 total prize costs).

If you draw 10 names each week, you will award about $40 worth of prizes weekly, or $400 over a 10-week CM period. If your CM program is in place longer than 10 weeks, then the costs will be increased accordingly (e.g., $800 if 10 names are drawn each week for 20 weeks).

Because you will not know how many people will be attending group each week, you cannot determine the exact cost, but you can estimate it, especially if you know the upper limit of the number of people who can attend the group. If no more than 20 patients are allowed in the group, and you draw 10 names each week for 10 weeks (i.e., if attendance is perfect), the maximal estimated costs are $400. If fewer than 20 people show up each week (which is likely), you will draw fewer than 10 names, and costs should average less than $400.

14.1.4 Distribution of Prizes During Groups

The bulk of the prizes should be locked and stored in a cabinet in a safe location (see Chapter 12). If this location is not the group room itself, it will not be possible or practical to carry all the prizes to a group room. The therapist should select a small subset of prizes to bring to the group room for each CM session. The therapist should bring in about x + two small prizes, two medium prizes, two large prizes, and one jumbo to each session (with x being the estimated number of names that will be drawn). Bringing in more prizes is better, but a balance between variety and practicality should be achieved.

Clinicians who have not brought sample prizes to group have reported poor enthusiasm about the prize CM procedure. In addition, clinicians who have been unable to shop for a while and had a small selection of prizes in the group or prize cabinet report poor response to the CM. The lack of a good response all goes back to the basic principles of CM; tangible reinforcement (things patients want and desire) needs to be provided as immediately as possible after the target behavior (attendance) occurs.

Once a patient draws a card from the prize bowl, she or he immediately selects from the subset of prizes of the appropriate value that were brought into the group room that day. Thus, the first person who draws a small gets to choose from the seven or so available smalls, and the next person who draws a small will get to select from the remaining six smalls and so on. The therapist should inform patients at EVERY session that if they do not like the prize they received in group that day, they can exchange it immediately after group from available prizes in the larger locked cabinet. Suggestions for additional prizes should also be solicited from the group, even those who did not win prizes that session. Be sure to have patients who win a prize sign for them on the Prize Release Form (see Table 12.3) as they select their prizes.

14.1.5 Remainder of Group Session

Once you and the patients get used to the Name-in-the-hat prize drawing procedures, the entire process should not take more that 10 minutes to complete. After the prize drawings occur, the remainder of the group session can proceed as usual.

At the end of the group, the therapist should inform group members that they will earn one more slip of paper with their name on it than they got this week if they attend group next week. Thus, the chances of their name being drawn next week will increase by one if they attend group the following week. The therapist should also remind patients that if they *do not* attend group the next week, the number of times their name will go into the hat will decrease to one for the next CM group session they attend.

14.1.6 Exchanging of Prizes

There will be a few extra prizes that will not be awarded each day in group, and those prizes should be returned to the prize cabinet immediately after the group session. Any patient who wants to exchange the prize(s) she or he received that day can do so when the remaining prizes are being locked up after session. This process is instituted to minimize the amount of time spent in group selecting among prizes (and because prize cabinets are often not located in the group rooms themselves). If you do have a prize cabinet in your group room and allow patients to select from it as soon as they win prizes, you will discover they may spend long periods of time deciding. It is better to award some prize immediately, and allow exchanges after group. However, be sure to inform patients that prize exchanges can only be done on the same day they are won; patients cannot exchange prizes a day, week, or month later.

14.2 DETAILED INSTRUCTIONS FOR THE NAME-IN-THE-HAT PRIZE CM PROCEDURE

After having reviewed the general instructions about the Name-in-the-hat prize CM procedure for increasing group attendance, you are now ready to learn about specific suggestions for implementing this procedure. Again, I base the details on the sample CM protocol highlighted throughout the book. Any minor modifications to this protocol should require only slight changes to the directions outlined below.

14.2.1 Introducing Name-in-the-Hat Prize CM to Patients

The Name-in-the-hat sample protocol that is described throughout this book implements CM for all new patients entering a treatment facility. The facility treats about 1,200 new patients per year, so about 100 new patients per month (or 20 to 25 a week) are seen for an intake evaluation and then scheduled to attend a 10-week outpatient group that meets once a week. Let's presume that a new group is started once a week at this clinic, and each group runs for 10 weeks. New patients who attend the intake evaluation are assigned to the new group beginning that week or the following week. Thus, each group would have up to 20 or 25 patients assigned to it, but experiences at the clinic reveal that only about 60% patients who come to the intake evaluation attend even one group, and even fewer become actively engaged in the groups. Average group attendance is seven patients prior to initiating CM.

For the purposes of this exercise, CM is going to be introduced with all new intakes and into all new groups beginning at this clinic over a one-month period—five groups in total and up to five groups × 20 patients, or 100 patients. The remainder of this chapter is directly relevant even if you are implementing Name-in-the hat prize CM into just a single group at your clinic rather than five groups. It is also relevant to rotating groups in which patients begin and end the CM group at different points in time. Moreover, the procedures are similar regardless of the patient population with which you are working, including adolescents, dual diagnosis patients, criminal justice system patients, or patients with specific needs (pregnant women, parenting groups, etc.). The only things that would change would be specific details of the CM intervention if they differ from those described herein (e.g., twice-weekly rather than once-weekly groups) and the types of prizes made available.

In this sample exercise, there is a two-part exposure to CM: (1) The patients get a priming reinforcer (Chapter 9) for attending the intake evaluation, and (2) they then can earn reinforcers for group attendance after the initial intake evaluation. Even if your CM protocol does not entail an individual CM session with patients prior to introducing the group-based CM, you can use similar verbal descriptions to inform patients about beginning a CM group.

14.2.1.1 Initial Description of CM to Eligible Patients

For this protocol, the intake coordinator would indicate the availability of CM to new patients scheduling appointments. After the typical discussions about concerns and reasons for seeking treatment, the intake coordinator may say over the phone to a patient who is appropriate:

> It sounds like our outpatient treatment program may be just right for you. What I'd like to do is schedule an appointment for you with our intake worker, Anne. Anne will meet with you for about two hours, and talk with you further about the issues you are having with cocaine, and how our treatment program may be able to help you. Can we set up that appointment for tomorrow? ... Okay, I do have an opening on Friday if tomorrow doesn't work for you. How about Friday from 10 am until noon? Great.
>
> If you come and meet with Anne on Friday at 10, you will also be eligible for our incentive program. You will get to draw a slip of paper from a bowl at your meeting with Anne, and you will win a prize. The prizes that you can win for coming to your scheduled appointment range from $1 items like fast food gift certificates, bus tokens, and toiletries such as toothpaste and soaps, to $5 items like T-shirts, gift cards, and notepads, to even larger $20 items like pot and pan sets, towels sets, watches, and CD players. And, there is even a chance you could win a $100 prize like a TV or stereo. Whatever prize category you draw from the bowl, you will get to choose a prize in that category, and you're guaranteed to win something. Not bad for just coming to an appointment, is it? ... Do you have any questions? ... We look forward to meeting with you on Friday.

14.2.1.2 Initial Exposure to CM

When the new patient arrives at the intake evaluation, the intake clinician will describe the CM program in the following way:

> As Sally described to you on the phone the other day, you get an incentive for coming in to treatment today. This is my prize bowl, and in it are 100 slips of paper. Each is associated with a prize— small, medium, large or jumbo. The small prizes are things worth about $1 in value, and if you draw a small you'll get to choose anything you'd like from this prize cabinet here in the small category. As you can see on this shelf, there are all sorts of toiletry items, gift cards to Dunkin' Donuts, bus tokens, pens and batteries,

and some food items. If you draw a medium, there are things like $5 gift cards to stores, T-shirts, coffee mugs, jewelry, and so on. A large prize would be $20 gift cards to movie theaters, music stores, clothing stores, or pot and pan sets, phone cards, some books, coffee makers, etc. And, there is also a chance you might win a TV or stereo system. You get one draw from this fishbowl for coming in today. Do you want to go ahead and do your draw now, and then I'll explain how you can win more chances to win prizes by coming to treatment? ... Okay, great, go ahead and draw one slip from the prize bowl, and let's see what you won today.

A small. Great! Here again are all the small prizes. Take a look, and once you decide what you'd like, I'll have you sign for it as I keep track of where all the prizes go.

Now I'll tell you about how you can get even more chances to win prizes by coming to treatment. Starting at your first group—next Tuesday—you will get the chance to win more prizes. We have found that offering patients prizes can be helpful for encouraging them to come to treatment and stop using drugs.

The prizes you can win at the Tuesday groups are just like those I showed you—the small, medium, large, and jumbo prizes. Each time you come to group, you will have a chance of winning these prizes. Each week, about half the people who come to group will win a prize. The more times in a row you come to group, the greater your chances will be of winning prizes.

The first week you come to group, your name will go into a hat ONE time. If you come to group two weeks in a row—this coming Tuesday and then the next one on March 14, your name goes in a hat TWO times that day. If you come to group three weeks in a row, your name goes in the hat THREE times, and so on. If you come to group all 10 weeks of the program, your name will go in the hat 10 times that last week.

At every group session, the counselor will draw some names from the hat. Those people whose names are drawn will get to draw from the prize bowl, just like you did a few minutes ago. It's the same prize bowl you just drew from. There are 100 slips in the bowl, and 69 state "small," 20 state "medium," 10 state "large," and one says "jumbo." So, if your name is drawn from the hat, you will win at least a small prize—like you just did, and most weeks at least one person will win a larger prize. You will get to select from available prizes in the category when you win, just like you did today.

If you attend groups regularly, you may win multiple prizes some weeks. For example, if you came to group 10 weeks in a row, your name may be drawn four times, or maybe even more, that 10th week in group, and you'd win that many prizes. The more you come to group, the greater your chances will be of winning prizes. Does this sound like something you'd be interested in?

Great. Here is a handout about the procedure, and I'll tell Jim, the therapist, that you will be coming to group on Tuesday at 4:00. I'll be keeping my fingers crossed that you win some good prizes. What did you see in the cabinet that really caught your eye?

It is unlikely that a patient would not be interested in a CM program when presented in the manner outlined above. Even if a draw is not being provided to all patients in an individual session before the beginning of your group CM procedure, the preceding script could still be used with just a few minor modifications. Rather than providing the patient with an actual prize during an adaptation of the preceding conversation, you could simply have him practice drawing from the bowl to gain exposure with it, and then look through the prizes in the cabinet to identify something he desired.

There is a CM fact sheet in Exhibit 14.2 that provides similar information that can be adapted for a handout and given to each patient.

Such a CM fact sheet should be provided to each patient who begins a CM program. It will remind patients of how name slips are earned and prize draws are won. In addition, it can be referred to if ever there is a misunderstanding or controversy about procedures. Please note that if you make any alterations to the CM protocol, you would need to reflect those changes in any such descriptive handout.

14.2.2 First Group CM Session

At the start of the first group CM session, you should describe the procedures regarding CM. Although all patients should have received a summary of the program on an individual basis prior to their first group CM session, a reiteration of this information is useful.

Patients should be handed their envelopes as they walk into the group room. As noted earlier, the envelopes need to be prepared ahead of time and should contain (a) the appropriate number of name slips to be placed in the hat (one for the first session) and (b) a form indicating why that slip was earned and how many slips are possible at the next session (Exhibit 14.3).

The first session may go something like this:

Therapist: Hi, Melissa, right? Glad you could make it today. Here is your first envelope for the prize draws, like Anne spoke with you about. You can open it up, and I'll explain everything to all to the group members in a few minutes, after more people arrive.

EXHIBIT 14.2   SAMPLE HANDOUT DESCRIBING THE NAME-IN-THE-HAT PRIZE CM PROGRAM FOR GROUP ATTENDANCE

Dear Patient,

Starting on ___(date)___, we will be offering you the chance to win prizes for coming to groups on ___(day of the week)___ at ___(time)___. Researchers have found that offering patients prizes can be helpful for engaging patients in treatment and reducing their substance use. We're trying this program in our clinic in hopes that more people will stick with the program and decrease drug use.

The prizes you can win range from small prizes, to medium, large, and jumbo prizes. Small prizes are things such as toiletry items like soaps, food and drink items, and $1 gift cards to fast food restaurants. Medium prizes are worth about $5 and include round-trip subway tokens, $5 gift cards to stores and restaurants, T-shirts, tools, etc. Large prizes are worth up to $20 and also include gift cards to a variety of stores, cameras, handheld CD players, cell phones, and kitchen items like pot and pan sets or dish sets. You may also win a jumbo prize by coming to treatment. A jumbo prize is your choice of a TV or stereo.

Each time you come to group, you will have a chance of winning these prizes. Each week, about half of the people who come to group will win a prize. The more times in a row you come to group, the greater your chances will be of winning prizes.

The first week you come to group, your name will go into a hat ONE time. If you come to group two weeks in a row, your name goes in a hat TWO times. If you come to group three weeks in a row, your name goes in the hat THREE times, and so on. If you come to group all _(10)_ weeks of the program, your name would go in the hat _(10)_ times that last week.

Each week in group, I will draw half as many names from the hat as there are people in group. Those people whose names are drawn get to draw from a prize bowl. The prize bowl contains 100 slips of paper, each representing a prize. Sixty-nine of the 100 slips in the prize bowl state "small," 20 state "medium," 10 state "large," and one states "jumbo." So, if your name is drawn from the hat, you will win at least a small prize, and many weeks at least one person in the group will win an even larger prize. You will get to select from all the available prizes in the category when you win.

If you ever miss a group session, your chances of winning prizes will be reduced. Failure to attend a group session without a pre-approved excused absence (e.g., for a doctor's or lawyer's appointment) will result in no name slips going into the hat that week, and a reset in the number of name slips down to one slip the next time you attend group. If you do reset to one name slip, you can increase the number of name slips you earn based on the number of weeks in a row you attend group.

If you attend groups regularly, you may win multiple prizes some weeks. For example, if you came to group 10 weeks in a row, your name may be drawn three or four times that week and you'd win that many prizes that day.

We hope you enjoy this program and look forward to your participation in group!

EXHIBIT 14.3   REMINDER SLIPS FOR NAME-IN-THE-HAT PRIZE CM FOR GROUP ATTENDANCE

Congratulations!

You earned ____ chances of winning a prize today
for attending group for ____ weeks in a row.
If you attend next week, you will earn ____ chances of winning a prize.

Good luck!

Therapist (to another patient): How are you today? Great. Here's your envelope that relates to the prize draws. Take a seat anywhere you'd like, and I'll explain how the prizes work in a couple of minutes.

Therapist: Good afternoon, Mike. You probably just heard me explaining that everyone gets an envelope, just like Anne mentioned to you at your intake appointment. Here is your envelope. Glad you came to group today, and we'll get started shortly.

Similar conversations can occur with each group attendee. Once the clock reaches five past the start time, or when all attendees appear to be settled in the group room, the therapist may state the following:

Therapist: Hi, everyone! I'm Jim. I want to welcome you all to our first group session. Why don't we briefly go around the room and everyone state their name. We'll do more formal introductions in a few minutes.

After all state their names, the therapist may describe the CM component of treatment.

Therapist: This is the Introductory Skills Group, and as you know, it lasts 10 weeks. So, we'll all be together for the next 10 weeks. We're going to start each session with an incentive procedure, similar to what you did with Anne during your initial evaluation. I've given each of you an envelope. It tells you how many slips you earned for coming to group today, and because this is our first session together, there is one for everyone in the room. That form also tells you how many slips you will earn next Tuesday if you come to group. For all of you, that number will be two. And, if you come next week, you'll get a form telling you that the following week, you will earn three slips for coming to group. The number of slips you earn will keep going up, so long as you keep coming to these groups. Can anyone guess how many slips you can get in our final group together if you come to all ten sessions?

Mike: Ten.

Therapist: Yes, that is correct, Mike. If you come to group every week for the next 10 weeks, you'll get 10 name slips on May 30; that's our last meeting date. You do want to earn more slips, because the more slips you earn, the better your chances are of winning prizes. At the beginning of each session, you all get to put into this hat all the name slips you've earned. So, today, you each get to put in your one name slip. Let's do that now, and I'll tell you what happens next.

Therapist: Great. There are 12 of you here today, and because you've each got one slip, that means there are 12 slips in this hat. What we do after all the slips are in is draw some names from the hat. We'll always draw half the number of names as there are people in the group that day. So, because there are 12 of you here today, we'll draw six names. If there's an odd number of people, we'll round up and do one extra draw. So, let's draw those six lucky names. Who wants to do the draws today? Let's have six volunteers, and you can each draw one name, for a total of six. How about we go in this circle here—Mike, Amy, Tom, Luis, Melissa, and Frank—each of you can reach in the hat, pull out one slip, and read that person's name out loud.

Six slips are drawn from the hat, and the names are each read aloud.

Therapist: So, we've got our six prize winners today. Each person whose name was drawn gets to draw from my prize bowl here—the same prize bowl you drew from when you met with Anne for your intake evaluation. Just like then, there are four categories of prizes in the bowl—small, medium, large, and jumbo. Whatever category you draw, you will get to select a prize from that category. Because I can't bring the entire prize cabinet into this group room, what I did was select a few prizes from each category. So, you can select a prize from the options I brought, or you can take one of these for now, and right after group come with me to the prize cabinet and exchange it for something else. Let me show you all what I brought today, and I'd be happy to take suggestions from the group for other prizes in the future. What I have here in my bag for smalls today are granola bars, a pair of socks, shampoo, a toothbrush, a tube of toothpaste, a candle, a bus token, a fancy pen, and a $1 gift card to Dunkin' Donuts or McDonald's. There are also lots of other things in the prize cabinet, just like you all saw with Anne. For mediums, I brought with me today a $5 gift card to Blockbuster and a $5 phone card, and there are lots of other gift cards in the cabinet. I also have as mediums this coffee mug and a baseball cap. For larges, I have right now with me a $20 gift card to the bookstore, a coffee maker, and this tool set. Over there in the corner is one of my jumbos—a stereo system—and we also have a TV, an iPod, and a window air conditioner in the prize cabinet, if anyone is so lucky to draw a jumbo today. Remember, you can choose something that I have with me right now or take something temporarily and come exchange it right after group if you want to see the larger selection of prizes. Any questions so far?

Melissa: Yeah, my name wasn't drawn. Does that mean I don't get a prize?

Therapist: Yes, each week we draw half as many names as there are people here. So, each person has a 50-50 chance of getting a prize today. Although you won't get a prize today, your name will be in the hat twice next Tuesday if you come to group, and hopefully, your name will be drawn then. I've never known anyone who has come to group regularly who hasn't had their name drawn. We just don't know when it will be drawn, and hopefully, you'll all want to keep coming back to increase your chances of winning prizes.

Melissa: Okay, I guess that's fair, except that I never win anything.

Therapist: I guess that is the beauty of this program. Even people who always feel like they are unlucky have good chances of winning in this program. And, I promise you that your name will be drawn at least once, and probably more times, if you come all 10 weeks.

Melissa: I might beat those odds.

Therapist: Let's think about that for a minute. If you came every week for 10 weeks in a row, your name would go in the hat 1+2+3+4+5+6+7+8+9+10 times. That adds up to 55 times. And, let's say we draw six names a week for 10 weeks; that's 60 names drawn over time, and you don't think it will ever be you?

Melissa: Not with my luck.

Therapist: Let's try it another way. If you came every week for the next 10, each week, you'd have at least a one-in-two chance of having your name drawn each time. To not have your name drawn for 10 weeks in a row would be $\frac{1}{2} \times \frac{1}{2} \times \frac{1}{2} \times \frac{1}{2} \times \frac{1}{2} \times \frac{1}{2} \times \frac{1}{2} \times \frac{1}{2} \times \frac{1}{2} \times \frac{1}{2} = 1/1024$ chance. I'd say the odds are with you, Melissa.

Melissa: How'd you do that math so quickly?

Therapist: Because other people have asked me the same question. So, I figured it out mathematically, and I've also watched people over time. I've never had anyone come to all the groups and not win at least a few prizes.

Okay, now Ellen, Amy, Frank, Mike, Tim, and Luis, each of you has had your name selected. So, one by one, we'll have you draw here from my prize bowl. You can go first, Ellen. Roll up your sleeve, show us all the palm of you hand, and go ahead and make a draw. Choose one slip from the prize bowl, and let's see what category you won.

Ellen: I got a small.

Therapist: Okay, great. Which of these would you like—a granola bar, a pair of socks, shampoo, a toothbrush, toothpaste, a candle, a bus token, a pen, or a $1 gift card to Dunkin' Donuts or McDonald's? Take your pick, and remember you can also exchange it later after group if you'd rather look for something else.

Ellen: I'll take the Dunkin' Donuts card.

Therapist: Excellent choice. I just need you to sign for it here on this sheet. … Great. Now, Amy, it's your turn to draw. Roll up the sleeves, show us your hand, and then make a draw as soon as I put Ellen's small slip back in so that chances of winning categories are always the same.

Amy: I got a small, too.

Therapist: Great. What would you like? A granola bar, shampoo, socks, toothbrush or toothpaste, a candle, a bus token, a pen, or a $1 McDonald's card?

Amy: Hmmm. I wanted the Dunkin' Donuts card, but Ellen took that.

Therapist: That is not a problem. I think I have more DD cards in the prize cabinet, so if you take something else now, you can exchange it after group for a DD card.

Amy: Never mind. I guess I need a bus token anyway. I'll take that instead.

Therapist: That is fine. Just sign here, and I'll put your small slip back in the prize bowl. Now, Frank, it's your turn to draw.

Frank: Come on, come on. I want it to be my lucky day. Give me a jumbo!

Therapist: Good luck, Frank. Roll up your sleeve, show me your palm. We're rooting for you!

Frank: Ah-ha. I got a medium!

Therapist: Good for you—what would you like? A Blockbuster card, a phone card, coffee mug, or baseball cap?

Frank: I'm going to take that cap for now, but I want to see the prize cabinet after group. There might be something better in there.

Therapist: Yes, that you can do. You can sign for this cap now, and if you decide you want to exchange it after group, we'll do so.

Therapist: Okay, I owe three more people draws. Mike, Tim, and Luis. You go next, Mike.

Mike: I got a small. I want the socks.

Therapist: Sounds good. Just sign here. And, now it's your turn, Tim.

Tim: Why are we pulling our sleeves up and showing hands?

Therapist: It's just my way of making sure no one tries to beat my system.

Carol: Yeah, I wouldn't trust you either!

Therapist: It's not about trust. It's just part of the program. Everybody does it. Okay, Tim, you ready to draw?

Tim: My sleeve is up, and I drew a small. Damn. I was hoping for a large.

Therapist: A small is not bad. Here's what I've got with me now: a granola bar, shampoo, toothbrush or toothpaste, a candle, or a pen.

Tim: I don't want any of that. I need a token.

Therapist: That is one thing I've always got extra of in the cabinet. Take one of these for now, and we'll exchange it for a token right after group.

Tim: Okay, give me that pen.

Therapist: Here it is, just sign here. And, last but not least, Luis.

Luis: The first shall be last, and the last the first. I got a large!

Therapist: Excellent! What would you like?

Luis: That tool set has my name on it!

Therapist: This is great. Six people won prizes today, and if you all come to group next Tuesday, you'll each have a 50-50 chance of winning a prize then. As Anne explained, our hope is that this prize system will keep you motivated to attend group and get the most out of treatment. I know sometimes it's hard to leave what you're doing at home or at work and get all the way here, especially when the weather is bad like today. But, if you're feeling unsure about coming or not to group, just remember the prizes. You never know if it'll be you're lucky day to win a large or even a jumbo. This prize system also seems to be fun for people, so I hope you enjoy it. Before we move on, let me get a sense from you all if you liked the types of prizes I brought with me today, or if anyone has suggestions for other things they'd like to see as prizes in any of the categories.

Carol: How about some of that hand soap?

Therapist: Sure, I can do that. Other suggestions?

Michelle: I'd like some lotions. And, maybe good Kleenex. The stuff here is scratchy.

Therapist: Those are excellent suggestions. Does anyone else have ideas for good prizes?

Melissa: How about something for kids? I've got kids and I'd like to win things for them.

Therapist: Sounds good. What kind of things do they like?

Melissa: You know, like stuffed animals, or those little figurines. My kids are little.

Therapist: I can do that. I'll also be sure to get a gift card to a toy store.

Melissa: Okay, good. Now I just need to win.

Therapist: I'll try to have more of those sorts of things next week, and anyone who wants to come look in the prize cabinet is welcome to come after group. You can see what I've got and give me additional suggestions then. Now, we're going to move on to what else we came here for—to talk about drug use and give one another advice on ways to break that cycle and improve problems that drug use is causing in your lives.

At this point, the group could move onto the usual content.

Although the preceding script may appear long, it will usually only take about 20 minutes out of group the first time CM is introduced, and thereafter become shorter and shorter. In estimates from over 20 clinics that have used this CM procedure, the entire duration of the CM is 10 minutes after the therapist and patients have become accustomed to it.

14.2.3 Subsequent Group CM Sessions

After patients have been introduced to the CM procedure, fewer explanations will be needed. However, even in closed group formats, sometimes patients new to the CM component will come to group for the first time. In those cases, a brief overview is useful. Below, I outline a sample dialogue for the second CM session, to which some patients who missed the prior week come. As in all group CM sessions, the therapist would greet patients as they arrive and hand them their envelopes containing their name slips and the form indicating the number of weeks in a row they've attended group and the number of slips they can earn the next week.

Therapist: I'm glad to see you all here today. You all did some really good work together last week, and I'm looking forward to another good session today. We have a couple of new members in group today. Let's briefly go around the room and say our first names.

After the introductions are finished …

Therapist: Now, we'll get to the prize draws before we move onto our topic of the day—coping with urges. I've given you each your envelopes— they contain your name slips for today, and they give you a reminder about how many slips you can earn next week if you come to group. Remember that your slips go up for each week in a row you attend group, and the more slips you get, the greater your chances are of having your name drawn. Let me also just remind you all that if ever you can't make it to group some week, it is really important that you let me know. If you have an excused absence for something like a doctor or legal appointment, I won't have to reset your name slips. But, if you just don't show some week or have an unexcused absence, you'll drop back down to one slip the next time you come to group. Does everybody understand that?

Mike: I've got a job interview next Tuesday? Does that count?

Therapist: Yes, a job interview can count for an excused absence. I would just need for you to tell me ahead of time and to bring back something from the interview—like a name card or brochure from the company.

If you can do that I won't reset your name slips when you come back to group in two weeks. You'd get three slips that day, rather than one if you didn't get the pre-approval for an excused absence. Let's talk after group, and anyone else who knows they've got something important planned for a Tuesday, be sure to speak with me as well.

Mike: Okay.

Therapist: Since we have a couple new members today, I'll just remind everyone how this works. Everyone put your name slips into the hat here—we'll pass it around. Once they are all in, we'll draw eight names from the hat today because we have 15 people here. We always draw half as many names from the hat as there are people in group, and we round up for odd numbers. I'll be giving out eight prizes today. Because some of you have your name in the hat more than once, some of you could win more than one prize today.

Therapist: Okay, we've got all the name slips in the hat. Now, I'll pass the hat around again to the first eight people starting with you, Tina. Each of you can draw ONE name from the hat, and read that name out loud. They are the people who will draw for a prize today.

As the hat goes to eight people starting with Tina, the following names are drawn: Amy, Mike, Frank, Melissa, Melissa, Luis, Tina, and Mark.

Therapist: We'll have people draw for prizes in the order their names were drawn, staring with Amy. Here is my selection of prizes today, which you can exchange for other things in the prize cabinet if you don't see anything here that catches your eye. For smalls, I brought with me a bus token, Dunkin' Donuts and Burger King cards, a hair clip, tweezers, a bottle of juice, a hand soap, and Kleenex—this is the soft kind! For mediums, I brought with me today a Big Book, a hand towel, and a gift card to CVS. For larges, I've got a $20 card to JCPenney, a towel set, and a cordless drill. The TV is too large for me to carry, so I brought an iPod for the jumbo today, but remember there are more things to choose from in the prize cabinet. What we do now is have everyone whose name was drawn select from the prize bowl, just like you all did at your intake evaluation with Anne. Everyone rolls up their sleeves and shows their hand before drawing, and we replace the prize slips that are drawn after each draw. Amy, you're first.

Amy: I got a small again. Today, I'll take that Dunkin' Donuts card. I love their coffee.

Therapist: Perfect, sign right here. Now, Mike, you're next.

Mike: I got a small again, too. Gimme the bus token.

Therapist (smiling): How about a "thank you?" Just sign here.

Frank: I'm next, and I got a small, too. Kleenex is good. I've got a cold.

Therapist: Okay, Melissa gets to draw twice, because her name was drawn two times today.

Lynn: Is that fair? My name didn't get drawn at all. Why should she get to pick twice?

Therapist: I'm glad you brought that up, Lynn. Let's take a minute to discuss it. Everybody's name goes into the hat based on the number of times in a row that they've come to group. Melissa, and some others, have come two weeks in a row, so their chances of having their name drawn increases. You've also been here two weeks in a row, so your name could have been drawn twice today, too. But, because it's based on probabilities, it's never exact on any given week. However, the more you come, the greater your chances are of having your name drawn. By the end of the 10-week program, if you come all 10 weeks, your name will be in the hat 10 times. You could win up to 10 prizes that day, and it would be pretty likely you'd win at least a couple of prizes that day. Melissa didn't have her name drawn last week, but she made up for it this week. We want to reward people for coming to group regularly, and even though odds are never perfect, your chances of having your name drawn next week will increase. You will get up to three tries.

Lynn: I do remember that. It's just weird she gets two draws, and some of us don't get any.

Therapist: It all tends to even out with time, especially if you keep coming to group. Are there other questions about how it works? No, okay, Melissa, are you ready to draw?

Melissa: Yes, I got a large! Yippee! I know what I want—that coffee maker you brought in last week. Mine broke, and I haven't bought another one, hoping I'd win one here.

Therapist: I did see that in the prize cabinet this morning. Why don't you take one of these large prizes for now, and we can exchange it after group.

Melissa: Okay, I'll take the towels for now, and I want to put this large slip back in the prize bowl before I draw again. Otherwise, it'll decrease my chances of getting another large today.

Therapist: Absolutely. We always replace the prize slips before each draw, so chances of winning each category remain the same. But, we also need to shake up the bowl.

Melissa: This time I got a small. I'll have the bus token.

Therapist: Just sign here for both your prizes. And, now, Luis, you are next.

Luis: Sleeves are up—here we go! I got a medium.

Therapist: Excellent. What would you like?

Luis: The CVS card is good.

Therapist: Just sign here, and now it is Tina's turn to draw.

Tina: Small.

Therapist: What would you like, Tina?

Tina: Hand soap. Thanks.

Therapist: Just sign here. And, finally, Mark. Your turn to draw for a prize.

Mark: Small. You don't have much left for me.

Therapist: But, you can take one of these now, and come to the cabinet with me after group. There are a lot more options there. These are just samples. Does anyone in the group have suggestions of what else you might like to see? I can try to bring it next week.

Mark: Okay, just give me the tweezers. I'll get something else later.

Therapist: Just sign here, please. Is everyone clear what will happen next week? All your names will go in the hat one more time than today, as indicated in the slip in your envelopes. The more you keep coming to group, the greater your chances are of winning prizes. And, the more you come to group, the more you will learn about your recovery. Questions? No? Okay, great, let's spend the rest of our time together talking about urges and cravings.

As noted in the preceding dialogue, the descriptions were less extensive than at the first session, but new group members were oriented to the procedure. Although most sessions proceed without concerns about "fairness," I provided reactions to such comments in case you receive such concerns from patients.

Dialogues similar to those in this section can be used throughout the remaining CM sessions. When the CM procedures are coming to an end, it is a good idea to remind patients about the termination of the prizes and what will happen afterward. In some cases, the groups may continue without CM, and in other cases, as in our example, patients will transfer to other levels of care (and different groups) once the CM component ends. The next sections describe some sample dialogue that can be used in the second to last and final CM sessions.

14.2.4 Ending of CM

In this sample CM protocol, the CM is in effect for 10 weeks. Therefore, in week nine, you should remind the patients about the ending of the CM procedure and describe post-CM plans from a treatment perspective. If patients are transferring out of the CM groups, the conversion may go as outlined below. This termination preparation conversation could occur immediately after the drawing procedure or at the very end of the group session.

Therapist: This is our ninth week together in this group, and I think you've all done some really good work here. I do just want to remind you that next week will be our last week together. Those of you who've come to all 10 sessions will get your names in the hat 10 times, and for everyone else it will be at least two or more times, depending on how many weeks in a row you've come and as noted in the form in your envelopes today. That will be our last prize drawing session together. Then, you will all be transferring to other groups. I think I've spoken to most of you about your discharge or aftercare plans. If anyone is unclear about those, please set up an appointment with me after group today.

In some CM programs, patients transfer out of a CM group at different times (e.g., rolling group admissions, in which each patient comes to the CM group for a set period of time and then transfers out after, for example, 12 weeks). In these cases, you could include a handwritten note at the bottom of the slip you place in the patients' envelope noting when their time in CM ends:

Dear Megan, I've enjoyed your contributions to group over the past 11 weeks. Next week will be your last week in the CM program. I'm hoping you'll get some good prizes, as your name will go in the hat 12 times for 12 weeks of perfect attendance! I know your primary counselor has discussed aftercare plans with you. Please make an appointment with her or me if you wish to discuss them further. Thank you for your contributions.

14.2.5 The Final CM Session

Whether all patients, or just some, are ending a CM group, it is important to acknowledge graduation from the program at the last session. In the example I've been detailing, the therapist may want to start the final CM session with a discussion such as the following:

Therapist: I see you've all received your envelopes from me, and today marks our last session together. We're going to do the final name draws and prize draws in a minute, and then we can reflect on how you've felt about these groups. I also just want to remind everyone to be sure to follow the aftercare treatment plans that your individual counselors have recommended to you. As you know, drug abuse treatment is an ongoing process, and although everyone has been doing really well in this group, it's important you stay with the program for your best chances of long-term recovery. I see there are 16 people here today, so we're going to do eight draws once we get all your names in the hat. Great. Kim—how about you draw all eight names today, and read them aloud as you pick them out?

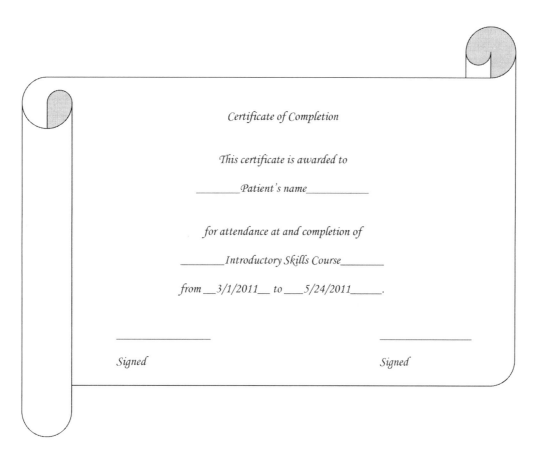

Certificate of Completion

This certificate is awarded to

_____*Patient's name*_____

for attendance at and completion of

_____*Introductory Skills Course*_____

from ___3/1/2011__ to ____5/24/2011_____.

_____   _____

Signed   *Signed*

FIGURE 14.1   Certificate of completion.

Kim: Mark, Melissa, Luis, Lynn, Melissa, Kevin, Tim, and one more—John.
Therapist: Great. Each of you will get one prize draw today, and two for Melissa, and then I have a little something for everyone in the group today.

After the prize drawings and selections occur, the therapist will provide all group members with a certificate of completion (see Figure 14.1).

Therapist: These are certificates, and I have one for each of you. I'm really proud of all the effort and hard work you've done to come to group and give good feedback and suggestions to one another, and for sharing your problems, and accomplishments, with us. You've all won some prizes here, which I hope will be reminders to you as you move through the next stages of recovery.

Note that in this dialogue, the therapist mentions the prizes and the draws, but focuses on recovery, tying in the prizes as reminders of a job well done. If an open-group CM format is being implemented, and just one or a few patients are ending time in a CM group, the conversation would be similar but would recognize specifically the patient(s) who are ending time in the CM group. An example is below.

Therapist: I see you've all received your envelopes from me, and today marks Michelle's last session with us. She is graduating from this program, and after we do the name and prize draws, I have a little something for Michelle. I see there are 17 people here today, so we're going to do nine draws once we get all your names in the hat. Great. Why don't we let Michelle draw all nine names today since it's her last group with us. Michelle, go ahead and draw nine name slips, and read out the names as you select them.

Michelle: Okay. Let's see. John, Tim, Lynn, Lynn, Luis—that's five, but what's with all these L names? Melissa, Michelle, yeah! Mark, and Lynn again.

Therapist: Those are our nine names for today. I'll show the prizes I brought with me today, and remember there is always the prize cabinet as well. Then, we'll do the draws.

After all the prize drawings are completed, the therapist may say,

> I have a special certificate of completion here for Michelle. It has her dates of attendance at our group and is signed by our director and me. Michelle, I hope you will remember our group and all the things you've learned over the past three months. You've made great contributions to our group, and we're really going to miss you. But, I am confident you are going to continue to do well in your aftercare groups. Does anyone have any thoughts they'd like to share with Michelle?

In this example, Michelle is acknowledged for her contributions to the group. The therapist brought extra attention to Michelle, by having her draw all the names at her last session. For patients who might be uncomfortable with that approach, therapists may forgo such attention and simply acknowledge their final session with the certificate. In either case, a certificate is a nice gesture to provide for all patients who successfully complete treatment.

14.3 ASSESSMENT OF YOUR CM PROGRAM

If delivered in the manner previously described, your CM program should increase group attendance. Please note, however, that there are two critical aspects to successful CM implementation. One is that you design a CM plan that follows appropriate behavioral principles. A second is that you implement CM in the intended manner, both in terms of awarding the correct number of slips and draws at every session to all patients and that you present the CM in the appropriate manner, with enthusiasm and confidence. As described in the next chapter, it is always a good idea to have a supervisor or colleague review your tracking forms and slips to make sure slips and draws are awarded as intended. Audiotaping the group is also encouraged, as review of CM delivery by a supervisor, colleague, and even yourself can be useful. Even if audiotaping is not possible, an honest self-appraisal of each session using the Contingency Management Competence Scale for Reinforcing Attendance, as described in Chapter 15, Exhibit 15.4, may be useful.

Although CM should be effective in improving group attendance, you should not expect that a CM program will work miracles or that all patients will respond. The response rate to CM is typically about 50%. If you have a group with a usual attendance rate of 40%, you should expect that CM would improve the attendance rate to about 60%. Note that if you have attendance rates of 80% or higher *without CM*, there is little point of adding CM to such a group, as there would be little room for noticeable improvement.

Keep in mind that CM may not work immediately. It will take some time for patients to get used to the procedures and to realize that they can really win prizes and that they can win more prizes the more often they attend. If you are not seeing any increases in attendance after three or four weeks in the program, talk with the patients who are coming as well as those who are not coming (by phone or in person) and find out why. Re-orient them to the prizes. If necessary, allow some new patients to join the CM program, and they may revive interest in the prizes.

If CM is not working to improve attendance after several weeks, then there is a very good chance that something is wrong with its implementation. You should make an honest appraisal of how well your CM design integrates important behavioral principles, and you should have a trusted colleague or supervisor review your protocol and your implementation, as outlined in Chapter 15. By determining what is wrong, you may be able to correct it.

Although it may be a good idea to make changes to how CM is introduced and administered to patients (in terms of verbal delivery and enthusiasm and choice of prizes), you generally should not change your CM protocol (the monitoring and reinforcement schedule) over the time period it was originally scheduled. You should consider your CM program to be a contract between you and the patients. You don't want to break that contract, or the next group of CM patients may not trust that you will keep your word with them either.

If for some reason your CM program isn't working to improve attendance by the end of the original number of weeks for which it was planned, you should have plenty of prizes left over to institute CM with a new group of patients. At that time, you may wish to make some modifications to the procedure, by increasing the number of names drawn from the hat at each group session, instituting it in a group that is likely to be more responsive, changing the duration of the program, buying more popular prizes, or making sure that you are presenting CM as novel and fun. By following your first CM program through, you will learn a lot about what you are doing right and what could be improved.

Chapter 15

Monitoring and Supervising Adherence and Competence in Contingency Management Delivery

If CM is implemented as described in this book, it ought to be effective in altering patient behavior. However, CM is not always administered as intended, often because of lack of experience, unexpected problems, or poor oversight. Things that can go wrong include patients failing to attend CM appointments, changes in intended frequencies of reinforcement, and not maintaining interesting reinforcers. Many of these issues relate to violations of key behavioral principles of CM. If you keep in mind the necessity of the three basic principles of CM (frequently monitor the target behavior, reinforce the behavior each time it occurs, and withhold reinforcement when it does not occur), you are likely to implement a successful CM program. To the extent these principles are not adhered to, the effectiveness of your CM program will suffer.

One of the biggest obstacles relates to maintaining monitoring and reinforcement regimens. If you are reinforcing abstinence and the patient has not achieved abstinence, he may be less likely to come in for monitoring. In these cases, you should continue to show him the prize cabinet and have him select item(s) of greatest interest to win. If a patient truly doesn't want to leave a sample, not forcing it is fine. However, you should continue to meet with him regularly, if even briefly to brainstorm methods for achieving initial abstinence and encouraging sample submission when one or two days of abstinence occurs. Once patients are able to provide a negative sample and start earning reinforcers, they may become re-engaged in the CM program.

If patients attend treatment but are unable to meet with you for monitoring or reinforcement (e.g., because you are busy or with another patient), they may weigh the pros and cons of waiting. Waiting more than 15 minutes for the chance of winning a prize that averages $2 may not be sufficiently valued. Minimizing "costs" for the patient for participating in CM involves reducing wait times, so you may need to consider how CM patients can been seen quickly or on demand, for example, by a dedicated CM staff member.

Another reason CM programs fail in community settings relates to clinicians either not being sufficiently enthusiastic about it or not implementing it correctly. To guard against inappropriate administration, the next section describes methods to assess appropriate CM administration.

Whether just a single clinician or multiple clinicians are implementing CM, it is important to ensure fidelity to the intended CM plan and competence in CM delivery. As when learning any new therapy, supervision and feedback are important and helpful in improving skills. In this chapter, I describe tools to monitor and ensure appropriate administration of CM. First, I outline these tools for use in CM protocols that reinforce abstinence, and second, I describe parallel forms and processes for CM protocols that reinforce group attendance. If you are reinforcing another behavior, you can adapt these procedures accordingly.

15.1 MEASURING ADHERENCE AND COMPETENCE IN DELIVERY OF CM THAT REINFORCES ABSTINENCE

Adherence refers to the delivery of an intervention in the intended manner. To ensure that the CM is delivered as intended, you should create checklists for each CM session. Examples of CM adherence checklists are in Exhibits 15.1 and 15.3. One is for a CM system that monitors and reinforces abstinence and the other is for group attendance. The forms could be altered to accommodate monitoring and reinforcing other behaviors. They need to be tailored to specific CM protocols if they differ from those detailed in this book.

15.1.1 Tracking Form for Abstinence

The tracking form for abstinence shown in Exhibit 15.1 has two columns, for two separate CM sessions. If you were instituting a twice-weekly CM program, you would use one sheet per week. If your program were for 12 weeks, you would use 12 sheets in total. A thrice-weekly monitoring and reinforcement system would best be represented by a sheet containing three columns, so that once again, each week could be contained on a single page.

As noted at the top of the form, the patient's name should be inserted. In the first box, there are also spaces for the date of the session (and for the rescheduled session, if applicable), session number, and CM therapist. In terms of dates, the date of the original scheduled session should be indicated. I suggest writing in the dates of scheduled sessions about a week ahead of time. I do not recommend writing in all scheduled sessions (e.g., all Tuesdays and Fridays for the next 12 weeks) at the beginning of the patient's participation in the CM program, as some patients may alter their testing schedules during the

EXHIBIT 15.1   TRACKING FORM FOR MONITORING AND REINFORCING ABSTINENCE

Patient: _____   Patient: _____

Date of scheduled session: _____   Date of scheduled session: _____

Date rescheduled (if applicable): _____   Date rescheduled (if applicable): _____

Session #: _____   Session #: _____

CM therapist: _____   CM therapist: _____

Attended?   Attended?
  Yes / No-unex / No-ex / No-resch   Yes / No-unex / No-ex / No-resch

  Reason excused, if applicable? _____   Reason excused, if applicable? _____

  _____   _____

  Attended rescheduled session?   Attended rescheduled session?
  Yes / No-unex / No-ex / NA   Yes / No-unex / No-ex / NA

If attended, sample collected? Yes / No   If attended, sample collected? Yes / No

If no, why not? _____   If no, why not? _____

  _____   _____

Methamphetamine results: Neg/Pos   *Methamphetamine results: Neg/Pos*

Discuss results, self-reports, and cravings   *Discuss results, self-reports, and cravings*

Draws due (0–8): _____ draws   Draws due (0–8): _____ draws

1 more than last session if negative, max   *1 more than last session if negative, max*
  of 8   *of 8*

Monitor draws-watch sleeves/hands   *Monitor draws-watch sleeves/hands*

Draw outcomes: Draw outcomes:

  Good job: _____   Good job: _____

  Small: _____   Small: _____

  Large: _____   Large: _____

  Jumbo: _____   Jumbo: _____

  TOTAL = _____   TOTAL = _____

Total Draw outcomes should equal   *Total Draw outcomes should equal*
  Draws due   *Draws due*

Prizes signed out on Prize Release Form?   Prizes signed out on Prize Release Form?

  Yes / No / NA   Yes / No / NA

(continued on next page)

273

Assess desire for future prizes.	*Assess desire for future prizes.*
Date of next session: _____	Date of next session: _____
Draws possible if negative*: _____	Draws possible if negative*: _____
* 1 more than Draws due today, but max of 8	* 1 more than Draws due today, but max of 8
Comments: _____	Comments: _____
_____	_____
_____	_____

course of treatment. If an agreed upon change occurred in week four, then all subsequent scheduled dates would need to be altered. If the date of testing were rescheduled (see Chapter 13, Section 2.4.4, "Excused Absences"), the date of the rescheduled session would be included in this top box as well. In most cases, sessions should not be rescheduled, so this line will usually contain "NA" for not applicable.

The session number (in this protocol, "1" to "24") should be indicated in this top box as well. For the first CM session of the program, the session number would be "1." For a 12-week, twice-weekly CM program, the numbers of sessions should go up consecutively from one to 24. Regardless of whether or not a session is rescheduled, the session number should be the same, as there should be exactly 24 sessions for this sample protocol I am outlining. The therapist who conducted the CM session should then be written in the appropriate space.

In the next box, the first item asks if the patient attended the scheduled session. A response should be circled: "Yes" if the patient attended the originally scheduled session, "No-unexcused" if the absence was unexcused, or "No-excused" if the patient failed to attend the scheduled CM session but that absence was excused and not rescheduled, or "No-rescheduled" if the absence was both excused and rescheduled. If the absence was excused, the next item asks the therapist to indicate the reason. Examples include therapist was sick, day was a holiday, or patient had a court or medical appointment. For an excused absence that is not rescheduled, no more markings on that day would be needed.

For an excused absence that is rescheduled, the next item asks if the patient attended the rescheduled session. Responses are "Yes," "No-unexcused," "No-excused," or "Not applicable," which would be the most often circled response, as most sessions ought not to be rescheduled.

For unexcused absences, whether they occurred in relation to the original session or a rescheduled session, the patient is NOT eligible for any draws that session, and at the next session, draws reset to the lowest number (i.e., one draw). To remind yourself of this reset, you should write "0" in the "Draws due" section if an unexcused absence occurs.

For an attended session, you next indicate whether a sample was collected or not. In rare cases, a patient may attend a CM session but refuse to provide a urine sample, or state they are unable to urinate and then not return later that day to provide a sample. If something like that happens, you would indicate what happened on the "If not, why not?" line. The results of the sample should then be recorded, with respect to the targeted (i.e., the reinforced) substance (in this case, methamphetamine). The next line, in italics, is a reminder line, so that you remember to discuss the results with the patient, along with any self-reports of drug use or cravings or urges to use (see Section 15.1.3, "Assessing Competence in CM Delivery" later in this chapter). If any self-reports of drug use occur, such information and your response to it can be indicated in the lowest box related to comments.

The next item relates to the draws due. The draws in our sample CM protocol range from zero (if the patient tested positive, had an unexcused absence, or refused to provide a sample) to a maximum of eight. Note that some CM protocols may have a different maximum number of draws and in these cases the tracking form would need to be altered. The draws due should be one more than the draws received at the last session (so long as the patient tested negative and has not reached the cap). Thus, if you are diligently completing these forms at each CM session, you can look back on the last CM session to see how many draws were earned and then and add one to it, unless the patient has already achieved the maximum number of draws (in this case, eight).

The next line reminds you to administer draws, and to monitor the drawing procedure to prevent any possibility of cheating (see Exhibit 12.3). You then record draw outcomes according to the prize categories. In our CM program, there are good job, small, large, and jumbo slips. So, if a patient earned four draws, and those draws resulted in two good jobs, one small, and one large, the appropriate numbers would be indicated, with zero included on the jumbo line. The total number of draw outcomes needs to match the total number of draws due, and the form tells you this.

The next section of the form asks you to indicate whether or not the patient signed the Prize Release Form. If you are administering CM correctly, the response to this item should be "Yes" every time a patient draws one or more prize slips. If the patient earned no draws that day, or if all his draws resulted in good job slips, then it would be appropriate to circle "NA" in response to that item. This section also reminds you to assess the patient's desire for prizes he wants to win in the future and to make suggestions for new prizes.

Finally, you are reminded to inform the patient about the date of the next CM session and the number of draws he can earn if he tests negative for the targeted substance. This number should be one more than he earned today, so long as he has not already reached the maximum number of draws, in which case the number would be the same as today's draws (i.e., eight).

In the very last section, you can write any comments related to clinical issues that may have arisen, self-reports of substance use or cravings that were discussed, or recommendations you may have made to the patient. As noted in the next sections, CM sessions are generally short, so it is fine to leave this section blank if nothing unusual arose in the session. If CM is integrated in the context of a longer individual session, usual progress notes should be kept, and this CM log can just be included as an adjunct form. The comments section here relates only to CM-specific issues, for example, rescheduling an appointment.

15.1.2 Monitoring Tracking Forms for Abstinence-Based Reinforcement

As you are implementing your CM program, you should be filling out this, or a similar, form for each CM session scheduled (e.g., 24 sessions for a twice-weekly 12-week CM program). You should review and become familiar with the forms prior to implementing CM, and check your forms regularly for completeness and accuracy. In addition, it is always a good idea to have a colleague or supervisor review your forms. If you make mistakes in reinforcement delivery, an extra set of eyes can help catch and correct mistakes for the future. Typically, I recommend that if a mistake in reinforcement occurs and it is in the patient's advantage (i.e., the patient got more draws than he was supposed to), then do not try to take away draws already made. If the mistake was caught prior to the next CM session, then you can explain the mistake to the patient and correct the draw schedule starting at the next session. You can also discuss with the patient that you made an error and that he benefited from that error in terms of draws last session. Clearly, most patients will be happy about the extra draws and respect you for your honesty. If you awarded too few draws in a session, then you can apologize to the patient, give him the missed draw(s), and return the draw schedule to the appropriate level at the next session. Checking tracking forms frequently should help in both regards.

However, if you don't uncover errors that were made until weeks later, it may be too late to correct the mistakes. A mistake in any given week can result in increases or decreases in draws due for many subsequent weeks. For example, if a patient in week three is awarded one more or fewer draw than he should have received, this mistake is likely to carry forward for the next several weeks. If you didn't catch the error until week eight, then you may be better off simply continuing the reinforcement schedule to which the patient was already accustomed. However, if you were making repeated errors over time (not resetting patients for positive or missed samples, or not escalating reinforcers at all), you would need to weigh the pros and cons of fixing the mistake for the future versus continuing to employ a suboptimal reinforcement schedule.

Consider a patient who regularly did not submit samples and who was never reset in terms of draws for his missed samples. If this patient was never reset for six missed samples over the past eight weeks and then all of a sudden you noticed the error and then tried to reset his draws for his next missed sample, the patient may get upset, and perhaps rightfully so. One way to handle this situation would be in week nine to explain to him that you were administering the reinforcement inappropriately for the past eight weeks, and he actually received a lot more draws than he should have. You could then state that henceforth, starting at subsequent sessions, any missed samples will result in a reset in draws earned. This would be much fairer to the patient, whose behavior of missing samples had already been shaped by the reinforcement contingencies previously in place (e.g., that missed samples result in no reinforcement loss).

In any case, frequent review of your tracking forms, by yourself and others familiar with the CM protocol in effect, ought to reduce the possibility of errors in CM adherence. During initial CM protocol implementation, I've found that therapists make errors with over 35% of patients! Therefore, monitoring tracking forms for adherence is critical for appropriate CM implementation. Once therapists' mistakes are pointed out, they subsequently make far fewer errors over time (Petry, Alessi, et al., 2010).

15.1.3 Assessing Competence in CM Delivery

To maximize effectiveness, your CM protocol should not only be delivered in the manner intended, utilizing the tracking sheet in Exhibit 15.1, but also with a high degree of quality or competence. Even in cases in which a CM therapist is appropriately using all the forms and keeping track of the prizes, CM may not necessarily be administered according to CM principles. One can correctly adhere to a therapy protocol without delivering the therapy competently. An inexperienced therapist, for example, may follow a CM protocol exactly, but she may convey little confidence in her own skill at delivering CM or lack enthusiasm for the intervention. Competence can be more difficult to achieve than adherence to many types of therapies. Fortunately, because of the relatively straightforward approach of CM, many therapists rapidly gain competence and a high degree of skill in delivering it.

Petry, Alessi, et al. (2010) and Ledgerwood & Petry (2010) developed a rating scale for measuring skill in CM delivery as it relates to prize CM protocols that reinforce abstinence. This scale, the Contingency Management Competence Scale for Reinforcing Abstinence (CMCS-Abstinence), appears in Exhibit 15.2.

EXHIBIT 15.2 COMPETENCE MEASURE FOR RATING DELIVERY OF PRIZE CM FOR ABSTINENCE

Tape # _____ Session # _____ Rater: _____

Date:___ ___/___ ___/___ ___Start time:_____

Therapist:_____Stop time: _____

Patient ID:_____Session duration:_____ min.

1 = Very Poor	The therapist's skill was non-evident (not addressed) or unacceptable, incompatible with the CM approach, and potentially counterproductive or toxic.
2 = Poor	The therapist addressed the issue, but in a poor or cursory manner; therapist demonstrated lack of competence, failure to understand issue or its context, or lack of expertise.
3 = Barely Acceptable	The therapist handled the issue in a manner somewhat consistent with the CM approach.
4 = Adequate	The therapist handled the issue in an acceptable way, consistent with CM, and in an average manner.
5 = Good	The therapist addressed the issue in a manner somewhat better than average.
6 = Very Good	The therapist's skill and expertise were very evident in delivering the intervention.
7 = Excellent	The therapist demonstrated exceptional mastery and excellence.

1. To what extent did the therapist discuss **outcomes of urine and breath sample monitoring**?   1 2 3 4 5 6 7

2. To what extent did the therapist state **how many draws were earned at this session**?   1 2 3 4 5 6 7

3. To what extent did the therapist state **how many draws would be earned at the next session** if the patient were abstinent?   1 2 3 4 5 6 7

4. To what extent did the therapist **assess the patient's desire for items in the prize cabinet**?   1 2 3 4 5 6 7

5. To what extent did the therapist **discuss the patient's self-report of substance use or urges/cravings to use**?	1	2	3	4	5	6	7	
6. If the patient self-reported substance use, to what extent did the therapist **relate self-report of substance use to objective indicators of substance use**?	1	2	3	4	5	6	7	NA
7. If the patient self-reported substance use, to what extent did the therapist **relate self-report of substance use to consequences of positive samples**?	1	2	3	4	5	6	7	NA
8. To what extent did the therapist **compliment or praise** the patient's efforts toward abstinence?	1	2	3	4	5	6	7	
9. To what extent did the therapist **communicate confidence** that the patient's efforts will yield success in the future?	1	2	3	4	5	6	7	

General Items

10. **General skillfulness/effectiveness** (demonstrates expertise, competence, and commitment; engages patient in discussion; makes interventions at appropriate times—not missed or too early)	1	2	3	4	5	6	7
11. **Maintaining session structure** (maintains session focus; sets appropriate tone and structure, appropriate level of therapist activity/directiveness, and appropriate duration)	1	2	3	4	5	6	7
12. **Empathy** (conveys warmth and sensitivity, demonstrates genuine concern and a non-judgmental stance, understands and expresses patient's feelings and concerns)	1	2	3	4	5	6	7

If CM sessions are audiotaped and rated, one can determine whether or not CM is being administered competently using this scale. A detailed manual (Ledgerwood & Petry, 2010), exists for rating each of the 12 items on the scale. It is available at http://contingencymanagement.uchc.edu/index.html.

These items assess how well therapists adhere to 12 issues relevant to CM. At least 10 of these issues should be addressed in every CM session (the remaining two items, labeled numbers "6" and "7," are relevant only when patients self-report substance use). Chapter 13 described competent administration of CM sessions that reinforce abstinence. By evaluating the therapists' dialogues in Chapter 13 in conjunction with the CMCS-Abstinence scale and detailed raters' manual (Ledgerwood & Petry, 2010), you can practice rating adherence.

Briefly, a CM session that contained the following aspects would be rated with high scores: discussion of results from toxicology testing, indication of draws earned and rationale for number of draws earned, reminders of draws possible at the next session, assessment of desired prizes, discussion of substance use or cravings/urges to use (and when applicable, relationship of self-reports to toxicology tests and reinforcement system in effect), compliments of the patient's efforts, and communication of confidence in the patient's future success. Sessions are also rated with respect to three general issues: general skillfulness, maintaining structure, and empathy.

An example of a dialogue that would score very high on the competence scale is shown here:

Therapist: John, as you can see here on the dipstick, your sample tests negative for methamphetamine today. Great job! You've provided all negative samples for three whole weeks in a row now. That is really something to be proud of.

John: Yeah, I am pretty happy about it. This is the longest I've gone without using in years.

Therapist: That is a real accomplishment. I knew you could do it! Since I saw you last, have you had any cravings or urges to use methamphetamine or other substances? I know alcohol has often been a trigger for you in the past.

John: I ran into an old buddy of mine on Wednesday. He wanted to go to a bar, but I just told him I was busy.

Therapist: That is great to hear. Being able to say no to an old friend can take a lot of courage and self control. Knowing that going to the bar would likely lead to drinking, which in turn could make you want to use methamphetamine, is part of the recovery process.

John: Yeah, I just knew I didn't want to end up using.

Therapist: It sounds like you really have your priorities straight. I also think you should bring up this issue in group later today, as I think a lot of other group members could learn from your experience. Because you were able to say no to that high-risk situation and you tested negative for methamphetamine again today, you are up to six draws. And, this means that next Tuesday, you will earn seven draws if you test negative for methamphetamine again then. Here is the reminder form stating how many draws you can get next Tuesday. And, now, let's get you your six draws for today.

John: Great. Six draws is a pretty good chance of getting a large like I did last week.

Therapist: It is—good luck!

John: Okay, my sleeves are up, and here I got a small, a good job, another good job, another good job, come on! A large—YES! And a good job.

Therapist: That's great! You got a large just like last time. Let me show you what I have in the cabinet today. If I remember correctly, there were several larges you were trying to decide between earlier, right?

John: Yup. I took the CD player last time, but I also really wanted that camera. Excellent. There it is. I'll take that.

Therapist: Good choice. Now, how about for your small?'

John: Well, the smalls aren't really great, you know. I don't really care much about that stuff. It's the larges I like. But, I'll take the bus token today.

Therapist: Good, here you go. What about for next time? Do you see anything else in there, anything you would like to work toward, or is there anything you could think of that you'd like but don't see now in the prize cabinet? I'll write your suggestions down, and we'll try our best to get those items in. We're always looking for ideas, especially for the small and large prizes.

John: Well, if I pick another large, I will definitely take that gift card to Best Buy. After that, I also want some tools, because I sold mine to buy drugs. Like a really good hammer or a cordless drill.

Therapist: Yes, I can get those things. They sound like good prizes. What about for smalls? Is there anything that interests you other than bus tokens?

John: Not really. I mean, tokens are good, because I can always use them. But, they're not a lot of fun. They also aren't really good to keep around as a reminder about staying clean.

Therapist: You bring up a good point about the reminders. Do the prizes help remind you about all the hard work you've done and keep you motivated to stay on track with this program?

John: Yes, I keep all the stuff I win in my apartment. Sometimes, when I think about using, I look at it, and I remember I wouldn't have gotten it if I had used.

Therapist: That is an important thing to keep in mind if you're tempted to use. A positive sample, or if you don't come to treatment someday when you're due to leave a sample, would result in no draws that day, and it would reset you down to one draw the next time you tested negative for methamphetamine.

John: Yeah, I remember that part.

Therapist: Good. Let's get back to these small prizes then. Is there anything you can think of that's little that might serve as a good reminder for you?

John: I can't think of anything. You can't buy much for a dollar.

Therapist: That is true, but maybe if we brainstorm a bit. … You said you sold all your tools. How about if I got in things like nails, or different size screws, painting tape.

John: Yeah! That would be good. I'd like that.

Therapist: I'll add it to my suggestion list, and I'll get it when I go shopping next week.

John: Perfect.

Therapist: Great. I'm glad we found some smalls you'll like. I'm also really proud of your efforts in abstaining from methamphetamine and alcohol. Keep up the good work, and I'm sure you will continue to succeed! See you on Tuesday.

In terms of the items on the CMCS-Abstinence form, this therapist did an excellent job of relating the results of the toxicology testing to the patient and informing him of the number of draws due that session and at the next session if he were to again test negative for the targeted substance. For all three of those items, the conversation was clear, succinct, and to the point, and at the same time caring and enthusiastic. The therapist queried about urges to use, and complimented the patient for his ability to resist an opportunity to drink, which in turn could lead to use of the drug targeted for reinforcement in this CM protocol. At the same time, the therapist appropriately guided the patient to further discussion of this episode in groups, as CM sessions themselves are intended to be brief. The therapist was enthusiastic and proactive about prize selections and inquired about desired prizes for the future. In sum, this therapist would have received excellent ratings on all items.

Contrast the preceding dialogue with one that would be rated generally average on the CMCS-Abstinence items, as detailed below.

Therapist: Hi, Mary. How are you today?

Mary: Pretty good, I guess.

Therapist: That's good. You tested negative again today.

Mary: Yup. I didn't use. How many draws do I get?

Therapist: Six.

Mary: Six? Okay, here goes. I got a small, good job, good job, small, small, and good job.

Therapist: What would you like today for your three smalls?

Mary: I guess I'll take more McDonald's coupons. I don't really like their food, you know. But, there's one right by my house, and they started selling salads that aren't bad. It's better than cooking. They're like $4, though, so I guess I don't have enough coupons yet.

Therapist: But, you'll have more chances to win draws at the next session.

Mary: That is true. I'm hoping to get a large or the jumbo, though.

Therapist: Yeah, one of these days you probably will. You wanted the TV, right?

Mary: The TV would be great. You still have it?

Therapist: Yes, it's still available, along with other things. Let's talk a little about the past few days. You haven't used any methamphetamine, right? Any temptations?

Mary: No, not in a while.

Therapist: Okay, good. You are doing a good job in this program.

Mary: Yeah, it's working for me this time, but it's almost time for group. I need to go.

Therapist: Yes, you have about five minutes. I'll see you next week.

Mary: Thanks, bye.

In this case, the therapist, although generally appropriate and somewhat encouraging, did not link the draws earned explicitly to the substance being tested. Instead, the therapist simply stated Mary was negative. Although draws earned was stated, there was no connection made between the number of draws earned to the behavior being reinforced. The therapist did state that Mary would have the opportunity to earn draws at the next session, but the therapist did not state the number of draws or explicitly link the behavior necessary for continued reinforcement. The therapist only briefly discussed Mary's desire for other prizes, and did not inquire about any large prizes that she wanted. A brief mention of drug use and temptations to use was made, but the therapist presumed that the patient hadn't used the targeted drug, and did not inquire about any possible use of other substances. Compared to the previous example, the patient in this scenario would be much less willing to bring up high-risk situations that may have arisen. Finally, the next CM session date was not explicitly stated, potentially leading to resets in reinforcement if the patient missed the meeting. In the preceding dialogue, each item on the CMCS-Abstinence would be rated about a "4" or average.

Finally, consider a dialogue between a therapist and a patient that would be rated very low (1s and 2s) on the Contingency Management Competence Scale.

Therapist: Megan, you're late. I told you in the beginning that if you can't get here in time, you need to call me or else I'm not going to give you any draws.

Megan: I know, but I tried my best to get in on time. I just missed the 12:15 bus, so I had to take the next one, and my cell phone got turned off. I couldn't call.

Therapist: Let's just get your sample.

Megan: I haven't used in almost two weeks! That's a long time.

Therapist: Not in the general scheme of things. You still have a lot of work to do—like planning your schedule better so you don't miss buses.

Megan: How many draws am I up to?

Therapist: Up to? You've gone a couple of days without using, and you think you should get more draws? You were late today, so the most I'm giving you is one draw, and frankly, I don't even think you should get that when you can't arrive on time.

Megan: Look. I already explained that. You told me in the beginning of this program that I'll get draws so long as I'm clean. And, I'm clean.

Therapist: I don't want to argue with you. I'll let you have one draw today. Here.

Megan: Good job. Figures … I never win anything.

Therapist: Maybe you ought to spend a little more time thinking about what is really important rather than focusing on draws. You'd better get to group now.

In this example, the therapist admonished the patient even though she came to treatment. The therapist also failed to correctly implement the CM procedure, and reset Megan's draws seemingly arbitrarily because of lateness. There was no discussion of reinforcement possible at the next session; nor was there any talk about substance use, urges, or cravings. The therapist never even mentioned the substance upon which the reinforcement system was based. The therapist did not show Megan the prizes available in the cabinet or solicit any suggestions from her regarding desired prizes. Moreover, the therapist was condescending and punitive and did not acknowledge Megan for the positive changes she was making. Finally, the therapist failed to state the day and time of the next CM session. A patient who experienced a CM session like that depicted in this dialogue would probably have little motivation to return to a CM session, and perhaps treatment even more generally.

Although it is unlikely that any therapist reading this book would deliver a CM session in the described manner, mistakes and oversights in CM delivery can occur. No therapist is expected to deliver a perfect CM session every time, but if continued problems in CM delivery arise (e.g., failure to assess desire for prizes or failure to accurately tie in self-reports of use to behavioral consequences), CM delivery will be less effective.

In an analysis of over 1,600 CM tapes from 35 therapists at community clinics who were learning to implement CM, this scale captured competence in CM delivery (Petry, Alessi, et al., 2010). Importantly, therapists' competence ratings rose significantly as they gained experience in CM delivery. In this project, a CM supervisor reviewed all the therapists' CM tapes, and met with therapists weekly for individual supervision, during which they reviewed tapes according to the rating scale outlined earlier. With this regular feedback, therapists reduced the number of mistakes they made and improved CM delivery over time. Moreover, scores on this competence scale correlated with measures of the therapeutic alliance, indicating that therapists who administered the CM most competently had better overall alliances with patients. Finally, scores on this competence scale were predictive of abstinence achieved. Therapists who most competently delivered CM had patients with the best treatment outcomes. Thus, competent CM delivery is important for patients' response to treatment.

In this study (Petry, Alessi, et al., 2010), 11 different raters were readily able to achieve high degrees of interrater reliability on every item on this competence scale. Thus, you and a CM supervisor or colleague should be able to similarly rate CM tapes with a high degree of concordance. Ideally, you should audiotape all CM sessions with your patients (with patient permission). After listening to the sessions, you can rate them to determine areas in which your CM delivery could be improved and areas in which you are administering CM appropriately. Your CM supervisor (or another colleague familiar with the CM protocol and rating system) could independently rate your audiotaped sessions and compare his or her ratings with your own. For items in which you have discrepant ratings, you can review the rating manual (Ledgerwood & Petry, 2010) and come up with a consensus. If items are consistently rated low (below acceptable), you can also review the detailed rating manual or Chapter 13 to get ideas about how to better implement CM.

After concordance in rating is established and you are administering CM with an adequate or better degree of competence on all 12 indices, you and your supervisor need not rate every session. Once competence is established, you can continue to record every session, but randomly select just one or two tapes per week for formal rating.

Even if you do not have other therapists available to evaluate your CM sessions, audiotaping them and reviewing and rating them yourself according to the guidelines should provide you with good ideas about what you are doing well and what aspects can be improved. Comparing your delivery of CM with that outlined in Chapter 14 and earlier in this section should also be useful.

15.2 MEASURING ADHERENCE AND COMPETENCE IN NAME-IN-THE-HAT PRIZE CM FOR GROUP ATTENDANCE

Similar types of forms and procedures have been developed and utilized in implementing group-based CM interventions that reinforce attendance. The tracking forms and competence rating scales are described in this section.

15.2.1 Tracking Form for Attendance

If you are tracking and reinforcing attendance in a group format, the tracking forms will look quite different from those described for individually reinforced behaviors. Exhibit 15.3 contains an example of a group attendance tracking

EXHIBIT 15.3 TRACKING FORM FOR NAME-IN-THE-HAT PRIZE CM FOR GROUP ATTENDANCE

Group leader(s):_____ Date:_____ CM session: _____

Patients Enrolled	# Slips Last Week	# Slips If Come This Week (1 more than last week)	Attended? Yes, No-Ex, No-Unex	# Slips Next Week If Attend	Times Name Drawn	Prize Category If Name Drawn
			Total attendees: _____		Total names drawn: _____	Total prizes awarded: _____

Draw ____ names from hat. This number should be equal to half as many as Total attendees.

Note: Each person whose name was selected from the hat gets to draw from the prize bowl as many times as their name was drawn. Total number of names drawn from the second to the last column should equal number of names drawn indicated in the blank at the bottom of the form. Total number of prizes awarded should also equal the total number of names drawn. Individuals whose names were drawn must sign for the prize they selected on the Prize Release Form.

sheet. On this form, there are spaces for up to 20 patients. Whether you are implementing CM in an open or closed group format will not matter. You will list patients who are enrolled in the group in the manner in which they join the group. In an open format, new group members' names will be added to lower rows over time as more patients enroll in the group. If it is a closed format group, the same patients will be listed on all forms throughout the duration of the CM intervention. In both cases, keep the order in which you list patients' names consistent week to week, as using the same order will help you keep track of slips awarded and due. When the order in which patients are listed is the same every week, it is easier to look back to prior weeks to determine the number of name slips due.

You will use one form for each week (or group session) that is reinforced. So, if you have designed a 10-week CM program with groups that meet weekly, you will have 10 forms in total. If it is a 10-week CM program that meets twice weekly, you will have 10 × 2 = 20 forms. In the far left column, you list the patients' names. Even if a patient withdraws from treatment (or the group), you should continue listing that patient's name to keep the order constant across sessions. As new patients join the group (in open group formats), new names are added to the lower rows.

In the second column, you list how many slips that patient earned at the last session. For the first session for each patient, the number is always zero. For subsequent sessions, you will look at the prior session's tracking sheet to determine the number of draws that were awarded at the last session they attended. If they had an unexcused absence at the most recent session, the number to be included in this column is zero, because they did not receive any name slips at the last session (even though they may have earned slips had they attended).

In the third column from the left, you write down the number of slips that the patient is due at this session if he attends. This number should be one more slip than he earned at the last session. So, for the first session for each patient, the number should be one (zero at last session + one = one this session). If a patient had previously attended four sessions in a row, the number would be five (four at the last session + one = five at this session). These three left-hand columns get completed BEFORE the group session occurs. You will also prepare envelopes containing the appropriate number of slips for each patient based on this tracking form as outlined in Chapter 14.

The middle column gets completed during group. It asks if the patient attended or not, and if not, if the absence was excused or not. In the case of an excused absence, the reason should be briefly listed.

The next column asks you to indicate the number of slips the patient will get if they attend the next session. This number will be one more slip than they received today. If they did not attend this session and had an unexcused absence, the number of slips they are due at the next session is one. In other words, they would have received zero slips today plus one next time, equaling one slip for the next session attended.

If a patient attended today's session, this number is the number he received today plus one more slip. Therefore, a patient who received five slips this session would be due six slips at the next session.

In the case of an **excused absence**, the patient should receive the same number of slips at the next session he attends as he would have gotten at the session for which he was excused. **Being late** to a CM group is a special case. If the patient came into the group after the draws had occurred, he would not earn any chance of winning a prize that week. Because he still attended, he is not penalized with respect to draws earned at the following session. Thus, for late attendance, the patient's number of slips due at the next session should still increase by one.

The two right-hand columns relate to the draw outcomes. As was described in Chapter 14, you will draw a certain number of names from the hat, and each of those patients will select from the prize bowl and win a prize. If you draw seven names from a hat, a total of seven patients should be denoted as having their names drawn in this column. In some cases, seven individual patients will each have their names drawn once, and then the number one would be indicated for each of those seven persons. In other cases, someone's name may be drawn more than once. For example, if Mike had his name in the hat five times, his name may be drawn two or more times (up to five times, ranging from zero to five). You would write the total number of times his name was drawn from the hat in the second to last column. Check to make sure the total number of names drawn adds to the total number of names indicated in the bottom text on the tracking form, where the blank is noted: "Draw ___ names from the hat." If you are drawing seven names from the hat, you write "7" there.

If seven names are drawn from the hat, seven prizes should be awarded. The right-hand column has you list the prize category for each type of prize(s) won for each patient whose name was drawn. In this column you would write "S" if he drew a small prize slip, "M" for a medium, "L" for a large, or "J" for jumbo. If a patient's name is drawn two or more times, then two or more prize categories ought to be listed for that patient. The total number of prizes awarded that session should match the total number of names drawn, and only patients whose names were drawn should have a prize category indicated.

These tracking sheets should be fairly universal in terms of their applicability to CM protocols that use the Name-in-the-hat prize CM procedure for reinforcing group attendance. However, aspects of the forms may need to be tailored to some specific CM interventions that modify parameters, such as how draws are awarded. By using these or similar forms to implement and monitor CM, you can be more assured that procedures are followed according to the intended structure. I recommend that someone other than the CM therapist also review your forms each week, especially during the first month of implementation, to ensure appropriate use and provide suggestions. Once you get accustomed to the forms, it should take no more than 30 minutes a week to prepare and review all the CM paperwork. Similarly, CM supervision should be rather straightforward and quick.

15.2.2 Use and Monitoring of Tracking Forms

Just as with individual CM protocols, weekly review of the group attendance tracking forms is important from an adherence perspective. Mistakes do happen. If the mistake in the number of draws earned or due is in the favor of the patients and you awarded more prize drawings than you should have, you may want to acknowledge the mistake to the group and not take away already awarded slips or draws. If you drew too few names from the hat one week, you could make up for it the next week, and draw the additional, previously missed number of names, at the next session. However, if the mistake is not recognized until two or more weeks later, it may be odd and confusing for the patients to try to correct it then. Again, if the tracking forms are reviewed regularly and independently by you and another person, mistakes ought to be noticed in close proximity to when they occurred and corrections would be easier to make.

If you make a mistake in terms of the number of name slips you provided to a patient(s), you would probably not want to address this in a group setting, unless the same mistake was made with most or all of the group members. In the case of awarding too few name slips to patient in a prior week, you could either talk individually with the patient affected and make up the appropriate number of name slips at the next session, or not address it with the patient if the miscalculation occurred weeks in the past. Awarding too many name slips on a given week also needn't be corrected or rectified in subsequent weeks, depending on how long it took to notice the error and how much the mistake impacted the patient's past and future chances of having his name drawn. Again, the key is to continuously monitor the tracking forms yourself and to have others check your work. Miscalculations in name slips awarded or draws done can be readily corrected if they are noticed soon after they occur. Mistakes that are not picked up for weeks or months may dramatically impact the reinforcement procedure, which in turn is likely to diminish the effectiveness of CM.

15.2.3 Competence in Delivery of Name-in-the-Hat Prize CM for Group Attendance

Not only must this CM procedure be delivered in the intended manner (i.e., in a manner that adheres to the CM protocol), but it must also be administered competently in order to be effective. As with individually based CM for abstinence, there is a manual available (Petry & Ledgerwood, 2010) that describes methods to monitor competence in group-based contingencies. It is available at http://contingencymanagement.uchc.edu/index.html.

The Contingency Management Competence Scale for Reinforcing Attendance (CMCS-Attendance) utilizes some of the same items as the scale that assesses abstinence-based reinforcement. However, because drug use is not being objectively tested, the items regarding toxicology monitoring are removed. In addition, items that assess reinforcement administration relate to the therapist's descriptions of how names go in the hat and how names in the hat translate to chances of winning prizes. Chapter 14 outlined excellent descriptions of CM in this regard and presented dialogues that would be rated very highly with respect to competence. Please review those descriptions and dialogues in conjunction with the CMCS-Attendance form outlined in Exhibit 15.4.

What follows is an example of a description of this type of CM that would be rated as adequate or average on most items of the competence scale.

Therapist: Welcome, everyone, to group today. It looks like there are eight of you here, so we'll draw four names from the hat. You each have your envelopes, and all your name slips are already in the hat, right? Anyone not put theirs in yet? Michelle, go ahead and pull out four names. Great. They are Matt, Evan, George, and Sandra. Each of you go ahead and draw for a prize from the prize bowl here. Matt, you can start. A small—would you like this juice container, a token, a pen set, a candle, or a small date book? The datebook, okay. Evan, your turn—another small. Which do you prefer? The pen set—here you go. George—a medium? I have a $5 gift card or a round-trip subway pass. Here's the subway pass. And Sandra, a small—the candle? Sure, here it is. And, don't forget that the number of slips you can earn next week is stated on the form in your envelope. Coming to treatment regularly will help increase your chances of winning more prizes.

This therapist delivered the CM as it was intended, but there was little to no enthusiasm for the procedure. In addition, most of the descriptions of the processes were fairly cursory. A new group member would have little idea about what was happening, or why, with respect to the reinforcement. Contrast the preceding example with the much more ideal ones provided in Chapter 14.

Finally, consider the next dialogue, which is lacking in many of the critical components on the CMCS-Attendance scale.

EXHIBIT 15.4   CONTINGENCY MANAGEMENT COMPETENCE SCALE FOR REINFORCING ATTENDANCE

Tape # _____ Session # _____ Rater: _____

Date:____ ___/___ ___/___ ___Start time:_____

Therapist:_____Stop time: _____

Patient ID:_____Session duration:_____ min.

1 = Very Poor   The therapist's skill was non-evident (not addressed) or unacceptable, incompatible with the CM approach, and potentially counterproductive or toxic.

2 = Poor   The therapist addressed the issue, but in a poor or cursory manner; the therapist demonstrated a lack of competence, a failure to understand the issue or its context, or lack of expertise.

3 = Barely Acceptable   The therapist handled the issue in a manner somewhat consistent with the CM approach.

4 = Adequate   The therapist handled the issue in an acceptable way, consistent with CM, and in an average manner.

5 = Good   The therapist addressed the issue in a manner somewhat better than average.

6 = Very Good   The therapist's skill and expertise were very evident in delivering the intervention.

7 = Excellent   The therapist demonstrated exceptional mastery and excellence in delivering the intervention.

1. To what extent did the therapist **inform patients of reinforcement earned at this session**?   1 2 3 4 5 6 7

2. To what extent did the therapist **inform patients of the reinforcement possible at the next session**?   1 2 3 4 5 6 7

3. How well did the therapist **administer reinforcement**?   1 2 3 4 5 6 7

4. To what extent did the therapist **assess patients' desire for prizes**?   1 2 3 4 5 6 7

5. To what extent did the therapist **compliment or praise patients' efforts toward attending treatment**?   1 2 3 4 5 6 7

(continued on next page)

6. To what extent did the therapist **tie attendance and the CM program to abstinence and other treatment goals?**   1 2 3 4 5 6 7

General Items

7. **General skillfulness/effectiveness** (demonstrates expertise, competence, and commitment; engages patients in discussion, makes interventions at appropriate times—not missed or too early)   1 2 3 4 5 6 7

8. **Maintaining session structure** (maintains session focus; sets appropriate tone and structure, appropriate level of therapist activity/ directiveness, and appropriate duration)   1 2 3 4 5 6 7

9. **Empathy** (conveys warmth and sensitivity, demonstrates genuine concern and a non-judgmental stance, understands and expresses patients' feelings and concerns)   1 2 3 4 5 6 7

Therapist: Hi, everyone! Let's have you all put your name slips in the hat. Excellent! Joe, draw out a few slips, okay? Mary, Steve, and Michael. That's good—that's enough. They'll each get to draw for prizes. Okay, Mary, you can draw now. Here you go. A small. The clinic's been short on cash flow, so I don't have much by way of smalls today, but you can pick something out next time I go shopping, okay? Steve—a medium—I think there might be a baseball cap in the cabinet. Do you want that? No, okay, like I said, I'll probably have more things in a couple of weeks. Michael, your turn to draw. A small. You can pick something out later. Great, now let's move on to the topic of the week.

Although this therapist was enthusiastic and not "toxic," she did not adequately explain the CM procedures. It would be likely that people in the group would not understand what was happening or why. There was no mention of attendance or how name slips were earned. There was no indication about why three names were drawn from the hat. The therapist brought no prizes into the group, and she suggested that patients just save up their wins for the next time she went shopping. She did not solicit suggestions for prizes. This therapist would have received scores of one or two on CMCS-Attendance items. If CM were implemented in the manner depicted in this dialogue, it is unlikely that it would increase patients' attendance at the group.

Unfortunately, situations such as this one take place when therapists, sometimes with the best of intentions, do not receive appropriate training or supervision in CM administration. The therapist in the previous dialogue, for example, may have thought she was being appropriate and helpful in encouraging patients to wait until she went shopping to select a prize when there would be greater availability of prizes. However, by placing a delay between the behavior of attendance and the positive reinforcer (the prize), the effectiveness of CM is likely to diminish greatly.

SUMMARY

The more you can practice CM before you implement it with real patients, and the more you try to mirror the examples of excellent CM administration outlined in this book, the greater your chances of successful implementation will be. Recording the CM sessions and reviewing them in conjunction with reviews of this chapter and Chapter 14, along with having others examine them, will help guard against potential pitfalls.

IV
Conclusion

Chapter 16

Conclusion

By this point, you should be well prepared to implement CM in practice. You have reviewed the background and efficacy of CM in research studies, and you can answer commonly voiced concerns about using CM. You have learned how to design effective CM programs and how to make appropriate modifications to existing CM protocols if needed. Whether you plan to implement or adapt a pre-existing CM protocol to reinforce abstinence or attendance at group sessions or to develop a unique CM program, you are positioned to initiate and institute reinforcement procedures. The worksheets and tracking sheets provided in Chapter 15 will help you ensure that CM is implemented in the manner in which it was intended. By carefully reviewing your protocol and referring back to relevant sections in this book throughout CM implementation, your CM program should be effective in instituting behavioral change and improvements among your patients.

Although the steps for successful CM design and implementation are spelled out in this book, mistakes still do happen. Often, clinicians forget to integrate some specific aspect of CM, or they do not think some features are important and intentionally delete some components. An example is a clinic in which the therapists thought it was easier to only provide gift cards as reinforcers; they felt all patients would desire gift cards. After a month or two of CM implementation, they realized CM was not having an effect on the desired behavior, which in this case was attendance. They mistakenly attributed the lack of a positive benefit to the erroneous belief that CM was simply not effective. However, had they been aware of the need for choice in reinforcers and considered the fact that many patients had limited or no transportation to use the gift cards, they may have come to the realization that it was not CM that was ineffective, but that the reinforcers they had chosen were inadequate for their population.

Another example of CM not working as intended is highlighted in the following example. In one clinic, a lead clinician attended an in-person CM training. She was convinced that CM would help with some of her clinic's groups that were suffering from high rates of attrition. She came back from the training and informed another clinician, who had very low attendance rates, about how to use the

Name-in-the-hat procedure for group attendance. That clinician was skeptical about CM; she had not attended the training and had not read any of the materials outlined in this book. She did as she was told by her supervisor, and implemented CM. No one with experience monitored or supervised her CM implementation. Within two weeks, the clinician told her supervisor that the patients in the group found CM to be demoralizing and belittling. The supervisor decided to cease CM in that clinician's group and implement it in another group, which was led by another therapist who had attended the same CM training and was enthusiastic about trying CM. In this second group, CM had strong beneficial effects on improving attendance. No patients found the procedures to be demoralizing or belittling. This example underscores the need for appropriate background, training, and supervision with respect to CM implementation. A clinician who does not believe in the approach is unlikely to administer it in its intended manner. Had the supervisor attended the first several groups or reviewed audiotapes of the CM administration, she would have quickly realized that the first clinician was not delivering CM in a competent manner (see Petry & Ledgerwood, 2010).

These examples highlight just a couple of the things that can go wrong with CM protocol design and implementation. If the CM protocol you implement is not having the desired effects on changing a behavior, it is likely that either some aspect of the CM design is inappropriate (e.g., the reinforcers are not of a high enough magnitude, or the monitoring and reinforcement schedule is inappropriate) or the CM is not being implemented with adherence (e.g., the correct procedures are not followed) or competence (e.g., the therapist is not appropriately enthusiastic). By reviewing various aspects of this book while implementing CM, you should be able to identify and correct problems that arise. As noted in the second case, instituting CM with a new group of patients may result in substantial improvements.

Although there are cautionary tales of things that can go wrong with CM administration, there are also many stories of substantial benefits that can be achieved with CM when it is correctly designed and implemented. Success stories of CM with patients, therapists, and clinics are plentiful. Patients can and do achieve substantial periods of abstinence, and they become engaged actively in groups. Therapists can find groups fun and rewarding to run, and they can develop better relationships with their patients. Clinics can achieve greater success rates, which in turn can result in higher reimbursement rates and better standing with insurers or public funders. Society at large may benefit from wider adoption of CM as well. Contingency management substantially reduces intravenous drug use and risky sexual behaviors (Ghitza, Epstein, & Preston, 2008; Hanson, Alessi, & Petry, 2008; Petry, Weinstock, Alessi, Lewis, & Dieckhaus, 2010), which in turn decreases the spread of HIV and other communicable diseases. Thus, everyone may stand to gain by more widespread implementation of CM.

Contingency management is an intervention built on substantial empirical evidence. If a CM protocol is designed in a manner consistent with research findings and implemented as intended and described in this book, it should bring about the very effects you are trying to achieve.

References

Alessi, S. M., Badger, G. J., & Higgins, S. T. (2004). An experimental examination of the initial weeks of abstinence in cigarette smokers. *Experimental and Clinical Psychopharmacology, 12,* 276–287.

Alessi, S. M., Hanson, T., Wieners, M., & Petry, N. M. (2007). Low-cost contingency management in community clinics: Delivering incentives partially in group therapy. *Experimental and Clinical Psychopharmacology, 15,* 293–300.

Alessi, S. M., Petry, N. M., & Urso, J. (2008). Contingency management promotes smoking reductions in residential substance abuse patients. *Journal of Applied Behavior Analysis, 41,* 617–622.

Amass, L., & Kamien, J. (2004). A tale of two cities: Financing two voucher programs for substance abusers through community donations. *Experimental and Clinical Psychopharmacology, 12,* 147–155.

Azrin, N. H. (1976). Improvements in the community-reinforcement approach to alcoholism. *Behavior Research and Therapy, 14,* 339–348.

Ball, J. C., & Ross, A. (1991). *The effectiveness of methadone maintenance treatment: Patients, programs, services, and outcomes.* New York: Springer-Verlag.

Bellack, A. S., Bennett, M. E., Gearon, J. S., Brown, C. H., & Yang Y. (2006). A randomized clinical trial of a new behavioral treatment for drug abuse in people with severe and persistent mental illness. *Archives of General Psychiatry, 63,* 426–432.

Bickel, W. K., Amass, L., Higgins, S. T., Badger, G. J., & Esch, R. (1997). Effects of adding behavioral treatment to opioid detoxification with buprenorphine. *Journal of Consulting and Clinical Psychology, 65,* 803–810.

Bijou, S. W., & Orlando, R. (1961). Rapid development of multiple-schedule control performances with retarded children. *Journal of the Experimental Analysis of Behavior, 4,* 7–16.

Budney A. J., Higgins S. T., Hughes, J. R., & Bickel W. K. (1992). The scientific/clinical response to the cocaine epidemic: A MEDLINE search of the literature. *Drug and Alcohol Dependence, 30,* 143–149.

Budney, A. J., Higgins, S. T., Radonovich, K. J., & Novy, P. L. (2000). Adding voucher-based incentives to coping skills and motivational enhancement improves outcomes during treatment for marijuana dependence. *Journal of Consulting and Clinical Psychology, 68,* 1051–1061.

Budney, A. J., Moore, B. A., Rocha, H. L., & Higgins, S. T. (2006). Clinical trial of abstinence-based vouchers and cognitive-behavioral therapy for cannabis dependence. *Journal of Consulting and Clinical Psychology, 74,* 307–316.

Calsyn, D. A., & Saxon, A. J. (1987). A system for uniform application of contingencies for illicit drug use. *Journal of Substance Abuse Treatment, 4,* 41–47.

Carroll, K. M., Easton, C. J., Nich, C., Hunkele, K. A., Neavins, T. M., Sinha, R., et al. (2006). The use of contingency management and motivational/skills-building therapy to treat young adults with marijuana dependence. *Journal of Consulting and Clinical Psychology, 74,* 955–966.

Carroll, K. M., Sinha, R., Nich, C., Babuscio, T., & Rounsaville, B. J. (2002). Contingency management to enhance naltrexone treatment of opioid dependence: A randomized clinical trial of reinforcement magnitude. *Experimental and Clinical Psychopharmacology, 10,* 54–63.

Cavallo, D. A., Cooney, J. L., Duhig, A. M., Smith, A. E., Liss, T. B., McFetridge, A. K., et al. (2007). Combining cognitive behavioral therapy with contingency management for smoking cessation in adolescent smokers: A preliminary comparison of two different CBT formats. *American Journal on Addictions, 16,* 468–474.

Chutuape, M. A., Silverman, K., & Stitzer, M. (1999). Contingent reinforcement sustains post-detoxification abstinence from multiple drugs: A preliminary study with methadone patients. *Drug and Alcohol Dependence, 54,* 69–81.

Committee on the Judiciary, United States Senate. (1990). *Hard-core cocaine addicts: Measuring and fighting the epidemic* (Publication No. 552-070-08156-9). Washington, DC: U.S. Government Printing Office.

Corby, E. A., Roll, J. M., Ledgerwood, D. M., & Schuster, C. R. (2000). Contingency management interventions for treating the substance abuse of adolescents: A feasibility study. *Experimental and Clinical Psychopharmacology, 8,* 371–376.

Dallery, J., Silverman, K., Chutuape, M. A., Bigelow, G. E., & Stitzer, M. L. (2001). Voucher-based reinforcement of opiate plus cocaine abstinence in treatment-resistant methadone patients: Effects of reinforcer magnitude. *Experimental and Clinical Psychopharmacology, 9,* 317–325.

DeFulio, A., Donlin, W. D., Wong, C. J., & Silverman, K. (2009). Employment-based abstinence reinforcement as a maintenance intervention for the treatment of cocaine dependence: A randomized controlled trial. *Addiction, 104,* 1530–1538.

Dolan, M. P., Black, J. L., Penk, W. E., Robinowitz, R., & DeFord, H. A. (1985). Contracting for treatment termination to reduce illicit drug use among methadone maintenance failures. *Journal of Consulting and Clinical Psychology, 53,* 549–551.

Drake, R. E., O'Neal, E. L., & Wallach, M. A. (2008). A systematic review of psychosocial research on psychosocial interventions for people with co-occurring severe mental and substance use disorders. *Journal of Substance Abuse Treatment, 34,* 123–138.

Drebing, C. E., Van Ormer, E. A., Krebs, C., Rosenheck, R., Rounsaville, B., Herz, L., et al. (2005). The impact of enhanced incentives on vocational rehabilitation outcomes for dually diagnosed veterans. *Journal of Applied Behavior Analysis, 38,* 359–372.

Drebing, C. E., Van Ormer, E. A., Mueller, L., Hebert, M., Penk, W., Petry, N. M., et al. (2007). Adding a contingency management intervention to vocational rehabilitation: Outcomes for dually diagnosed veterans. *Journal of Rehabilitation Research and Development, 44,* 851–866.

Dutra L., Stathopoulou, G., Basden S. L., Leyro T. M., Powers M. B., & Otto M. W. (2008). A meta-analytic review of psychosocial interventions for substance use disorders. *American Journal of Psychiatry, 165,* 179–187.

Elk, R., Schmitz, J., Spiga, R., Rhoades, H., Andres, R., & Grabowski, J. (1995). Behavioral treatment of cocaine-dependent pregnant women and TB-exposed patients. *Addictive Behaviors, 20,* 533–542.

Epstein, D. H., Hawkins, W. E., Covi, L., Umbricht, A., & Preston, K. L. (2003). Cognitive-behavioral therapy plus contingency management for cocaine use: Findings during treatment and across 12-month follow-up. *Psychology of Addictive Behaviors, 17,* 73–82.

Ferster, C. B., & Skinner, B. F. (1957). *Schedules of reinforcement.* Acton, MA: Copley.

Festinger, D. S., Marlowe, D. B., Croft, J. R., Dugosh, K. L., Mastro, N. K., Lee, P. A., et al. (2005). Do research payments precipitate drug use or coerce participation? *Drug and Alcohol Dependence, 78,* 275–281.

Ford, J., Hawke, J., Alessi, S. M., Ledgerwood, D., & Petry, N. M. (2007). Psychological trauma and post-traumatic stress symptoms as predictors of substance dependence treatment outcomes. *Behavior Research and Therapy, 45,* 2417–2431.

García-Rodríguez, O., Secades-Villa, R., Higgins, S. T., Fernández-Hermida, J. R., & Carballo, J. L. (2008). Financing a voucher program for cocaine abusers through community donations in Spain. *Journal of Applied Behavior Analysis, 41,* 623–628.

Gawin, F. H., & Kleber, H. (1987). Issues in cocaine abuse treatment research. In S. Fisher, A. Raskin, & E. H. Uhlenhuth (Eds.), *Cocaine: Clinical and biobehavioral aspects* (pp. 174–192). New York: Oxford University Press.

Ghitza, U. E., Epstein, D. H., & Preston, K. L. (2008). Contingency management reduces injection-related HIV risk behaviors in heroin and cocaine using outpatients. *Addictive Behaviors, 33,* 593–604.

Ghitza, U. E., Epstein, D. H., Schmittner, J., Vahabzadeh, M., Lin, J. L., & Preston, K. L. (2007). Randomized trial of prize-based reinforcement density for simultaneous abstinence from cocaine and heroin. *Journal of Consulting and Clinical Psychology, 75,* 765–774.

Gilbert, D. G., Crauthers, D. M., Mooney, D. K., McClernon, F. J., & Jensen, R. A. (1999). Effects of monetary contingencies on smoking relapse: Influences of trait depression, personality, and habitual nicotine intake. *Experimental and Clinical Psychopharmacology, 7,* 174–181.

Glover, A. C., Roane, H. S., Kadey, H. J., & Grow, L. L. (2008). Preference for reinforcers under progressive- and fixed-ratio schedules: A comparison of single and concurrent arrangements. *Journal of Applied Behavior Analysis, 41,* 163–176.

Godley, S. H., Godley, M. D., Wright, K. L., Funk, R. R., & Petry, N. M. (2008). Contingent reinforcement of personal goal activities for adolescents with substance use disorders during post-residential continuing care. *American Journal on Addictions, 17,* 278–286.

Gonzalez, G., Feingold, A., Oliveto, A., Gonsai, K., & Kosten, T. R. (2003). Comorbid major depressive disorder as a prognostic factor in cocaine-abusing buprenorphine-maintained patients treated with desipramine and contingency management. *American Journal of Drug and Alcohol Abuse, 29,* 497–514.

Hanson, T., Alessi, S. M., & Petry, N. M. (2008). Contingency management reduces drug-related human immunodeficiency virus risk behaviors in cocaine-abusing methadone patients. *Addiction, 103,* 1187–1197.

Heil, S. H., Higgins, S. T., Bernstein, I. M., Solomon, L. J., Rogers, R. E., Thomas, C. S., et al. (2008). Effects of voucher-based incentives on abstinence from cigarette smoking and fetal growth among pregnant women. *Addiction, 103,* 1009–1018.

Heil, S. H., Tidey, J. W., Holmes, H. W., Badger, G. J., & Higgins, S. T. (2003). A contingent payment model of smoking cessation: Effects on abstinence and withdrawal. *Nicotine & Tobacco Research, 5,* 205–213.

Helmus, T. C., Saules, K. K., Schoener, E. P., & Roll, J. M. (2003). Reinforcement of counseling attendance and alcohol abstinence in a community-based dual-diagnosis treatment program: A feasibility study. *Psychology of Addictive Behaviors, 17,* 249–251.

Henggeler, S. W., Chapman, J. E., Rowland, M. D., Halliday-Boykins, C. A., Randall, J., Shackelford, J., et al. (2007). If you build it, they will come: Statewide practitioner interest in contingency management for youths. *Journal of Substance Abuse Treatment, 32,* 121–131.

Henggeler, S. W., Chapman, J. E., Rowland, M. D., Halliday-Boykins, C. A., Randall, J., Shackelford, J., et al. (2008). Statewide adoption and initial implementation of contingency management for substance-abusing adolescents. *Journal of Consulting and Clinical Psychology, 76,* 556–567.

Henggeler, S. W., Halliday-Boykins, C. A., Cunningham, P. B., Randall, J., Shapiro, S. B., & Chapman, J. E. (2006). Juvenile drug court: Enhancing outcomes by integrating evidence-based treatments. *Journal of Consulting and Clinical Psychology, 74,* 42–54.

Higgins, S. T., Badger, G. J., & Budney, A. J. (2000). Initial abstinence and success in achieving longer-term cocaine abstinence. *Experimental and Clinical Psychopharmacology, 8,* 377–386.

Higgins, S. T., Budney, A. J., Bickel, W. K., Badger, G. J., Foerg, F. E., & Ogden, D. (1995). Outpatient behavioral treatment for cocaine dependence: One-year outcome. *Experimental and Clinical Psychopharmacology, 3,* 205–212.

Higgins, S. T., Budney, A. J., Bickel, W. K., Foerg, F. E., Donham, R., & Badger, G. J. (1994). Incentives improve outcome in outpatient behavioral treatment of cocaine dependence. *Archives of General Psychiatry, 51,* 568–576.

Higgins, S. T., Budney, A. J., Bickel, W. K., Hughes, J. R., Foerg, F., & Badger, G. (1993). Achieving cocaine abstinence with a behavioral approach. *American Journal of Psychiatry, 150,* 763–769.

Higgins, S. T., Delaney, D. D., Budney, A. J., Bickel, W. K., Hughes, J. R., Foerg, F., et al. (1991). A behavioral approach to achieving initial cocaine abstinence. *American Journal of Psychiatry, 148,* 1218–1224.

Higgins, S. T., Heil, S. H., Dantona, R., Donham, R., Matthews, M., Badger, G. J. (2007). Effects of varying the monetary value of voucher-based incentives on abstinence achieved during and following treatment among cocaine-dependent outpatients. *Addiction, 102,* 271–281.

Higgins, S. T., Heil, S. H., Solomon, L. J., Bernstein, I. M., Lussier, J. P., Abel, R. L., et al. (2004). A pilot study on voucher-based incentives to promote abstinence from cigarette smoking during pregnancy and postpartum. *Nicotine & Tobacco Research, 6,* 1015–1020.

Higgins, S. T., Sigmon, S. C., Wong, C. J., Heil, S. H., Badger, G. J., Donham, R., et al. (2003). Community reinforcement therapy for cocaine-dependent outpatients. *Archives of General Psychiatry, 60,* 1043–1052.

Higgins, S. T., Wong, C. J., Badger, G. J., Ogden, D. E. H., & Dantona, R. L. (2000). Contingent reinforcement increases cocaine abstinence during outpatient treatment and one year of follow-up. *Journal of Consulting and Clinical Psychology, 68,* 64–72.

Hunt, G. M., & Azrin, N. H. (1973). A community-reinforcement approach to alcoholism. *Behavior Research and Therapy, 11,* 91–104.

Iguchi, M. Y., Belding, M. A., Morral, A. R., & Lamb, R. J. (1997). Reinforcing operants other than abstinence in drug abuse treatment: An effective alternative for reducing drug use. *Journal of Consulting and Clinical Psychology, 65,* 421–428.

Jones, H. E., Haug, N., Silverman, K., Stitzer, M., & Svikis, D. (2001). The effectiveness of incentives in enhancing treatment attendance and drug abstinence in methadone-maintained pregnant women. *Drug and Alcohol Dependence, 1,* 297–306.

Jones, H. E., Haug, N. A., Stitzer, M. L., & Svikis, D. S. (2000). Improving treatment outcomes for pregnant drug-dependent women using low-magnitude voucher incentives. *Addictive Behaviors, 25,* 263–267.

Kadden, R. M., Litt, M. D., Kabela-Cormier, E., & Petry, N. M. (2007). Abstinence rates following behavioral treatments for marijuana dependence. *Addictive Behavior, 32,* 1220–1236.

Kadden, R. M., Litt, M. D., Kabela-Cormier, E., & Petry, N. M. (2009). Increased drinking in a trial of treatments for marijuana dependence: Substance substitution? *Drug and Alcohol Dependence, 105,* 168–171.

Kahneman, D. R., & Tversky, A. (1979). Prospect theory: An analysis of decision under risk. *Econometrica, 40,* 263–291.

Kamon, J., Budney, A., & Stanger, C. (2005). A contingency management intervention for adolescent marijuana abuse and conduct problems. *Journal of the American Academy of Child & Adolescent Psychiatry, 44,* 513–21.

Katz, E. C., Chutuape, M. A., Jones, H., Jasinski, D., Fingerhood, M., & Stitzer, M. (2004). Abstinence incentive effects in a short-term outpatient detoxification program. *Experimental and Clinical Psychopharmacology, 12,* 262–268.

Katz, E. C., Gruber, K., Chutuape, M. A., & Stitzer, M. L. (2001). Reinforcement-based outpatient treatment for opiate and cocaine abusers. *Journal of Substance Abuse Treatment, 20,* 93–98.

Kellogg, S. H., Burns, M., Coleman, P., Stitzer, M., Wale, J. B., & Kreek, M. J. (2005). Something of value: The introduction of contingency management interventions into the New York City Health and Hospital Addiction Treatment Service. *Journal of Substance Abuse Treatment, 28,* 57–65.

Kirby, K. C., Marlowe, D. B., Festinger, D. S., Lamb, R. J., & Platt, J. J. (1998). Schedule of voucher delivery influences initiation of cocaine abstinence. *Journal of Consulting and Clinical Psychology, 66,* 761–777.

Knealing, T. W., Wong, C. J., Diemer, K. N., Hampton, J., & Silverman, K. (2006). A randomized controlled trial of the therapeutic workplace for community methadone patients: A partial failure to engage. *Experimental and Clinical Psychopharmacology, 14,* 350–360.

Kosten, T., Oliveto, A., Feingold, A., Poling, J., Sevarino, K., McCance-Katz, E., et al. (2003). Desipramine and contingency management for cocaine and opiate dependence in buprenorphine maintained patients. *Drug and Alcohol Dependence, 70,* 315–325.

Krishnan-Sarin, S., Duhig, A. M., McKee, S. A., McMahon, T. J., Liss, T., McFetridge, A., et al. (2006). Contingency management for smoking cessation in adolescent smokers. *Experimental and Clinical Psychopharmacology, 14,* 306–310.

Ledgerwood, D. M., Alessi, S. M., Hanson, T., Godley, M., & Petry, N. M. (2008). Contingency management for attendance to group substance abuse treatment administered by clinicians in community clinics. *Journal of Applied Behavior Analysis, 41,* 617–622.

Ledgerwood, D. M., & Petry, N. M. (2006). Does contingency management affect motivation to change substance use? *Drug and Alcohol Dependence, 83,* 65–72.

Ledgerwood, D. M., & Petry, N. M. (2010). *Rating contingency management sessions using the Contingency Management Competence Scale.* Unpublished treatment manual. Available at http://contingencymanagement.uchc.edu/index.html

Lester, K. M., Milby, J. B., Schumacher, J. E., Vuchinich, R., Person, S., & Clay, O. J. (2007). Impact of behavioral contingency management intervention on coping behaviors and PTSD symptom reduction in cocaine-addicted homeless. *Journal of Traumatic Stress, 20,* 565–575.

Lott, D. C., & Jencius, S. (2009). Effectiveness of very low-cost contingency management in a community adolescent treatment program. *Drug and Alcohol Dependence, 102,* 162–165.

Lussier, J. P., Heil, S. H., Mongeon, J. A., Badger, G. J., & Higgins, S. T. (2006). A meta-analysis of voucher-based reinforcement therapy for substance use disorders. *Addiction, 101,* 192–203.

Marlowe, D. B., Festinger, D. S., Dugosh, K. L., Arabia, P. L., & Kirby, K. C. (2008). An effectiveness trial of contingency management in a felony preadjudication drug court. *Journal of Applied Behavior Analysis, 41,* 565–577.

McCarthy, J. J., & Borders, O. T. (1985). Limit setting on drug abuse in methadone maintenance patients. *American Journal of Psychiatry, 142,* 1419–1423.

McCorry, F., Brandau, S., & Morone, J. (2009). *A case study of the New York single state agency's infrastructure to improve practice. Final report.* Unpublished manuscript.

Milby, J. B., Schumacher, J. E., McNamara, C., Wallace, D., Usdan, S., McGill, T., et al. (2000). Initiating abstinence in cocaine abusing dually diagnosed homeless persons. *Drug and Alcohol Dependence, 60,* 55–67.

Milby, J. B., Schumacher, J. E., Raczynski, J. M., Caldwell, E., Engle, M., Michael, M., et al. (1996). Sufficient conditions for effective treatment of substance abusing homeless persons. *Drug and Alcohol Dependence, 43,* 39–47.

Milby, J. B., Schumacher, J. E., Vuchinich, R. E., Freedman, M. J., Kertesz, S., & Wallace, D. (2008). Toward cost-effective initial care for substance-abusing homeless. *Journal of Substance Abuse Treatment, 34,* 180–191.

Milby, J. B., Schumacher, J. E., Wallace, D., Freedman, M. J., & Vuchinich, R. E. (2005). To house or not to house: The effects of providing housing to homeless substance abusers in treatment. *American Journal of Public Health, 95,* 1259–1265.

National Institute on Drug Abuse. (1989). Household survey. In *NIDA Notes, 4,* 42–43 (DHHS Publication No. ADM 89-1488). Washington, DC: U.S. Government Printing Office.

National Institute on Drug Abuse. (1990). *National household survey on drug abuse: Main findings 1988* (DHHS Publication No. ADM 90-1682). Washington, DC: U.S. Government Printing Office.

Oliveto, A., Poling, J., Sevarino, K. A., Gonsai, K. R., McCance-Katz, E. F., Stine, S. M., et al. (2005). Efficacy of dose and contingency management procedures in LAAM-maintained cocaine-dependent patients. *Drug and Alcohol Dependence, 79,* 157–165.

Olmstead, T. A., & Petry, N. M. (2009). The cost-effectiveness of prize-based and voucher-based contingency management in a population of cocaine- or opioid-dependent outpatients. *Drug and Alcohol Dependence, 102,* 108–115.

Olmstead, T. A., Sindelar, J. L., Easton, C. J., & Carroll, K. M. (2007). The cost-effectiveness of four treatments for marijuana dependence. *Addiction, 102,* 1443–1453.

Olmstead, T. A., Sindelar, J. L., & Petry, N. M. (2007). Cost-effectiveness of prize-based incentives for stimulant abusers in outpatient psychosocial treatment programs. *Drug and Alcohol Dependence, 87,* 175–182.

Peirce, J. M., Petry, N. M., Stitzer, M. L., Blaine, J., Kellogg, S., Satterfield, F., et al. (2006). Effects of lower-cost incentives on stimulant abstinence in methadone maintenance treatment: A National Drug Abuse Treatment Clinical Trials Network study. *Archives of General Psychiatry, 63,* 201–208.

Petry, N. M. (2000). A comprehensive guide to the application of contingency management procedures in clinical settings. *Drug and Alcohol Dependence, 58,* 9–25.

Petry, N. M. (2005). *Pathological gambling: Etiology, comorbidity, and treatment.* Washington, DC: American Psychological Association Press.

Petry, N. M., & Alessi, S. M. (2010). Prize-based contingency management is efficacious in cocaine-abusing patients with and without recent gambling participation. *Journal of Substance Abuse Treatment, 39,* 282–288.

Petry, N. M., Alessi, S. M., Carroll, K. M., Hanson, T., MacKinnon, S., Rounsaville, B., et al. (2006). Contingency management treatments: Reinforcing abstinence versus adherence with goal-related activities. *Journal of Consulting and Clinical Psychology, 74,* 592–601.

Petry, N. M., Alessi, S. M., Hanson, T., & Sierra, S. (2007). Randomized trial of contingent prizes versus vouchers in cocaine-using methadone patients. *Journal of Consulting and Clinical Psychology, 75,* 983–991.

Petry, N. M., Alessi, S. M., Ledgerwood, D. M., & Sierra, S. (2010). Psychometric properties of the contingency management competence scale. *Drug and Alcohol Dependence, 109,* 167–174.

Petry, N. M., Alessi, S. M., Marx, J., Austin, M., & Tardif, M. (2005). Vouchers versus prizes: Contingency management treatment of substance abusers in community settings. *Journal of Consulting and Clinical Psychology, 73,* 1005–1014.

Petry, N. M., & Bohn, M. J. (2003). Fishbowls and candy bars: Using low-cost incentives to increase treatment retention. *Science: Practice and Perspectives, 2,* 55–61.

Petry, N. M., Kelley, L., Brennan, M., & Sierra, S. (2008). What happens when contingency management treatment ends? A tale of two clients. *American Journal on Addictions, 17,* 241–244.

Petry, N. M., Kolodner, K. B., Li, R., Peirce, J. M., Roll, J. M., & Stitzer, M. L. (2006). Prize-based contingency management does not increase gambling. *Drug and Alcohol Dependence, 83,* 269–273.

Petry, N. M., & Ledgerwood, D. M. (2010). *The Contingency Management Competence Scale for Reinforcing Attendance.* Available at http://contingencymanagement.uchc.edu/index.html

Petry, N. M., & Martin B. (2002). Low-cost contingency management for treating cocaine and opioid-abusing methadone patients. *Journal of Consulting and Clinical Psychology, 70,* 398–405.

Petry, N. M., Martin, B., Cooney, J. L., & Kranzler, H. R. (2000). Give them prizes and they will come: Variable-ratio contingency management for treatment of alcohol dependence. *Journal of Consulting and Clinical Psychology, 68,* 250–257.

Petry, N. M., Martin, B., & Finocche, C. (2001). Contingency management in group treatment: A demonstration project in an HIV drop-in center. *Journal of Substance Abuse Treatment, 21,* 89–96.

Petry, N. M., Martin, B., & Simcic, F. (2005). Prize reinforcement contingency management for cocaine dependence: Integration with group therapy in a methadone clinic. *Journal of Consulting and Clinical Psychology, 73,* 354–359.

Petry, N. M., Peirce, J. M., Stitzer, M. L., Blaine, J., Roll, J. M., Cohen, A., et al. (2005). Effect of prize-based incentives on outcomes in stimulant abusers in outpatient psychosocial treatment programs: A national drug abuse treatment clinical trials network study. *Archives of General Psychiatry, 62,* 1148–1156.

Petry, N. M., & Stitzer, M. (2003). *Contingency management: Using motivational incentives to improve drug abuse treatment.* New Haven, CT: Yale University Psychotherapy Development Center.

Petry, N. M., Tedford, J., Austin, M., Nich, C., Carroll, K. M., & Rounsaville, B. J. (2004). Prize reinforcement contingency management for treatment of cocaine abusers: How low can we go, and with whom? *Addiction, 99,* 349–360.

Petry, N. M., Tedford, J., & Martin, B. (2001). Reinforcing compliance with non-drug related activities. *Journal of Substance Abuse Treatment, 20,* 33–44.

Petry, N. M., Weinstock, J., Alessi, S. M., Lewis, M. W., & Dieckhaus, K. (2010). Group-based randomized trial of contingencies for health and abstinence in HIV patients. *Journal of Consulting and Clinical Psychology, 78,* 89–97.

Piotrowski, N. A., Tusel, D., Sees, K., Reilly, P. M., Banys, P., Meek, P., et al. (1999). Contingency contracting with monetary reinforcers for abstinence from multiple drugs in a methadone program. *Experimental and Clinical Psychopharmacology, 7,* 399–411.

Prendergast, M. L., Hall, E. A., Roll, J., & Warda, U. (2008). Use of vouchers to reinforce abstinence and positive behaviors among clients in a drug court treatment program. *Journal of Substance Abuse Treatment, 35,* 125–136.

Prendergast, M. L., Podus, D., Finney, J., Greenwell, L., & Roll, J. (2006). Contingency management for treatment of substance use disorders: A meta-analysis. *Addiction, 101,* 1546–1560.

Preston, K. L., Ghitza, U. E., Schmittner, J. P., Schroeder, J. R., & Epstein, D. H. (2008). Randomized trial comparing two treatment strategies using prize-based reinforcement of abstinence in cocaine and opiate users. *Journal of Applied Behavior Analysis, 41,* 551–563.

Preston, K. L., Silverman, K., Umbricht, A., DeJesus, A., Montoya, I. D., & Schuster, C. R. (1999). Improvement in naltrexone treatment compliance with contingency management. *Drug and Alcohol Dependence, 54,* 127–135.

Preston, K. L., Umbricht, A., & Epstein, D. H. (2000). Methadone dose increase and abstinence reinforcement for treatment of continued heroin use during methadone maintenance. *Archives of General Psychiatry, 57,* 395–404.

Rawson, R. A., Huber, A., McCann, M. J., Shoptaw, S., Farabee, D., Reiber, C., et al. (2002). A comparison of contingency management and cognitive-behavioral approaches during methadone maintenance treatment for cocaine dependence. *Archives of General Psychiatry, 59,* 817–824.

Rawson, R. A., McCann, M. J., Flammino, F., Shoptaw, S., Miotto, K., Reiber, C., et al. (2006). A comparison of contingency management and cognitive-behavioral approaches for stimulant-dependent individuals. *Addiction, 101,* 267–274.

Resetar-Volz, J. L., & Cook, C. R. (2009). Group-based preference assessment for children and adolescents in a residential setting: Examining developmental, clinical, gender, and ethnic differences. *Behavior Modification, 33,* 778–794.

Reynolds, B., Dallery, J., Shroff, P., Patak, M., & Leraas, K. (2008). A web-based contingency management program with adolescent smokers. *Journal of Applied Behavior Analysis, 41,* 597–601.

Ries, R. K., Dyck, D. G., Short, R., Srebnik, D., Fisher, A., & Comtois, K. A. (2004). Outcomes of managing disability benefits among patients with substance dependence and severe mental illness. *Psychiatric Services, 55,* 445–447.

Rigsby, M. O., Rosen, M. I., Beauvais, J. E., Cramer, J. A., Rainey, P. M., O'Malley, S. S., et al. (2000). Cue-dose training with monetary reinforcement: Pilot study of an antiretroviral adherence intervention. *Journal of General Internal Medicine, 15,* 841–847.

Rhodes, G. L., Saules, K. K., Helmus, T. C., Roll, J., Beshears, R. S., Ledgerwood, D. M., & Schuster, C. R. (2003). Improving on-time counseling attendance in a methadone treatment program: A contingency management approach. *American Journal of Drug and Alcohol Abuse, 29,* 759–773.

Robles, E., Crone, C. C., Whiteside-Mansell, L., Conners, N. A., Bokony, P. A., Worley, L. L., et al. (2005). Voucher-based incentives for cigarette smoking reduction in a women's residential treatment program. *Nicotine & Tobacco Research, 7,* 111–117.

Roll, J. M. (2005). Assessing the feasibility of using contingency management to modify cigarette smoking by adolescents. *Journal of Applied Behavior Analysis, 8,* 463–467.

Roll, J. M., Chermack, S. T., & Chudzynski, J. E. (2004). Investigating the use of contingency management in the treatment of cocaine abuse among individuals with schizophrenia: A feasibility study. *Psychiatry Research, 125,* 61–64.

Roll, J. M., & Higgins, S. T. (2000). A within-subject comparison of three different schedules of reinforcement of drug abstinence using cigarette smoking as an exemplar. *Drug and Alcohol Dependence, 58,* 103–109.

Roll, J. M., Higgins, S. T., & Badger, G. J. (1996). An experimental comparison of three different schedules of reinforcement of drug abstinence using cigarette smoking as an exemplar. *Journal of Applied Behavioral Analysis, 29,* 495–505.

Roll, J. M., Higgins, S. T., Steingard, S., & McGinley, M. (1998). Use of monetary reinforcement to reduce the cigarette smoking of persons with schizophrenia: A feasibility study. *Experimental and Clinical Psychopharmacology, 6,* 157–161.

Roll, J. M., Petry, N. M., Stitzer, M. L., Brecht, M. L., Peirce, J. M., McCann, M. J., et al. (2006). Contingency management for the treatment of methamphetamine use disorders. *American Journal of Psychiatry, 163,* 1993–1999.

Roll, J. M., Reilly, M. P., & Johanson, C. E. (2000). The influence of exchange delays on cigarette versus money choice: A laboratory analog of voucher-based reinforcement therapy. *Experimental and Clinical Psychopharmacology, 8,* 366–370.

Roozen, H. G., Boulogne, J. J., van Tulder, M. W., van den Brink, W., De Jong, C. A., & Kerkhof, A. J. (2004). A systematic review of the effectiveness of the community reinforcement approach in alcohol, cocaine and opioid addiction. *Drug and Alcohol Dependence, 74,* 1–13.

Rosen, M. I., Dieckhaus, K., McMahon, T. J., Valdes, B., Petry, N. M., Cramer, J., et al. (2007). Improved adherence with contingency management. *AIDS Patient Care and STDs, 21,* 30–40.

Schmitz, J. M., Rhoades, H., & Grabowski, J. (1995). Contingent reinforcement for reduced carbon monoxide levels in methadone maintenance patients. *Addictive Behaviors, 20,* 171–179.

Sigmon, S. C., & Higgins, S. T. (2006). Voucher-based contingent reinforcement of marijuana abstinence among individuals with serious mental illness. *Journal of Substance Abuse Treatment, 30,* 291–295.

Sigmon, S. C., Steingard, S., Badger, G. J., Anthony, S. L., & Higgins, S. T. (2000). Contingent reinforcement of marijuana abstinence among individuals with serious mental illness: A feasibility study. *Experimental and Clinical Psychopharmacology, 8,* 509–517.

Silverman, K., Chutuape, M. A., Bigelow, G. E., & Stitzer, M. L. (1996). Voucher-based reinforcement of attendance by unemployed methadone patients in a job skills training program. *Drug and Alcohol Dependence, 41,* 197–207.

Silverman, K., Chutuape, M., Bigelow, G., & Stitzer, M. L. (1999). Voucher-based reinforcement of cocaine abstinence in treatment-resistant methadone patients: Effects of reinforcement magnitude. *Psychopharmacology, 146,* 128–138.

Silverman, K., Higgins, S. T., Brooner, R. K., Montoya, I. D., Cone, E. J., Schuster, C. R., et al. (1996). Sustained cocaine abstinence in methadone maintenance patients through voucher-based reinforcement therapy. *Archives of General Psychiatry, 53,* 409–415.

Silverman, K., Svikis, D., Robles, E., Stitzer, M. L., & Bigelow, G. E. (2001). A reinforcement-based therapeutic workplace for the treatment of drug abuse: Six-month abstinence outcomes. *Experimental and Clinical Psychopharmacology, 9,* 14–23.

Silverman, K., Svikis, D., Wong, C. J., Hampton, J., Stitzer, M. L., & Bigelow, G. E. (2002). A reinforcement-based therapeutic workplace for the treatment of drug abuse: Three-year abstinence outcomes. *Experimental and Clinical Psychopharmacology, 10,* 228–240.

Silverman, K., Wong, C. J., Higgins, S. T., Brooner, R. K., Montoya, I. D. Contoreggi, C., et al. (1996). Increasing opiate abstinence through voucher-based reinforcement therapy. *Drug and Alcohol Dependence, 41,* 157–165.

Silverman, K., Wong, C. J., Needham, M., Diemer, K. N., Knealing, T., Crone-Todd, D., et al. (2007). A randomized trial of employment-based reinforcement of cocaine abstinence in injection drug users. *Journal of Applied Behavior Analysis, 40,* 387–410.

Silverman, K., Wong, C. J., Umbricht-Schneiter, A., Montoya, I. D., Schuster, C. R., & Preston, K. L. (1998). Broad beneficial effects of cocaine abstinence reinforcement among methadone patients. *Journal of Consulting and Clinical Psychology, 66,* 811–824.

Simpson, D. D., Joe, G. W., Fletcher, B. W., Hubbard, R. L., & Anglin, M. D. (1999). A national evaluation of treatment outcomes for cocaine dependence. *Archives of General Psychiatry, 56,* 507–514.

Sindelar, J., Elbel, B., & Petry, N. M. (2007). What do we get for our money? Cost-effectiveness of adding contingency management. *Addiction, 102,* 309–316.

Sindelar, J. L., Olmstead, T. A., & Peirce, J. M. (2007). Cost-effectiveness of prize-based contingency management in methadone maintenance treatment programs. *Addiction, 102,* 1463–1471.

Sinha, R., Easton, C., Renee-Aubin, L., & Carroll, K. M. (2003). Engaging young probation-referred marijuana-abusing individuals in treatment: A pilot trial. *American Journal on Addictions, 12,* 314–323.

Sorensen, J. L., Haug, N. A., Delucchi, K. L., Gruber, V., Kletter, E., & Batki, S. L. (2007). Voucher reinforcement improves medication adherence in HIV-positive methadone patients: A randomized trial. *Drug and Alcohol Dependence, 88,* 54–63.

Squires, D. D., Gumbley, S. J., & Storti, S. A. (2008). Training substance abuse treatment organizations to adopt evidence-based practices: The Addiction Technology Transfer Center of New England Science to Service Laboratory. *Journal of Substance Abuse Treatment, 34,* 293–301.

Stanger, C. Budney, A. J., Kamon, J. L., & Thostensen, J. (2009). A randomized trial of contingency management for adolescent marijuana abuse and dependence. *Drug and Alcohol Dependence, 1,* 240–247.

Stitzer, M. L., Bickel, W. K., Bigelow, G. E., & Liebson, I. A. (1986). Effect of methadone dose contingencies on urinalysis test results of polydrug-abusing methadone-maintenance patients. *Drug and Alcohol Dependence, 18,* 341–348.

Stitzer, M. L., & Bigelow, G. E. (1983). Contingent payment for carbon monoxide reduction: Effects of pay amount. *Behavior Therapy, 14,* 647–656.

Stitzer, M. L., & Bigelow, G. E. (1984). Contingent reinforcement for carbon monoxide reduction: Within-subjects effects of pay amounts. *Journal of Applied Behavior Analysis, 17,* 477–483.

Stitzer, M. L., Bigelow, G. E., & Liebson, I. (1980). Reducing drug use among methadone maintenance clients: Contingent reinforcement for morphine-free urines. *Addictive Behavior, 5,* 333–340.

Stitzer, M. L., Iguchi, M. Y., & Felch, L. J. (1992). Contingent take-home incentive: Effects on drug use of methadone maintenance patients. *Journal of Consulting and Clinical Psychology, 60,* 927–934.

Svikis, D. S., Lee, J. H., Haug, N. A., & Stitzer, M. L. (1997). Attendance incentives for outpatient treatment: Effects in methadone- and nonmethadone-maintained pregnant drug dependent women. *Drug and Alcohol Dependence, 48,* 33–41.

Thompson, W., Gordon, N., & Pescatello, L. S. (2009). *American College of Sports Medicine (ACSM's) guidelines for exercise testing and prescription* (8th ed.). Baltimore: Lippincott Williams & Wilkins.

Tidey, J. W., Mehl-Madrona, L., Higgins, S. T., & Badger, G. J. (1998). Psychiatric symptom severity in cocaine-dependent outpatients: Demographics, drug use characteristics, and treatment outcome. *Drug and Alcohol Dependence, 50,* 9–17.

Tidey, J. W., O'Neill, S. C., & Higgins, S. T. (2002). Contingent monetary reinforcement of smoking reductions, with and without transdermal nicotine, in outpatients with schizophrenia. *Experimental and Clinical Psychopharmacology, 10,* 241–247.

Tracy, K., Babuscio, T., Nich, C., Kiluk, B., Carroll, K. M., Petry, N. M., & Rounsaville, B. J. (2007). Contingency management to reduce substance use in individuals who are homeless with co-occurring psychiatric disorders. *American Journal of Drug and Alcohol Dependence, 33,* 253–258.

Vandrey, R., Bigelow, G. E., & Stitzer, M. L. (2007). Contingency management in cocaine abusers: A dose-effect comparison of goods-based versus cash-based incentives. *Experimental and Clinical Psychopharmacology, 15,* 338–343.

Volpp, K. G., John, L. K., Troxel, A. B., Norton, L., Fassbender, J., & Loewenstein, G. (2008). Financial incentive-based approaches for weight loss: A randomized trial. *Journal of the American Medical Association, 300,* 2631–2637.

Volpp, K. G., Loewenstein, G., Troxel, A. B., Doshi, J., Price, M., Laskin, M., et al. (2008). A test of financial incentives to improve warfarin adherence. *BMC Health Services Research, 8,* 272.

Weinstock, J., Alessi, S. M., & Petry, N. M. (2007). Regardless of psychiatric severity the addition of contingency management to standard treatment improves retention and drug use outcomes. *Drug and Alcohol Dependence, 87,* 288–296.

Wolf, M., Risley, T., & Mees, H. (1964). Application of operant conditioning procedures to the behavior problems of an autistic child. *Behavior Research and Therapy, 1,* 305–312.

Wong, C. J., Sheppard, J. M., Dallery, J., Bedient, G., Robles, E., Svikis, D., et al. (2003). Effects of reinforcer magnitude on data-entry productivity in chronically unemployed drug abusers participating in a therapeutic workplace. *Experimental and Clinical Psychopharmacology, 11,* 46–55.

Index